TEACHING YOUNG CHILDREN

Choices in Theory and Practice

For Ted and all lifelong learners

TEACHING YOUNG CHILDREN

Choices in Theory and Practice

Glenda MacNaughton & Gillian Williams

Open University Press
McGraw-Hill Education
McGraw-Hill House
Shoppenhangers Road
Maidenhead, Berkshire
England SL6 2QL

email: enquiries@openup.co.uk
world wide web: www.openup.co.uk

Open University Press edition first published 2004

A catalogue record of this book is available from the British Library

ISBN 0 335 21371 5

Library of Congress Cataloging-in-Publication Data

Senior Acquisitions Editor: Nicole Meehan
Senior Project Editor: Kathryn Fairfax
Senior Editorial Coordinator: Jill Gillies
Copy Editor: Marie-Louise Taylor
Proofreader: Tom Flanagan
Indexer: Frances Wade
Cover and internal design by Ellie Exarchos
Cover photograph from Photodisc
Typeset by Midland Typesetters, Maryborough, Vic.

Printed in Malaysia

Contents

Part Three: Specialist Teaching Techniques

Part Four: Educational Philosophies, Goals and Teaching Techniques

Preface

We have been very fortunate in having many forms and sources of support during the process of writing this book. Acknowledging them at this point in the book's life is one of the more pleasurable writing tasks.

In writing this book we were very lucky to be able to draw on the professional skills of many staff in the Department of Early Childhood Studies, The University of Melbourne, as we wrote this book. The library staff always provided very swift responses to our constant requests for articles, books and information, and were incredibly patient with our often overdue books. Ruth Coulson provided an instant and clear response to our scientific question about hair, Debra Thompson shared her very busy printer with us and Sofia Tsai and Veronica Plozza worked incredibly hard on the permissions brief for the book. We would like to thank each of these people for their professionalism, good will and personal warmth in providing us with support at different points in bringing the book to light.

This edition has drawn on additional people from the Centre for Equity and Innovation in Early Childhood (CEIEC) at the University of Melbourne who we would like to acknowledge. Ruth Callum was a multi-skilled administrative officer with the CEIEC who provided enthusiastic and careful support in the final stages of word processing and proofing the book. She did this when many additional demands were being made on her time and she always managed our demands with good will and calm. Rosemary Jones provided research assistance that supported us in updating the research for this second edition. She did this in such a calm, organised and careful way that it made the integration of contemporary research into this second edition a pleasure rather than a task to be accomplished.

Finding good photographs of work with children is difficult. We would like to thank children and staff from the Early Learning Centre at Melbourne University, Swanston Street Children's Centre, Carlton Child Care Centre, Kew Primary School, the LaTrobe University occasional care, Claire, Jude and David, Mimi, Fergus, Eliza and Hannah, and the Davis Street Kindergarten, all of whom allowed Gillian to photograph them at work and play for this edition of the book.

We would also like to thank Playworks Disability Resource Centre, Melbourne, for the time and effort they spent in providing us with information about other disability services and about current views on preferred terms for people with specific forms of disability.

The final stages before submission were hectic and there never seemed to be enough time in the day to do all that was needed. We would like to thank Patrick Hughes for his invaluable help with proofreading the first edition.

It was a pleasure and a privilege to work with Pearson Education Australia staff on the book. Their professionalism, enthusiasm and commitment made working with them a delight. Particularly Nicole McMeehan and Kathryn Fairfax have been supportive, flexible and highly professional throughout. We thank them for that and for bearing with us through the production process.

On a more personal note, Glenda would again like to thank Patrick for his unfailing emotional, political and intellectual support throughout the writing of the book. It was a particularly challenging time personally and without that support this book would not have seen the light of day. Gillian thanks her family: David for his steadfast belief in her abilities, and Amy, Mary, Hannah, Eliza, Mimi and Fergus for their real-life demonstrations of teaching and learning.

Introduction

It has been our experience that early childhood students and staff are often frustrated by the lack of specific guidance on how to teach young children. There is a plethora of books that can be used to develop early childhood programs and that explore issues in curriculum implementation. Typically, these books explain the theories and principles of early childhood education, present some process for curriculum development and implementation, and contain ideas about how to structure specific learning experiences to enhance children's development. They also contain information about how to incorporate specific discipline-based learning from the arts and the sciences into the curriculum.

While these books provide staff and students with essential knowledge about early childhood education, they provide scant information about the specific teaching techniques they can use to support children's learning. The sparseness of information makes it difficult for staff to evaluate the theory and practice of their own teaching, and to extend and enrich their repertoire of useful and appropriate teaching techniques. The detailed information on teaching techniques is often scattered through journals that are difficult for students and staff to access, or written in very academic and inaccessible language. For these reasons, we felt it was timely to write a book that would present students and staff with an accessible and detailed discussion on the how and why of teaching in early childhood settings. We hope that this book will affirm the response to our initial decision to develop a book focused on the interaction between adult teaching techniques and young children's learning.

This book presents early childhood students and staff with a broad and diverse range of teaching techniques to support children's learning. We do not want to 'tell' staff what to do but to provide them with options that they can test in practice and integrate into their own teaching repertoire. We examine eighteen general teaching techniques commonly mentioned in early childhood texts and eleven specialist techniques that offer diverse theoretical perspectives on teaching. The techniques range from simple methods such as describing and listening through to more complex techniques such as deconstruction and scaffolding.

Each chapter presents one technique. It discusses what the technique is, how staff can use it in their work with children, and when and why they might use it. In thinking about when and why staff might (or might not) opt for a particular technique we have explored current early childhood theory and practice and discussed how this impacts on the goal relevance of the technique and the developmental and equity considerations we consider relevant to the technique. Developmental considerations cover babies, toddlers, preschoolers and children in the early years of school. The specific equity considerations we explore are gender, 'race' and culture, and disability. The word 'race' is in single inverted commas throughout the text to indicate that 'race' is a socially and politically constructed categorisation of people rather than an inherent (biological) fact and to remind readers of the contested nature of this construction. Vignettes and examples show how early childhood staff can use the techniques to support children's learning and help to bring the discussion of each technique to life.

In the final chapter we argue for a strategic approach to selecting teaching techniques which link educational philosophy with choices about specific teaching techniques. We examine the links between the techniques presented in the earlier chapters and specific educational philosophies and goals. To explore this link, we present several approaches to childhood curriculum highly regarded in the international early childhood field: the Anti-Bias Curriculum, the High/Scope Preschool Curriculum, Montessori Education, the Reggio Emilia Approach, and Steiner and Waldorf Schooling.

The organisation of the chapters should make it possible for early childhood students and staff to dip in and out of the book as they need to. While the book is not intended to be read sequentially, students and staff will find it easier to understand the specialist techniques in Part 3 if they are familiar with Parts 1 and 2. The final chapter is also more likely to have meaning once readers have explored the earlier parts of the book.

ANALYSING TEACHING IN EARLY CHILDHOOD SETTINGS

What is teaching?

> In some respects teaching is like lighting a fire. We bring heat to paper to enable it to start combining with oxygen in its environment. In the classroom our function is similar; we bring to bear various teaching devices with a view to producing a 'flash' between each child and some part of his [and her] environment. (Hughes and Hughes 1937, p. 355).

The daily interactions between staff and children in an early childhood setting provide a myriad of opportunities for such 'flashes'. Skilful staff draw on a wide repertoire of teaching 'devices' during these interactions to maximise children's learning. In this book we will look at how several general and specialist teaching 'devices' can 'light the fire' of children's learning and 'fan its flame'. For ease of access we have grouped the general and specialist 'devices' or, as we prefer, 'techniques' alphabetically.

General verbal and non-verbal techniques

While teaching is a complex, highly interactive process, much of the teaching process involves the continuous use of very simple and subtle verbal interactions that may only last moments. Many of these interactions rely on what we refer to as generic, everyday verbal teaching techniques, such as describing, questioning, recalling and telling. Despite the subtlety and simplicity of such teaching techniques they can be powerful in shaping children's learning. They also form the foundations on which the more complex specialist teaching techniques build.

Non-verbal teaching techniques contribute an important element to the overall tone, texture and meaning within staff's daily interactions with children. For example, listening to children can help contribute to a tone of respect for their ideas and efforts, it can help contribute to a sense of calm within the group and it can help staff to understand more precisely what children are thinking, feeling and learning. Many simple non-verbal teaching techniques such as helping, listening and demonstrating also form the foundation of several of the more complex specialist techniques discussed in this book (for example, scaffolding and task analysis).

The simplicity of many of the non-verbal techniques discussed in this book means that they are easy to learn and easy to use. However, the simplicity of these techniques also means that they can be overlooked or overused. Successful use of these techniques relies on knowing when to use them (timing) and what can be accomplished (or not) by using them.

Timing

Good teaching relies on good timing. Knowing just when a comment, question or suggestion might be useful can be difficult to judge. So, timing the right moment to intervene in children's learning is hard. Staff need to make judgments by thinking about what will be gained and what will be lost through their intervention. The following questions can help staff decide if the gains from intervening might outweigh the losses.

➡ Will the children learn more effectively and more enjoyably if I intervene?
➡ Is the children's learning and enjoyment at risk if I don't intervene?
➡ Is this the best moment to intervene?

These questions, and the answers to them, often need to be posed and answered in a split second. Careful observation of the children, knowledge of how they best learn, and experience of what works best, all combine to help staff judge if and when to intervene.

Choosing the optimum moment and method of intervention is a fundamental art of teaching. As Edwards (1993, p. 159) writes:

. . . you are always afraid that you are going to miss that hot moment. It's really a balancing act. I believe in intervention, yet personally I tend to wait because I have noticed that children often resolve the problem on their own, and not always in the way that I would have told them to! Children often find solutions that I would never have seen. But sometimes waiting means missing the moment. So it's a decision that you have to make very quickly.

The decision about if, how and when to intervene in children's learning depends on several factors. However, once staff choose to intervene they have another set of choices about how to do so. These choices form the substance of this book.

Choosing the best teaching technique for a specific child or learning experience is complex. Your choice can be affected by many factors. In this book we will consider how your choice of a teaching technique might be influenced by:

➡ your chosen teaching goals
➡ a child's developmental age and stage
➡ research knowledge about how children's learning can best be enhanced
➡ the desire for equity for boys and girls, children from diverse racial and cultural backgrounds, and children with disabilities.

In the following chapters we consider the relevance of each of these factors in developing excellence in teaching. In this consideration we take an anti-discriminatory (anti-bias) approach to equity issues. This approach rests on the belief that the best way to ensure an excellent education for all children is to actively promote positive acceptance of and respect for diversity. This involves challenging discrimination when it occurs and working to empower children to be active in creating a fair and just world.

TEACHING AND EXCELLENCE

All children deserve good teaching (Hatton 1994, p. xv).

We would argue that all children deserve excellent teaching. But, how do staff know what excellent teaching is? This book aims to help early childhood staff to think about the best way to teach young children and to become better teachers.

Teaching is a process through which early childhood staff assist and encourage children's learning. It is a highly complex and dynamic process in which staff make decisions about how to best respond to children to best support their learning.

To choose the best response for each child, staff need to reflect on:

- what they are going to do
- what they are going to say
- whether they need to do or say anything
- how they will set up the environment.

In early childhood settings excellent teaching involves basing these decisions on knowledge of and understanding about:

- child development
- individual children's characteristics
- the cultural values of the children's families
- parental desires for their children's learning
- the knowledge required to function effectively in a specific society (NAEYC and NAECSSDE 1991)
- a sense of what is ethical.

In this book we believe that teaching is a process which aims to optimise children's learning. It is an interactive process between child and teacher that is extremely complex, dynamic and demands that early childhood staff reflect on children's responses to their program and respond in the ways that they believe will most assist children's learning. It is, therefore, a highly value-based process.

EXCELLENCE AND INTERVENTION: A NECESSARY COALITION?

> However interested children are in their work, some teaching is necessary. Some skilful teachers apparently give very little teaching. The fact is, however, that they are continuously teaching in many subtle ways . . . (Hughes and Hughes 1937, p. 357).

In the early childhood field there is considerable debate about what is the best way to respond to children to optimise learning. Much of this debate centres on the question of how much and what kind of adult intervention is needed to promote young children's learning. Some people argue for minimal adult intervention and believe that indirect teaching methods are the most appropriate for early childhood settings. Others are convinced that direct, highly interventionist techniques are more appropriate in these settings. As Edwards (1993, p. 152) says, teachers can choose to work 'inside' the group of children or 'just around' them. Several differing views on the level of intervention needed to promote children's learning are reflected in the following quotes.

- In interactionist approaches . . . the role of the adult is critical to children's learning, providing structure and support, with meaning-making the paramount focus. (Makin 1996, p. 76)
- The role of the adult is above all one of listening, observing, and understanding the strategy that children use in a learning situation. The teacher has . . . a role as dispenser of occasions . . . not a judge but a resource. (Edwards 1993, p. 153)

➡ It is the task of the teacher to stand between the known and unknown. The teacher must see where students are and lay the stepping stones to new knowledge surely and safely so that the students come to trust themselves, their teachers and the educational process. (Jonquiere 1990, p. 292)

➡ Adults will observe children interacting with the environment, listen to them, ask questions, demonstrate possible solutions and know when to withdraw and allow the child to make a discovery. (Department of Human Services 1996, p. 6)

➡ I try to stand aside and allow . . . [the children] to speak for themselves. It is not easy to wait and listen. (Paley 1986, p. xv)

While there are many different views about the precise level and type of intervention that is most likely to optimise children's learning there seems increasing agreement that some form of adult intervention is necessary.

INTERVENTION AND REFLECTIVE TEACHING

Irrespective of staff beliefs about intervention in children's learning, all staff do and must intervene in the daily actions and decisions of the children in their care. As Spodek (1987, p. 5) reminded us:

> Early childhood education, like all education, is a deliberate intervention in the lives of young children. It results from a belief that children growing up naturally might not come to know all the things we want them to know.

We believe that excellent teaching is most likely to occur when staff make informed choices about their interventions and see excellent teaching as reflective teaching.

Reflective teachers think carefully about what they are doing and saying or not saying in the daily interactions with children and question what children have or have not learnt from these interactions. Reflective teachers are committed to improving their teaching through regular evaluation of their teaching techniques. They question what has or has not worked to enhance children's learning and make changes in their approach accordingly.

Careful and critical reflection on teaching choices contributes to excellence in teaching in several ways.

➡ There is considerable evidence that children across different class, gender, ethnic and ability groups (see Hatton 1994) experience unequal educational outcomes. Staff, therefore, need to carefully consider how they can best intervene to reduce such inequalities in educational outcomes and to promote greater equality of outcomes for all children in their care.

➡ Research into teachers' choice of teaching methods suggests that many teachers have a 'fairly narrow and conservative repertoire of teacher behaviours' (Hatton 1994, p. 7) which often mimic those teaching methods they experienced in their own schooling. Access to information about a broad and diverse repertoire of teaching methods can increase the likelihood that staff will choose the best rather than the most familiar way to further children's learning.

➡ According to Denscombe (1982; cited in Hatton 1994) the practical daily need to control children in an orderly fashion often means that teachers rely on a few tried and tested teaching methods to accomplish this. They also become reluctant to try alternative methods of assisting children's learning. This can lead to well-behaved children but often works against excellence in teaching.

 Teaching is full of dilemmas, successes and failures for both experienced and inexperienced staff alike (McLean 1933). These dilemmas are increasingly born of tensions between teachers' own beliefs and practices and the practices they believe are required of them through state-mandated curricula (Adcock & Patton 2001). Knowledge of a broad and diverse range of teaching methods can help staff reflect on alternative ways to assist children's learning when the more familiar methods fail. It can also assist them to critically engage with state-mandated curriculum practices and the curriculum policy debates that are increasingly evident internationally (Adcock & Patton 2001).

 High-quality early childhood education can produce lasting cognitive and social benefits throughout later years of schooling for children (Schweinhart and Weikart 1993). High-quality education rests on having 'good' teachers working with this age group who reflect on their practice (Bowman, Donovan and Burns 2001).

 Early childhood staff can expect to have over 1000 interpersonal interactions with young children during a day (Goodfellow 1996). While many of these are unplanned, it is important that staff know how they can make the most of their interactions to support children's learning. Imagine the power of a thousand 'good' teaching interactions daily within an early childhood setting!

There is a growing interest in giving teachers a 'voice' in research on teaching and learning (see, for example, Halliwell 1992; Brown 1996; Adcock & Patton 2001). The argument of those wanting to prioritise teachers' theories of teaching and learning is that the answers to what works best can be found in real-life settings with real-life teachers and children (McCully Wilucki 1990). In line with this interest, and a commitment in this book to being 'practical', we will draw on early childhood staff's experiences and theories of what works best, not just on formal academic research.

However, we are mindful that written instructions about what constitutes best teaching practice is just one part of the story of ensuring excellence in teaching for all children. Excellence in teaching relies on early childhood staff making informed decisions about what to do and say, based on their own reflections and analysis of their day-to-day teaching. We strongly support Isenberg's (1990, p. 325) view that:

> Thoughtful teaching is central to professional growth. When teachers reflect upon instruction, they can analyse the result of their decisions on students. Classroom teachers who are active problem-solvers are key agents in school reform . . . Teachers engaged in inquiry about their own practice must become an increasingly important aspect of the continuing development of teachers.

Teaching Young Children is not a recipe book to be followed uncritically, but an 'aide-memoir', an 'idea starter' and an 'enricher' to the daily practices and theories of early childhood students and staff. Techniques should be used, modified and/or rejected on the basis of careful evaluation of practice. Excellence in teaching relies on such careful testing and on critical reflection of what best supports young children's learning.

In summary, reflection on teaching involves thinking about what you have said and done (or not said and done) with the children. It also involves thinking about what you can learn from your actions (and inactions) to improve the effectiveness of your teaching for children's learning. We believe that when staff have critically informed access to a diverse range of teaching techniques, children and staff benefit: children are more likely to experience excellent teaching and staff are more likely to find their work satisfying.

WHO CAN TEACH? THE THORNY ISSUE OF CARE AND EDUCATION

Education is a process not a place. It can occur within a diverse range of places including child care settings. There is nothing magical about the institutions of kindergartens or schools that gives them the sole prerogative over claiming their work is educational. It is the teaching practices, not the institutions that make interactions educational. To argue that only people called 'teachers' can teach is misguided, given the particular stage we have reached in training early childhood staff across all service types to deliver flexible, developmentally appropriate services for young children.

We need to move beyond our concern about teaching only happening when people called 'teachers' do it, to a concern with maximising the contribution of all who work in services for young children to fostering excellence and meaning in every interaction they have with young children. In this move we need to ensure that teaching is understood as a deliberate, thoughtful process based on knowledge of how children learn and a set of beliefs about what it is important for them to learn. When this happens we will be optimising learning and possibilities for all children. We hope this book offers a useful contribution to this process.

CONCLUSION

The principles underpinning the approach to teaching in this section, on which the rest of this book is based, are:
1 All children deserve excellent teaching.
2 Teaching is a highly complex and dynamic decision-making process about how to best respond to children to support their learning.
3 Teaching involves intervention in children's lives.
4 Teaching is value-based.
5 There is no single correct way to respond to children to optimise learning.
6 Careful and critical reflection on teaching choices contributes to excellence in teaching.
7 Choosing the optimum moment and method of intervention is the fundamental art of teaching.
8 Teaching techniques should be relevant to teaching goals.
9 Teaching techniques should be relevant to all children. This means they must be developmentally appropriate, culturally appropriate, acknowledge the different learning styles of girls and boys and of children with disabilities.
10 Teaching techniques should be anti-discriminatory.
11 Education is a process not a place, therefore teaching can occur within a diverse range of settings including those of child care.
12 Drawing on information about best practice from research and from international developments in the early childhood field contributes to excellence in teaching.

REFLECTING ON THE NATURE OF TEACHING AND LEARNING

1 How would you define teaching?
2 How would you define excellent teaching?

3 Haberman (1994, p. 24) believes that 'good' teaching involves 'drawing out rather than stuffing in'. What do you think this means? Do you agree? How would you define 'good' teaching?

4 What do you see as the relationship between teaching, timing and observation?

5 To what extent do the quotes on pages 5 and 6 emphasise working 'inside' or 'around' the children? Which of the above quotes most closely represent your view of intervention? What factors have influenced your views on intervention? Are there some times or situations in which a higher or lower level of intervention might be appropriate? Does the age group you work with influence how you feel about intervention?

6 What do you think is meant by reflecting on teaching? What do you think can be learned by regular reflection?

7 To what extent do you agree with the following statement? How might administrators and managers demonstrate 'trust' and 'respect' for teacher choices and decision-making?

'Teachers need to feel trusted and respected as professionals, free to make choices and decisions' (Conzemius, 1999, p. 34).

Further references

Adcock, S.G. & Patton, M.M. 2001, 'Voices of effective early childhood educators regarding systematic constraints that affect their teaching', *Journal of Research in Childhood Education*, 15(2), pp. 194–208.

Cartwright, S. 'What makes good early childhood teachers?', *Young Children*, 54 (4), pp. 4–7.

Edwards, C. 1993, 'Partner, Nurturer and Guide: The Roles of the Reggio Teacher in Action', in C. Edwards, L. Gandini and G. Foreman, eds, *The Hundred Languages of Children: The Reggio Emilia Approach to Early Childhood Education* (pp. 151–69), Norwood, New Jersey, Ablex Publishing Company.

Hatton, E. 1994, *Understanding Teaching: Curriculum and the Social Context of Schooling*, Sydney, Harcourt Brace.

McLean, V. 1993, 'Learning from teachers' stories', *Childhood Education*, 69(5), pp. 265–8.

References

Adcock, S.G. & Patton, M.M. 2001, 'Voices of effective early childhood educators regarding systematic constraints that affect their teaching', *Journal of Research in Childhood Education*, 15(2), pp. 194–208.

Bowman, B., Donovan, M. and Burns, S. 2001, *Eager to Learn: Educating Our Preschoolers*, Washington, DC., National Academy Press.

Brown, R. 1996, 'Teacher reflections on educational theory and practice', in *Weaving Webs: Collaborative Approaches to Teaching and Learning in the Early Childhood Curriculum*, Melbourne, Australia, 11–13 July.

Department of Human Services 1996, Babies, Toddlers and Two-Year-Olds: A Curriculum Resource for Developing Child-Centred Programs for Children Under Three, Melbourne, Government of Victoria.

Conzemius, A. 1999, 'Ally in the office', *Journal of Staff Development*, 20, pp. 31–34.

Edwards, C. 1993, 'Partner, Nurturer and Guide: The Roles of the Reggio Teacher in Action', in C. Edwards, L. Gandini and G. Foreman, eds, *The Hundred Languages of Children: The Reggio Emilia Approach to Early Childhood Education* (pp. 151–69), Norwood, New Jersey, Ablex Publishing Company.

Goodfellow, J. 1996, *Weaving Webs of Caring Relationships*. Paper presented to the Weaving Webs: Collaborative Learning and Teaching in the Early Childhood Curriculum Conference, Melbourne, Australia, 11–13 July.

Haberman, M. 1994, 'The pedagogy of poverty versus good teaching', in E. Hatton, ed., *Understanding Teaching: Curriculum and the Social Context of Schooling* (pp. 17–25), Sydney, Harcourt Brace.

Halliwell, G. 1992, 'Practical curriculum theory, describing, informing and improving early childhood practices', in B. Lambert, ed., *Changing Faces. The Early Childhood Professional in Australia* (pp. 122–32), Canberra, Australian Early Childhood Association.

Hatton, E. 1994, *Understanding Teaching: Curriculum and the Social Context of Schooling*, Sydney, Harcourt Brace.

Hughes, A. and Hughes, E. 1937, *Learning and Teaching: An Introduction to Psychology and Education*, London, Longmans.

Isenberg, J. 1990, 'Teachers' Thinking and Beliefs and Classroom Practice', *Childhood Education*, 66(5), pp. 322–7.

Jonquiere, H. 1990, 'My beliefs about teaching', *Childhood Education*, 66(5), pp. 291–3.

Makin, L. 1996, 'Play and the language profiles and scales', in M. Fleer, ed., *Play through the Profiles: Profiles through Play* (pp. 68–84), Watson, ACT, Australian Early Childhood Association.

McCully Wilucki, B. 1990, 'Autonomy: the goal for classroom teachers of the 1990s', *Childhood Education*, 66(5), pp. 279–80.

McLean, V. 1993, 'Learning from teachers' stories', *Childhood Education*, 69(5), pp. 265–8.

NAEYC and NAECSSDE 1991, 'Guidelines for appropriate curriculum content and assessment in programs serving children age 3 through 8', *Young Children*, 46(3), pp. 21–38.

Paley, V. 1986, *Mollie is Three: Growing up in School*, Chicago, University of Chicago Press.

Schweinhart, L. and Weikart, D. 1993, *A Summary of Significant Benefits: The High Scope Perry Preschool Study Through Age 27*, Ypsilanti, Michigan, Highscope, UK.

Spodek, B. 1987, 'The knowledge base of kindergarten education', in *Five Year Olds in School Conference*, Minesota, ED280569.

Part One
Teaching and the Environment

Chapter 1

Positioning equipment and materials

Position: the place, situation or location of a person or a thing.

(*Collins Dictionary of the English Language*, p. 1143)

A place for everything and, everything in its place.

Samuel Smiles (late 19th century)
cited in Cohen and Cohen 1960

. . . teachers add materials in order to support or set the stage for the use of other teaching techniques. They add a material to illustrate an explanation or to encourage further questions from a child.

(Allen and Hart 1984, p. 255)

WHAT?

Positioning is the process of placing objects in relation to each other or in relation to people. As a teaching technique, positioning involves placing learning materials in ways that safely support and enhance children's learning.

HOW?

Staff need to think about several interrelated facets of the physical organisation of inside and outside space so that they may place materials to safely assist children's learning.

Overall physical organisation of the learning areas

Staff need to decide how they will place materials and equipment in the physical learning environment to best assist children's learning. Specifically, they need to decide:

 the equipment, materials and spaces they will make available in the inside and outside play areas

- ➲ the balance between the different types of closed and open spaces and materials
- ➲ the boundaries between the different areas within the centre
- ➲ the ways in which materials will be grouped together
- ➲ the ways in which the placement of materials will encourage movement and interaction between children
- ➲ the ways in which the placement of materials will allow for quiet moments of reflection
- ➲ the ways in which spaces will allow for robust physical exploration of materials.

There can be considerable advantage to having multi-use spaces that can be quickly adapted to children's changing interests and projects and that allow staff to respond flexibly to what emerges during a day with children. As Wanerman (1999, p. 17) explained:

> Life can be frustrating when you try to control everything. As with life in general, improvisation and accident can be as important to a curriculum as planning and preparation.

Overall social organisation of the learning areas

Staff need to decide how they will place materials and equipment to facilitate social interaction within the learning environment. For instance, they need to think about how they will make places available for adults and/or children to sit individually, sit in groups, sit on the floor, sit on chairs, stand and move about. They need to decide what equipment will be placed within easy reach of the children, what equipment only adults will be able to access, how possible it will be for children to work in small and large groups, how large the groups will be and what spaces will encourage individual exploration and thinking.

Daily placement of learning materials

While staff may have an overall plan for organising the inside and outside learning environments, daily changes can enrich and extend children's learning. For instance, placing materials near where a child is working can prompt children's interests and can make their play more elaborate. Staff need to think about when and where they will place new materials and how they might alter the placement of existing materials to encourage children's active involvement in the program and excite their interest in it. In the following example staff placed materials to excite children's interest in making things.

> In a classroom for five-year-olds, an area is defined for what the children call 'making'. A large table with chairs around it is positioned near several shelves holding tools such as staplers, tape, paste, a hole-puncher, string, pencils, crayons, needles and threads; and resources for creative and engineering work, such as paper of different colours, sizes and textures, boxes, cotton reels, buttons, pieces of plastic and so forth. The children are able to help themselves to anything that they need from the shelves.

When deciding how to place people and materials, staff should seek to create and maintain a safe, secure, interesting and pleasurable learning environment for children and adults. To do this, staff need to:

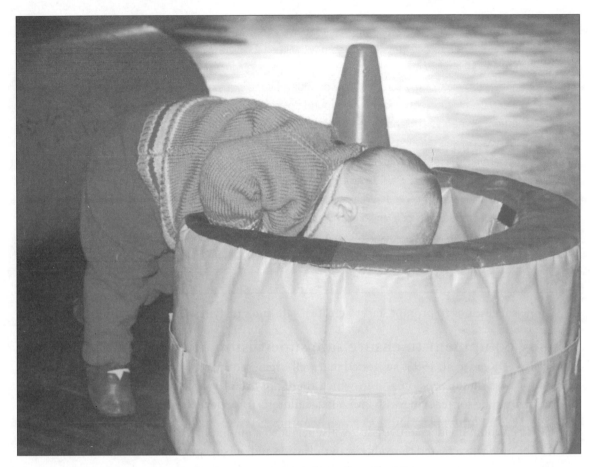

Equipment in easy reach for safe exploration.

- ❯ place people to ensure safe supervision of all children and safe work conditions for all
- ❯ place equipment to meet children's and their own health and safety needs. For example a member of staff can make a safety check every day before the first child arrives and a staff member can always be scheduled to be near the climbing equipment to assist children if needed
- ❯ place equipment to enhance the aesthetic appeal of the environment, thus maximising children's, parents' and staff's enjoyment of it
- ❯ place equipment to ensure that children gain a feeling of security and competence in their learning environment
- ❯ place equipment and materials to stimulate children's curiosity and interest by providing elements of surprise and novelty
- ❯ place equipment and adults to support equity of access to and participation in the program by all children
- ❯ place equipment to stimulate brain development.

The following discussion illustrates how one staff member balanced the need for novelty with need for security in her approach to placing equipment in a toddlers' room.

A group of teachers are having a discussion at a seminar about environments. Jenny, a new graduate from teachers' college, is in charge of a room with fifteen toddlers. She is enthusiastic and energetic and is keen to try new ideas.

Jenny: 'I'm sick of my room, I have changed all the equipment around three times in two months and the children seem to wander around doing nothing!'

Silvana: 'I used to find that when I changed the environment around too much, the children became unsettled and didn't stay in one area for very long. Now, I keep the main areas the same—that is, the home area, the messy play area, the book corner and so forth—and I add different things to these areas from time to time. Last week I added scarves to the home area with the hats. I put pictures of the children doing finger painting in the "messy area". I added some vinyl squares to the blocks. I find that the children like the security of everything in its place but they also like the novelty of additions.'

Jenny: 'You've given me food for thought. I can see that the children in my room have become a bit unsettled recently—perhaps I could try your idea and move some things around from time to time, not everything at once!'

Some suggestions to prompt staff to create a safe and satisfying learning environment follow.

Placing equipment to ensure safe supervision of children

Research (see Read et al. 1993) suggested that well-organised space, in which equipment placement allows for ease of supervision and in which there are broad visible pathways, gives staff more discretionary time for teaching with individual children. To achieve these goals, staff need to:

- keep room dividers above adult waist height to a minimum
- be able when seated to readily scan the inside and outside play areas
- ensure semi-transparent materials (for example, lace curtains) are used to create children's secret spaces so that staff can still see the children.

Placing equipment to ensure children's and staff's health and safety

To promote health and safety for everyone in the centre, staff need to ensure that:

- play spaces are well lit
- there are comfortable temperatures and fresh air
- there is room to move around freely (for example, when using a wheelchair or walking frame)
- equipment can be reached easily and safely
- there are no sharp edges that children might knock against
- there is ready access to a space for the recycling of material and to enable the clearing of rubbish from the floor
- there are non-slip surfaces in the 'wet' areas
- there is ready access for staff to all equipment without their straining muscles
- dangerous substances are out of children's reach.

Staff should be alert to potential hazards when they are placing equipment. Equipment should be:

- away from electrical hazards such as leads and plugs
- away from heating appliances on which children can burn themselves
- away from glass and mirrors that can splinter and break (Plested 1993).

Placing equipment to enhance the aesthetic appeal

The lighting, colour, texture, size and density of materials, space, furnishing and equipment contribute to the aesthetic feel of a space. However, people's tastes about what is pleasing are culturally based and, therefore, value-based. In trying to place equipment in a tasteful and pleasing way staff will need to negotiate with children, parents and other staff to develop an aesthetic style that is pleasing to all who use the centre. In general, an aesthetically pleasing space will be one in which:

- ➔ equipment and materials are deliberately and carefully placed, and this arrangement is maintained
- ➔ the environment evolves over time, with changes reflecting the changing interests of those who work in it
- ➔ there are soft areas that encourage people to relax, reflect and rest
- ➔ sounds and aromas are placed as carefully as objects—wind-chimes, music and perfumed oils and plants have a place in the program
- ➔ texture, shape and colour are used with care and thought to provide enjoyment, stimulation and relaxation
- ➔ visual images are hung and treated with care and respect
- ➔ there are artefacts, crafts, art and memorabilia that are culturally familiar to the children and adults, and that are displayed with care and respect
- ➔ lighting is used to add atmosphere to the room.

Staff can develop and maintain an aesthetically pleasing space in many ways. A large preschool in Melbourne is aware of the importance of an aesthetic environment. In order to cater for differences in taste and values, each member of staff is on a two-weekly roster to design and organise the entrance area of the centre so that it is aesthetically appealing to parents and children from different backgrounds. Feedback is sought from the children, parents and staff, and is used to good effect.

Consider the following descriptions by Gandini (1994) of careful positioning of materials to enhance the aesthetic appeal of a learning area in a school in Reggio Emilia, Italy.

. . . there is in these schools a great deal of attention paid to the beauty and harmony of design. This is evident in both the functional and pleasing furnishings, often invented and built by teachers and parents together. It is also evident in the colours of the walls, the sunlight streaming through large windows, the healthy green plants (p. 140).

When samples of the colourful fall leaves are brought in and pressed, each one's favourites can be placed in small, transparent pockets with other coloured treasures. All these packets are put together and placed on the glass wall to make a large display that catches the light and creates arresting shadows (p. 141).

Source: Edwards, Gandini & Formant (eds), *The Hundred Languages of Children: The Reggio Emilia Approach to Early Childhood Education*, 1994, Ablex Publishing Company, New Jersey. Reproduced by permission of Greenwood Publishing Group.

Children's artwork is carefully displayed in the foyer.

Wilson Gillespie (2000) described several changes made to the learning environment in six Head Start centres that decided to explore the implications of Reggio Emilia for their work with children. She points to ways in which enhancing the aesthetics of the environment enriched the play and deepened the involvement of the children. Examples included:

- adding silk flowers and tablecloths to the home-corner area
- replacing all commercially made decorations with those made by the children and staff
- storing materials in clear plastic containers so that they were more visible to the children and so their options were clearer.

Placing equipment to enhance children's sense of security and competence

To achieve this staff need to ensure that:

- there are regular major traffic paths in the environment
- children can readily access child-safe cleaning materials and equipment
- everyday materials which children use, such as sticky-tape, glue-sticks, scissors, etc. are readily accessible to the children
- everyday materials are placed in a way that avoids congestion when several children at once want access
- materials used regularly have an obvious home. Briggs and Potter (1995) suggested that all containers, shelves and storage bins are labelled with names or symbols to show children where everything belongs

> ➜ children have a personal storage space for their special projects and personal belongings
>
> ➜ children have access to child sized furniture and equipment when needed.

Placing equipment and materials to stimulate children's curiosity

There are many ways to do this. One simple method is to place some materials 'out of place'. For instance, staff can make a simple change such as placing a book in the block corner to stimulate particular types of building or placing paints near the nature table to suggest the possibility of painting nature or using nature in paintings. A more complex change can also prompt new discoveries and learning. Raczynski and Stevenson (1996, p. 330) reported how a group of staff placed materials to stimulate children's exploration of their environment as part of a project in which children were encouraged to practise their negotiating skills with each other:

> . . . we collected a range of fabrics different in colour, surface, and that illustrated different techniques of decoration . . . we covered the door with a large flannel sheet for the children to enter the room. Desks were turned upside down and pieces of fabric were arranged at different heights.

Children explored the space and materials in pairs. In each pair, one child was 'blindfolded' and the pairs had to share their descriptions of the materials with each other.

Greenman (1988) suggested that spaces which promote learning are those that allow for involvement, for children to spread out, and for moments of peace, and that reduce the need to share continuously.

Placing equipment to support equity of access and participation

Staff can create equity of access and participation by ensuring that:

> ➜ children of differing physical abilities can move around easily. For example, consider how readily a child using a wheelchair or a walking frame can move around the area
>
> ➜ children of differing physical abilities can participate in a range of experiences
>
> ➜ children of differing abilities, sizes and ages can easily see and touch display areas
>
> ➜ children from differing cultural backgrounds can recognise their own culture in the materials and staff available to them.

Placing equipment to stimulate brain development

There is increasing evidence that the early years really do matter to young children's learning and that brain stimulation enhances brain development in very specific ways (Bowman et al. 2001). Applying some of the findings from neuroscientific understandings of the brain, Schiller (1999) offers the following advice on placing equipment to maximise early brain development:

> ➜ ensure children have access to plenty of water to reduce the likelihood of brain dehydration, which can lead to children being 'bored, listless and drowsy' (p. 49)
>
> ➜ introduce aromas into the classroom to increase children's learning in several ways. Floral odours can increase 'the ability to learn, create and think . . . Peppermint, basil, lemon, cinnamon, and rosemary are linked to mental alertness. Lavendar, chamomile, orange, and rose are used for relaxation and calming.' (p. 50)

> ⊘ introduce novelty into the environment to increase children's memory. Schiller suggested rotating toys, equipment, books and shelving, and placing things in surprising places.

WHEN AND WHY?

In any early childhood program, staff decisions about how to position staff, children and materials will be influenced by their approach to curriculum and their specific teaching and learning goals for the children.

Goal relevance

In general, staff can position equipment and materials near someone or something to:

> ⊘ gain and maintain children's attention during a specific learning experience. Introducing a 'popular' piece of equipment at the beginning of an experience or adding a new piece of equipment to an experience at a key moment can help gain and maintain children's interest.
>
> ⊘ increase children's concentration on specific experiences. Placing equipment to allow children to have moments for quiet reflection helps their concentration.
>
> ⊘ ensure safe supervision of children's learning. This means that staff need to place themselves, furniture and equipment in a way that allows them to see the children. For example, sitting down facing into a room makes scanning the room on a regular basis easy.
>
> ⊘ encourage children's participation in a specific experience. For instance, adding a child's favourite toy to a specific area may encourage a reluctant child to participate in a new experience. Adding an object that is culturally familiar to a child may encourage exploration of experiences the child has been avoiding.
>
> ⊘ encourage social interaction between children. For example, placing several spades in the mud-patch or a very large box in the block area can make it easy and possible for several children to explore the experience. Children's ability and desire to share will be greater and conflict lessened when there is sufficient equipment for each child to enjoy a particular experience (Stephen 1993).
>
> ⊘ create an open and inviting environment for children and families (Wanerman 1999).
>
> ⊘ help children to learn to practise reflective listening. For example, creating a Peace Table as a site in the classroom where conflicts are negotiated through children practising reflective listening and problem-solving with each other. Hintz and Stomfay-Stitz (1999) talk of examples that include the use of a 'decorated felt blanklet on the floor' (p. 4) that acts as a site for conflict resolution, and specific tables or desks allocated to the purpose of peace.

Developmental considerations

The positioning of equipment to encourage interactions between children of mixed abilities can have positive effects on children's learning. Bennett and Cass (1988; cited in Edwards and Knight 1994) suggested that placing children of mixed age and/or mixed ability in small groups could enhance their learning. Staff should consider the possibility that placing toddlers and babies or toddlers and preschoolers in small groups enhances each child's skills.

When babies lie in their cots, in hammocks, or on the floor they spend considerable portions of their time looking at the spaces that are above them or to the side of them. Babies' interest, wonder, enjoyment and curiosity about their physical environment can be encouraged by careful positioning of artefacts and materials to capture their attention. Their attention can be maintained by choosing items with surfaces that reflect the light, that change as different lights play on them and that enable babies to see the movement of other people. Gandini (1994, p. 143) described how staff from one of the schools in the district of Reggio Emilia in Italy positioned objects and windows to capture and maintain babies' interests:

> None is considered marginal space; for example, the mirrors in the washrooms and bathrooms are cut in different shapes to inspire the children to look in a playful way at their image. The ceilings are used as host to many different types of aerial sculptures or beautiful mobiles all made with transparent, coloured, and unusual material, built by children and set up by teachers. There are glass walls to create a continuity between interior garden and outside gardens; they contribute much natural light and give an occasion for playing with transparencies and reflections.

By three months of age babies can use their hands and feet to 'bat and swipe' (Honig 1990) at mobiles or similar items. Placing such items within reach will encourage them to physically explore them and begin to teach them about cause and effect and how to make things happen. Once babies show an interest in rolling over, staff can occasionally place toys just out of a baby's reach to encourage stretching and exercise. This helps to strengthen their muscles (Honig 1990) and increases mobility. There are many ways to do this. For example, one child care worker in a room placed a slightly elevated board across part of the room so that the babies could crawl over and along it.

Toddlers are active, they move about quickly, they are unpredictable, love exploring how things work and want to do lots of things by themselves. Equipment needs to be positioned carefully to ensure that toddlers' emerging skills are fully supported and their learning is enriched. Toddlers will need plenty of space to carry things around, push them around and drop them unexpectedly (Arthur et al. 1996). It is, therefore, important that staff are not too concerned with maintaining clear boundaries between different spaces such as a book area and a block area—some mingling of areas is inevitable with this age group. However, it can be helpful to organise the environment to allow toddlers space by themselves for uninterrupted play so they do not feel crowded by other children. This can help to reduce conflicts between toddlers (Schreiber 1999).

Preschoolers are growing in social autonomy and initiative but still need considerable support to manage their social relationships. Placing equipment and materials to promote social interaction between the children can help them to learn the skills such as negotiation and sharing which they need to create and maintain positive peer relationships (Arthur et al. 1996). For instance, placing one wheelbarrow with several shovels in it near the mud-play area means that when several children can be involved in digging and moving the mud at the one time, they will have to negotiate over when, how and who can use the wheelbarrow.

In the preschool years children are becoming increasing physically competent. They can run, jump, hop and balance and can co-ordinate a variety of physical movements (large and small) with increasing ease. In placing equipment and materials staff should provide children with the opportunity to acquire, practise and consolidate a variety of physical skills (Arthur et al. 1996). Successful use of large and small motor skills helps children to feel a sense of mastery and control over their environment. This in turn promotes a sense of competence and well-being that positively supports learning across all domains of development. Preschoolers need equipment that will support and extend their physical development and that is positioned to allow for consolidation of their existing skills and for challenges which encourage them to develop new skills.

The placement of equipment is also very important in encouraging preschooler's cognitive development. It encourages children's acquisition of problem-solving skills (see Chapter 25), and helps them to imagine, create and recognise relationships between events and objects in their environment. In the following anecdote, the teacher placed equipment in the outdoor shed in ways that enabled children to make choices and supported their dramatic play.

> The children wanted to build a cubby house on the platform at the top of the climbing frame. They are discussing how to make the walls. Their teacher reminds them to look in the outdoor shed, which contains different materials and equipment. The children discuss among themselves what they need and choose some old bedspreads and some sheets of masonite.

Children's early numeracy and mathematical thinking can also be supported through the innovative placement of equipment in the classroom. Traditional classrooms in which desks are placed in rows and children learn maths using formal worksheets and rote learning can produce 'maths anxiety' (Perlmutter et al. 1993, p. 20). In contrast, classrooms in which the placement of equipment and materials creates interest centres that children can explore through independent and group maths projects can lead to an enjoyment of maths. One teacher described how this works:

> Every day each child is expected to design and carry out some form of investigation that varies week by week . . . including geometry, numeration, estimation, measurement, patterns, classification, sequencing and money . . . During large group meetings, Burrell introduces a specific topic and gives sample investigations that can be done in the area . . . Investigations always include recording of results and thus are part of the children's writing experience.

Children learn maths through making their own discoveries and using maths as a tool to help them solve problems in their project.

For children of all ages, the choice of equipment can be important to their imaginative worlds and the play that they build in them. Research has shown that realistic props, such as plastic food, detailed uniforms, real trucks, etc., can restrict rather than enhance children's imagination and imaginative play. Describing a project designed within a Vygotskian framework, Bodrova and Leong (2001, pp. 17–18) described the importance of non-realistic, minimal props to children's dramatic play:

> In the Tools of the Mind project, teachers try to wean children from the need for specific props by introducing games in which children think of different ways to play with ordinary objects. They brainstorm ways in which a wooden block can be used—as a baby, a ship or a chair for a doll. Teachers transition children from using realistic props to using minimal props.

EQUITY CONSIDERATIONS

'Race' and culture

The placement of materials can provide children with very important messages about what is valued and how adults understand the relationships between different objects and events. When staff place items of equipment or images next to each other, they should avoid tokenistic placement of images. Tokenism means making a superficial or minimal gesture towards representing and respecting cultural diversity. For instance, having one picture representing Aboriginal Australian families in a display of Australian family diversity would be tokenistic. This is because it would only provide children with a small amount of information about Aboriginal Australian families. One image cannot convey the diversity and complexity of the kinship arrangements of Australian Aboriginal cultures. However, it can tend to reinforce stereotypes by suggesting that all Aboriginal families live in the way depicted in the picture.

Staff can also use unusual positioning of photographs of activities and people to explore preschooler's attitudes to cultural diversity. Ramsey (1987) suggested showing people involved in daily tasks such as eating using a variety of implements such as chopsticks and knives and forks to provoke discussion among children about what is 'normal'.

It is important to have places where children who are bilingual can play alongside other children without always needing to use language to interact (Arthur et al. 1996). This helps bilingual children participate in play without the pressure to use language. Jenny van Oosten (1988) found that music and movement experiences where the verbal component of the experience is minimal allow positively for such interactions between English speaking and non-English speaking children.

Thoughtful positioning of items and prompt cards can enable children learning English as a second language to make requests and to participate in decisions about what the group or individuals might do next. For instance, van Oosten (1988) used song cards in the music corner to ensure that children with little or no English could request songs merely by pointing to or picking up a particular card.

Gender

In groups of four-year-old children it is not unusual for girls and boys to develop boys-only and girls-only play spaces (Browne and Ross 1991). Often these spaces are developed in traditionally gender-stereotyped ways, with construction toys such as blocks and Lego in the boys' areas and domestic play areas such as home corner in the girls' areas (MacNaughton 1997). Disrupting the normal placement of materials in these areas, by, for example, placing the dolls in the blocks area, removing physical dividers between home corner and blocks area or adding Lego to the home corner can encourage more mixed-gender play. Staff need to monitor such changes carefully to ensure that the gender-stereotyped play patterns do not merely transfer to new areas.

Children's understandings of what is normal for males and females to do, think and feel can also be challenged by careful positioning of images within the centre. Consider placing an image of a man performing caring, nurturing tasks alongside a woman doing these things. Similarly, always place a female involved in physically challenging tasks or traditional male areas of employment alongside any traditional images you have. Children can be stirred to question and discuss gender roles by cutting and pasting images in ways that challenge their understandings about normality. Consider placing a male head on a female body and vice-versa and discussing with children how they know which picture is of a male and which is of a female.

Children's understandings about normality can also be challenged by offering them lots of images of non-traditional family lifestyles. Children can be stirred to question and discuss family roles and lifestyles by cutting and pasting images in ways that challenge their understandings about what is a normal family. Consider asking the children to cut and paste families where dad does all the work at home or where there are two mums and one mum is in paid work and the other mum is at home caring for the children, and discussing how there are lots of different types of families. There are single-parent families, families where people have divorced and mum and dad no longer live in the same house, gay and lesbian families, and families in which grandparents, aunts and uncles and children all live together. Understanding diverse family lifestyles helps children broaden their understanding of gender roles by seeing that there are lots of ways to be dads and lots of ways to be mums.

Disability and additional needs

The placement of materials and pathways should enable children with disabilities to move about safely and with comfort. Materials and equipment should be positioned to ensure that children with disabilities can participate in the key experiences in the program. The nature and type of each child's disability will determine what this means in practice.

As discussed above, careful positioning of images within the centre can challenge children's understandings of what is normal male and female behaviour. Consider creating similar challenges to children's understandings of disability by placing images of children and adults with different disabilities performing a variety of potentially unexpected tasks alongside images of non-disabled people performing these tasks. An example of this would be using images from the Para Olympics. Staff can use such images to interest the children in people's differing abilities and disabilities and challenge their understandings about what is a normal way to be, think, see, move, hear and feel.

Careful placement of materials can also enhance engagement between children with autism and their environment. McGee et al. (1991) have found that developing a toy rotation play which adds novelty and interest to materials available helps the integration of children with autism into mainstream early childhood settings. They instigated a fortnightly rotation plan of toys to produce novelty and interest in their classrooms and found that novelty helped increase the engagement of the children with autism with the toys.

REFLECTING ON POSITIONING TECHNIQUES

1 Consider the following quote from Gandini (1994, p. 149):

> We think that the space has to be a sort of aquarium that mirrors the ideas, values, attitudes, and cultures of the people who live in it.

Do the centres you are familiar with position people, objects and artefacts to accomplish these goals? Do you think they should? Why? How could they achieve these goals? How relevant is Gandini's statement to issues of equity and anti-bias in the placement of equipment and materials?

2 How might equipment and materials be positioned to encourage preschoolers' emerging interest in the world of print and the associated skills of reading and writing?

3 How could you use the positioning of equipment and materials to encourage social interaction and conversation between preschool children and babies?

4 What are the key precautions you need to take when positioning equipment to ensure a safe learning environment for all ages?

5 How might your philosophy on adult intervention in children's learning influence the positioning of equipment in the inside learning area?

6   Briggs and Potter (1995) believed that the positioning of space and material can enhance chil-
    dren's learning through:

- ➲ encouraging movement and interaction
- ➲ encouraging deep involvement
- ➲ promoting independence and self-direction
- ➲ encouraging the use of specific skills
- ➲ increasing or decreasing concentration
- ➲ encouraging co-operation between children
- ➲ stimulating curiosity and problem-solving.

Use the following table to reflect on how you could position materials in the sand-play area to encourage children to be involved in these processes.

Aim of positioning	Positioning equipment Babies	Positioning equipment Toddlers	Positioning equipment Preschoolers
Movement and interaction Deep involvement Independence and self-direction Skills Concentration Co-operation			

IMPROVING TEACHING IN PRACTICE

1   Sketch the layout of the inside and outside learning areas in an early childhood centre and take photographs of these areas.
2   How well did placement of equipment support easy supervision of children?
3   How well was equipment placed to support a safe and healthy environment?
- ➲ Were play spaces well lit?
- ➲ Was there fresh air and were temperatures comfortable?
- ➲ Was there room to move around freely (for example, when using a wheelchair, callipers, walking frames, guide dog, etc.)?
- ➲ Could equipment be reached easily and safely by children?
- ➲ Were sharp edges kept away from areas where children might knock against them?
- ➲ Was there ready access to a space for recycling of material and clearing rubbish from the floor?
- ➲ Were there non-slip surfaces in the 'wet' areas?
- ➲ Could staff readily access all equipment without straining muscles?

4   To what extent did the current placement of equipment enhance the aesthetic appeal of the centre?
- ➲ Were equipment and materials deliberately and carefully placed?
- ➲ Was the careful placement of materials and equipment maintained?
- ➲ Did the environment evolve over time?

- ➡ Were there soft areas that encouraged people to relax, reflect and rest?
- ➡ Were sounds placed as carefully as objects?
- ➡ Were texture, shape and colour used with care and thought to provide enjoyment, stimulation and relaxation?
- ➡ Were visual images hung and treated with care and respect?
- ➡ Were artefacts, crafts, art and memorabilia culturally familiar to the children and adults?

5 Was equipment placed to enhance children's sense of security and competence?
- ➡ Were there regular major traffic paths in the environment?
- ➡ Could children readily access child-safe cleaning materials and equipment?
- ➡ Were everyday materials children use such as pencil sharpeners, sticky-tape, glue-sticks, scissors, etc. readily accessible to the children?
- ➡ Were everyday materials placed so as to avoid congestion when several children want access at once?
- ➡ Did materials used regularly have an obvious home?
- ➡ Did children have a personal storage space for their special projects and personal belongings?
- ➡ Did children have access to child-sized furniture and equipment for several of their experiences?

6 How was equipment placed to stimulate children's curiosity?

7 Did the placement of equipment and adults support equity of access and participation?
- ➡ Could children of different physical abilities move around easily?
- ➡ Could children of different physical abilities participate in a range of experiences?
- ➡ Could children of different abilities and ages easily see and touch display areas?
- ➡ Could all children in the group irrespective of their cultural background recognise their own culture in the materials and staff available to them?

8 How and how well were developmental considerations taken into account in the placement of equipment and materials?

Further reading and resources

Briggs, F. and Potter, G. 1995, *Teaching Children in the First Three Years of School*, second edn, Sydney, Longman, Chapters 7 and 8.

Brown, K. 1994, 'Adaptive equipment and positioning for mobility: focus on infants and toddlers', *ED393228*.

Crook, S. and Farmer, B. 1996, *Just Imagine*, Melbourne, TAFE Publications.

Fowler, M. and McDougall, M. 1990, *Cost Effective Child Caring Places and Spaces*, Canberra, Australian Early Childhood Association.

Gandini, L. 1994, 'Educational and caring spaces', in C. Edwards, L. Gandini and G. Forman eds, *The Hundred Languages of Children: The Reggio Emilia Approach to Early Childhood Education*, New Jersey, Ablex Publishing Corporation [refer to pp. 135–50].

Greenman, J. 1988, *Caring Spaces, Learning Places: Children's Environments that Work*, Redmond, Washington, Exchange Press.

Harrison, L. 1996, *Planning Appropriate Learning Environments for Children Under Three*, revised edn, Watson, ACT, Australian Early Childhood Association.

Plested, D. 1993, 'Health and safety in early childhood centres', *Australian Early Childhood Association Resource Book Series* (3), pp. 1–16.

Read, K., Gardner, P. and Mahler, B. 1993, *Early Childhood Programs: Human Relationships and Learning*, ninth edn, Forth Worth, TX, Holt, Rinehart and Winston Inc. [refer to pp. 49–67].

Talbot, J. and Frost, J. 1989, 'Magical playscapes', *Childhood Education*, 66(1), pp. 11–19.

Taylor, B. 1989, *Early Childhood Program Management: People and Procedures*, Toronto, Merrill [refer to pp. 129–54].

Wanerman, T. 1999, 'The open door policy: enhancing community in a part-time preschool program', *Young Children*, 54(2), pp. 16–17.

Video/CD-ROM

Creating a Child Care Environment for Infants and Toddlers: Space to Grow, California State Department of Education, 1988.

Early Childhood Training: Guidance and Discipline in the Learning Environment, Setting Environment Vol. 1, Magna Systems Inc., Illinois, 1995.

Equity Adventures in Early Childhood, MacNaughton, G., Campbell, S., Smith, K. and Lawrence, H., Centre for Equity and Innovation in Early Childhood, University of Melbourne, Australia, 2002.

Learning Environment, Early Childhood Training Series, Magna Systems, 1995/2002, available from Marcom Projects at www.marcom.com.au

Routines from Lunch to Bed, Australian Early Childhood Association, Lady Gowrie Children's Centre, Melbourne, Australia, 1998.

Setting up the Learning Environment, A curriculum videotape from High Scope Press, 1992.

Websites — extending learning online

http://www.edfac.unimelb.edu.au/LED/CEIEC/

References

Allen, K. and Hart, B. 1984, *The Early Years: Arrangements for Learning*, New Jersey, Prentice Hall.

Arthur, L. 1995, 'Linguistic diversity', in B. Creaser and E. Dau eds, *The Anti-Bias Approach in Early Childhood* (pp. 85–113), Sydney, Harper Educational.

Arthur, L., Beecher, B., Docket, S., Farmer, S. and Death, E. 1996, *Programming and Planning in Early Childhood Settings*, second edn, Sydney, Harcourt Brace and Co.

Bodrova, E. and Leong, D. 2001, *Tools of the Mind: A Case Study of Implementing the Vygotskian Approach in American Early Childhood and Primary Classrooms*, Switzerland, International Bureau of Education.

Bowman, B., Donovan, M. and Burns, S. 2001, *Eager to Learn: Educating Our Preschoolers*, Washington DC, National Academy Press.

Briggs, F. and Potter, G. 1995, *Teaching Children in the First Three Years of School*, 2nd edn, Sydney, Longman.

Browne, N. and Ross, C. 1991, '"Girls' stuff, boys' stuff": young children talking and playing', in N. Browne ed., *Science and Technology in the Early Years* (pp. 37–51), Milton Keynes, Open University Press.

Cohen, J. and Cohen, M. 1960, *The Penguin Dictionary of Quotations*, Middlesex, Penguin Books.

Edwards, A. and Knight, P. 1994, *Effective Early Years Education: Teaching Young Children*, Milton Keynes, Open University Press.

Gandini, L. 1994, 'Educational and caring spaces', in C. Edwards, L. Gandini and G. Forman eds, *The Hundred Languages of Children: The Reggio Emilia Approach to Early Childhood Education* (pp. 135–50), New Jersey, Ablex Publishing Corporation.

Greenman, J. 1988, *Caring Spaces, Learning Places: Children's Environments that Work*, Redmond, Washington, Exchange Press.

Hintz, B. F. and Stomfay-Stitz, A. 1999, Peace education and conflict resolution through expressive arts in early childhood education and teacher education, Paper presented at the *Annual Conference of the Eastern Educational Research Association*, Hilton Head, SC, February 26, ED433105.

Honig, A. 1990, 'The baby: birth to 12 months', in E. Surbeck and M. Kelly eds, *Personalizing Care with Infants, Toddlers and Families* (pp. 10–22), Wheaton, MD, Association for Childhood Education International.

McGee, G., Daly, T., Izeman, S., Mann, L. and Risley, T. 1991, 'Use of classroom materials to promote preschool engagement', *Teaching Exceptional Children* (Summer), pp. 44–7.

MacNaughton, G. 1997, 'Who's got the power? Rethinking gender equity strategies in early childhood', *International Journal of Early Years Education*, 5(1), pp. 57–66.

Perlmutter, J., Bloom, L. and Burrell, L. 1993, 'Whole maths through investigation', *Childhood Education*, 70(1), pp. 20–4.

Plested, D. 1993, 'Health and safety in early childhood centres', *Australian Early Childhood Association Resource Book Series* (3), pp. 1–16.

Raczynski, B. and Stevenson, C. 1996, 'It's curtains to the quilt project: reflection on a small collaborative project with 7 and 8 year olds', in *Weaving Webs: Collaborative Teaching and Learning in the Early Years Curriculum* (pp. 327–44), Melbourne, 11–13 July.

Ramsey, P. 1987, *Teaching and Learning in a Diverse World: Multicultural Education for Young Children*, New York, Teachers' College Press.

Read, K., Gardner, P. and Mahler, B. 1993, *Early Childhood Programs: Human Relationships and Learning*, ninth edn, Forth Worth, TX, Holt, Rinehart and Winston Inc.

Schiller, P. 1999, 'Turning knowledge into practice', *Child Care Information Exchange*, March 126, pp. 49–52.

Schreiber, M. 1999, 'Time out for toddlers: is our goal punishment or education?', *Young Children*, 54(4), pp. 22–6.

Stephen, H. 1993, 'Conflict resolution with young children', *Australian Early Childhood Association Resource Book Series* (2), pp. 1–16.

van Oosten, J. 1988, 'Integrating Music in the Program', *Resource*, 56, July, no page specified.

Wanerman, T. 1999, 'The open door policy: enhancing community in a part-time preschool program', *Young Children*, 54(2), pp. 16–17.

Wilkes, G. (ed.) 1979, *Collins Dictionary of the English Language*, Middlesex, Penguin Books.

Wilson Gillespie, C. 2000, 'Six Head Start classrooms begin to explore the Reggio Emilia Approach', in *Young Children*, 55(1), pp. 21–27.

Chapter 2

Collecting

Collect: to gather together.

(*Collins Dictionary of the English Language*, p. 297)

There are displays of pine cones, shells, or pebbles arranged by size, shape, or color. These displays record events in the children's lives. They contain treasures that children have gathered on special outings or regular walks.

(Gandini 1993, p. 141)

. . . children . . . [drew and wrote] a catalog of the international toys they collected. Math skills were enhanced by graphing the kinds of toys in the collection as well as the countries of origin.

(Swiniarski 1991, p. 162)

WHAT?

Collecting is the process of gathering things together. As a teaching technique, collecting is a deliberate process of gathering together objects, information and ideas to help generate children's interest in and learning about their natural and their social and cultural world. Collecting can help children to learn how to sort, classify, match and organise their world. In doing so, collecting enhances numerous skills across all areas of development.

HOW?

Collecting can be initiated by staff or by children. It may involve individuals, small groups or the whole group. It may begin simply with something found by a child, for instance a leaf in the garden. When shared with others this prompts them to search for more. Staff can encourage children's enthusiasm for collecting by using their interest in something and simply saying, 'Why don't we see if we can find some more like it? I wonder who would like to help?'. In contrast, staff may begin a collection by introducing something they have found, such as seeds from their own garden, and asking children if they have seen any similar ones at home or on the way to the centre. On some occasions, staff may have something they would like the children or an individual child to explore in more detail. For example, one child's interest in an overseas stamp on a letter that arrives at the centre may prompt staff to ask the children to bring in anything they have from overseas.

All sorts of objects can be collected. Staff can develop collections from things in the natural world or the social and cultural world. Items from the natural world that can be collected include rocks, leaves, plants, shells, seeds, feathers, bones, etc. Items from our social and cultural world that are easily collected include memorabilia and cultural artefacts (photos, diaries, clothes, ornaments, tickets, models) and items from popular culture such as music, records, tapes, books, magazines, comics, toys, etc. Recycled and found objects can also provide lots of ideas about collecting.

Display—a collection of shells.

The following anecdote shows how one teacher capitalised on the potential of collecting to enhance children's learning.

The teacher of a class of five-year-olds knows that during the school holidays many of the children will be visiting the beach. She talks to the children about collecting shells and seaweed during their holidays to bring back to school the following term. She reinforces this by sending an informal note to the parents. At the beginning of the next term, the children bring along several kinds of shells and seaweeds. These form the basis of a display and promote much discussion, comparing and contrasting, classifying and so forth.

Collections do not need to be limited to objects. Interesting collections can also be made from:

 sounds using tape-recordings of traffic noises, sounds in the bush, etc.

 jokes. Young children love having fun, and collecting the things they find funny can be developmentally valuable. Children's humour generally derives from what they find incongruous (Bergen 1992). This may be a sound that seems odd (ants barking), an action that is incongruous (dogs flying) or word play (Mousey Mick instead of Mickey Mouse). Seeing and understanding such 'mistakes' can assist the development of higher level cognitive skills; as children search for what is funny and try to create their own 'mistakes' they need to problem-solve and create new language.

Staff can follow some simple principles to ensure that collecting is a positive and productive learning experience for the children. They should:

- set aside a special place for the collected objects to be displayed and investigated by the children
- have reference books available to the children. Children can use the reference books to label their 'finds' and to compare and contrast different items in the collection. This can enrich their learning by extending their vocabulary and by enabling them to gain more in-depth understandings of how things grow or work
- keep a special box of tools for investigating the objects collected in more detail. This could include a magnifying glass, rulers, simple balance scales, a colour chart and a shape chart
- have some tools handy with which children can record their discoveries. Pencils and paper are obvious, but a camera can be a useful way to record the different ways in which children sort objects and allows several different sortings to be tried. The pros and cons of using different properties such as size or weight to sort objects can then be discussed via the photographs
- display objects with care to encourage children to take care of them
- develop clear rules and limits about who can use the collection and how. If the collection includes things that are rare, expensive, irreplaceable and/or personally precious to people, staff should carefully supervise their use
- take time to think about some of the discoveries that a collection might encourage and how they can use questions and comments to encourage such discoveries
- be available to the children to answer questions, to ask questions and to prompt the children to explore the collection
- ensure that the collection links with or reminds the younger children of real-life experiences
- ensure that all of the objects collected can be handled safely by the children.
- avoid collecting flora and fauna which are on the endangered or protected species lists and avoid collecting objects from the natural world that might be home to animals and plants
- avoid collecting becoming a competition about who brings the best or the most of something.

Collecting becomes a worthwhile learning experience when children are encouraged to explore, sort and classify the objects they or the staff have collected. Children can look for a number of properties that differentiate objects from each other or group them together. Shape, size, colour, texture, smell, weight and function can each be used to explore, sort and classify. Asking children to think about how to sort things and what they might call the categories into which they can be sorted can add fun, interest and conceptual challenges to the experience of collecting.

Matthew, a kindergarten director in the outer eastern suburbs of Melbourne, has a passion for wood-working. One day a child came to the kindergarten with an old, hand-made nail (her parents were renovating their house). With Matthew's guidance the children discussed the difference between the old nail and the nails that they had at the kindergarten. This quickly led to an interest in different kinds of nails. The children made a collection of nails that their parents had at home. The nails were categorised as long, short, round-headed, flat-headed, fat, thin, different metals of different weights and different colours. The nails were displayed on an 'interest' table, where the children were able to touch them and to begin to notice differences and to discuss functions.

WHEN AND WHY?

Whether collecting begins spontaneously or in a planned way by staff or by children, it may last minutes, hours, days or months. Collections can stimulate socio-dramatic play, scientific discovery or a long-term group project on a specific theme or issue. Collections can help children to develop wonder about their world by encouraging them to sort and to explore the physical or social properties of objects in the world about them. In doing so, children develop new concepts and new language through which to describe and to understand the world about them.

In some parts of Australia, autumn is a wonderful time to collect leaves in and out of the playground. These can be sorted according to colour, size, shape, etc. Leaves can be used to see changes in properties, for example leaves change in colour and texture as they dry. Leaves can also be used for artwork, collage, pressing between wax paper and then displaying on windows so that the light passes through them.

Goal relevance

Collecting develops children's cognitive skills by encouraging children to classify and match objects (Beaty 1996). Staff can use open questions to encourage children to think about the similarities and differences between objects. For instance:

- ➔ How does this object look like the others we collected?
- ➔ What is the difference(s) between these two objects?
- ➔ Can you find a picture in the book of an object like this?
- ➔ Where could we find more objects like this?

Beaty (1996) argued that collecting natural objects is an important part of inducting children into the scientific mode of inquiry because it helps children to:

- ➔ create and maintain a sense of wonder in the world about them
- ➔ question and find out about their world
- ➔ learn to take care of the things in the world about them.

Collecting can also develop children's socio-symbolic competencies. Staff can use what Dowd (1990) called 'jackdaws' to develop and extend children's understandings of particular stories and enrich the children's socio-dramatic play. 'Jackdaws' are collections of items related to a particular book and its setting. They can be items in the story or items that might be found in a place or time in which the story is set. The staff generally place the 'jackdaw' in a special place (in a box or on an interest table) so that the children can explore it alone or in small groups. This exploration can

Classifying is engaging for these boys.

extend children's understandings of the story, enhance their vocabulary and lead to individual or group project work related to the story.

Collecting can be a group activity that promotes social competence through providing children with the opportunity to share discoveries, to help others to find things, to feel the enjoyment of working with a group towards a common goal and to practise contributing to group projects. Collecting can create a real sense of excitement within the group as each child finds something to add to the collection and the children make discoveries about the properties of each item.

Collections also contribute to specific curriculum domains such as mathematics and literacy. For instance, collections of objects from the natural world of similar objects (seeds, stones, shells, leaves) that are of different sizes can assist in building children's knowledge of and skills in seriation:

> Laura also brought to the classroom her own collection of 17 pinecones—from giant Sequoia cones from California to very tiny pinecones. They enjoyed putting them in order from the smallest to the biggest and vice versa . . . The inclusion of vocabulary like first, second, third and so forth helped the children to develop representational knowledge of seriation. (Kirova and Bhargava 2002, p. 12)

A collection can also be used to build children's counting skills. Willis (1999) noted that not all children will necessarily use items in a collection in the same way to achieve specific mathematical outcomes. She discussed how many Indigenous Australian children, and some non-Indigenous children, particularly from working-class backgrounds, could count just by looking at a collection of objects. It is therefore important to be flexible in how collections are used to teach specific skills to specific children.

Collections of books that represent different perspectives on a topic, experience, feeling or way of being can help build children's critical literacy skills. Swindler Boutte (2002, p. 148) suggest collecting books that:

- ❯ represent various ethnic groups, genders, religions, ages, lives, family structures
- ❯ represent historical and contemporary depictions of different people
- ❯ describe different holidays and cultural rituals and traditions
- ❯ share fairytales from different cultures
- ❯ show different gender roles being performed by men and women, boys and girls
- ❯ are written in different languages and different dialects.

These books can be used to discuss with children the different ways in which people think and act and different points in history and in different cultural groups. Having a diverse range of books enables comparisons to be made, stereotypes to be critically discussed and simplistic and tokenistic views of who we are to be explored through comparisons and contrasts offered within the books.

Developmental considerations

Collecting is a useful teaching technique for all age groups. However, the younger the child, the more the collecting needs to be done by the staff for the children. The children's developmental stage is likely to influence the types of objects of interest they collect themselves or have others collect for them. A good rule of thumb is to collect diverse objects that introduce young children to different sensory experiences. Some possibilities would be:

- ❯ different smells from a collection of aromatherapy oils, herbs and spices
- ❯ different textures from objects in the constructed and natural worlds
- ❯ objects with different plays of light on them such as glass pebbles, mirrors and mobiles
- ❯ objects with sounds from the natural and constructed worlds including audio-tapes and CDs.

Toddlers are interested in themselves and what they can do; have a great interest in the here and now; are grappling with object permanence so enjoy things that appear and disappear; want to learn the names of the things about them; and, are fascinated by how things work (Arthur et al. 1996). Collections that are likely to interest toddlers would include:

- ❯ personal items such as 'my toys' or 'my bed-time things'
- ❯ items in the natural world that they can readily name (for example, insects, rocks and shells)
- ❯ things that appear and disappear (jack-in-the-box toys, pop-up books or cards)
- ❯ simple mechanical items that have clear workings (hole punchers, hand-held flour sieves)
- ❯ things that can be taken apart and put together again easily (torches, watering cans with removable nozzles, large padlocks and keys, pairs of shells, large seed pods, fasteners, zippers, 'nests' of things such as Russian dolls, measuring spoons and jars).

Clarissa is a staff member in a child care centre in a small country town in Victoria. She encouraged the parents of the children in the toddler room to bring several types of padlocks to the centre so she could develop a padlock collection for the children to play with. The children enjoyed undoing the locks. Clarissa was able to use this time with the children to enhance their language development and to foster their social skills. She talked about the different shapes and sizes of the padlocks and how they were made of different types of metal. The children were encouraged to take turns at opening and closing the locks and to watch others practising their skills.

Toddlers have a few basic characteristics that could influence the success of collecting:

- Their understandings of right and wrong are just beginning to evolve, so staff should not expect them to follow complex rules about how to use and care for items in the collection.
- They enjoy finding out how things work and what things can and cannot do. This means they explore objects in somewhat enthusiastic and unconventional ways. Keeping collections to objects that can 'handle' this is one way forward. However, it is also important for toddlers to learn how to care for precious things. If there are items in the collection that could be easily damaged or broken there should always be an adult present to reinforce simple rules about how to care for these items.
- They can sometimes find it difficult to share. When collections are built from objects that toddlers have collected themselves, they will need help to share these with the group.
- Their fine motor skill control is erratic so staff should remember to choose objects that they can handle easily.
- They find out about how things work by, among other things, putting them in their mouths. Adult supervision should be constant around such objects that could be dangerous if swallowed or tasted.

Preschool children are becoming increasingly developmentally adept in all areas of development. They are gaining more control over their fine motor skills so they can handle a variety of objects with care and will enjoy objects that they can explore using their fine motor skills. Collections of things that can be taken apart and put together such as nuts and bolts and keys and padlocks can offer preschoolers the opportunity to practise and consolidate their fine motor skills.

By four and five years of age children's moral development has reached a point where they can understand the differences between what is fair or not fair and between what is kind or unkind in everyday situations (Arthur et al. 1996). Consequently, collections of objects can be used to help children share and to negotiate use of the objects in the collection. It also becomes more possible to collect objects and images that develop critical thinking about stereotypes (see below) and which can encourage children to think about what is fair and unfair, kind and unkind.

Beginning readers can benefit from access to a vibrant collection of Big Books. When teachers read aloud to beginning readers from Big Books children's interest in the relationship between print and language increases, their enjoyment in reading times improves and they are more vividly able to recall words and storylines from within the book (Cassady 1988). In addition to buying commercially published Big Books teachers can make their own books from events in the classroom which combine children's artwork with teacher print. Teachers need to ensure that their collection of Big Books includes lots of stories that have repetitive phrases or are written in rhyme so that beginning readers can readily recall the words and begin to associate them with the text within the books.

EQUITY CONSIDERATIONS

'Race' and culture

Collecting cultural artefacts and memorabilia can help children to share their own culture and help them to learn about cultures of other children in their group. Everyday objects express many aspects of a group's culture, including what it celebrates, how it celebrates, its art and craft traditions, its folk mythology, its language, its family structures and its ways of valuing others. Collections of photos, ornaments, clothes and household items can all stimulate discussions about many aspects of the different cultural lifestyles of children in the group.

If children have things from their culture on display in a centre this can help build a sense of belonging and a sense that they are being valued. Seeing things from other people's daily lives can help increase children's understandings of the similarities and differences in their own cultural background and that of other people. However, such collections should not be 'one-off' events that reinforce what Dermon-Sparks et al. (1989) called a 'tourist approach' to cultural diversity. Such approaches invite children to 'visit' a culture for a day or a week by looking at clothes, food, etc. of cultures different to their own. This can make the other cultures seem exotic destinations to be visited rather than an important and everyday part of living in a multicultural society.

Collecting and sharing children's family history and current traditions can build respect and acceptance of diversity within the group (Partington and McCudden 1992). However, this should be done with care and thought. It should always be discussed with *all* children's parents before starting such a project. Some parents may feel comfortable sharing their family history within the group, others may not. Sharing family history can raise painful memories such as the violent death of loved ones in war-torn countries or enforced migration to Australia. Some refugee families may have lost much of the record of their lives and have little in the way of memorabilia. For children of these families, being unable to 'bring in' things to share may result in them feeling isolated and marginalised. They may also feel confused when their request for them brings sadness to their family. Families may have many complex reasons for not participating in such projects. Staff need to remember all families have a right to privacy.

Some Aboriginal children may find that collections of family memorabilia help them build relationships more quickly within the group. By encouraging the group to share personal history and interests such collections can in part reflect what happens in their own communities when people who don't know each other meet. On these occasions:

> . . . they share information about themselves and to whom they are related, as a way of establishing relationships . . . These relationships need to be recognised as in Aboriginal communities emphasis is placed on the extended family and a complex kinship system. (Colbung and Glover 1996, p. 36)

Such processes of getting to know each other should be reciprocal: staff should be prepared to share who they are with the Aboriginal children. This will help build positive relationships more quickly.

Collections of photographs of people can be a particularly positive way of representing and talking about ethnic diversity. Children can become familiar with and comfortable about physical diversity by looking at and comparing the facial characteristics and expressions of the people in the photographs. There is some evidence that children will make less stereotyped comments about photographs than they will about other images of ethnic diversity (Ramsey 1987).

When collections of photographs are used to introduce a homogeneous group of children to diversity, the photo should be carefully chosen. Staff should be careful to ensure that the photos contain contemporary images of each ethnic group and do not reinforce stereotypes prevalent in the centre (Ramsey 1987). Particular care should be taken over the use of photographs of Aboriginal Australians on two counts. Firstly, several Aboriginal groups find it offensive to publicly display images of people who have died. Secondly, many images of Aboriginal people are highly stereotyped and represent a very limited range of Aboriginal lifestyles. The checklist on vetting images in children's books in Chapter 14 can be used when choosing pictures for the collection.

Children may bring in images or objects for a collection that staff believe are racist. Staff should tell children why they want to exclude them from the collection or should create a collection of racist images to discuss with the children. To do this requires considerable thought and care.

When staff collect natural materials from their local environment it is also important that they try to use reference books that give accurate information about Australian natural environments.

Gender

Collecting can be a useful technique for teaching preschool children about gender-role stereotyping and sexism and helping them to think critically about these issues. Askew and Ross (1988) used collecting as a way of helping six-year-old boys to think critically about traditional forms of masculinity and violence. They asked the boys to collect images from television, comics and magazines about heroes. Once the boys had a collection of images of heroes, they thought about what it means to be a hero and decided that to be a hero you had to be brave. Askew and Ross (1988) then asked the boys to use their collection of images to find out what it meant to be brave. The boys found that lots of 'brave' heroes were involved in violence and hurting others. This formed the basis of a discussion between staff and children about whether this was a 'good' way to be a hero and what other things you could do to be a hero.

Staff can use such a process to raise many issues about stereotyping with young children. For instance, staff could ask children to collect images of girls being heroines, men being caring, the jobs that women do, etc. to begin discussions with the children about male and female roles and the pros and cons of these. Staff can also talk about why it is hard to find images of particular things—for example, women being 'brave'.

Disability and additional needs

Collecting and collections need to be accessible to children in the group with disabilities. It is also important that staff offer sufficient variability in the objects collected, the ways they can be collected and how they are displayed to enable children with disabilities to find a personally appropriate way of exploring the collection (Winter et al. 1994). To ensure that all children can collect and explore the collection staff need to provide a safe environment. Children with disabilities often require more floor space for freedom of movement (Winter et al. 1994) and this should be taken into account when collecting in the centre and when displaying the collection. In addition, floor placement of the collection can facilitate easy access for those children who have difficulty with balance and bending. Consider collecting things that will demonstrate the special abilities of children with visual or hearing impairment. Anastasia's work shows how this might be done.

Anastasia is working with visually impaired children in a special setting. Most of the children have little or no sight. She encourages the children to bring their soft toys from home. Eventually they formed a collection of these toys. Anastasia taped open shoe boxes together and put them on a low table. Into each of the boxes she put one soft toy. The children were encouraged to pick up each toy, to notice the texture of the material, the shape, the smell, how hard and soft the toys were, and to notice similarities and differences. A good deal of learning took place, their expressive language was increased and they had many opportunities for social interaction.

Developing collections of visual aids and props that can help staff to talk easily with children about a variety of disabilities is a positive way to use collecting to enhance anti-discriminatory attitudes in the group. For instance, Playworks (Victoria, Australia) has developed a range of 'DD dolls' (Diversity Dolls) that could be gradually collected to represent a full range of disabilities and to provide a basis for discussion with children from as young as two years of age. Involving the children in collecting images that represent people with disabilities can heighten children's awareness of, interest in and understanding of disability. Sorting images broadly into major areas of disability, such as people with visual impairment, or people with mobility impairment, can encourage children to explore the similarities and differences between these people. They can learn that not all people who are blind look the same, and begin to talk about different degrees of sight. Some people who are blind use guide-dogs to help them see, some use a white stick, some need very strong glasses, etc. Children can also be encouraged to think about how they find images of people with less obvious disabilities such as hearing impairment or epilepsy. For instance, 'What does a person with epilepsy look like?', 'Can you tell from a picture that a person has epilepsy?'.

REFLECTING ON COLLECTING TECHNIQUES

1 Define collecting.
2 What are the key factors that contribute to successful teaching through collecting with young children?
3 What are ten recycled objects that you could collect and use with babies?
4 What sort of objects might preschoolers like to collect and why?
5 What everyday objects express your group's culture?
6 Make a list of the items you could collect when you first work with a group of children to ensure that your area creates a sense of belonging for all children in the group.
7 What cultural artefacts or memorabilia do you have in your home that represent your personal history and current traditions? Which of these could be used to begin a collection with young children? Would they be suitable to use with all age groups of children?
8 What sort of images could you collect that you could use to challenge traditional gender-role stereotypes with three-year-old children?
9 What are the key factors you would need to consider when involving a four-year-old child with hearing impairment in a group collecting project?

IMPROVING TEACHING IN PRACTICE

1 Develop a list of the type of visual aids and props you could collect that could be used to easily talk with children about a variety of disabilities.

2 Start a collection of images that you could use to promote positive attitudes to cultural and racial diversity with children.

3 Choose one storybook you could use with two-year-old children and one storybook you could use with four-year-old children. Begin a 'Jackdaw' collection for each of the books.

4 Visit an early childhood centre and evaluate its approach to collecting. Did it:

> set aside a special place for the collected objects to be displayed and investigated by the children?

> have reference books available to the children?

> keep a special box of 'tools' for investigating the objects collected in more detail?

> have some 'tools' handy to help children record their discoveries?

> display objects with care to encourage children to take care of them?

> develop clear rules and limits about use of the collection?

> have staff available to the children to answer questions, to ask questions and to prompt their exploration?

> ensure that all of the objects collected were safe for the children to handle?

> avoid collecting flora and fauna on endangered or protected species lists and avoid collecting objects from the natural world that might be home to animals and plants?

> avoid turning collecting into a competition about who brings the best or the most of something?

Further reading and resources

Dowd, F. 1990, 'What's a Jackdaw doing in our classroom?' *Childhood Education*, 66(4), pp. 228–31.

Moyer, E. (ed.) 1995, *Selecting Educational Equipment and Materials for School and Home*, Washington DC, Association for Childhood Education International.

Swiniarski, L. 1991, 'Toys: universals for teaching global education', *Childhood Education*, 67(3), pp. 161–3.

References

Arthur, L., Beecher, B., Dockett, S., Farmer, S. and Death, E. 1996, *Programming and Planning in Early Childhood Settings*, second edn, Sydney, Harcourt Brace and Company.

Askew, S. and Ross, C. 1988, *Boys Don't Cry*, Milton Keynes, Open University Press.

Beaty, J. 1996, *Skills for Preschool Teachers*, fifth edn, New Jersey, Prentice Hall Inc.

Bergen, D. 1992, 'Using humour to facilitate learning', *Childhood Education*, 69(2), pp. 105–6.

Cassady, J. 1988, 'Beginning reading with big books', *Childhood Education*, 65(1), pp. 18–23.

Colbung, M. and Glover, A. 1996, 'In partnership with Aboriginal children', in M. Fleer, ed., *Conversations about Teaching and Learning in Early Childhood Settings* (pp. 33–40), Canberra, Australian Early Childhood Association.

Dermon-Sparks, L. and the Anti-Bias Task Force, 1989, *The Anti-Bias Curriculum*, Washington DC, National Association for the Education of Young Children.

Dowd, F. 1990, 'What's a Jackdaw doing in our classroom?', *Childhood Education*, 66(4), pp. 228–31.

Gandini, L. 1993, 'Educational caring spaces', in C. Edwards, L. Gandini and G. Foreman, eds, *The Hundred Languages of Children: The Reggio Emilia Approach to Early Childhood Education* (pp. 135–49), New Jersey, Ablex Publishing Company.

Kirova, A. and Bhargava, A. 2002, 'Learning to guide preschool children's mathematical understandings: a teacher's professional growth', *Early Childhood Research and Practice*, 4(1), pp. 1–20.

Partington, G. and McCudden, V. 1993, *Ethnicity and Education*, Sydney, Social Science Press.

Ramsey, P. 1987, *Teaching and Learning in a Diverse World: Multicultural Education for Young Children*, Columbia, Teachers' College Press.

Swindler Boutte, G. 2002, 'The critical literacy process: guidelines for examining books', *Childhood Education*, 78(3), pp. 147–52.

Swiniarski, L. 1991, 'Toys: universals for teaching global education', *Childhood Education*, 67(3), pp. 161–3.

Wilkes, G. (ed.) 1979, *Collins Dictionary of the English Language*, Middlesex, Penguin Books.

Willis, S. 1999, 'Numeracy and outcomes in the early years', *Every Child*, 5(1), pp. 8–9.

Winter, S., Bell, M. and Dempsey, J. 1994, 'Creating play environments for children with special needs', *Childhood Education*, 71(1), pp. 28–32.

Chapter 3

Scheduling

Schedule: a plan of procedure for a project, allotting the work to be done and time for it.

(*Collins Dictionary of the English Language*, p. 1304)

Time is something which teachers say they do not have.

(Lally 1991, p. 179)

Time, it is clear, can be managed in many ways.

(Jones and Reynolds 1992, p. 24)

WHAT?

Scheduling, as a teaching technique, involves taking decisions about how to organise the tempo and duration of current and future interactions between children, between children and adults, and between people and materials. The aim is to organise the day to ensure there is a balanced, productive and pleasing momentum to these interactions, and that children's learning is enhanced through careful use of time. This means that staff need to consider how to plan time for key events such as arrivals, departures, transitions and meals, and how this time meshes with the remainder of the day.

While a centre schedule should be planned well in advance, it should also be flexible. For example, on a hot day the children may need to go to sleep earlier than usual because they may be more tired; on a rainy day the indoor playtime may be extended if the children have had long periods of 'inside time'.

HOW?

Staff need to consider several, interrelated dimensions of how they and the children use time if they are to produce a productive and pleasing learning environment.

Organisation of time during the day: the timetable

Staff need to develop a plan for how they can best use their time to enrich and extend children's learning. To do this they need to organise time to:

 maximise enjoyment and sense of well-being of children, parents and staff

 ensure that children gain a feeling of security and competence in their learning environment

➲   support children's differing learning styles and patterns

➲   support equity of access to and participation in the program for all children.

The following discussion at a staff meeting shows how scheduling can help children feel secure in a new environment.

A new group of three-year-olds is about to start the kindergarten year and the staff are discussing ways in which they can help the children to settle in.

Dean: 'Let's decide on a timetable for the day and keep this for the first weeks of the term'.

Andrea: 'That's a good idea. It'll help the children, and it'll help me, too, because I don't have to think too much about what we're going to do next. I'm always so busy with the children at the start of a new term—they seem to need so much individual attention!'

Dean: 'I think that inside time is best done first; that way the children get used to the room'.

Organising time for children's and staff's sense of enjoyment and well-being

Staff can achieve a sense of enjoyment and well-being for both children and staff in the centre by:

➲   organising time flexibly to cater for their own and the children's changing interests and levels of concentration and energy during the day (Briggs and Potter 1995)

➲   organising time to create a relaxed, unhurried, non-regimented tempo to the day (Jones and Reynolds 1992)

➲   planning time to ensure that children are not kept waiting for the next part of the day, for example, for lunch (Beaty 1996)

➲   organising time to allow staff to have in-depth conversations with children and to actively explore things with them

➲   organising time to allow staff to become actively involved with the children as well as doing 'housekeeping' tasks. Harrison (1996) suggests that the time spent on these tasks can be reduced by involving children in them

➲   planning quiet times for rest and recovery in between, or after more intense and active experiences for staff and children (Briggs and Potter 1995)

➲   planning time to allow for the unhurried transition between one experience or part of the day and another. As Hendrick (1990, p. 51) reminds us, '. . . little children do not "hurry" well'

➲   organising time so children can just 'be'. Children develop as 'thinkers, wonderers and builders . . . who at the same time are confident, resilient and tough' (Talbot and Frost 1989, p. 19) when they have time to daydream and reflect.

Organising time for children's sense of security and competence

Staff can help children by ensuring that:

➲   there is a regular pattern to the children's day, providing them with predictability. An illustrated daily timetable kept at the children's eye level can help children to understand the daily sequence (Beaty 1996)

⊙ there are blocks of time for children to improve their competence through practising new and old skills.

Organising time to support children's differing learning styles and patterns

Children's learning styles can be supported by staff who organise time to:

⊙ take account of children's differing levels of concentration
⊙ enable children to finish activities in their own time rather than in pre-set time periods
⊙ allow time to offer challenging extensions to children's experiences (Briggs and Potter 1995)
⊙ allow children to follow their interests at length and in depth (Lally 1991)
⊙ enable children to make their own decisions about when to have snacks, when to rest and when to be involved in inside or outside activities (Lally 1991)
⊙ meet the changing needs of the children as the year progresses
⊙ meet the demands and challenges of changing weather patterns during the year by, for example, taking account of children's and their own differing energy levels in hot and cold weather
⊙ allow ample opportunities for children to make choices during the day.

At the Little People Centre, staff have a schedule that allows the children to finish their projects and to work in their own time without the pressure that is often imposed by having to 'pack up' at pre-arranged times.

They have an informal snack time in the morning and in the afternoon. The snack—fruit or biscuits and drink—is set out on a table and the children help themselves over a period of about forty-five minutes. A staff member sits at the table during this time to cut up the fruit, to help the children pour drinks and to encourage social interaction. This arrangement allows the children to decide for themselves if they are hungry and thirsty at this time of the day.

Organising time to support equity of access and participation

Staff can ensure that:

⊙ children of differing physical abilities have the time to move around easily
⊙ children of differing physical abilities have the time to participate in a range of experiences
⊙ children of differing abilities have similar amounts of quality time with them
⊙ children of differing abilities and ages can explore experiences and materials for lengths of time commensurate with their differing levels of concentration
⊙ children in the group, irrespective of their cultural background, have time with them
⊙ boys and girls have similar amounts of quality time with them.

WHEN AND WHY?

Staff's approach to curriculum and their specific teaching and learning goals for the children will influence their scheduling decisions.

Snack time—a time to be together.

Goal relevance

In general, staff can use scheduling to ensure that children have time to:

- ❯ explore a balanced variety of experiences from within the arts and the sciences
- ❯ develop and practise skills and dispositions across a broad range of developmental domains
- ❯ experience personal control over their learning
- ❯ wonder and just 'be'
- ❯ satisfy their routine needs for eating, drinking, resting and toileting.

Developmental considerations

During their first twelve months of life, babies have widely differing patterns of sleeping, eating and toileting, and the daily timetable must take account of this. Staff will face considerable difficulties if they try to ensure that all babies in a group eat, sleep and have their nappies changed at the same time! Babies can react with anger, distress and fussiness or irritability if they are forced into a routine that does not suit their own individual rhythms (Honig 1990). On the other hand, when the daily timetable takes account of the differing rituals and routines of individual children then positive attachments between babies and staff can grow (Sims and Hutchins 1999). Positive attachments between babies and early childhood staff are critical to a baby's well-being.

Scheduling time for one-on-one interactions between individual staff and individual babies is also critical to a baby's well-being. If individual staff have time to actively and positively respond to a specific baby's cues and 'know them well enough to be able to respond in ways that work for them' (Rolfe 2002, p. 10) then babies will feel secure and cared for. Hence, building time to be caring into a day working with babies is critical.

Organising toddler programs involves 'slowing down, taking more time, adjusting to "toddler time" ' (Psaltis and Stonehouse 1988, p. 79). Toddlers generally dislike being hurried and are only just beginning to master the skills needed to be independent in routines and play experiences (Department of Human Services 1996). Thus, there should be sufficient time in the toddler program for each of the daily routines and for each of the learning experiences. Transition from one experience or routine to another will be easier if staff warn toddlers that they will soon need to bring their activity or routine to a close (Psaltis and Stonehouse 1988). In addition, staff should organise sufficient time for toddlers to watch others and to contemplate what is happening (Department of Human Services 1996). This helps them make sense of their daily world.

However, as the following example indicates, creating such flexibility in toddler settings often means innovative use of staff time.

A child care centre attached to a factory in the outer eastern suburbs decided that their toddler program could best meet the children's developmental needs by employing an extra member of staff to be present during routines and transition times. This would enable the children to take their time eating, dressing and going to sleep. The addition of a further member of staff would allow the children to finish activities at their own pace, to dress and undress themselves with help and to eat more slowly or quickly. The director approached the committee with well-thought-out arguments and obtained funding for an extra three hours of staff time per day.

Staff also need to plan for continuity from one day to the next. Recent work stimulated by an interest in the programs of Reggio Emilia in Italy has shown that children as young as two and three years of age can work in-depth over several months on projects of interest to them (LeeKeenan and Nimmo 1994; New 2000).

There are many different approaches to organising timetables for preschool children. Beaty (1996) and Arthur et al. (1996) provide several practical examples of approaches to scheduling. They call for a program which balances leisure, concentration, activity, wondering and exploring with the routines of eating, resting and toileting. Irrespective of how staff approach scheduling for preschoolers, they should plan for their increased competence and concentration. Time for in-depth and focused work is essential to create learning challenges for this age group.

A similar balance is also important for children in the early years of schooling. They share many of the same ways of learning as do preschool children (Arthur et al. 1996). However, children's ability and desire to concentrate on the same project for a considerable period of time can grow as their cognitive skills grow. Children in the early years of schooling also need time for in-depth work on projects that offer learning challenges for them. For example, their ability to invent increasingly complex games and follow rules is best supported by scheduling that allows them to work on their inventions over several days (Castle 1990). This principle applies to many other areas of project work with children of this age. Children in the early years of schooling can also benefit from recall time being planned into each day. This can be a time in which children 'explain and describe to other children what they have done and/or learnt in the course of an activity' (Fisher 1998, p. 40) and this can assist teachers to assess their learning. It can also offer children practice in sharing their experiences and ideas with others.

David talks to Jude's mother when she picks him up.

All children can benefit from time during which they experience control over their own learning and direct it. Research suggests that lack of personal control over learning can lead to anxiety in children in the early years of schooling (Broadhead 2001). The timetable can be used to counter the development of anxiety in young children by providing them with extended periods of time in which they direct their own learning activities and initiate and follow through on social relationships with each other.

A timetable that also allows time for children and teachers to experience pleasure in learning and in classroom relationships is important. Too often haste to move through routine times, such as meal times, can lead to coercive relationships in which the adult's power over the child dominates and the experience of pleasurable relationships between child and adult is diminished (Phelen 1997). Allowing time to deviate from the normal routine of the day can free children and adults to experience greater power over their lives with each other, to 'win back children's—as well as their own—rights to their bodies and desires' (Leavitt and Bauman Power 1997, p. 71).

EQUITY CONSIDERATIONS

'Race' and culture

Adults' use of time sends clear messages to children about who is most valued in the group. Consequently, staff should monitor how much time they are spending with each child. If there are children with whom they tend to spend superficial or minimal time, staff need to ask themselves, 'Who are these children?'. For example, staff decisions about how they spend their time can unintentionally reinforce racism: when staff spend only token amounts of time with particular children or on their specific interests, those children can believe that they are less valued than other children in the group. Staff need to monitor their interactions with all children in the group to avoid such tokenism. Consider the following scenario.

> The Greenfields child care centre in an outer suburban area had a small number of Aboriginal Australian children. The staff wanted the Aboriginal children to feel included in the group and decided that one way to do this was to make time to say something to each Aboriginal child each day. However, as they reflected on this idea, they felt that it was tokenistic. It would not give the Aboriginal children in-depth time with staff and it could result in staff spending only small amounts of time with Aboriginal children, indicating that these children were not valued as highly as other children in the centre.

Cook and Porter (1996) believe that staff working with families from culturally and linguistically diverse backgrounds need to plan very carefully to ensure that the organisation of the day meets these families' needs. They suggest that staff give particular attention to:

- creating time for a new family to settle into the centre's culture
- scheduling time to speak with parents, preferably with a bilingual staff member
- ensuring children have time with a bilingual staff member.

Increasingly, early childhood staff are working with children and families from culturally and linguistically diverse backgrounds who have experienced war-driven dislocation and refugee-related trauma. It is particularly important when working with these people that there is time for children and families to have bilingual support and time to settle into new routines and expectations without experiencing hurrying or stress (Sims and Hutchins 2001). Bilingual support workers should not be suddenly withdrawn from children and families. Instead there should be a carefully planned transition in which early childhood staff take increasing responsibility for building relationships with the child and the family.

Staff also need to be conscious of how cultural marginalisation can lead to a different sense of time and to different priorities in using time. Consider the comments by Treppte (1994, p. 19) about planned meeting times in an early childhood project involving German and Lebanese women:

> [The] . . . Lebanese women . . . proposed that each week, one of them should be phoned by the teacher on the morning of the day that they were expected to come. They argued that in the situation they live in— . . . with nothing to do and nowhere to go—they find it difficult to remember the day of the week . . . Of course, we take it for granted that our way of organising and defining sequences of time is rational and the only possible way to do so. Yet, it is not.

Treppte (1994) argued that while the Lebanese women did not have a different sense of time to the German teachers in the project, they were so marginalised in German society that time had a different meaning to them. For similar reasons, staff need to consider if time might have a different meaning for some families in their specific early childhood setting.

Many Australian early childhood centres set aside time in their yearly schedule to celebrate special festivals and events. These times often include Christmas and Easter, but York (1991) cautioned against unthinking inclusion of these and other celebrations and holidays in a centre's annual schedule. She argues that celebrating some holidays and not others can lead to a sense of cultural supremacy and to competition between children. Some holidays can be seen by the children as more important than others and some ways of celebrating holidays and festivals can be seen as more interesting or exciting than others. York (1991) advised that all holidays celebrated in the programs should be given equal importance and that staff should choose holidays relevant to the lives of the children in their program. She also suggested that it is important for children to learn that different families celebrate holidays differently and that some families choose not to celebrate some holidays.

A detailed discussion of the issues involved in celebrating holidays and festivals within an anti-discriminatory perspective in Australia can be found in Barnes (1995). Similar discussions about such celebrations in the United States can be found in York (1991), and Millam (1996) discusses these issues in a UK context.

It takes regular amounts of in-depth time to make anti-discriminatory perspectives work, and staff should recognise this when timetabling specific work to learn about and respect cultural and 'racial' diversity. As Greenman (1992, p. 145) put it:

> Diversity is the spice of life. It also makes us sneeze a lot. If we believe in diversity, we have to take the time to think it through for our programs.

Further, it takes time to develop the knowledge and skills to work in anti-discriminatory ways (Dermon-Sparks et al. 1989). Thus, as staff plan regular time for the children to learn about cultural and 'racial' diversity and to work with them against any biases they may have, they should ensure that this work develops slowly and with care.

Gender

Research has consistently shown that boys and girls spend their time differently in early childhood centres. Girls tend to remain longer than boys with single items of equipment; boys tend to spend more time than girls in high levels of physical activity and in less-stable social groupings (Davies and Bremner 1994); and boys often demand and get more staff time than girls (MacNaughton 1995). Staff can alter these gendered patterns of involvement in the early childhood program by spending time with boys to extend and enhance their concentration and with girls to enhance their interest in higher levels of physical activity (Davies and Bremner 1994). In such work it is important for staff to monitor the amount of time they are spending in these tasks with boys and girls. West (1992) recounted her experiences of watching staff spend far more time encouraging boys into domestic roles than in encouraging girls into non-traditional female roles.

Some early childhood staff have organised the timetabling of specific activities to ensure equal access to, and involvement in them by boys and girls. Dermon-Sparks et al. (1989) discussed ways of doing this, including having an 'everybody plays with blocks' day, a 'girls-only' block time once a week and having a 'boys-only' sewing time or art time. Research (for example, Epstein 1995; MacNaughton 1997) has shown that such techniques will lead to girls being more involved with blocks but organising children's time in this way can also create difficulties. MacNaughton (1997) identified two difficulties. First, once girls-only time was stopped, the children reverted to their 'old' patterns. Second, during girls-only times, groups of boys tried to disrupt the play through what one practitioner described as 'seek and destroy' missions. This involved boys making very swift forays into the girls' play and disrupting it through the use of loud voices, or aggressive actions. Often, this occurred when staff were otherwise occupied. Hence, staff need to carefully monitor such techniques to ensure that they achieve the planned gender equity outcomes for all children.

Disability and additional needs

Children with disabilities may need special equipment or care. As Palmer (1995) emphasised, staff should have a positive attitude to the time and effort needed to give special care to children with disabilities and to support use of their special equipment. Staff who resent this time will teach children with disabilities that they are not valued and will teach children without disabilities to devalue those with disabilities.

Alongside the need to plan time for any special care and attention needed by specific children with disabilities, it is also important to plan time in which children in the group without disabilities can become familiar with any special care and equipment needs of children in the group who have disabilities. Palmer (1995, p. 77) suggested planning in-depth time when children and staff can express their feelings about working and living in an environment where everyone has differing needs and abilities. She argued that one-off sessions are of little value:

> Video material or brief, one-off visits from guests with disabilities encourage children to focus on novel differences without providing real opportunities to make sense of what they see.

Ongoing interaction and discussion between children and staff of differing abilities can offer children positive attitudes to people with disabilities and can teach them to confront bias in a constructive and meaningful way (Crary 1992).

REFLECTING ON SCHEDULING TECHNIQUES

1 Define scheduling.
2 Consider the following quote from Lally (1991, p. 78):

> The routine in a nursery class should be more concerned with the establishment of flexible daily patterns rather than with set times for whole group activity. A whole class approach is clearly not consistent with a developmental approach where individual needs are of paramount concern . . .

3 Do the centres you are familiar with organise time for a whole group approach? Do you think that they should? Why? How could they achieve these goals?
4 How might time be organised to encourage toddlers to practise independent decision-making?
5 How could you use the organisation of staff time to encourage social interaction and conversation between preschool children and babies?
6 How might your philosophy on adult intervention in children's learning influence how you organised your daily timetable?
7 Beaty (1996) believed that there are three keys to the productive organisation of time within an early childhood centre. These are:
   - providing an orderly sequence of events
   - ensuring that children experience a minimum of waiting
   - ensuring that children have a maximum amount of time for doing what they want to do.

Use the following table to reflect on one thing you could do to accomplish these tasks during a long day-care program for children of different ages.

Keys to good timing	Babies	Toddlers	Preschoolers
Provide an orderly sequence of events. Ensure children experience a minimum of waiting. Ensure children have a maximum of time for doing what they want to do.			

IMPROVING TEACHING IN PRACTICE

1 Note the daily and weekly timetables of an early childhood centre.
2 How well does the centre's organisation of time enable children to develop their own learning styles and patterns?
3 To what extent does the current organisation of time enhance a sense of enjoyment and well-being for staff and children?
4 Note the times when children are required to wait.
5 Was equipment used to enhance children's sense of security and competence?
6 Did the organisation of adult time support equity of access and participation?
7 How and how well were developmental considerations taken into account in the way staff organised their time?
8 To what extent was there time for pleasure in the day?

Further reading

Arthur, L., Beecher, B., Dockett, S., Farmer, S. and Death, E. 1996, *Programming and Planning in Early Childhood Settings*, second edn, Sydney, Harcourt Brace and Company [refer to pp. 269–77].

Brewer, J. 1992, *Introduction to Early Childhood Education: Preschool through Primary Grades*, Boston, Allyn and Bacon [refer to pp. 146–53].

Cook, C. and Porter, C. 1996, *Babies and Toddlers: Considering Multicultural Perspectives*, Melbourne, FKA Multicultural Resource Centre [refer to pp. 29–30].

Harrison, L. 1996, *Planning Appropriate Learning Environments for Children Under Three*, revised edn, Watson, ACT, Australian Early Childhood Association.

Hendrick, J. 1990, *Total Learning: Developmental Curriculum for the Young Child*, third edn, Toronto, Merrill Publishing Company [refer to Chapter 3].

Leavitt, R. and Bauman Power, M. 1997, 'Civilizing bodies: children in day care', in J. Tobin, ed., *Making a Place for Pleasure in Early Childhood Education* (pp. 40–75), New Haven and London, Yale University Press.

Psaltis, A. and Stonehouse, A. 1988, 'Toddler-centred routines', in A. Stonehouse, ed., *Trusting Toddlers: Programming for One to Three Year Olds in Child Care Centres* (pp. 79–100), Watson, ACT, Australian Early Childhood Association.

York, S. 1991, *Roots and Wings: Affirming Culture in Early Childhood Programs*, Minnesota, Toys'n Things Press.

Video

The Daily Press, The High Scope Press 1989.

Getting in Time. Creating Nurturing Relationships with Infants and Toddlers, California Department of Education 1990.

Learning Environment, Early Childhood Training Series, Magna Systems 1995/2002, available from Marcom Projects at www.marcom.com.au

Respectfully Yours: Magda Gerber's Approach to Professional Infant/Toddler Care, California, Realtime Videos, 1987.

Routines from Lunch to Bed, Australian Early Childhood Association, Lady Gowrie Children's Centre, Melbourne, Australia.

References

Arthur, L., Beecher, B., Dockett, S., Farmer, S. and Death, E. 1996, *Programming and Planning in Early Childhood Settings*, second edn, Sydney, Harcourt Brace and Company.

Barnes, S. 1995, 'Festivals, holidays and community celebrations: do they still have a place in early childhood programmes', in B. Creaser and E. Dau, eds, *The Anti-Bias Approach in Early Childhood* (pp. 175–83), Sydney, Harper Educational.

Beaty, J. 1996, *Skills for Preschool Teachers*, fifth edn, New Jersey, Prentice Hall Inc.

Briggs, F. and Potter, G. 1995, *Teaching Children in the First Three Years of School*, Melbourne, Longman.

Broadhead, P. 2001, 'Investigating sociability and cooperation in four and five year olds in reception class settings', *International Journal of Early Years Education*, 9(1), pp. 23–36.

Castle, K. 1990, 'The second year: 12–24 months', in E. Surbeck and M. Kelly, eds, *Personalizing Care with Infants, Toddlers and Families* (pp. 23–32), Wheaton, MD, Association for Childhood Education International.

Cook, C. and Porter, C. 1996, *Babies and Toddlers: Considering Multicultural Perspectives*, Melbourne, FKA Multicultural Resource Centre, pp. 29–30.

Crary, E. 1992, 'Talking about differences children notice', in B. Ncugcbauer, ed., *Alike and Different: Exploring our Humanity with Young Children* (pp. 11–15), Washington, National Association for the Education of Young Children.

Davies, J. and Bremner, I. 1994, 'Morning and afternoon nursery sessions: can they be equally effective in giving children a positive start to school?', *International Journal of Early Years Education*, 2(2), pp. 43–53.

Department of Human Services, 1996, *Babies, Toddlers and Two Year Olds: A Curriculum Resource for Developing Child-Centred Programs for Children Under Three*, Melbourne, Government of Victoria.

Dermon-Sparks, L. and the Anti-Bias Task Force, 1989, *The Anti-Bias Curriculum*, Washington DC, National Association for the Education of Young Children.

Epstein, D. 1995, 'Girls don't do bricks', in J. A. I. Siraj-Blatchford, ed., *Educating the Whole Child: Cross-curricula Skills, Themes and Dimensions* (pp. 56–69), Milton Keynes, Open University Press.

Fisher, J. 1998, 'The relationship between planning and assessment', in I. Siraj-Blatchford, ed., *A Curriculum Handbook for Early Childhood Educators*, pp. 15–44, London, Trentham Books.

Greenman, J. 1992, 'Diversity and conflict: the whole world will never sing in perfect harmony', in B. Neugebauer, ed., *Alike and Different: Exploring our Humanity with Young Children* (pp. 140–5), Washington DC, National Association for the Education of Young Children.

Harrison, L. 1996, *Planning Appropriate Learning Environments for Children Under Three*, revised edn, Watson, ACT, Australian Early Childhood Association.

Hendrick, J. 1990, *Total Learning: Developmental Curriculum for the Young Child*, third edn, Toronto, Merrill Publishing Company.

Honig, A. 1990, 'The baby — birth to twelve months', in E. Surbeck and M. Kelley, eds, *Personalizing Care with Infants, Toddlers and Families* (pp. 10–22), Wheaton, MD, Association for Childhood Education International.

Jones, E. and Reynolds, G. 1992, *The Play's the Thing: Teachers' Roles in Children's Play*, New York, Teachers' College Press.

Lally, M. 1991, *The Nursery Teacher in Action*, London, Paul Chapman Publishing.

Leavitt, R. and Bauman Power, M. 1997, 'Civilizing bodies: children in day care', in J. Tobin, ed., *Making a Place for Pleasure in Early Childhood Education* (pp. 40–75), New Haven and London, Yale University Press.

LeeKeenan, D. and Nimmo, J. 1994, 'Connections: using the project approach with 2- and 3-year-olds in a university laboratory school', in C. Edwards, L. Gandini and G. Forman, eds, *The Hundred Languages of Children: The Reggio Emilia Approach to Early Childhood Education* (pp. 251–67), New Jersey, Ablex Publishing Corporation.

MacNaughton, G. 1995, 'The gender factor', in B. Creaser and E. Dau, eds, *The Anti-Bias Approach in Early Childhood* (pp. 51–70), Sydney, Harper Educational.

——1997, 'Who's got the power? Rethinking gender equity strategies in early childhood', in *International Journal of Early Years Education*, 5(1), pp. 57–66.

Millam, R. 1996, *Anti-Discriminatory Practice: A Guide for Workers in Childcare and Education*, London, Cassell Books.

New, R. 2000, 'Reggio Emilia: Catalyst for change and conversation', *ERIC Digest*, ED447971.

Palmer, A. 1995, 'Responding to special needs', in B. Creaser and E. Dau, eds, *The Anti-Bias Approach in Early Childhood*, Sydney, Harper Educational.

Phelen, A. 1997, 'Classroom management and the erasure of teacher desire', in J. Tobin, ed., *Making Place for Pleasure in Early Childhood Education* (pp. 76–100), New Haven and London, Yale University Press.

Psaltis, A. and Stonehouse, A. 1988, 'Toddler-centred routines', in A. Stonehouse, ed., *Trusting Toddlers: Programming for One to Three Year Olds in Child Care Centres* (pp. 79–100), Watson, ACT, Australian Early Childhood Association.

Rolfe, S. 2002, *Promoting Resilience in Children*, Watson, ACT, Australian Early Childhood Association.

Sims, M. and Hutchins, T. 1999, 'Positive transitions', *Australian Journal of Early Childhood*, 24(3), pp. 12–16.

Sims, M. and Hutchins, T. 2001, 'Transition to child care for children from culturally and linguistically diverse backgrounds', *Australian Journal of Early Childhood*, 26(3), pp. 7–11.

Talbot, J. and Frost, J. 1989, 'Magical playscapes', *Childhood Education*, 66(1), pp. 11–19.

Treppte, C. 1994, 'Multicultural approaches in education: a German experience', *International Journal of Early Childhood*, 2(2), pp. 5–30.

West, B. 1992, 'Children are caught — between home and school, culture and school', in B. Neugebauer, ed., *Alike and Different: Exploring our Humanity with Young Children* (pp. 127–39), Washington DC, National Association for the Education of Young Children.

Wilkes, G. (ed.) 1979, *Collins Dictionary of the English Language*, Middlesex, Penguin Books.

York, S. 1991, *Roots and Wings: Affirming Culture in Early Childhood Programs*, Minnesota, Toys'n Things Press.

Part Two
General Teaching Techniques

Chapter 4
Demonstrating

Demonstrate: to show.

(Collins Dictionary of the English Language, p. 395)

Watching a skilled movement being made helps a learner to acquire skill . . . by deliberately imitating other people, they get the feel of the movement and the learning process is accelerated.

(Hughes and Hughes 1937, p. 221)

Extensions of the demonstration method are to have the children practise the demonstration while the professional supervises and to ask a child to demonstrate to other children.

(Morrison 1995, p. 480)

WHAT?

To demonstrate something is to show how it is done. As a teaching technique, demonstrating can help children's learning by showing them how to use materials and special tools or how to accomplish a particular task. Simply moving in and showing a child how to approach a task can be a very effective way of reminding a child how to do something that they may have forgotten or of teaching them a new skill. It can also help children to learn alternative and more effective ways of approaching a problem.

HOW?

Demonstrating will most effectively support children's learning when staff:

- ➲ use clear, unambiguous verbal instructions to support the demonstration
- ➲ break a skill or task into small, sequential steps. This is particularly important when staff are demonstrating complex techniques to children. For instance, as toddlers can only remember two or three steps at a time (Kowalski 1996), it is best to plan demonstrations accordingly. Task analysis (see Chapter 28) will assist in this
- ➲ keep the demonstration brief to allow for children's often short attention span (Benelli and Yongue 1995)
- ➲ are familiar with the steps involved in the skill or technique they are demonstrating so they do not confuse children. For instance, if staff can turn on a new hose-nozzle with ease, their demonstrations are likely to effectively teach children the technique.

➔ review with children what they have learnt so that additional demonstrations can be planned if necessary (Benelli and Yongue 1995)

➔ provide the children with lots of opportunities to practise the skill or technique being demonstrated (Benelli and Yongue 1995).

Staff may also find it helpful to support their demonstration of key skills or techniques with visual aids. At a later date, children can refer to the visual aids to refresh their memory of the sequence involved in a particular task. Chris has found this useful in supporting children's learning in the woodworking area.

> Chris has brought a new piece of equipment — a vice — to the centre's woodworking area. She is aware that the children have never used a vice before, so she demonstrates how to use it in several small steps: first put the wood in the vice; then turn the screw to tighten it; finally saw the wood. Next to the woodworking area, Chris places a three-step diagram of how to use the vice, so that the children can look at the pictures and remind themselves how to use it properly.

WHEN AND WHY?

Demonstrating will be most appropriately used as a teaching technique when:

➔ children are keen to learn the skill or technique

➔ children have the necessary competence to learn the new technique or skill with minimal adult support and with a minimum of frustration

➔ children's own creativity and experimentation with skills and techniques are not be hampered by an adult direction. Hughes's and Hughes's caution of almost 70 years ago is still pertinent:

> The moment when a child is absorbed in creative work that is giving him intense satisfaction is obviously not an occasion for attempting to teach him technique. (Hughes and Hughes 1937, p. 224)

Goal relevance

There are many occasions when simply showing children how to do something can be the most effective way to assist their learning. In general, demonstration can be used to teach children how to do something that requires specific skills or techniques that they lack. Here are some examples of such occasions:

➔ When children need help with a task or technique but staff cannot talk to them at that precise moment because they are talking with another child or an adult. Here, a quick demonstration of how to approach the task or technique can provide a child with the information and attention they need to proceed.

➔ When children have reached a point in doing something or using something when support or encouragement will assist with success or perseverance.

➔ When children are exploring new equipment or materials that require skills or techniques that are new to them. For instance, if the hose for the sandpit has a new hose-nozzle that requires a special technique for releasing water, it will be helpful to demonstrate how the hose works.

'This is how you do it!'

● When children's learning will benefit from knowing the most effective and safe way to use a tool such as a hammer or a saw. Some techniques will be more effective and less dangerous than others.

● When children want to learn a new skill or technique to help complete a task or solve a problem. For instance, if staff demonstrate the most effective way to hold scissors or to use sticky-tape, children at the collage table can concentrate on when to use them and not become frustrated by learning how to use them.

● When children need reminding about how to do something. For instance, children may need reminding that the stapler works best if it is placed on the table and the top is pressed down firmly.

● When adults want to increase children's technical competence in a particular area. For instance, Edwards (1993, p. 164) described how Paola Notari, a teacher in the Reggio Emilia district, used demonstration to increase children's skill at working clay:

Finishing the new slab [of clay], she takes it over to the girl needing it. Seeing her first piece, Paola comments, 'Look at that marvel! Now you have to think about what else you want to do. You could put the same marks in it [the new slab] you did before. Or you could place these pieces folded, or standing up'. She demonstrates, using little strips of clay.

Maria Montessori believed that demonstration was a particularly useful technique for helping children to learn basic daily living skills, such as preparing food and setting the table. In addition, she believed that learning these skills nurtured the young child's need to constantly improve their daily living skills (Oriti and Kahn 1994). (Refer to Chapter 29 for additional information on Montessori's approach to early childhood education.) Demonstration is also seen as a useful technique for teaching children to respect the environment. When staff demonstrate to the children their enjoyment of nature, children learn to respect the environment (Wilson 1993).

Research has shown that demonstration can be important in developing young children's scientific literacy if it is combined with questions that probe children's understandings of what has been demonstrated (Klein et al. 2000). However, the researchers highlighted that not all children learn equally well with a strongly teacher-directed approach to science and that using diverse teaching techniques adapted to individual children is important.

Children's emergent literacy skills can also be enhanced through demonstration in specific contexts. For instance, when adults demonstrate how to use text and other visual resources within dramatic play, children's knowledge of text and its uses is enhanced (Arthur and Makin 2001). When teachers physically guide children's early writing attempts, it can also support children in building their writing skills. Demonstration was identified by children who were beginning writers as helpful to them (Martello 1999).

Developmental considerations

Babies constantly try to make sense of the world about them by acting on it. When babies reach the point of exploring objects by hitting, banging, sucking and grasping them, they also begin to be able to intentionally imitate other people (Morrison 1995). From this point in a baby's development, staff can use simple demonstrations of how to do things to help develop a baby's concentration on an experience. Staff can show babies how to hold, push and pull objects to make interesting sounds, sights and events, thus extending the babies' interest in the experience. Puna often uses simple demonstrations to support the learning of the babies in her room:

> Puna sits on the floor with Aisha, who is seven months old. Aisha is between Puna's legs to give her extra support as she is presented with different equipment to enjoy. Puna presents Aisha with a toy that has a large button on the top. As she demonstrates how to press the button to make the toy squeak, she says, 'Look Aisha, you press the button like this'. The baby imitates her action, the toy squeaks and Aisha gurgles with delight.

Toddlers are keen to gain greater control over themselves and their bodies. They are also keen to use their increasing physical competence to help them explore their environment. With so much to do and so much to learn, toddlers often forget how to do something they learnt just recently. For instance, they may forget how to make the blocks balance or how to open the door of the stove in the imaginative play area. Toddlers' active exploration of their environment also means that they often meet situations that require a skill or a technique that they have not tried before. For instance, they may decide to fill a screw-top container with water and be unsure as to how to screw the top on.

Toddlers' ability to imitate the actions of others means that by demonstrating a new or momentarily forgotten skill or technique, staff can easily provide the support toddlers need to succeed or to maintain their efforts. However, toddlers generally cannot remember a complex

'Look what happens when you shake it.'

sequence of events, so staff should keep the demonstration short and simple. In addition, toddlers have ever-changing needs and interests and quickly move on to new challenges, so demonstrating a new skill or technique will be most effective if it happens at the moment the toddler needs it. Molly is alert to the importance of this in her work:

An old child care centre in the middle of Melbourne has had a face lift and the children's bathrooms now have taps with handles which swing to the side rather than turn. Molly is in the bathroom to make sure that the four-year-old children, who are using the bathroom for the first time, become familiar with the new environment. As the children come to wash their hands after toileting, Molly demonstrates to each one how to use the new taps. She then asks each child to do it by themselves so that she can check if they are able to turn them on and off.

Preschoolers gain increasing competence in using their fine motor skills by doing a wide range of activities such as drawing, pasting, painting, sewing, cutting, joining and using computer keyboards. In the preschool years, children need many of these skills to complete tasks or solve problems. For instance, children involved in dramatic play in which they have decided to set up a Real Estate office might want to use a saw to cut a piece of wood to make a 'For Sale' sign. They may also want to join two pieces of wood together to make their sign stand up by itself and they may want to write 'For Sale' on the sign. If staff demonstrate the most effective way to saw the wood and to join it, the children can concentrate on developing their dramatic play rather than having to work out for themselves how to saw and join the wood. Having said this, it is often appropriate that staff allow children the time and opportunity to solve such problems for themselves. Therefore, the time staff save by demonstrating how to do things needs to be balanced against the need for children to solve problems for themselves.

Gaining new technical skills can enhance children's work on a particular project and as children become older there are a wider range of techniques they can use to express their meanings to others. Teachers working with young primary school children on an ecology project about paper recycling introduced children to paper-making techniques to enhance their understanding of recycling. The children were shown how to make new paper from recycled paper. To do this staff demonstrated the steps involved in paper-making to the children and then supported the children's use of this skill with additional demonstrations (Cole 1992).

EQUITY CONSIDERATIONS

'Race' and culture

In a program based on strong multicultural perspectives, children are likely to encounter tools and utensils from a wide variety of cultures. Just some of the tools and utensils that may be seen in early childhood programs are chopsticks, a wok, bamboo steamers, a tortilla press, spatulas, a coffee pot, tongs, a *tava*, a *degchi*, a *karai*, *thali* plates, a coconut grater, a souffle dish, a chatty, a mortar and pestle (*nuoc cham* in Vietnamnese), *wajan*, boomerangs, hammers, clap sticks.

Children should learn how to use these tools and utensils appropriately for two reasons. First, understanding how a tool or utensil is used within a culture avoids children learning negative values of supremacy. Values of supremacy develop when children believe that, '. . . a certain country or a specific group of people is better than another . . .' (York 1991, p. 151). When children are unfamiliar with correct ways to use a tool from another culture they may use it incorrectly, fail to make it work and learn to see the tool and the culture it is from as 'silly'. Demonstrating correct uses of the tool can prevent this from happening.

Second, understanding how a tool or utensil is used within a culture builds respect for that culture and helps to counter stereotypes about it. Staff should not include in their program a range of tools from a culture other than their own without knowing what the tools are for and how to use them. It implies that they don't care about other cultures or are not prepared to take the time to learn about them. If staff demonstrate to the children how to use the tools or utensils correctly, they also demonstrate interest and respect for diversity.

When staff introduce tools and utensils from a particular culture into a centre, they can use children who are familiar with the items to help demonstrate to the group how to use them correctly. Using children's specialist knowledge and skill in this way can help build their self-esteem. However, it is important that staff do not stereotype children and assume, for example, that all children from a Chinese background know how to use chopsticks with confidence or that all children from an Indonesian background have a *wajan* (flat metal cooking pot like a wok) in their home. To avoid such stereotyping, staff should check with children and/or their parents what children use within their own homes. Maybe an Anglo-Australian child has a *wajan* in their home because their parents love Indonesian food and bought one on their recent trip to Indonesia.

Gender

Gender differences often exist in children's technical competence in using tools and utensils. Many four- and five-year-old boys may be very competent in using tools such as spades and hammers, while many girls of the same age find these tools difficult to use. Conversely, girls will often be more competent than boys in using needles for sewing and in the fine and detailed cutting of materials (Lopez 1991). These differences are the result of the often-different expectations, opportunities and experiences which boys and girls have, rather than any genetic differences between them. Boys are often expected to be good with spades and hammers but rarely expected to be good at sewing. The opposite is often true for girls.

Consequently, children can often lack confidence when using tools that are normally associated with the other gender. Boys can lack confidence when sewing and girls can lack confidence when hammering. This lack of confidence sometimes combines with a belief that boys don't sew or girls don't hammer. The result is a 'learned helplessness' around tasks traditionally associated with the other gender (McDonald and Rogers 1995). Research has shown that overcoming 'learned helplessness' can be difficult because, as Browne and Ross (1991, p. 44) found:

> When children were operating beyond their perceived gender domain their confidence was very easily undermined.

Staff can support and encourage boys and girls to test out tools traditionally associated with the other gender by demonstrating the most effective way to hold and use the tool. Such demonstrations can reduce the possibility that children will not achieve what they hoped to because they used the tool inappropriately. If a girl successfully uses a spade to dig a hole, she is more likely to return to the activity another time. However, if her attempts to dig a hole flounder because she has used the spade inappropriately, she may not feel confident to try again.

There is considerable evidence (Browne and Ross 1991; Epstein 1995) that boys and girls try to undermine each other when they move into areas traditionally associated with the other gender. Boys will often tease girls when they begin to use tools such as hammers and spades and girls will tease boys as they learn to sew and cook. Using same-gender groups to demonstrate the use of tools can avoid this possibility to a large extent. For instance, staff may find it helpful to demonstrate how to use spades in girls-only groups and how to use needle and thread in boys-only groups. Once the children become confident and competent users within their same-gender group, they will readily apply their new skills and techniques in play with the other gender (Browne and Ross 1991).

Disability and additional needs

Demonstration is one way to enhance children's skills. The Department of Employment, Education and Training (DEET) (1994, p. 30) suggested that when thinking about how and when to build the skills of children with severe disabilities, staff should remember that these children, '. . . will normally learn fewer skills than other children and this learning will take longer . . .' and should ask the following questions:

- ➲ Is the skill or activity valued by the child's parents and by society in general?
- ➲ Does the skill or activity contribute to the child's positive interactions with their peers?
- ➲ Is the skill or activity appropriate for the child's age?
- ➲ Does the child have an interest in, or preference for, the skill or activity?
- ➲ Is it likely that the child will acquire the skill or activity, given reasonable time and resources?
- ➲ Are there opportunities to practise the skill or activity?

➔ Will the skill or activity enhance the child's physical well-being?

➔ Will the skill or activity be required in the child's later life?

Once staff feel confident that it is worthwhile to teach a particular skill to a child with disabilities and that demonstration is a useful technique for such teaching, it is important to demonstrate the skill or technique in small, manageable parts. Task analysis (refer Chapter 28) can assist in this process.

Reflecting on demonstrating techniques

1 Define demonstration.

2 To what extent do you think that Hughes's and Hughes's caution of almost 70 years ago (see quote below) is still pertinent when thinking about when and how to demonstrate a skill or a technique to a child?

> The moment when a child is absorbed in creative work that is giving him intense satisfaction is obviously not an occasion for attempting to teach him technique. (Hughes and Hughes 1937, p. 224)

3 How could demonstrating be used to help a three-year-old child learn to use a magnifying glass? What would be the pros and cons of using this technique?

4 Would demonstrating be appropriate to help a toddler learn how to construct a tall block tower? Why?

5 Which of the following goals for children's learning could be supported through adult demonstration? Why?

➔ Goal 1—for the children to learn how to put blocks away.

➔ Goal 2—for the children to practise co-operation with each other.

➔ Goal 3—for the children to learn how to mix colours.

➔ Goal 4—for the children to express their ideas through movement.

6 How could you use demonstrating to overcome a five-year-old boy's 'learned helplessness' at bathing a baby?

7 The following extract presents a teaching episode with preschool children. How has the teacher used demonstrating to support children's learning in this episode? Do you believe this was an appropriate technique to use? Why?

> Some children were building haphazard piles of blocks and knocking them down. I sat alongside them on the floor and silently began to sort through a container of plastic animals, putting them in identical pairs to form a long queue. The children stopped what they were doing and joined in my play. (Skinner 1996, p. 62)

8 Read Paley (1986, pp. 8–9). To what extent is the use of demonstration to show Mollie how to make green successful? Was demonstration an appropriate teaching technique in this instance? Why?

9 How might you use demonstration to help the children in Christopher's group to learn to communicate with him?

> We do a lot of massage on each other's hands and feet, and this gives the children an awareness of their bodies and body parts. This is particularly important for Christopher because he tends to stiffen up because of his disability. His hands just close tight. (DEET 1994, p. 33)

IMPROVING TEACHING IN PRACTICE

1 Videotape the teaching interactions you have with children during a five-minute teaching period on several different occasions.

2 When using demonstration to support children's learning did you:
> use clear, unambiguous verbal instructions to support the demonstration?
> break the skills or tasks into small, sequential steps?
> ensure that you were familiar with the steps involved in the skill or technique you were demonstrating?

3 How and how well did you take account of developmental considerations in how you demonstrated skills and techniques to the children?

4 Did your demonstrations support equity of access and participation in the program?

5 What are your strengths and weaknesses in using demonstrating to promote children's learning?

6 How can you work to improve your demonstrating techniques in practice?

Further reading and resources

Benelli, C. and Yongue, B. 1995, 'Supporting young children's motor skill development', *Childhood Education*, 71(4), pp. 217–20.

Cole, P. and Chan, L. 1990, *Methods and Strategies for Special Education*, New Jersey, Prentice Hall Inc., [refer to pp. 203–20].

Edwards, C. 1993, 'Partner, Nurturer and Guide: The Roles of the Reggio Teacher in Action', in C. Edwards, L. Gandini and G. Forman, eds, *The Hundred Languages of Children: The Reggio Emilia Approach to Early Childhood Education* (pp. 151–69), Norwood, New Jersey, Ablex Publishing Company.

References

Arthur, L. and Makin, L. 2001, 'High quality literacy programs', *Australian Journal of Early Childhood*, 26(2), pp. 14–19.

Benelli, C. and Yongue, B. 1995, 'Supporting young children's motor skill development', *Childhood Education*, 71(4), pp. 217–20.

Browne, N. and Ross, C. 1991, '"Girls' stuff, boys' stuff": young children talking and playing', in N. Browne, ed., *Science and Technology in the Early Years* (pp. 37–51), Milton Keynes, Open University Press.

Cole, E. 1992, 'Art and learning: fostering ecological awareness', *Childhood Education*, 68(5), pp. 285–9.

Department of Employment, Education and Training (DEET), 1994, *Like Any Child: Planning for Children with Disabilities*, Melbourne, DEET and Brotherhood of St. Lawrence.

Edwards, C. 1993, 'Partner, Nurturer and Guide: The Roles of the Reggio Teacher in Action', in C. Edwards, L. Gandini and G. Forman, eds, *The Hundred Languages of Children: The Reggio Emilia Approach to Early Childhood Education* (pp. 151–69), Norwood, New Jersey, Ablex Publishing Company.

Epstein, D. 1995, 'Girls don't do bricks', in J. and I. Siraj-Blatchford, eds, *Educating the Whole Child: Cross-curricula Skills, Themes and Dimensions* (pp. 56–69), Milton Keynes, Open University Press.

Hughes, A. and Hughes, E. 1937, *Learning and Teaching: An Introduction to Psychology and Education*, London, Longmans.

Klein, E. R., Hammrich, P., Bloom, S. and Ragins, A. 2000, Language development and science inquiry: a child-initiated and teacher-facilitated program, paper presented at the *Annual Meeting of the American Education Research Association*, New Orleans, April, ED 440756.

Kowalski, H. 1996, 'What should we do with toddlers?', *Every Child*, 2(1), pp. 8–9.

Lopez, E. 1991, 10th July, 'Switches or stiches, it's still science', *The Age*.

Martello, J. 1999, 'In their own words: children's perceptions of learning to write', *Australian Journal of Early Childhood*, 24(3), pp. 32–7.

McDonald, L. and Rogers, L. 1995, Who waits for the White Knight? Training in 'nice', Paper presented to the *Annual Meeting of the American Education Research Association, San Franciso* (18–22 April).

Morrison, G. 1995, *Early Childhood Education Today*, sixth edn, New Jersey, Merrill.

Oriti, P. and Kahn, D. (eds) 1994, *At Home with Montessori*, Cleveland Heights, OH, North American Montessori Teachers Association.

Paley, V. 1986, *Mollie is Three: Growing up in School*, Chicago, University of Chicago Press.

Skinner, P. 1996, 'Play and the mathematics profile', in M. Fleer, ed., *Play through the Profiles: Profiles through Play* (pp. 57–66), Canberra, Australian Early Childhood Association.

Wilkes, G. (ed.) 1979, *Collins Dictionary of the English Language*, Middlesex, Penguin Books.

Wilson, R. 1993, 'The importance of environmental education at the early childhood level', *International Journal of Environmental Education and Information*, 12(1), pp. 15–24.

York, S. 1991, *Roots and Wings: Affirming Culture in Early Childhood Programs*, Minnesota, Toys'n Things Press.

Chapter 5

Describing

Describe: to give an account or representation in words.

(*Collins Dictionary of the English Language*, p. 401)

The purpose and problems of describing as a teaching procedure are quite unlike those of casual description.

(Hogg and Foster 1973, p. 218)

. . . the effectiveness of narration and description depends very largely on a child's previous knowledge and on the way in which the new knowledge is connected with it.

(Hughes and Hughes 1937, p. 368)

WHAT?

When we describe something to someone we try to paint a word-picture of how something or someone feels, looks, sounds, tastes or moves. We do this by recalling the key features or characteristics of the event, object or feeling. As Hogg and Foster (1973, p. 218) stated:

> It [describing] is a process of using language to convey an idea or image of an object, event, or the properties of objects or events being described, from one person to a second person, in such a way that the second person can recognise what is being described.

A person knows they have successfully described something when it is recognised by the person to whom they are describing it.

The purpose of using description as a teaching technique is to help children to see increasingly finer and more complex distinctions between events, people and things in their daily world. Good descriptions help children to expand their understandings of the world. Good descriptions draw children's attention to the features, properties or characteristics of events, people and things that they may not have noticed or that they themselves may lack the language to describe.

HOW?

Staff can have their powers of description tested regularly by children's interest in the world about them and their disposition from an early age to ask, 'Why?'. A staff member's descriptive powers can be challenged by children's questions, such as: 'What is a flood?', 'What happens when dogs die?', 'How does that man get out of his wheelchair into bed?'.

Staff can increase the effectiveness of their descriptive powers with young children by:

- ensuring that they are familiar with what is to be described
- thinking about the key features to be described
- trying not to describe every single feature or property of something. Staff need to focus on the main characteristics of what they are describing: a lot of detail at once can confuse young children
- thinking about what is unique or specific to what they are describing and what will help the children to recognise what is being described
- using language as clearly and precisely as possible. A description is only useful if the children understand what is being said
- being prepared to rephrase a description if children do not understand it. Children may not immediately recognise what is being described because they have focused on different features to those that staff have focused on. It may also be that they have not understood the description
- checking with the children that they have understood the description
- remembering that people do not always 'see' things in the same way. Two people can describe the same event, person or object, but their descriptions can be very different because each person focuses on features that are of importance to them
- ensuring that description is used as part of conversations in which children have a chance to interact with and respond to adults.

Yvonne and Sasha are two early childhood staff who are trying to improve their powers of description:

> Yvonne was working on a project about sound with her five-year-old students. That day, she went home and studied how people hear and how the ear works, anticipating that the next day the children would ask questions about listening and hearing.
>
> Sasha asked David, a four-year-old, to tell her what he has understood about magnets. She then paraphrases and builds on what he has already described to her.

WHEN AND WHY?

Describing something to children only begins their process of understanding it (Allen and Hart 1984). By itself, an adult's description is rarely sufficient to create total understanding of an event or person by the young child. It is a teaching technique that must be supplemented by opportunities for children to explore in a practical and concrete way the things being described.

Goal relevance

As a teaching technique, description can be used to:

- heighten children's awareness of the characteristics of particular things. Describing what children are doing or looking at can be a useful technique for developing their competence in using descriptive language (Feeney et al. 1991). Talking about what is happen[...] what children are doing can help them to become more specific and precise in t[...] use of descriptive language. For example, describing is an effective teaching technique in creative movement sessions. Staff descriptions of children's movements can help children to internalise them. It can also help them to know that the movements they are making are appropriate to what they have been asked to do (Andress 1991; cited in Beaty 1996). Often such descriptions will be very simple:

> I can see Clara sliding to the violin music. Now she is stamping to the drum music.
>
> A group of three-year-olds is playing in the sand with water. Neil, their teacher, is sitting with them. His aim is to encourage the children to use descriptive language by using the language for them: 'Look what happens when the water is mixed with the sand — the sand becomes darker in colour!'

➲ extend children's vocabulary. Staff can do this by using appropriate adjectives and by encouraging children to use words to describe their world. Access to a wide range of descriptive words and phrases increases our ability to convey our meanings to others. When staff use descriptive words and phrases, they can increase children's awareness of and familiarity with an increasingly large descriptive vocabulary. Describing what children are doing as they are doing it provides them with concrete experiences of how new words can be used, extending their vocabulary in a meaningful way. However, as Susan realises below, staff need to develop a wide range of descriptive words and phrases:

> Susan, a student teacher, is working in a prep grade during her teaching rounds. She is aware that her own descriptive vocabulary is limited and decides to broaden it and to use it with the children. She asks her supervising teacher to give her specific feedback on this each day.

➲ enable children to share their knowledge and understandings with others. When children are asked to describe an event or an object with which they are familiar, they have an opportunity to share with others what they know and to gain a sense of competence and of belonging within the group
➲ build children's listening skills. Guessing games in which staff describe the key features of an event or an object can build children's ability to listen. Children's analytical listening skills can be supported by games which require them to assess the information provided and to make judgements about what is being described.

Developmental considerations

There are many challenges in a baby's daily world. One of the early challenges is how to match spoken words with objects (Willis and Riccuiti 1975). Chatting with babies and describing what is being touched, played with and looked at can help them to match words and objects. When descriptions accompany babies' actions they can be sung or chanted (Department of Human Services 1996). Such descriptions need to be brief and simple, and should be part of incidental and reciprocal daily interactions with individual babies. In those interactions it is important to remember that

Showing and discussing at work.

repetition is a cornerstone of how babies learn new skills, including language skills. It is also important to remember that repetition best promotes a baby's learning and well-being when it is not
forced in any way but arises naturally from playful interactions that are unhurried and sensitive
(Thompson 2001).

As adults describe events in the babies' world to them, babies begin to learn that language can
be used to give and receive information (Willis and Ricuitti 1975; Thompson 2001). Such learning
is most effectively supported if descriptive talk is part of a responsive and caring relationship
between adult and baby. If a baby is interested by an adult's descriptions of things or events around
them or of what they are seeing and feeling, the adult should respond by repeating the description
and elaborating on it. This helps babies to learn that language is an important part of how people
interact. It also helps introduce babies to the sounds of new words. Research shows that babies
enjoy novelty and that new sounds will help build their capacity to remember, understand cause
and effect and make sense of their world (Thompson 2001).

A key developmental task for children in their first three years of life is to develop a sense of
themselves as autonomous, capable and independent people (Harrison 1996; Thompson 2000,
2001). Successful accomplishment of this task means that they can tell other people what is happening and can understand other people's descriptions. By two and a half years of age, children can
begin to use words to describe mental and personal properties. They can talk about being careful,
scared, worried, glad, happy and better, and about thinking, liking, disliking, being surprised and

promising (Hinchcliffe 1996). Adding these words to the descriptive language to which toddlers are exposed will strengthen their ability to describe how they are thinking and feeling. This, in turn, strengthens their ability to feel autonomous. For example, toddlers can learn to tell others how they feel rather than relying on others to do so for them.

> Justine, two years old, was feeling sad because her mother had gone away for a few days. The staff at the centre were aware of this and were able to encourage Justine to express how she felt by asking her questions and paraphrasing what she said. They listened to her words and gave her new descriptive words to express how she was feeling. They talked with her about feeling sad, unhappy and how when you are unhappy it feels like crying inside.

However, it is important to remember that description relies on words and is based on symbolic thinking. It involves the ability to substitute words for objects and still understand what is being talked about (Seefeldt 1980). As such, it is a teaching technique that gains additional power when children begin to think symbolically. Preschool children are becoming increasingly adept at symbolic thought, as demonstrated by the increasing complexity of their socio-dramatic play. In this play, they regularly substitute one object for another, substitute objects for ideas and use increasingly complex language structures. This means that descriptions can become more intricate, varied and less repetitive than with the toddler age group.

In the preschool years, descriptions can also begin to cover a wider range of concrete and less concrete events in children's lives. They are most likely to engage preschoolers' interests when they are relevant to their interests (Thompson 2001). Tizard and Hughes (1984, p. 261) found that preschool children were interested in anything that impinged on their daily lives, including 'the neighbours, money, electric lights, the structure and arrangement of houses, parents' work, God, the death of pets and doctors'. Faced with this range of interests, the challenge for staff using description as a teaching technique is two-fold: to use description appropriately and to use description incidentally in response to children's queries.

Children who are developing their literacy skills in the early years of schooling can benefit from opportunities to have the books they read described to them. Such descriptions aid several areas of literacy development, including format literacy, visual literacy, content literacy and verbal literacy (Camp and Tompkins 1990). Descriptions of how the book is presented, how the images relate to the text, and how the book presentation helps give it meaning, aid children's critical awareness of the relationships between text and meaning. Teachers can initiate such descriptions and then involve the children in developing their own descriptions of the books they read or listen to.

EQUITY CONSIDERATIONS

Our descriptions of ourselves and of other people provide children with the vocabulary to describe themselves and other people. Using non-biased language to describe social diversity to young children is an important aspect of implementing an anti-bias approach to teaching and learning.

'Race' and culture

When describing people's cultural and racial backgrounds, it is important that adults provide children with accurate terms with which to describe physical and cultural diversity, and that the language they use with children is non-culturally biased and non-racist. This means that staff must learn to avoid reinforcing tokenism, inaccuracies and stereotypes in their descriptions of cultural and racial difference. Some basic principles that can help staff develop an anti-bias approach to description are:

- Staff can learn from parents the correct cultural and language group names of children attending their centre.
- Staff can learn from parents the correct cultural descriptors for the clothes, hairstyles, skin tones, dialects, country of origin, celebrations, etc. of the children attending their centre, and can learn how to describe these simply and accurately to the children in their group.
- Staff can learn from parents the correct words for all aspects of a culture they are describing to children, including its traditions, rituals, symbolic forms, norms and values.
- Staff can ask people from cultural and racial groups other than their own what features of their particular culture should be shared and how best to do so. This helps staff to learn the correct words to use in their descriptions to children.
- Staff can ensure that they are describing the contemporary life of cultural groups and that they are not assuming all people within the group live identical lives.
- When a word which describes an idea, musical instrument or tradition, is not easily translated into English, staff can learn its correct pronunciation and spelling and teach this to the children.

As staff apply these principles to their cultural and racial descriptions, they can use the following pointers to judge their success. Anti-discriminatory descriptions will:

- enhance all children's understanding of cultural and racial diversity
- reinforce children's self-esteem and their pride in their cultural and racial identity
- present positive messages about cultural and racial diversity. Staff should describe diversity to children in ways which focus on the strengths, joys and richness of living with diversity. For example, staff can focus on the benefits of living in a country with cultural and racial diversity by describing what they like about such diversity and by encouraging the children to talk about what they like about it
- be accessible to all the children in the group. For example, when English-speaking staff are using words to describe something to children from a non-English-speaking background, their descriptions may help to extend the children's vocabulary, but they may also serve to confuse them. Staff should think about how to use visual cues and gestures alongside words to ensure that their descriptions are understood. Describing actions which children are making can assist them to acquire English as a second language (Clarke 1992)
- encourage children to value each others' backgrounds. For example, it is important that staff do not present one particular lifestyle as more important or more interesting than another by giving it more time or by describing it in more detail. Staff can research children's backgrounds so that they can teach children the words and ideas that describe each others' lifestyles
- encourage children to empathise with each other. For example, when talking with children about physical differences, staff can also focus on the similarities in what makes us happy or sad
- avoid words and ideas that are offensive to particular cultural and racial groups. By three years of age children can match, label and identify people by racial groupings, so it is

important that they are provided with inoffensive descriptive language with which to do so. Terms to describe different 'racial' groups are extremely problematic: distinctions between people on the basis of physical traits have been the basis and justification of a number of discriminatory practices.

Ramsey (1987) pointed to the difficulties that arise from the following ways of describing 'racial' diversity. Words such as 'black', 'white', 'coloured', 'brown' and 'yellow' do not accurately describe people's skin tone and they ignore the other physical characteristics such as hair and facial features that contribute to our physical diversity. Despite this, some groups choose to use such words to describe 'racial' diversity. As Brown (1995, p. 10) explained:

> We use the term 'black' in an oversimplified way to refer not only to those people of African, Caribbean, or South Asian origins who are most immediately perceived as 'black' by most white people, but also to those of Chinese, Cypriot, Arab, Malaysian or Latin American backgrounds who also experience differential treatment as a result of being perceived as so-called 'non-white'. It is important to acknowledge that this usage is not acceptable to all such groups themselves. Difference of culture both within and between different ethnic groups must not be overlooked just because of their common experience of discrimination in Britain.

Many groups prefer words which refer to their continent of origin, such as 'Asian', 'Australian', 'African' and 'American'. However, they do not accurately describe the origins of many people whose immigration history does not neatly fit into such 'boxes'. Nor do they accurately describe children and immigrants who are from 'racially mixed' backgrounds.

In several countries, indigenous people have specific words to describe who they are, and these are often different from the labels they have been given historically. It is important to find out what these are to avoid causing offence. For example, the term 'native' is no longer acceptable to indigenous peoples in Australia. They prefer to be called Aboriginal Australians or to be identified through reference to their specific language group. 'Indian' is no longer acceptable to the indigenous peoples of North America. They may prefer to be called 'Native Americans', 'American Indians' or 'People of the First Nations' (Ramsey 1987). The following extract highlights some of the complexities of using labels to describe people:

> I am sometimes asked, 'Are you Indians? Native Americans? What do you prefer to be called?' . . . By race, I am an American Indian; by citizenship, I am an American citizen. (I have also been told that by treaty with the Sioux nations and Canada, I'm also a Canadian citizen.) By nationality, I am an enrolled member of the Oglala Sioux nation. I am also a hereditary member of the Cheyenne and Arapaho nations in Okalahoma (GossMan 1992, p. 146).

When in doubt about which descriptors to use, staff should always ask others who can advise. These may be parents, other staff, or advisory staff from specialist resource services such as a multicultural resource agency.

Gender

Description relies on language and language is not neutral. The language we use has many in-built assumptions and values which shape our understandings of the world about us. Among other things, our language shapes our understandings of ourselves as male and female, and our understandings of

Avoid	Term preferred	Reasons for preferred term
Slang names such as 'wop', 'spic', 'nigger', 'wog' and 'dago' (offensive).	Use country of origin labels such as 'Italian heritage', 'Anglo-Greek' and 'Vietnamese Australian'.	Is more objective, descriptive and is less subjective and offensively value-laden.
Terms such as 'coloured' (offensive).	Use colour labels terms 'black' or 'white', or people of colour.	Whites have historically used 'coloured' to describe 'other than-white' and the term is offensive to many black people. It was prevalent during the slavery era in America.
Terms such as 'part-Aborigine', 'quarter-Aborigine' (misleading and outdated).	'Person of Aboriginal or Torres Strait Islander descent.'	Being Aboriginal is a cultural, social and historical self-identification that involves more than blood relationships.
The term 'migrant' once a person has settled in Australia. This should only be used to describe a person in a state of transition from one country to another.	'Greek Australian', 'Vietnamese Australian', etc.	'Migrant' is inaccurate once a person has settled and it gives the impression that they do not really belong in their new country.

gender relations. Much of the language we use on a daily basis has gender-stereotyped assumptions and values built into it. Consider the following statements and their related gender assumptions:

Statement: 'Last night politicians and their wives attended . . .'
Assumption: All politicians are men.
Statement: 'Last night politicians and their husbands attended . . .'
Assumption: All politicians are women.

Which statement is more common?

As young children learn about their own gender and other people's, it is important that staff use language that broadens children's views of themselves rather than narrowing them. Words, phrases and meanings that stereotype and denigrate must be avoided. When describing people, the things they do, how they feel and what they think, staff should use gender-inclusive language, using descriptions that will:

➲ expand children's views of masculinity and femininity
➲ reinforce boys' and girls' self-esteem and pride in their own gender identity. This is particularly important for girls and for those boys who adopt non-traditional ways of being masculine. Traditionally, masculine boys are already likely to have a strong sense of self-esteem and pride in their gender identity
➲ present positive messages about different ways of being masculine and feminine. The descriptions of gender diversity that staff use with children should focus on the strengths, joys and richness of being with different sorts of boys and girls. For example, preschoolers can learn that some boys like dancing, some boys like pink or some girls like climbing. We do not all have to be the same. It's more interesting if we are different

- encourage boys and girls to empathise with each other
- avoid unnecessary gender suffixes or modifiers which demean and belittle women and girls, such as 'the little woman', 'the lady doctor', 'the fair sex' or 'the weaker sex'
- avoid words and ideas that denigrate or restrict girls' and women's capabilities. The table below offers some guidance on how to do this.

Avoid	Term preferred	Reasons for preferred term
'Policeman', 'fireman', 'ambulanceman'.	'Police officer', 'firefighter', 'paramedic'.	Provides children with the message that men and women can do all types of work.
'Lady doctor', 'woman lawyer'.	'Doctor', 'lawyer'.	Provides children with the message that men and women can do all types of work.

Disability and additional needs

Children with disabilities may have their ability to hear, see, move, think, touch or feel impaired in some way, and staff may not be able to rely as much on oral language to describe the world to these children. For example, to describe what is happening to a child with a hearing disability, staff may need to rely more on visual language and gesture. Similarly, they may need to emphasise touch and sound when describing something to a child with a visual disability.

Staff who are trying to develop an anti-discriminatory approach to people with disabilities in their centres can use descriptions of similarities and differences between people to provide children with appropriate language and ideas about human diversity. When describing people with disabilities, staff should provide positive messages about disability which are acceptable to such people. Some examples of preferred terms to describe people with disabilities include:

Avoid	Term preferred	Reasons for preferred term
Abnormal, subnormal, defective or deformed.	Specify the disability.	Less negatively value-laden.
Afflicted with . . .	The person has . . . (a disability).	Affliction is a very negative word.
Confined to a wheelchair.	Uses a wheelchair.	A wheelchair provides mobility not restriction.
Mongol.	Person with Down's syndrome.	More specific and less offensive to Mongolian people.
Spastic.	Person with cerebral palsy.	Less negatively value-laden and places the person at the centre.

REFLECTING ON DESCRIBING TECHNIQUES

1 Define describing.
2 What does research suggest are the keys to using describing to optimise children's learning?
3 When do you think description should be used in your teaching?

4   Are there any times when you think that the use of description is inappropriate with young children?

5   How could descriptions be used to promote communicative competence with infants? What sort of descriptions could you use to achieve this aim?

6   What items do you think toddlers would enjoy having descriptions of?

7   What are the most interesting descriptions that you have heard other adults provide for four-year-old children?

8   Imagine you were working with a group of three-year-olds who were going to visit an art gallery for the first time. What words could you use to describe the gallery to the children?

9   Develop a plan for a learning experience for four- to five-year-old children in which you wanted to increase their descriptive vocabulary in relation to feelings. How could you use description as a teaching technique to do this?

10   Imagine you were working in a mixed group of two- to five-year-old children. One of the three-year-olds had just returned from overseas and you were discussing the journey with the group. One of the four-year-old children asked what the inside of an aeroplane looked like. What words could you use to describe the inside of an aeroplane that the children might be familiar with? What new language might you need to use and explain in your description?

IMPROVING TEACHING IN PRACTICE

1   Record (using a tape-recorder or written notes) the descriptions you provided during several half-hour teaching periods.

2   What is your current style of describing? Do you:

- ➤   ensure you are familiar with whatever you describe to the children?
- ➤   think in advance about the key features you would describe?
- ➤   focus on the main characteristics?
- ➤   identify what is unique or specific to what you describe?
- ➤   use clear and precise language?
- ➤   rephrase your description when children don't understand?
- ➤   check with the children that they understand the description provided?

3   How and how well did you take account of developmental and equity considerations?

4   What are your strengths and weaknesses in using description to promote children's learning?

5   How can you work to improve your description techniques in practice?

6   Make a list of the words you could use to describe anger, happiness, joy, sadness.

Further reading

Curriculum Corporation 1995, *Early Moves: Primary Gender Inclusive Curriculum Units*, Melbourne, Curriculum Corporation [refer to pp. 68–70].

GossMan, H. 1992, 'Meeting the needs of all children: an Indian perspective', in B. Neugebauer, ed., *Alike and Different: Exploring our Humanity with Young Children* (pp. 146–51), Washington, National Association for the Education of Young Children.

Klein, E. R., Hammrich, P., Bloom, S. and Ragins, A. 2000, Language development and science inquiry: a child-initiated and teacher-facilitated program, Paper presented at the *Annual Meeting of the American Education Research Association*, New Orleans, April, ED 440756.

Ramsey, P. 1987, *Teaching and Learning in a Diverse World: Multicultural Education for Young Children*, Columbia, Teachers' College Press [refer to pp. 15–35].

References

Allen, K. and Hart, B. 1984, *The Early Years: Arrangements for Learning*, New Jersey, Prentice Hall Inc.

Beaty, J. 1996, *Skills for Preschool Teachers*, fifth edn, New Jersey, Prentice Hall Inc.

Brown, B. 1995, *All Our Children: A Guide for Those who Care*, 3rd edn, London, British Broadcasting Commission Education.

Camp, D. and Tompkins, G. 1990, 'The Abecedarius: soldier of literacy', *Childhood Education*, 66(5), pp. 298–302.

Clarke, P. 1992, *English as a 2nd Language in Early Childhood*, Melbourne, FKA Multicultural Resource Centre.

Department of Human Services 1996, *Babies, Toddlers and Two-Year-Olds: A Curriculum Resource for Development of Child-Centred Programs for Children Under Three — May 1996*, Melbourne, Department of Human Services, Government of Victoria.

Feeney, S., Christensen, D. and Moravcik, E. 1991, *Who am I in the Lives of Children? An Introduction to Teaching Young Children*, fifth edn, New York, Macmillan Publishing Company.

GossMan, H. 1992, 'Meeting the needs of all children: an Indian perspective', in B. Neugebauer, ed., *Alike and Different: Exploring our Humanity with Young Children* (pp. 146–51), Washington, National Association for the Education of Young Children.

Harrison, L. 1996, *Planning Appropriate Learning Environments for Children Under Three*, revised edn, Watson, ACT, Australian Early Childhood Association.

Hinchcliffe, V. 1996, 'Fairy stories and children's developing theories of mind', *International Journal of Early Years Education*, 4(1), pp. 35–46.

Hogg, A. and Foster, J. 1973, *Understanding Teaching Procedures*, Sydney, Cassell Australia.

Hughes, A. and Hughes, E. 1937, *Learning and Teaching: An Introduction to Psychology and Education*, London, Longmans.

Ramsey, P. 1987, *Teaching and Learning in a Diverse World: Multicultural Education for Young Children*, Columbia, Teachers' College Press.

Seefeldt, C. 1980, *Teaching Young Children*, New Jersey, Prentice Hall Inc.

Thompson, R. 2000, 'The legacy of early attachments', *Child Development*, 71, pp. 141–52.

—— 2001, 'Development in the first years of life', *The Future of Children*, 11(1), pp. 21–33.

Tizard, B. and Hughes, M. 1984, *Young Children Learning: Talking and Thinking at Home and at School*, London, Fontana.

Wilkes, G. (ed.) 1979, *Collins Dictionary of the English Language*, Middlesex, Penguin Books.

Willis, A. and Riccuiti, H. 1975, *A Good Beginning for Babies: Guidelines for Group Care*, Washington DC, National Association for the Education of Young Children.

Chapter 6

Encouraging, praising and helping

Help: to assist or aid (someone to do something).

> (*Collins Dictionary of the English Language*, p. 682)

Praise: the act of expressing commendation, admiration, etc.

> (*Collins Dictionary of the English Language*, p. 1151)

Encourage: to inspire (someone) with the courage or confidence (to do something).

> (*Collins Dictionary of the English Language*, p. 482)

The positives in adults' behaviour with children are usually a mixture of praise, rewards, and encouragements.

> (Laishley 1983, p. 66)

If praise is given too liberally, it becomes a meaningless habit, and ultimately, an irritant.

> (Briggs and Potter 1995, p. 263)

WHAT?

To encourage someone means to reassure and to support them when they are having difficulty with a task or experience. This reassurance and support might be verbal or non-verbal. Staff use encouragement as a teaching technique to reassure and support children attempting new or difficult activities. The aim of such encouragement is to help children persevere with the task and to learn new skills or dispositions.

Verbal encouragement and praise

To praise someone means to show that you approve of what they have done and that their act deserves acclaim. As a teaching process, praise shows children that they deserve recognition, acclaim and approval.

Some early childhood texts confuse 'praise' and 'encouragement' and often use them interchangeably. However, in terms of children's learning, there are very significant differences between the two terms. Encouragement is given while a child is doing something to support them to continue it and to show appreciation of their efforts. Praise is given after a child has completed part or all of a task to show them that their achievement is worthy of your approval. Laishley explained the difference further:

> . . . spoken praise . . . emphasises the child. Encouragement tends to emphasise what the child is doing (Laishley 1983, p. 67).

The research literature suggests that children's learning is best supported through encouragement rather than praise (Hitz and Driscoll 1988).

Non-verbal encouragement and helping

To physically help someone is to assist them, to aid and contribute to what they are doing. Help can take many forms and may last for moments or for much longer. Physically helping a child with a task might involve holding their hand as they attempt to enter a situation about which they feel apprehension, or helping them to use a piece of equipment by holding it steady. Such help can encourage children to continue with their task and can assist them to achieve success. Non-verbal forms of encouragement such as holding a child's hands can be just as valuable in supporting children's learning as verbal encouragement. The following example shows how simple such non-verbal support can be:

> To make Jaya feel safe as he jumps, Miklosh holds Jaya's hands on the jumping board.

However, it is important for staff to remember that helping is about doing something with someone, not doing it for them. Helping involves doing a task with a child, not taking over the task from the child and completing it for them.

> Lois, a volunteer from the local secondary school, is sitting with some children at the drawing table. The children are three-year-olds and are at different levels of ability and skill. Damien asks Lois to draw him a person. Lois obliges and draws a 'stick figure'. At the end of the session with the children, Andrew, the teacher has a discussion with Lois about drawing for them. He explains how Lois can help the children to draw their own pictures so that they need not rely on adults to do it for them. Andrew gives her some suggestions on how to encourage them to do their own work, including phrases such as, 'Can you show me how you would draw a person?', or 'Let's think about what you need to have in a drawing of a person', and 'I think you could draw a very interesting person if you try. I'll come and look when you've finished.'

HOW?

Verbal encouragement

Verbal encouragement can act as a positive motivator for children's learning if some basic rules are followed. Staff need to ensure that their encouragement is very specific and that it focuses on how a child is undertaking a specific task. This is best done when the child and the adult are alone, rather than part of a large group, because this prevents the adult's comments embarrassing the child in front of other children (Hitz and Driscoll 1988). It is also important to ensure that comments on a child's performance do not involve comparison with other children, such as, 'Look how much better you are doing than . . .', thus avoiding competition between them (Catron and Allen 1993).

Words of encouragement should extend children's learning rather than reduce it. Schwartz (1995, p. 400) argued that '. . . emphasizing the process of thinking, rather than the product, extends the thinking'. For example, a comment such as, 'Great job!' focuses on the product and does not extend the child's thinking. In contrast, a comment such as, 'I wonder how we could make that happen again, it looked really interesting' not only tells the child that what they have done is worthy of interest and comment, but also encourages them to think about how to extend what has happened.

Praise

Staff can prevent their praise becoming meaningless or irritating by drawing on the following guidance offered by Briggs and Potter (1995):

- ➲ Use praise sparingly. Praise can reduce children's ability to judge their own work and can create anxiety in the children about whether their efforts will meet with staff approval. It can also encourage them to focus on external rather than intrinsic rewards (Schiller 1999).
- ➲ Praise children equitably. Research (Briggs and Potter 1995) suggests that teachers tend to praise only those children who they think are high achievers.
- ➲ Praise children only for new achievements or consistent effort. Praising children for accomplishing tasks that require little effort can encourage them to try less difficult tasks.

Non-verbal encouragement and physical help

There are several simple non-verbal ways of offering encouragement and physical help to a child. These include:

- ➲ moving a toy closer to a child
- ➲ moving yourself closer to a child
- ➲ offering a helping hand
- ➲ finding a special tool or item that will enrich a child's play
- ➲ handing a child a toy that is out of reach
- ➲ sitting by a child to offer support when needed
- ➲ smiling at the right moment.

Staff can support children's learning through non-verbal encouragement and physical help if they:

- ➲ ask the child if they would like assistance
- ➲ provide help appropriate to the level of difficulty a child is having. For example, if a child needs help to complete a puzzle, merely placing one piece of the puzzle correctly might be sufficient to help the child complete the task themselves. On the other hand, if a child is trying to construct a large and complex collage, staff may need to help at several points in the process

➡ ask the child if they would like any additional assistance

➡ encourage children to help each other by providing positive models of helping behaviour and by commenting positively on children's helping behaviours.

These guidelines have helped Jemma to provide just the right amount of verbal and non-verbal encouragement to Ursula:

> Jemma is sitting at the collage table with five four-year-old preschoolers. The children are all busily constructing their own creations. They are talking with each other and with Jemma as they work. Jemma notices that Ursula is having trouble with the tape. She offers assistance: 'Can I help you, Ursula? That tape looks hard to get off.' Ursula responds that she would like help. Jemma moves around to hold the tape dispenser for Ursula and says: 'I'll hold it and then it will be easier for you to break a piece off.'

Angela uses verbal and non-verbal encouragement
as Nam moves across the monkey bars.

WHEN AND WHY?

Goal relevance

There are many moments during a child's day when a small amount of encouragemen[t] adult can make the difference between an enjoyable and satisfying learning outc[ome] child or a frustrating and disappointing one. For example, encouragement by a[n] essential to a toddler who had climbed to the top of a climbing frame but was becoming upset because she could not find her way down again. In these circumstances, withholding help could be dangerous both to the toddler's safety and to their emotional well-being.

Staff can use physical help and verbal encouragement as a teaching strategy to:

➲ support and reassure children as they tackle a particular task or become involved in a particular experience. As Laishley (1983, p. 67) explained:

> Encouragement is used to help a child try out new activities and to persevere when she is finding something difficult, or when she is beginning to fail.

➲ increase the likelihood that children will behave in pro-social ways, such as helping each other to tidy up or sharing materials with each other (Laishley 1983; Warner and Lynch 2002/03)

➲ extend children's thinking about an event, an idea or a material (Schwartz 1995)

➲ help children practise complex skills and techniques (Schwartz 1995)

➲ support children's expression of their ideas through movement and music, visual arts, etc.

➲ provide children with positive attention to accentuate children's positive behaviours within the group (Warner and Lynch 2002/03).

When offering non-verbal encouragement and physical help, staff need to strike a balance between allowing children to solve problems for themselves and by themselves, and in helping them to do so. Physical help should always be provided when children's safety and well-being is at risk, but beyond this, staff's individual philosophy on adult intervention in children's learning will guide when and how often help is provided.

> At the weekly staff meeting at the Little Geese Children's Centre, the director, Heather, expresses some concerns about staff members' styles of helping. Staff have fallen into the habit of doing things for the children rather than helping them or encouraging them to do things for themselves. Heather gives several examples: dressing the children, putting things away, completing puzzles when the children have abandoned them, pushing children on the wheel toys rather than encouraging them to use their feet to move themselves along. She encourages the staff to discuss what they want for the children and gently reminds them of the Centre's mission statement, which states that, 'The centre aims to help the children to become autonomous'. She then facilitates a discussion about useful techniques thro..gh which staff can help the children to do things for themselves. She also gives the
> ...al advice.

...onsiderations

...bal ways through which staff can encourage babies to actively explore their ...hese are examined in Chapters 1 and 12. Verbal encouragement is an effec- ...the emerging communicative competence of babies in their first twelve ...lieves that one key skill to encourage is that of combining vowels and con- ...s 'mu-mu' and 'ba-ba', because it enables babies to develop their own

Binh sings with Oliver.

language through which to express their needs. Babies can learn to use 'mu-mu' to ask for milk or 'ba-ba' to ask for their bottle. If adults respond with similar sounds whenever babies produce them, babies are strongly encouraged to repeat their sounds and to experiment with new vowel–consonant combinations.

During their second year of life, young children become increasingly sensitive to the reactions of the adults around them. More specifically, they become '. . . increasingly sensitive to standards set by adults' (DeCooke and Brownell 1987, p. 1). Thus, staff need to be especially careful to encourage rather than praise toddlers. Too much praise can quickly lead toddlers to become dependent on adult approval of their performance. Schwartz (1995) cautioned that overemphasis on praise can foster dependence rather than autonomy in children's thinking and can restrict their learning rather than extend it.

The preschool years are a time of considerable growth in the complexity of children's imaginative play and children rapidly build their social and communication skills through this play. During sequences of socio-dramatic play, staff can use verbal encouragement to increase children's '. . . social interaction, make-believe, role-playing and verbal communication . . .' (Ward 1994, p. 9). For example, if a group of children is preparing to have a party but is unclear about what to do next, staff could comment on how well their preparations are going and extend the play through posing a question such as, 'I wonder what would happen if you did . . . ?'. Ward (1994, p. 12) argued that such intervention in children's play is essential for children to develop into what she called 'master players'.

Staff can develop their own skills in using verbal encouragement through sharing ideas with each other:

At a children's centre in Hobart there is a list in the staff tea room on which the staff write down examples of how to verbally encourage children. In this way the staff share different ways of speaking to the children and increase their own 'encouraging' vocabulary and behaviours. The list includes: focus comments on the child's process of learning, not their products; comment on how children are achieving success; ask questions that show interest in how children could extend their achievements; use words that show children you have confidence in their abilities to problem-solve, achieve and extend themselves.

Children who are learning to write need lots of technical practice at writing. They need practice at forming letters on paper and at choosing the correct letters and putting them in the correct order. The experience can be frustrating and children will generally know when they have 'got it wrong' or 'messed it up'. A well-placed word of encouragement can help children persevere with the acquisition of their technical writing skills. The more they can be encouraged to refine these skills through repetition the more pleasure they will derive from them.

EQUITY CONSIDERATIONS

'Race' and culture

Children gain a sense of their racial and cultural identity through interacting with others. Also, children develop a strong and positive racial and cultural identity and feel good about who they are if there are strong and positive images of their own racial and cultural group around them. Children who lack such positive images can quickly develop a poor sense of identity and low self-esteem. There is a strong risk of this happening for children from racial and cultural groups who experience racism in the wider society (Ramsey 1987), as they will regularly confront negative images of their own group. In Australia, such children would be those with Aboriginal or Torres Strait Islander backgrounds and children of parents whose background is from countries in Southeast Asia, Africa and the Pacific Islands.

Low self-esteem can damage children's thirst for learning in a number of ways. For instance, Millam (1996, p. 190) argued that it can result in children:

> . . . not mixing with other children, or wanting to be by themselves; not wanting to be cuddled and avoiding physical contact . . . [and] . . . not trying to do things in case they get it wrong.

For these reasons, staff encouragement is particularly important when children with black and ethnic minority backgrounds explore new experiences, practise existing skills and do things for themselves. Support and reassurance can make the difference between persevering and feeling good about their efforts or giving up and feeling bad about what they have not done. When staff help children with black and ethnic minority backgrounds to feel good about their own efforts, they also help them to:

 counter the racist images and messages they have experienced in the wider society
 develop a positive racial and cultural identity during their time in the centre; and
 build self-esteem with which to counter a negative attitude towards their racial and cultural identity.

As with any child, the encouragement of children of black and ethnic minority groups will be most effective when it is specific to the task or skill. This helps the children to learn that they are being encouraged for effort, rather than for who they are. Encouragement also needs to extend children's learning rather than reduce it, making it more likely that the children will want to take on new challenges. Talking with parents to ensure that staff efforts at encouragement and praise are culturally relevant and sensitive will support the skill development of children (McCay and Keyes 2001/02).

Gender

There is evidence to suggest that within the early childhood environment, boys and girls are encouraged to do different things and take on different challenges (Ebbeck 1985; Dunn and Morgan 1987; Alloway 1995). For example, boys are often verbally encouraged to become actively involved in a variety of gross motor activities such as running, jumping and climbing. Girls, on the other hand, are often verbally encouraged to become actively involved in the quieter and more passive fine motor activities such as making collage, solving puzzles, drawing and painting. Staff who want gender equity in their program will need to carefully monitor their interactions with the children to ensure that they are encouraging both boys and girls to fully explore all aspects of the program. Research (Ebbeck 1985; Dunn and Morgan 1987; Alloway 1995) suggests that staff should guard against:

- ❯ encouraging girls but not boys to help with packing away. For example, staff may comment on how well the girls have helped with the task but not comment on the boys' involvement or lack of involvement
- ❯ encouraging boys but not girls to extend their climbing skills. For example, staff may move over to the boys when they are being active on the climbing frame and comment on their skill in climbing so high, but not when girls accomplish similar feats
- ❯ encouraging girls in their domestic play but not similarly encouraging boys in this play. For example, staff may positively comment on how well the girls have worked together to bake a cake but not when boys successfully work together in domestic play
- ❯ encouraging boys but not girls to engage in messy mud play. For example, staff may comment on how deep a hole the boys have dug but not comment on girls' achievement in the digging area
- ❯ encouraging girls but not boys to be involved in quiet, table activities. For example, staff may comment on how quiet the girls have been while they completed a puzzle but not comment on similar success by boys.

Staff need to ensure that they expend equal effort on girls and boys as part of the process of encouraging them to try different activities. West (1992) noted that in some centres staff made great efforts to encourage boys to explore non-traditional roles but not the girls.

Disability and additional needs

Children without disabilities are likely to develop a number of misconceptions about children with disabilities as they interact with them (Brown 1995). As part of the process of developing an antibias approach to disability, staff should counter these misconceptions with accurate information about people with disabilities. However, staff cannot counter misconceptions unless they are aware of them, and a good way to bring misconceptions into the open is to encourage children without disabilities to ask questions about children with disabilities. Staff can encourage open discussion by responding to children's questions with comments that extend their interests in each other rather than closing them off. For example, if a child asks why another child has to wear glasses, by responding that 'It's rude to ask such questions' staff would close their interest and allow misconceptions to develop. In contrast, responding with comments such as, 'I'm glad you asked that question. It shows that you have been thinking about Tim. How could we find out if he can see very far without his glasses?' is likely to encourage further interest in Tim and what makes him special.

Children with severe disabilities often face considerably greater challenges than other children in acquiring the basic skills required in daily living. Children with severe disabilities who can understand verbal feedback can be powerfully supported via verbal encouragement in their efforts and successes to acquire these basic skills. In addition, it is important for staff to encourage children with disabilities to become as independent as possible in the classroom, ensuring that there is the time and opportunity for the children to build the skills required for independent classroom learning. This includes specifically assigning children tasks, allowing them choices and providing time for independent exploration (McCay and Keyes 2001/02).

Encouragement can be a powerful strategy to support children with cognitive disabilities who demonstrate challenging behaviours in the classroom (for example, biting, kicking and screaming) by helping them adapt to build pro-social behaviours. For example, a synthesis of 100 research studies of children with cognitive disabilties has shown that frequent encouragement and reinforcement of positive behaviours and redirection of anti-social behaviours can help to build pro-social behaviours with these children (Warger 1999).

REFLECTING ON TECHNIQUES FOR ENCOURAGING CHILDREN

1   Define encouragement.
2   What are the differences between verbal and non-verbal encouragement?
3   What does research suggest are the keys to encouraging and optimising children's learning?
4   When do you think encouragement should be used in your teaching?
5   Are there any times when you think that the use of encouragement is inappropriate with young children?
6   How would you explain the differences between praise and encouragement?
7   When do you think it is appropriate to praise young children?
8   Imagine you are working with a group of three-year-olds who are just beginning to share their toys each other. What forms of encouragement would you use to support their sharing behaviours?
9   Develop a plan for a learning experience for four- to five-year-old children in which you wanted to increase their balancing skills. How would you use encouragement as a teaching strategy to do this?
10 Which of the phrases below represent encouragement and which represent praise?
    ❸   Sally, thank you for your help today, it made it much easier for us to pack away before lunchtime.
    ❸   Anu, you are such a tidy girl.
    ❸   Good boy, Richard.
    ❸   Calamity, I can see that you are working really hard on that collage. It must have been difficult to make the boxes stick together.

IMPROVING TEACHING IN PRACTICE

1 Record (using a tape-recorder or written notes) the encouragement you provide to children during several half-hour teaching periods.

2 What is your current style of verbal encouragement? Do you:
- ➲ ensure your encouragement is very specific?
- ➲ ensure your encouragement focuses on how a child is undertaking a specific task?
- ➲ encourage children individually or in group settings?
- ➲ ensure that your encouragement extends children's learning rather than reduces it?
- ➲ use praise sparingly?
- ➲ praise children equitably?
- ➲ only praise children for new achievements or consistent effort?

3 What is your current style of physical encouragement and help?

4 How and how well did you take account of developmental and equity considerations?

5 What are your areas of strength and weakness in using encouragement to promote children's learning?

6 How can you work to improve your encouragement techniques in practice?

7 What do you see as the hardest part of improving your encouragement techniques?

Further reading

Catron, C. and Allen, J. 1993, *Early Childhood Curriculum*, New York, Macmillan Publishing Company [refer to pp. 70–71].

Hitz, R. and Driscoll, A. 1988, 'Praise or encouragement? New insights into praise: implications for early childhood teachers', *Young Children*, 6–13 July.

Laishley, J. 1983, *Working with Young Children: Encouraging their Development and Dealing with Problems*, London, Edward Arnold [refer to pp. 66–68, 135–6 and 97].

Schwartz, S. 1995, 'Hidden messages in teacher talk: praise and empowerment', *Teaching Children Mathematics*, (March), pp. 396–401.

References

Alloway, N. 1995, *Foundation Stones: The Construction of Gender in Early Childhood*, Melbourne, Curriculum Corporation.

Briggs, F. and Potter, G. 1995, *Teaching Children in the First Three Years of School*, Melbourne, Longman.

Brown, B. 1995, *All Our Children: A Guide for Those Who Care*, 3rd edn, London, British Broadcasting Commission Education.

Catron, C. and Allen, J. 1993, *Early Childhood Curriculum*, New York, Macmillan Publishing Company.

DeCooke, P. and Brownell, C. 1987, Help-seeking in toddlers: possible precursors of a problem-solving skill, Paper presented to the *American Educational Research Association*, April.

Dunn, S. and Morgan, V. 1987, 'Nursery and infant school play patterns: sex-related differences', *British Educational Research Journal*, 13(3), pp. 271–81.

Ebbeck, M. 1985, 'Pre-school teachers' interactions with boys as compared with girls: a report of an observation study', *Australian Journal of Early Childhood*, 10(2), pp. 26–30.

Hitz, R. and Driscoll, A. 1988, 'Praise or encouragement? New insights into praise: implications for early childhood teachers', *Young Children*, 6–13 July.

Honig, A. 1990, 'The baby — birth to twelve months', in E. Surbeck and M. Kelley, eds, *Personalizing Care with Infants, Toddlers and Families* (pp. 10–22), Wheaton, MD, Association for Childhood Education International.

Laishley, J. 1983, *Working with Young Children: Encouraging their Development and Dealing with Problems*, London, Edward Arnold.

McCay, L. and Keyes, D. 2001/02, 'Developing social competence in the primary schools', *Childhood Education*, 78(2), pp. 70–8.

Millam, R. 1996, *Anti-Discriminatory Practice: A Guide for Workers in Childcare and Education*, London, Cassell Books.

Ramsey, P. 1987, *Teaching and Learning in a Diverse World: Multicultural Education for Young Children*, Columbia, Teachers' College Press.

Schiller, P. 1999, 'Turning knowledge into practice', *Child Care Information Exchange*, March (142), pp. 49–52.

Schwartz, S. 1995, 'Hidden messages in teacher talk: praise and empowerment', *Teaching Children Mathematics* (March), pp. 396–401.

Ward, C. 1994, Adult intervention: appropriate strategies for enriching the quality of children's play, Paper presented to the *Annual Conference of the Southern Early Childhood Association*, New Orleans, 11–16 April.

Warger, C. 1999, 'Positive behaviour support and functional assessment.' *ERIC Digest*, ED0-99-8.

Warner, L. and Lynch, S. 2002/03, 'Classroom problems that don't go away', *Childhood Education*, 79(2), pp. 97–100.

West, B. 1992, 'Children are caught — between home and school, culture and school', in B. Neugebauer, ed., *Alike and Different: Exploring our Humanity with Young Children* (pp. 127–39) Washington DC, National Association for the Education of Young Children.

Wilkes, G. (ed.) 1979, *Collins Dictionary of the English Language*, Middlesex, Penguin Books.

Chapter 7

Facilitating

Facilitate: to make easier: to assist the progress of.

(Collins Dictionary of the English Language, p. 521)

Teachers best facilitate creative thought in a flexible but well-planned, well-organized environment where children's ideas are valued and where curriculum ideas are generated by children as well as teachers.

(Catron and Allen 1993, p. 39)

Teachers facilitate learning by creating a learning environment and offering learning experiences that are relevant and interesting to the children.

(Spodek and Saracho 1994, p. 15)

WHAT?

As a teaching technique, facilitating refers to the process of making children's learning easier. Facilitation, therefore, refers to all the things that staff do to make children's learning more possible, such as scheduling, selecting materials, organising space, and interacting verbally and non-verbally with them. In other words, it concerns the majority of the teaching techniques discussed in this book! However, facilitating is also about careful observation and thoughtful timing to ensure that learning is appropriate to the children's needs and interests.

HOW?

> We can . . . facilitate children's learning by providing the appropriate space, time and resources (Arthur et al. 1996, p. 242).

How staff arrange the learning environment will contribute to their ability to facilitate children's learning. Facilitation supports children's learning by paying attention to what materials they are offered, how space is used, how their time is organised and how people are used. Staff can facilitate specific children's learning on specific occasions through regularly:

 observing how children approach a specific task and identifying the elements of the task with which they have difficulties

➲ reflecting on how they can make a task easier for the child but with minimal intervention. Specifically, staff need to think about what changes to the use of people, space, time and materials might be made to make a task easier for the child. Such changes might include ensuring that distractions, such as loud noises or other children, are kept to a minimum by redirecting the other children to alternative tasks, placing a tool nearby that might make the task easier, expanding the space available for the activity by moving furniture and joining two tables together, or moving another adult nearby to assist with a particularly tricky negotiation between the children. The following anecdote shows how simply this can be done:

> Randolf has started to play with his puzzle on the floor outside the bathroom. However, he is having difficulties concentrating on it because he is distracted by the children walking around him on their way to the bathroom. His teacher suggests that he may be able to do a better job if he moves himself to the quiet corner set aside for this type of work. She carefully helps him to carry his puzzle over to the quiet area and stays with him for a moment until he is absorbed in his task.

➲ waiting a few seconds after they have made changes in the organisation of space, time, materials and people to see if additional changes are needed; then monitoring at regular intervals.

Facilitating children's learning also involves constantly assessing the environment to see if more significant changes are needed in the positioning of people (Chapter 12), the positioning of equipment and materials (Chapter 1), or the scheduling of the day (Chapter 3).

WHEN AND WHY?

Goal relevance

Staff generally facilitate children's learning through using equipment, time, materials, space and people. Staff do this when they are encouraging children to be independent learners and to learn through self-discovery. A supportive and helpful learning environment will make it more likely that these goals will be achieved and that children will be self-motivated learners.

> Students who feel supported in their striving toward autonomy have greater internal motivation, higher achievement, and healthier adjustment (Sands and Doll 1996, p. 69).

Staff can also use facilitation to:

➲ increase the complexity of children's fantasy play through ensuring that they spend lots of time in the outdoor play space. In particular, boys' fantasy play tends to be more complex in the outdoor play area than in the inside play area (Pelligrini and Boyd 1993)

➲ increase children's social play with each other through ensuring that they have lots of time in the outdoor play space. Research has shown that playing outdoors leads to more social play than playing indoors (Ladd and Coleman 1993)

➲ increase children's co-operative play through participating in it and using language to model to children how to extend their play and negotiate and share roles (Hintz and Stomfay-Stitz 1999)

Sarah facilitates fantasy play outside by adding a new boat and spending time with the children in it.

→ increase children's sense of autonomy through ensuring that they can make choices about when, where, with whom and with what they play

At a meeting in a bayside suburb of Melbourne, teachers are discussing how to help children in their centres to become more autonomous. Susie has some concerns. She feels that she has not been able to facilitate the children's transition from being told what to do throughout the session at the beginning of the year, to choosing their own activities now, six months later.

Susie: 'I have not let them become independent. After two terms, they still rely on me to tell them what to do. Now I think it's too late for them to be any other way.'

Shaun: 'How about starting off by giving them choices about what they might do and then progress to giving them complete freedom of choice, so that they can cope with small changes at a time? You could ask them if they want to play inside or outside and then progress to informing them that they can play where they like.'

Susie. 'That sounds like a good idea! That way, we can all get used to the change gradually.'

→ increase the confidence of children learning English as a second language through ensuring that there are opportunities for solitary fantasy play. Research has shown that solitary fantasy play provides a safe space for children learning English as a second language to practise their new language (Pelligrini and Boyd 1993)

In a kindergarten in one of the outer suburbs of Brisbane where there is a large proportion of NESB families, Greta makes sure that she provides plenty of opportunities each day for the children to engage in solitary dramatic play. An area of the room is set up for this purpose. Greta presents such things as a sandbox with small animals and people in it, a collection of interesting objects with stimulus pictures or some magnets. She regularly talks with parents to ensure that the objects she uses are of particular interest to the children learning English.

increase peer interactions between children by providing small spaces within the play area. Research has shown that children engage in more conversational and pro-social play in play spaces that are divided into small areas (Ladd and Coleman 1993)

 increase children's capacity to learn by providing lots of opportunities for quiet contemplation and concentration. 'The most important process needed for learning is that of attention' (Wieder and Greenspan 1993, p. 83)

 support children's experimentation with writing. Children need adults to '. . . ensure an atmosphere conducive to exploration and to good feelings about writing' (Atkins 1984, p. 6). This involves providing children with the tools they need for writing (for example, paper and pencils) and the time to experiment with using these for writing

 support young children's science literacy development by providing an environment that enables them to explore and create and by 'relating experiences and answering personal questions when appropriate' (Klein et al. 2000, p. 12). When techniques of facilitation are combined with explicit teaching of scientific knowledge, children's science literacy is significantly enhanced (Klein et al. 2000)

 encourage children to share ideas while using computers by placing computers side by side (Bowman et al. 2001).

Additional goals that can be achieved through facilitation are discussed in the chapters on organising the environment (Chapters 1 to 3).

Developmental considerations

Babies are more likely to pay attention to adult faces and sounds when they are calm and rested than when they are excited, tired or distracted (Wieder and Greenspan 1993). Paying attention to adult faces and sounds helps a baby learn to communicate with others. Through watching an adult's face and listening to the sounds they make, a baby learns that the things they can do, such as cooing, can attract an adult's attention and that adults will respond with coos or smiles. This is the beginning of babies learning that communication is a two-way process with a logic and a sequence. To facilitate this early form of two-way communication in an early childhood setting, staff need to spend time with babies when the babies are calm and rested. Staff also need to organise space and equipment to create places and spaces in which staff and babies can attend to each other without distraction. Staff at the Tiny Tots Children's Centre have made sure that part of the floor in the babies' room is set aside for a member of staff to simply sit and be available to the children for unplanned verbal and physical interaction.

Toddlers become increasingly mobile and adept at using their growing physical competence to explore the world around them. They are keen to gain control over their bodies and to use this control to become more independent. However, they are only just beginning to acquire many motor skills such as learning to walk up and down stairs with ease, kicking and throwing balls, building with small blocks, turning handles, turning pages of books, rolling and squeezing play dough and clay, and wrapping and unwrapping things (Catron and Allen 1993). To acquire these skills, toddlers need to practise them repeatedly. Staff can facilitate this by providing plenty of space for toddlers to practise their gross motor skills, lots of time for them to try their skills out over and over again, and lots of equipment that allows them to use their developing skills. Part of this will involve having equipment '. . . remain in place for some time to allow for practice and repetition . . .' (Olsson 1988, p. 132).

> Peta, a teacher education student, was set the task of encouraging the toddlers to use their gross motor skills. Each day she set up the area in new and exciting ways. Peta was given some feedback from her supervising teacher about this. Her teacher explained that the children do not necessarily need novel equipment each day. It was more important that they had her support and the time to practise their skills over and over.

There is some evidence to suggest that preschool children's abilities to adapt to novel situations and to deal with transitions, such as that from an early childhood setting to school, is helped by '. . . regular exposure to peers in unstructured community contexts . . .' (Ladd and Coleman 1993, p. 63). Such 'unstructured community contexts' include museums, libraries, parks and swimming pools, and early childhood staff can organise visits and outings to facilitate the development of these abilities. This may be especially beneficial for preschoolers to prepare for their transition to school.

Preschool children are able to make and maintain stable friendships over a long period of time. Up to 70 per cent of the friendships children make in child care settings will last for over twelve months (Howes 1988). Staff can facilitate the development of friendships among children through careful selection of materials and experiences that promote quality peer interaction. Dramatic play experiences are more likely to promote social interaction than experiences such as painting and playing with sand and water. Similarly, large motor equipment such as climbing frames are more likely to promote social interaction than small motor equipment such as puzzles (Ladd and Coleman 1993).

In the early years of schooling, children are increasingly being exposed to computers in the classroom. To facilitate children's acquisition of computer skills in ways that support rather than hinder learning, Clements and Nastasi (1993) suggested that staff:

- ❯ select software that children can use with minimal adult support
- ❯ provide lots of support and guidance when children first use new software
- ❯ encourage group use and co-operative problem-solving over time
- ❯ ensure that all children get a fair go with using the equipment
- ❯ use computers as a means of learning new things
- ❯ question children about their thinking skills as they are using the computers.

Explanations of how to approach new situations or unfamiliar problems can also act to facilitate successful problem-solving and generalisation skills with children in the early years of schooling (Crowley and Steigler 1999).

EQUITY CONSIDERATIONS

'Race' and culture

Children with a positive sense of self engage in early childhood programs with enthusiasm and confidence. Developing a positive sense of self can be difficult for children who have experienced negative reactions to their skin colour and physical characteristics. This is particularly likely to be the case for black children. Children's self-esteem is enhanced when they learn to be competent decision-makers and to be independent learners (Sands and Doll 1996). Facilitating opportunities for black children to make decisions and to become independent learners can be one important way to build their self-esteem.

Staff can facilitate children's acceptance of cultural and racial diversity by creating an environment in which children can notice and talk about such diversity. If there is racial diversity within a group of children, they will notice and talk about it as they learn about each other. However, in a predominantly white group of children, staff need to facilitate other opportunities for them to notice and to talk about racial diversity. Having posters, dolls, books, puzzles and pictures that represent the full racial diversity of a specific country is a simple but effective way to do this. More specific information on how to organise the environment to facilitate positive attitudes to racial diversity is provided in Chapters 1 and 2.

In culturally diverse classrooms teachers can facilitate a sense of welcome and safety for all children if they ensure the images, symbols, sounds and languages of the children's cultural background are infused throughout the classroom. When children can recognise their identities reflected within the classroom it affirms who they are and their culture (Adler Matoba 2001).

Gender

Children's fantasy play is influenced by the gender composition of play groups and by the props available to them. When preschool boys and girls play together using stereotypically masculine props or gender-neutral props, boys tend to choose the fantasy play storylines (Pelligrini and Boyd 1993; MacNaughton 1997, 2000). Staff can facilitate girls' ability to choose the fantasy play storylines by encouraging girls-only groups when they want to play with stereotypically masculine or gender-neutral props, and by encouraging the use of stereotypically feminine props in mixed group play. For example, adding lots of dolls to the block area makes it more likely that the girls may be able to choose the storyline when they are playing with the boys in this area.

Staff can facilitate a more equitable gender climate in their classrooms in the early years of schooling by ensuring that girls receive recognition for their achievements, that they remember the girls' names and use them, and by regularly sitting with the girls to support their work. Corson (1993) argued that these simple steps help children learn that girls and their ideas are important because it shows that the person with power in the classroom (the teacher) takes girls seriously and is interested in their achievements.

Disability and additional needs

Developing a positive sense of self is as important for children with disabilities as it is for other children. However, developing a positive sense of self can be difficult for children who have experienced negative reactions to their disabilities. This is particularly likely to be the case for children who have visible disabilities.

As indicated earlier, children's self-esteem is enhanced when they learn to be competent decision-makers and to be independent learners (Sands and Doll 1996). Facilitating opportunities for children with disabilities to make decisions and to become independent learners can be one important way to build their self-esteem. This can be difficult to do when staff feel uncertain about a child's specific strengths and abilities. Staff need to talk with parents and learn about the special abilities of children with disabilities. Providing lots of open-ended materials that have no inherently right or wrong way to use them can be a useful way forward. Sometimes a simple adaptation to the physical environment is all that is needed to facilitate a child's successful involvement in an experience.

> One of the modifications we made for him was to create a sand tray which was elevated from the ground. Instead of him going down to the sand, we brought the sand up to him (Department of Employment, Education and Training 1994, p. 28).

Staff can facilitate children's acceptance of diverse abilities and needs by creating an environment in which children can notice and talk about their own abilities and disabilities. When there are children within the group who have visible disabilities, the children will notice and talk about diversity as they learn about each other. However, in a group of predominantly able-bodied children, staff will need to facilitate other opportunities for children to notice and talk about disability and diversity. Having posters, dolls, books, puzzles and pictures that represent a range of visible disabilities is a simple but effective way to do this.

More specific information on how to organise the environment to facilitate positive attitudes to people's diverse abilities is provided in Chapters 1 and 2. Ways of talking with children about the differences between them are detailed in Chapters 5 and 14.

REFLECTING ON FACILITATION TECHNIQUES

1 Briefly define facilitating.
2 What do you think is the major difference between helping and facilitating?
3 List ten non-verbal ways of facilitating children's learning. Would each of these processes be suitable for use with babies?
4 What are most successful ways that you have seen other adults help toddlers build self-esteem through facilitation?
5 What are three ways in which you could facilitate children's social play?
6 What are three ways in which you could facilitate girls' ability to choose the storylines for their fantasy play?
7 The following extract presents a teaching episode with preschool children. Has the teacher used facilitation to support children's learning in this episode?

> Some children were building haphazard piles of blocks and knocking them down. I sat alongside them on the floor and silently began to sort through a container of plastic animals, putting them in identical pairs to form a long queue. The children stopped what they were doing and joined in my play (Skinner 1996, p. 62).

8 Observe a child in an early childhood setting who has a visible disability. How and how well have staff facilitated the child's learning?
9 Observe a group setting for babies. How and how well does the organisation of space, time, materials and people facilitate two-way communication between the babies and the staff?

IMPROVING TEACHING IN PRACTICE

1 Videotape the non-verbal teaching interactions you have with children during several five-minute teaching periods.
2 How and how well did you facilitate children's learning? Did you:
   ❯ observe how the children were approaching a specific task and identify the elements of the task they were having difficulties with?
   ❯ focus on what you could do to make the task easier for the children with minimal intervention?
   ❯ wait a few seconds after you had made changes in the organisation of space, time, materials and people to see if additional changes were needed?
   ❯ monitor the need for additional facilitation at regular intervals?

3   What are your areas of strength and weakness in using facilitation as a teaching technique to promote children's learning?

4   How can you work to improve your facilitation techniques?

Further reading

Arthur, L., Beecher, B., Dockett, S., Farmer, S. and Death, E. 1996, *Programming and Planning in Early Childhood Settings*, second edn, Sydney, Harcourt Brace and Company [refer to p. 242].

Catron, C. and Allen, J. 1993, *Early Childhood Curriculum*, New York, Macmillan Publishing Company, [refer to p. 39].

Haigh, K., Rodriguez, D. and Schroeder, G. 2002, 'A study of hands: Chicago Commons explores Reggio Emilia', *Child Care Information Exchange*, 144(3), pp. 42–5.

Video

Supporting Children's Active Learning: Teaching Strategies for Diverse Settings, The High Scope Press 1992.

References

Adler Matoba, S. 2001, 'Racial and ethnic mirrors: reflections on identity from an Asian American educator', in S. Grieshaber and G. Cannella, eds, *Embracing Identities in Early Childhood Education: Diversity and Possibilities* (pp. 148–57), New York, Teachers' College Press.

Arthur, L., Beecher, B., Dockett, S., Farmer, S. and Death, E. 1996, *Programming and Planning in Early Childhood Settings,* second edn, Sydney, Harcourt Brace and Company.

Atkins, C. 1984, 'Doing something constructive', *Young Children* November, pp. 3–6.

Bowman, B., Donovan, M. and Burns, S. 2001, *Eager to Learn: Educating Our Preschoolers*, Washington DC, National Academy Press.

Catron, C. and Allen, J. 1993, *Early Childhood Curriculum*, New York, Macmillan Publishing Company.

Clements, D. and Nastasi, B. 1993, 'Electronic media and early childhood education', in B. Spodek, ed., *Handbook of Research on Early Childhood Education* (pp. 251–75), New York, Macmillan Publishing Company.

Corson, D. 1993, *Language, Minority Education and Gender: Linking Social Justice and Power*, London, Multilingual Matters.

Crowley, K. and Steigler, R. S. 1999, 'Explanation and generalisation in young children's learning strategy', *Child Development*, 70(2), pp. 304–16.

Department of Employment, Education and Training 1994, *Like Any Child: Planning for Children with Disabilities*, Melbourne, DEET and the Brotherhood of St Lawrence.

Hintz, B. F. and Stomfay-Stitz, A. 1999, Peace education and conflict resolution through expressive arts in early childhood education and teacher education. Paper presented at the *Annual Conference of the Eastern Educational Research Association*, Hilton Head, SC, February 26, ED433105.

Howes, C. 1988, 'Peer interaction of young children', *Monographs of the Society for Research in Child Development*, 53(1), Serial No. 217.

Klein, E. R., Hammrich, P., Bloom, S. and Ragins, A. 2000, Language development and science inquiry: a child-initiated and teacher-facilitated program, Paper presented at the *Annual Meeting of the American Education Research Association*, New Orleans, April, ED 440756.

Ladd, G. and Coleman, C. 1993, 'Young children's peer relationships: forms, features and functions', in B. Spodek, ed., *Handbook of Research on the Education of Young Children* (pp. 57–76), New York, Macmillan Publishing Company.

MacNaughton, G. 1997, 'Who's got the power? Rethinking gender equity strategies in early childhood', *International Journal of Early Years Education*, 5(1), pp. 57–66.

—— 2000, *Rethinking Gender in Early Childhood*, Sydney, Allen & Unwin; New York, Sage Publications; London, Paul Chapman Publishing.

Olsson, B. 1988, 'Experiences for toddlers: some practical suggestions', in A. Stonehouse, ed., *Trusting Toddlers: Programming for One to Three Year Olds in Child Care Centres* (pp. 132–9), Watson, ACT, Australian Early Childhood Association.

Pelligrini, A. and Boyd, B. 1993, 'The role of play in early childhood development and education: issues in definition and function', in B. Spodek, ed., *Handbook of Research on the Education of Young Children* (pp. 105–21), New York, Macmillan Publishing Company.

Sands, D. and Doll, B. 1996, 'Fostering self-determination is a developmental task', *The Journal of Special Education*, 30(1), pp. 58–76.

Skinner, P. 1996, 'Play and the mathematics profile', in M. Fleer, ed., *Play through the Profiles: Profiles through Play* (pp. 57–66), Canberra, Australian Early Childhood Association.

Spodek, B. and Saracho, O. 1994, *Right from the Start: Teaching Children Ages Three to Eight*, Boston, Allyn and Bacon.

Wieder, S. and Greenspan, S. 1993, 'The emotional basis of learning', in B. Spodek, ed., *Handbook of Research on the Education of Young Children* (pp. 77–87), New York, Macmillan Publishing Company.

Wilkes, G. (ed.) 1979, *Collins Dictionary of the English Language*, Middlesex, Penguin Books.

Chapter 8

Feedback

Feedback: to offer or suggest (information, ideas etc.) in reaction to an inquiry, experiment etc.

(Collins Dictionary of the English Language, p. 533)

. . . a teacher's positive feedback to children is the basis for the effectiveness of all the other teaching strategies.

(Allen and Hart 1984, p. 261)

Children learn a broad range of information, ideas, values, attitudes and skills from others . . . It occurs daily through interaction, observation, practice, and feedback from others.

(Robison and Schwartz 1982, p. 107)

WHAT?

Feedback is the provision of information before, during and after an experience. This feedback may be verbal, such as a comment on how a child has approached a task; or it may be non-verbal, such as a smile to show a child that you have appreciated their efforts during a task. Staff assist in children's learning by using verbal and non-verbal feedback as a teaching technique to give them information about what they have done. Feedback can provide children with information through which to clarify what they are doing, to decide if what they are doing is right and to evaluate their own actions (Seefeldt 1980). Feedback supports children's learning most effectively when it provides them with clear and specific information that helps them think about what to do next.

On most occasions, children will gain more useful information from verbal feedback than from non-verbal feedback because verbal feedback can be clearer and more precise. For example, a child can find it harder to identify the precise action or event to which non-verbal feedback refers.

Consider the following example of a child who has successfully put the final pieces in a puzzle after several attempts. She was finally successful because she decided to match the colours on one side of the puzzle piece with the colours in the puzzle. Staff could give feedback on her success through a smile or through comments such as 'You must be pleased to have found how the piece fits after so many tries. It seemed to work when you put the same colours together.' Words are more likely to help the child learn from her experience because a smile cannot tell her why she was successful, and so it does not help her to build strategies that can help her when she next tries to do a puzzle. For this reason we will concentrate mainly on verbal feedback.

How?

Feedback should be appropriate to each child's learning style and developmental abilities. Some children are more likely to be supported in their learning through verbal feedback while other children may gain more support through non-verbal feedback. Staff need to be familiar with the learning styles and developmental abilities of each child in their group if they are to judge which form of feedback might be more appropriate.

As a general rule, Seefeldt (1980) believed that verbal feedback is most successful when it:

 describes what the child is doing rather than placing a value judgement on it

 describes specific events, interactions and behaviours

> Oskar (a four-year-old) is using indoor blocks to construct a large building. Kylie, his teacher, sits close to him. After a period of observation she remarks, 'I like the way you have used the long blocks at the bottom. This has made your building stronger. You have been working here for a long time this morning and I can see that you have been concentrating hard.'

 is given soon after the actions to which it refers. The importance of this is emphasised in the following discussion among teachers about ways of giving feedback to children:

> Christie: 'I always give positive feedback when the children are concentrating well. I hope that this encourages them to stay at one activity for more than a minute and a half!'
>
> Carol: 'That's right. I always give feedback when I think the children are making an effort to do something they haven't tried before.'
>
> Anne: 'I guess that I always give feedback when the children are showing any kind of prosocial behaviour like helping another child, or sharing or taking turns. But when I look at it, I'm not really describing what it is they've done right, I'm just praising them for doing it.'
>
> Christie: 'I see what you mean, yes. I'm going to put more description into my feedback from now on. Instead of saying, "I like the way you finished the puzzle, Jack", I will say something like, "I like the way you looked carefully at each piece before you put it into the puzzle". I can see that this will be more useful to him because he will know what he did right.'

More detailed information on feedback and its special role in reinforcement and scaffolding can be found in Chapters 26 and 27.

When and why?

Goal relevance

Staff generally use verbal feedback to encourage children in what they are doing (Allen and Hart 1984; Slee 1998). Feedback actively responds to children's actions in order to positively reinforce them. It may also be used as a negative reinforcer (Slee 1998). Specifically, feedback as a positive reinforcer:

- ➲ enables children to learn the likelihood that what they're doing will be successful (Wieder and Greenspan 1993). For example, the comment, 'Tina, I think the cart will make it up the hill this time if you keep pushing it with both hands' tells Tina that her current approach to pushing the cart should achieve her goal. The feedback will, hopefully, encourage Tina to keep trying

- ➲ allows children to learn about their level of progress in developing their skill or interactions with people or materials (Wieder and Greenspan 1993). For example, the comment, 'Sipho, sharing that towel with Tim was really helpful. It meant he could dry his doll as well' tells Sipho that his actions were appreciated and welcomed. The feedback will, hopefully, encourage Sipho to share again

- ➲ allows children to learn that staff take an interest in their achievements. For example, the comment, 'Sandy, I was interested to see how you used the really long nails to join those two pieces of wood together for your boat' tells Sandy that her hard work was appreciated by the adult. The feedback will, hopefully, encourage Sandy to try different ways to join wood

- ➲ supports the development of self-concept in preschool children (Penn 2000)

- ➲ encourages children's scientific theory making when teachers use feedback to validate children's theories and elaborate on the effects of children's experimentation (McWilliams 1999)

- ➲ Supports the development of the internal motivation to succeed in young children's exploration of the world about them (Klein et al. 2000).

Children's early writing skills are supported by staff feedback on how their writing is progressing. Such feedback encourages children's writing because it indicates to them that staff have an interest in their efforts at writing and helps them decide how to progress with their writing (Atkins 1994). Staff can also use verbal feedback to check their own understandings of what is happening to a child. For example, staff could ask, 'Ashley, I thought you looked very sad after Bill left today. Was that how you felt?'. The feedback will, hopefully, provide the staff member with accurate information about Ashley's feelings.

Staff could use verbal feedback as a teaching technique when they think that children will benefit from their support and reassurance as they tackle a particular task or as they become involved in a particular experience.

> Lettie is new to the children's centre. She appears shy and withdrawn and is hesitant to try the activities that the staff have put out for the children. Griselda has been allocated to help Lettie to feel more comfortable as she settles in. She deliberately uses verbal feedback to help Lettie to become more involved. For example, she says, 'Lettie, you've tried painting and playing with the puzzles this morning, I'm happy to see you experimenting with new things. Well done!'.

Staff can also use feedback to help children understand how their learning is progressing and to provide them with explicit information on how they are learning. This form of feedback has been shown to expand the range of ways in which children learn and to support the development of young children's independence in learning (Hendy and Whitebread 2000).

Di gives Sam verbal feedback about his writing.

Developmental considerations

Infants and toddlers develop the foundations of self-esteem by having a sense of personal control and personal competence (Marshall 1989). Children feel good about themselves when they know that they can make things happen, and staff can help infants and toddlers to feel good about themselves by giving non-verbal feedback—for example, by using mirrors. Marshall (1989, p. 47) suggested that:

> When infants can see both themselves and their image moving at the same time, they can learn about the effects of their own actions and their ability to control their world.

Toddlers are able to read both positive and negative non-verbal feedback. They can tell if a gesture or look is one of approval or disapproval (Wieder and Greenspan 1993). Staff can draw on this ability to provide toddlers with positive feedback about their accomplishments. For example, at meal time a staff member might say, 'I like the way you're eating with the spoon today'.

Preschool children are just developing the ability to predict whether or not they might succeed at a task, so their predictions are somewhat erratic (Sands and Doll 1996). Staff can support the development of more accurate predictions through giving children feedback on their efforts. For example, when a staff member observes a block building getting higher and higher, they could say, 'This building has been built with strong foundations, so I'm sure it will stand up'.

Feedback is also helpful for older children who are trying to refine their writing skills. Teachers can provide feedback on where commas might go, how exclamation marks might help the children give emphasis to their statement and how well children's writing is conveying what they intend it to say (Amos Hatch 1991).

EQUITY CONSIDERATIONS

'Race' and culture

Toddlers can notice differences between people such as hair colour and texture, skin colour and facial characteristics. They notice that some people have darker skin than others, some people have curlier hair than others, some have flat noses and some people have long noses. When toddlers notice these physical differences, staff can help them to understand and enjoy diversity by giving clear, accurate, descriptive feedback about what they have seen. If staff describe to toddlers the differences they are seeing in simple words, they can reduce the possibility that they will develop fear or discomfort about people who are different to themselves.

For example, when a toddler from an Anglo-Australian background stares at a black child from northern Africa, staff can give verbal feedback such as: 'Sally, you have just seen Sasha. She has very dark skin. Sometimes people are born with light skin like yours, sometimes they are born with dark skin like Sasha's.' Associating such observations with simple stories and games to familiarise children with differences between people and discussions consolidates their understandings of physical diversity. Giving feedback to children during these experiences is an important part of such consolidation.

York (1991) listed a wide range of activities that help children learn about racial differences and similarities, including:

- ➜ collecting nylon stockings in lots of different shades and encouraging children to try them on hands and feet till they find a shade that matches their skin tones. Staff's descriptive feedback can give children words to help them name and talk about skin tone. For example, 'Timmy, you're wearing a coffee-coloured stocking, but your skin looks much more like a caramel colour to me. What do you think? Can you find a stocking that is more like caramel?'
- ➜ mixing batches of play dough in different colours and encouraging children to mix the colours until they create colours that match their skin tones. Staff's descriptive feedback can give children words to help them name and talk about skin tone. For example, 'Jessie, your dough looks dark and shiny just like the colour of molasses. Do you think your skin is as dark and shiny as molasses?'
- ➜ collecting pictures of people from a variety of racial groups and encouraging children to find people like themselves in the pictures. Once again, staff's descriptive feedback can give children words to help them name and talk about skin tone. For example, 'This person in the picture has skin like golden wheat. Does anyone here have skin like golden wheat?'.

These activities can be an especially good way to begin to talk about the similarities and differences between children in mixed-race groups. However, in mono-racial groups, children will also be likely to discover differences in their skin tones and can learn words that help them to name their own specific skin tone.

'What colour is your hand?'

Gender

Adults' ideas about how boys and girls should behave influence in several ways the feedback they give to children. Adults who have traditional views about gender roles tend to give feedback to girls about their appearance and feedback to boys about their physical achievements (Leipzig 1992). Adults with traditional views about gender roles are also likely to give feedback to girls in a different tone than they use to give feedback to boys. They tend to give feedback to girls in gentle and quiet tones and to boys in strong and confident tones. Staff who want to expand girls' and boys' understanding of what it is possible to do as a boy and as a girl should be alert to these tendencies. They should look for opportunities to give feedback to girls on their accomplishments rather than their appearance and to give feedback to boys which concerns their moments of caring for others as well as their physical achievements.

However, staff should be very careful about when and how they give feedback to girls on their achievements. There is some evidence that girls learn that they need to do very little in non-traditionally female play areas such as Lego and blocks to receive positive feedback. Staff eager to support girls' exploration of construction materials can inadvertently encourage underachievement by giving girls positive feedback for merely putting a couple of pieces of Lego together (Browne and Ross 1991). If girls are to increase their confidence in the science and technology areas of the curriculum, they need to receive positive feedback on their hard work and problem-solving attempts. There is strong research evidence to suggest that girls tend to have less confidence than boys in their mathematical abilities and so feedback that supports the building of confidence in girls is important to their success in mathematics (Sleeter and Grant 1999).

Disability and additional needs

Toddlers notice differences between people with visible disabilities and those without them. They notice that some people use wheelchairs, some people have one arm shorter than the other, some people wear very thick glasses and some people have had their windpipe removed (tracheotomy). When toddlers notice these differences, staff can help them to '. . . develop a comfortable awareness of others' (Dermon-Sparks et al. 1989, p. 22) by providing them with immediate and '. . . simple feedback that supports their observations and helps sort out what is happening' (Dermon-Sparks et al. 1989, p. 23). If staff can use simple words to describe to the toddler what they have seen, they can reduce the possibility that toddlers will develop fear or discomfort about people with disabilities.

For example, when a toddler stares at someone who has no fingers on one hand, staff can give verbal feedback such as, 'Suzy, you have just seen a person who has no fingers on one of her hands. Sometimes people are born with no fingers on their hands, sometimes they have no fingers because they have had an accident.'

However, providing descriptive verbal feedback to toddlers when they notice people with visible disabilities should be just the beginning of helping them to feel comfortable with diversity. Simple stories and discussions can consolidate children's early understandings of ability and diversity.

REFLECTING ON FEEDBACK TECHNIQUES

1   Define feedback.
2   What are the keys to using feedback to optimise children's learning?
3   When do you think feedback should be used in your teaching?
4   Are there any times when you think the use of feedback is inappropriate with young children?
5   How could feedback be used to promote communicative competence with infants? What sort of feedback could you use to achieve this aim?
6   What things do you think toddlers would enjoy having feedback about?
7   What are most meaningful forms of verbal feedback that you have heard other adults provide to four-year-old children?
8   Develop a plan for a learning experience for four- to five-year-old children in which your goal is to increase children's problem-solving skills. How could you use feedback as a teaching technique to do this?
9   What words could you use to give a toddler feedback when she first observes a person in a wheelchair?
10 Observe staff working with babies. To what extent do they use verbal and non-verbal feedback to encourage babies' two-way communication competence?

IMPROVING TEACHING IN PRACTICE

1   Record (using a tape-recorder or written notes) the verbal feedback you give children during several half-hour teaching periods.
2   What is your current style of giving feedback? Do you:
    ➋   describe what the child is doing rather than place a value judgement on it?
    ➋   describe specific events, interactions and behaviours?
    ➋   provide feedback close to the time the child is doing the act?

3   How and how well did you take account of developmental and equity considerations?
4   What are your areas of strength and weakness in using verbal feedback to promote children's learning?
5   How can you work to improve your feedback techniques in practice?

Further reading

Cole, P. and Chan, L. 1990, *Methods and Strategies for Special Education*, New Jersey, Prentice Hall Inc. [refer to pp. 96–7].

References

Allen, K. and Hart, B. 1984, *The Early Years: Arrangements for Learning*, New Jersey, Prentice Hall Inc.

Amos Hatch, J. 1991, 'Developing writers in the intermediate grades', *Childhood Education*, 68(2), pp. 76–80.

Atkins, C. 1994, 'Doing something constructive', *Young Children*, November, pp. 3–6.

Browne, N. and Ross, C. 1991, '"Girls' stuff, boys' stuff": young children talking and playing', in N. Browne, ed., *Science and Technology in the Early Years* (pp. 37–51), Milton Keynes, Open University Press.

Dermon-Sparks, L. and the Anti-Bias Task Force. 1989, *The Anti-Bias Curriculum*, Washington DC, National Association for the Education of Young Children.

Hendy, L. and Whitebread, D. 2000, 'Interpretations of independent learning in the early years', *International Journal of Early Years Education*, 8(3), pp. 245–54.

Klein, E. R., Hammrich, P., Bloom, S. and Ragins, A. 2000, Language development and science inquiry: a child-initiated and teacher-facilitated program, Paper presented at the *Annual Meeting of the American Education Research Association*, New Orleans, April, ED 440756.

Leipzig, J. 1992, 'Helping whole children grow: non-sexist childrearing for infants and toddlers', in B. Neugebauer, ed., *Alike and Different: Exploring our Humanity with Young Children* (pp. 32–41), Washington, National Association for the Education of Young Children.

Marshall, H. 1989, 'The development of self-concept', *Young Children*, 44(5), pp. 44–51.

McWilliams, M. 1999, Fostering wonder in young children, Paper presented at the *Annual Meeting of the National Association for Research in Science Teaching*, Boston, MA, March 28–31, ED444833.

Penn, C. 2000, An evaluation of the impact of attributional feedback on the self-concept of children aged four to six years of age, EDD, Queensland University of Technology.

Robison, H. and Schwartz, S. 1982, *Designing Curriculum for Early Childhood*, Boston, Allyn and Bacon Inc.

Sands, D. and Doll, B. 1996, 'Fostering self-determination is a developmental task', *The Journal of Special Education*, 30(1), pp. 58–76.

Seefeldt, C. 1980, *Teaching Young Children*, New Jersey, Prentice Hall Inc.

Slee, J. 1998, 'Understanding and responding to children's anti-social behaviour', *Every Child*, 4(2), pp. 8–9.

Sleeter, C. and Grant, C. 1999, *Making Choices for Multicultural Education: Five Approaches to Race, Class and Gender*, third edn, New Jersey, Merrill Prentice Hall.

Wieder, S. and Greenspan, S. 1993, 'The emotional basis of learning', in B. Spodek, ed., *Handbook of Research on the Education of Young Children* (pp. 77–87), New York, Macmillan Publishing Company.

Wilkes, G. (ed.) 1979, *Collins Dictionary of the English Language*, Middlesex, Penguin Books.

York, S. 1991, *Roots and Wings: Affirming Culture in Early Childhood Programs*, Minnesota, Toys'n Things Press.

Chapter 9

Grouping

Grouping: a number of persons or things located close together, or considered or classed together.

(*The Concise Oxford Dictionary of Current English*, p. 522)

A social group is simply a number of people who interact with each other on a regular basis.

(Giddens 1989, p. 275)

The study of groups and of individuals in groups, as well as the study of individuals by themselves, is necessary for a full understanding of the arts of learning and teaching.

(Hughes and Hughes 1959, p. 2)

Erickson and Shultz (1992) report research from the anthropology and history of education. In traditional societies, they note, individual rather than group instruction is often the norm.

(cited in Pinar et al. 1995, p. 783)

WHAT?

Grouping, as a teaching technique, involves taking decisions about how and when to bring children together to assist their learning. The aim is to organise the children in ways that best facilitate learning. Studies have shown that group size does affect children's learning. Smaller group sizes are associated with:

- ➲ 'more opportunities for teachers to work on extending language, mediating children's social interactions, and encouraging and supporting problem-solving (Bowman et al. 2001, p. 145)
- ➲ cognitive gains on IQ tests when there is also a high staff–child ratio (Bowman et al. 2001).

Groups may be informal or formal. They may be curriculum-based, age-based or project-based. They may be temporary or fixed for a period of time. As most early childhood staff work with more than one child they have to actively decide how to group children, when to do so and why. If staff know what can be accomplished through different types of grouping, they can be proactive in matching their approach to grouping children with their teaching and learning intent.

HOW?

There are several different ways of grouping children to support the development of productive and pleasing learning relationships, and in doing so maximise children's well-being and their learning. Informal groups are those that arise spontaneously. Formal groups are those that are deliberately constructed by staff to meet specific teaching and learning goals. Some ways of grouping children for learning include age grouping, multi-age grouping, ability grouping, mixed-ability grouping, small task-based groups, whole groups and project groups.

Informal grouping

Informal groups may form and reform during a specific learning experience or project, and membership of the group will be flexible and determined by the children rather than by the staff. Allowing time for children to create and maintain informal groups is important for their learning on several counts. Membership of informal groups can:

- ➲ support literacy learning when children are involved in dramatic play that is rich with literacy resources (Arthur and Makin 2001)
- ➲ help develop well-being and social competence in young children when they enable children to share, work together and experience friendship and kindness within the group (Corrie and Leitao 1999)
- ➲ help children to build close relationships and a sense of community if they enable children to share stories with each other (Phillips 2000).

Multi-age grouping

Multi-age groups are formed when children of different ages are brought together in the same room or classroom. The children will be at least one year apart in age. They are also referred to as mixed-age groupings and in school settings may be called ungraded or non-graded classrooms (Goldstein 1997) or family groupings.

> Multi-age groupings give children the opportunity to be both a younger and an older in the same classroom; they provide opportunities for cross-age tutoring; and they are developmentally appropriate, fostering flexibility and responsiveness to the individual needs of the particular students. (Goldstein 1997, p. 40)

Research exploring peer interactions in preschool children's fantasy play has shown that multi-age grouping can benefit preschool children because 'more capable peers do scaffold activity in play in such a way that learning and development take place' (Fimreite et al. 1999, p. 9). Studies have also consistently found that multi-age groupings can improve children's social skills, reduce discipline problems, increase co-operative problem-solving between children and improve literacy outcomes (Ong et al. 2000).

The benefits to young children's well-being and learning in multi-age groups rests on staff using specific learning strategies with children. Ong et al. (2000) detailed the following strategies as important to effective multi-age grouping:

- peer tutoring
- cognitive scaffolding
- co-operative learning
- heterogeneous grouping
- emphasis on socio-emotional goals.

Mixed-ability or mixed culture and gender grouping and inclusive classrooms

Mixed grouping (or heterogeneous grouping):

- supports the development of multicultural learning (Grenot-Scheyer et al. 1998)
- supports literacy learning. For instance, 'using mixed groups of children that include children without language delay may provide additional modelling opportunities for children with language delay' (Lonigan et al. 1999, p. 318). Specifically, in shared reading sessions with children of mixed reading abilities there were positive gains in children's oral language skills, print knowledge and phonological sensitivity for children considered at risk (Lonigan et al. 1999)
- supports the development of positive interactions between peers with and without disabilities if staff actively model pro-social behaviours for children (Hewitt 1999).

One model of group investigation that has been widely adapted for use in heterogenous classrooms was described Joyce and Weil in 1972. It still has considerable currency (see Sleeter and Grant 1999) and it is used to support learning within heterogeneous groups. Children are required to complete a task or produce a product together drawing on the different skills within the group.

- Phase 1—encounter puzzling situation (planned or unplanned).
- Phase 2—explore reactions to the situation.
- Phase 3—formulate study task and organise for study (problem definition, role, assignments, etc.).
- Phase 4—independent and group study.
- Phase 5—analyse progress and process.
- Phase 6—recycle activity. (Joyce and Weil 1972, pp. 237–8).

Sleeter and Grant (1999) described two other models for group investigation in heterogeneous groupings:

- A jigsaw model in which two groups are required to complete a task. They are each given different aspects of the task to complete via questions or topics that enable them to become experts in complementary but separate aspects of the task. The two groups then come back together, each as experts on different aspects of the task. They then share their learning. Commenting on this model Sleeter and Grant (1999, p. 97) wrote:

  Many teachers like this particular model of cooperative learning because when students get to their second group, everyone has an important piece to contribute that the rest of the group members need. Even the lowest academic achievers have some expertise to share.

Team games in which children in different groups compete. It requires that each member of the group support each other to learn as much as possible before each of the teams meet and compete against each other.

Strategies that help support learning in mixed-ability groups include:

 encouraging children to give and receive explanations to each other about what is working or not, how to approach a task or what to do next (Lou et al. 2001)

 encouraging a co-operative learning atmosphere to help children focus on learning and how to complete tasks rather than on comparing themselves favourably and unfavourably with other children (Klein et al. 2000).

Issue response groups

A specific issue or experience within a group of children may best be explored within a small group. Some examples of where staff may choose to bring children together in small groups to discuss specific experiences or issues include:

 helping children to cope with a traumatic event such as the experience of war, forced migration, violence and/or abuse. When children have the opportunity to share their ideas and feelings with each other it can reduce the fears and anxieties that are often associated with experiences of trauma (Alat 2002)

 working on building peaceful ways to resolve conflicts. Small group drama and socio-dramatic play can help children learn how to work with others in small teams and to co-operate in the execution of a task. Hintz and Stomfay-Stitz (1999) described how dramatic play and creative drama can be used to complement other aspects of peace education.

A specific form of an issue response group is the classroom meeting or, as some call it, 'circle time' or group time. The classroom meeting is a time when the whole of the class comes together to discuss events of the day, issues and challenges, and to share concerns and problem-solve. This is a regular event at the Crossley Heath primary school in the reception class:

> Some of the children in the class have complained to the teacher (Malcolm) that they are not getting a fair go at the computer learning centre in the classroom. The teacher decides to open their daily classroom meeting with a question that will enable children to share their concerns with the whole class and asks the whole group the question, 'How is work going at the computer learning centre?'. There is silence. He asks the question in a different way, 'I wondered if everyone was happy with how work is going at the computer learning centre?'. One of the children who complained to him about it earlier wriggles and then quietly says, 'I like the computers but it's hard to get to play there'. At this point, other children contribute their views and Malcolm continues asking children how they feel and what they think they might do. The discussion brings the group to a consensus about the way forward.

According to Glasser (1969) (cited in Joyce and Weil 1972) the classroom meeting aims to provide a place where mutuality grows through group problem-solving. Joyce and Weil (1972, p. 209) described the phases in a classroom meeting with these aims:

The Classroom Meeting Model for social problem-solving includes six phases: (1) establishing a climate of involvement; (2) exposing the problem for discussion; (3) making a personal value judgement; (4) identifying alternative courses of action; (5) making a commitment; and (6) behavioural follow-up. These phases may take place during one or more meetings or they may be quickly accomplished in a single meeting, even for several problems.

Staff can adapt these phases of involvement to construct their approach to group meetings and as a point of reflection on how effectively they led the group meeting. For instance, each of the six phases can be used to produce the following questions for staff to use in developing group discussions:

➲ How will I or how did I establish a climate of involvement for each of the children?
➲ How will I or how did I expose the problem for discussion? What are the comments I will or did make? What are the questions I led or will lead with? Will I or did I use a story, image or piece of writing to begin the discussion?
➲ What is it I value here? How will I or how did I explain that to the children?
➲ How will I or how did I identify alternative courses of action? What do I see these as being? Will I or did I generate these with the children?
➲ How will I or how did I make a commitment to act as a result of the discussion? Is a commitment to act necessary?
➲ How will I or how did I follow up with the children on what we agreed as an action?

Same-age groupings

The assumption in the organisation of children into groups of the same age (such as baby, toddler and preschool groups) is that children of the same age have similar developmental needs, interests and learning capacities. This assumption is not, however, borne out by research (Ong et al. 2000).

At the Strahan Park Community Child Care Centre the co-ordinator Pieta is wanting to change from same-age groupings to mixed-age groupings in the centre. Some staff are not feeling comfortable with the move:

> Shira: I think the babies will have a really hard time having their needs met in a mixed-age group. I don't know how we will keep track of their individual needs.
>
> Benny: I agree. How are we going to set up our rooms in ways that are developmentally relevant for babies, toddlers and the preschoolers? They each have such different interests.
>
> Paula: I have similar concerns but I think we will just have to be creative. The preschool children in my group have different interests now and different capacities developmentally. I have to plan for diverse children now anyway. I am not sure this will be so different.
>
> Pieta: I think it could give us more flexibility in how we use each room in the centre. We could have a room just for art and one just for natural materials if we don't have to cater for all the children in one room. Children could move from space to space irrespective of their age.
>
> Shira: I like that idea, but how will we keep track of individual children?
>
> Paula: That's going to be really important. We could invite staff from one of the other centres locally who have moved to mixed-age groups to talk with us about what they have done.

In all small group work where children are being asked to work together it is important that they have a clear sense of their roles and responsibilities. Staff can support successful group work if they explain what the group is going to do, who is going to do what (roles), set limits and take responsibility for debriefing the group (Hintz and Stomfay-Stitz 1999).

WHEN AND WHY?

Staff members' approaches to curriculum and their specific teaching and learning goals for the children will influence their grouping decisions. For instance, multi-ability grouping can be of most benefit to children's learning when the task is complex and children can bring their joint skills, knowledge and resources to bear on the task (Lou et al. 2001).

Goal relevance

In general, staff can use grouping to support children's learning in several ways.

- ➲ Studies show that children's learning using computers is positively enhanced when they are learning in small groups compared to learning as individuals (Lou et al. 2001).
- ➲ Early childhood programs can serve as a bridge for children between home and school by providing exposure to the varied interaction styles (large group, small group, one-on-one learning) that the children will encounter in school (Bowman et al. 2001, p. 179).
- ➲ The self-esteem and independence of children with disabilities in inclusive classrooms can be enhanced if there is an emphasis on the goals of interdependence and collaboration through small group work (Okagaki and Diamond 2000).
- ➲ Sharing memories and stories in small groups can help children construct a positive sense of themselves and enable children to integrate the different parts of their lives (Grey 2002).
- ➲ Children's cognitive development can be enhanced when they work in small groups where there is group discussion and collaboration. Although it should be noted that one study (Murphy and Messer 2000) found that children between five and seven years of age when working alone on a task were more able to transfer the learning from that task to a similar task.
- ➲ Co-operative learning can reduce stereotyping and social rejection for children with disabilities, children from different racial backgrounds and between genders (Sleeter and Grant 1999).

Developmental considerations

Children can benefit developmentally from mixed-age and same-age grouping (Avgitidou 2001) at all ages. Babies can learn from watching each other when they are in small groups and when they have sensitive, responsive and reciprocal relationships with the key carers in their lives. It is important for staff to remember that one-to-one interaction benefits babies by helping them build secure and caring relationships with key people in their lives. When babies are in groups it is important these key adults are with them, can support their interactions and respond to any signs of distress or discomfort a baby experiences in a group setting.

Toddlers learn from each other even when they cannot talk to each other. They learn through watching each other, listening to each other's sounds and focusing on each other's body language. They also teach each other using the same strategies (Pratt 1999). Therefore it is important that toddlers have the opportunity to be in small groups with each other for some part of their day and to have the chance to meet with the minds of others (Rayna 2001, p. 114). If the group size is small it is possible for staff to readily support toddlers as they attempt to interact with each other and in the moments when conflicts arise. Small groups also help toddlers to form friendships and gain from the well-being and confidence that being friends with someone brings (Bleiker 1999).

Preschoolers take a lively interest in their peers and having opportunities to interact with them is crucial to their learning. The chance to build informal groups and friendships is critical to their learning. Children can experience learning difficulties in schooling and their academic achievement can be disrupted if they lack friends and positive social interactions with their peers (Coplan et al. 2001). Dramatic play offers staff a powerful vehicle to create opportunities for preschool children to interact socially with their peers. It should be noted that a study in the United Kingdom found that dramatic play involved more complex and richer peer relations when it occurred in the outside play area where less structured play materials were available and less adult intervention occurred (Shim et al. 2001).

In the early years of schooling children begin to gain a stronger sense of what is needed to create and maintain a social group. They can see and make sense of more subtle and complex cues from their peers and begin to problem-solve in groups more effectively (Broadhead 2001). However, they will benefit by staff supporting them to learn different ways to enter group play, select and act in different roles in the group and in building a shared sense of direction for the group with others.

EQUITY CONSIDERATIONS

Working in heterogeneous groups is often seen as a key strategy for reducing bias and prejudice between specific groups of children. However, it is important to note the caution on grouping for equity offered by Sleeter and Grant (1999, p. 96):

> Depending on how a teacher structures group work, it can be either very successful or disastrous. Some teachers mistakenly believe that contact by itself among members of different groups is beneficial. Actually, contact by itself can encourage stereotyping, prejudice, and social rejection.

To avoid group work reinforcing bias and rejection it is critical that staff have clear protocols in place for building a co-operative approach to being in groups. These include developing listening skills, conflict management and sharing ideas (refer to the ideas above for working effectively to promote co-operative learning).

'Race' and culture

Cultural assumptions can be made by staff about how best to group children to support their learning. Furthermore, a child's cultural background can affect the extent to which they will be encouraged to learn in groups or to learn independently of others. Some cultural groups value independence and self-reliance, while others value collective and collaborative learning. A study of young children in child care settings explored the effects of cultural expectations on children's conflict resolution skills and group behaviour. It compared how children from Holland and Andalusia negotiated conflict and found cultural differences in the extent to which children were prepared to disrupt the group to maintain their own point of view (Sanchez Medina et al. 2001). The researchers concluded that cultural values determined the extent to which children focused on maintaining group harmony in their interactions with other children. Taking note of this research, staff need to be alert to the different ways in which the children they are working with may understand their role in groups and the goals they may prioritise in their group interactions.

Research suggests that not all children learn equally well in groups and that specific forms of grouping benefit some groups of children more than others. For instance, multi-age grouping was found to benefit the mathematics and literacy learning of non-Hispanic school age children more than Hispanic children (Ong et al. 2000). As with all teaching techniques, it is important that staff reflect on the effects of their grouping decisions.

Questions which can assist in that reflection could include:

➲ Which children are actively engaged in this group?
➲ Are there different levels of engagement for children from different ethnic and 'racial' backgrounds?
➲ Which children have their ideas listened to by other children?
➲ Which children take a leadership role? Is this role always taken by the same children?

Gender

There is considerable discussion about the extent to which different forms of grouping children benefit one gender over the other. For instance, differences in the mathematics and literacy achievement of girls and boys remained constant in both multi-age and single-age groups in a study of primary school children's achievement (Ong et al. 2000). However, other studies point to the reduction of gender bias when children are involved in co-operative learning (Sleeter and Grant 1999).

Some research evidence indicates that adults call on boys more than girls to answer questions in small group discussions. It is important for staff to reflect on their interactions with children in small group discussions and small group work and work against any gender biases that they see occurring in their own behaviours (Marshall et al. 1999).

Classroom meetings can be adapted to explore gender dynamics and perspectives within the classroom, as the following extract discussing a study of teaching for gender equity highlights:

> Isabel often was observed using workshare, a classroom ritual where students' work is highlighted and discussed in a public forum, to bring gender issues to the foreground of the curriculum . . . Not only did Isabel encourage students to talk about their individual understandings of gender, but she also worked dialectically with students, drawing from her own and others' experiences, to further challenge gender norms. By manipulating and orchestrating workshare to include competing, and often biased, understandings about gender, Isabel encouraged students to question and confront narrow assumptions of gender. (Ryan et al. 2001, p. 53)

Questions which can assist staff to reflect on the gender dynamics of grouping in their classroom include:

➲ Which children are actively engaged in this group?
➲ Are there different levels of engagement for boys and girls? Is there any pattern to which girls and boys seem differently engaged?
➲ Which children have their ideas listened to by other children?
➲ Which children take a leadership role? Is this role always taken by the same children?
➲ How do I avoid gender biases in whose voice I invite to be heard in group discussions?

Disability and additional needs

In multi-ability grouping staff need to be alert to the power relations in the play between children of different abilities. Differential power relations have been found between children with disabilities and other children in some studies.

> When sighted and children who are visually impaired are playing with each other it can be difficult for the latter children to have their ideas taken up in the play; their ideas tend to be ignored by the sighted children. This can lead to the child who is visually impaired withdrawing and playing alone. However, sighted children do respond positively to requests for help by children who are blind (Janson 2001).

It is also important for staff to take account of the different capacities of young children with disabilities to engage in group activities and co-operative learning. Roe (2001, p. 11) explains in relation to children with Autism Spectrum Disorder:

> In a group situation they are often the 'loners' who stay outside the group or move to a table by themselves. Some children just appear to ignore other children altogether . . . The child with a milder Autism Spectrum Disorder may be able to play co-operatively for short periods, but finds it very difficult when others wish to play something they have not chosen or cannot control.

In these instances it will be important for staff to work with children to help them understand social cues and practise social skills through drama, cartoons and rehearsing behaviours they may need in social situations (Roe 2001).

Questions which can assist staff to reflect on the disability dynamics of grouping in their classroom include:

- ❯ Which children are actively engaged in this group?
- ❯ Are there different levels of engagement for children with and without disabilities?
- ❯ Which children have their ideas listened to by other children?
- ❯ Which children take a leadership role? Is this role always taken by the same children?

REFLECTING ON GROUPING TECHNIQUES

1 Define grouping.
2 Consider the following quote from Goldstein (1997, p. 40):

> Ungraded classrooms . . . deal honestly with the vicissitudes of child development, allowing children to learn and grow at their own pace.

To what extent do you agree with this statement?

3 Do the centres you are familiar with organise time for small group learning? Do you think they should? Why?
4 How might groups be organised to encourage toddlers to practise friendship building?
5 How could you use mixed-age grouping to encourage social interaction and conversation between preschool children and babies? What might the benefits of this be? What might the challenges be?
6 How might your philosophy on adult intervention in children's learning influence how you group children and when you group them for learning?
7 Review the extract by Ryan et al. (2001) earlier in this chapter, in the section on gender. To what extent do you think Isabel's use of workshare would contribute to gender equity in the classroom? How might you group children to support your efforts to work for gender equity with young children?

Improving teaching in practice

1 Note the grouping strategies of an early childhood centre, and if and/or how they change during a day or during a week.

2 Discuss with staff the pros and cons of their approach to grouping for individual children within the service.

3 How does the grouping of children support equity of access and participation?

> How and how well were developmental considerations taken into account in how staff organised their groupings of children for learning?

> To what extent were there opportunities for children to have time by themselves?

> To what extent did you see positive social interaction between the children? How did the nature of the grouping link to this?

Further reading

Barbour, N. and Seefeldt, C. 1993, *Developmental Continuity Across the Preschool and Primary Grades: Implications for Teachers*, Wheaton, MD, Association for Childhood Education International [refer to pp. 33–5].

Lonigan, C., Anthony, J., Bloomfield, B., Dyer, S. and Samwel, C. 1999, 'Effects of two shared reading interventions on emergent literacy skills of at-risk preschoolers', *Journal of Early Intervention*, 22(4), pp. 306–22.

Sleeter, C. and Grant, C. 1999, *Making Choices for Multicultural Education: Five Approaches to Race, Class and Gender*, third edn, New Jersey, Merrill Prentice Hall [refer to pp. 95–107].

References

Alat, K. 2002, 'Traumatic events and children: how early childhood educators can help', *Childhood Education*, 79(1), pp. 2–7.

Allen, R. (ed.), 1990, *The Concise Oxford Dictionary of Current English*, Oxford, Clarendon Press.

Arthur, L. and Makin, L. 2001, 'High quality early literacy programs', *Australian Journal of Early Childhood*, 26(2), pp. 14–19.

Avgitidou, S. 2001, 'Peer cultural and friendship relationships as contexts for the development of young children's pro-social behaviour', *International Journal of Early Years Education*, 9(2), pp. 145–52.

Bleiker, C. 1999, 'Toddler friendship: the case of Hiro and John', *Young Children*, 54(6), pp. 18–23.

Bowman, B., Donovan, M. and Burns, S. 2001, *Eager to Learn: Educating Our Preschoolers*, Washington DC, National Academy Press.

Broadhead, P. 2001, 'Investigating sociability and cooperation in four and five year olds in reception class settings', *International Journal of Early Years Education*, 9(1), pp. 23–36.

Coplan, R., Wichmann, C. and Lagace-Seguin, D. 2001, 'Solitary-active play behaviour: a marker variable for maladjustment in preschool?', *Journal of Research in Childhood Education*, 15(2), pp. 164–72.

Corrie, L. and Leitao, N. 1999, 'The development of well-being: young children's knowledge of their support networks and social competence', *Australian Journal of Early Childhood*, 24(3), pp. 25–31.

Fimreite, H., Flem, A. and Gudmundsdottir, S. 1999, 'Peer interactions among preschool children in play', Paper presented at *The 8th European Conference for Research on Learning and Instruction*, August 24–28, Goteborg, Sweden.

Giddens, A. 1989, *Sociology*, London, Polity Press.

Goldstein, L. 1997, *Teaching With Love: A Feminist Approach to Early Childhood Education*, New York, Peter Lang Publishing.

Grenot-Scheyer, M., Schwartz, I. and Meyer, L. 1998, 'Blending best practices for young children: inclusive early childhood programs', *Every Child*, 4(2), pp. 4–5.

Grey, A. 2002, 'Children's earliest memories: a narrative study', *Australian Journal of Early Childhood*, 27(4), pp. 1–5.

Hewitt, V. M. 1999, 'A case study of an inclusive early childhood setting', *Early Education and Development*, 10(4), pp. 532–49.

Hintz, B. F. and Stomfay-Stitz, A. 1999, Peace education and conflict resolution through expressive arts in early childhood education and teacher education, Paper presented at the *Annual Conference of the Eastern Educational Research Association*, Hilton Head, SC, February 26.

Hughes, A. and Hughes, E. 1959, *Learning and Teaching*, third edn, London, Longmans.

Janson, U. 2001, 'Togetherness and diversity in preschool play', *International Journal of Early Years Education*, 9(2), pp. 135–44.

Joyce, B. and Weil, M. 1972, *Models of Teaching*, third edn, New Jersey, Prentice Hall International.

Klein, E. R., Hammrich, P., Bloom, S. and Ragins, A. 2000, Language development and science inquiry: a child-initiated and teacher-facilitated program, Paper presented at the *Annual Meeting of the American Education Research Association*, New Orleans, April, ED 440756.

Lonigan, C., Anthony, J., Bloomfield, B., Dyer, S. and Samwel, C. 1999, 'Effects of two shared reading interventions on emergent literacy skills of at-risk preschoolers', *Journal of Early Intervention*, 22(4), pp. 306–22.

Lou, Y., Abrami, P., and d'Apollonia, S. 2001, 'Small group and individual learning with technology: a meta-analysis', *Review of Educational Research*, 71(3), pp. 449–521.

Marshall, N., Robeson, W. and Keefe, N. 1999, 'Gender equity in early childhood education', *Young Children*, 54 (4), pp. 9–13.

Murphy, N. and Messer, D. 2000, 'Differential benefits from scaffolding and children working alone', *Educational Psychology*, 20(1), pp. 17–31.

Okagaki, L. and Diamond, K. 2000, 'Responding to cultural and linguistic differences in the beliefs and practices of families with young children', *Young Children*, 55(3), pp. 74–80.

Ong, W., Allison, J. and Haladyna, T. 2000, 'Student achievement of 3rd graders in comparable single-age and multiage classrooms', *Journal of Research in Childhood Education*, 14(2), pp. 205–15.

Phillips, L. 2000, 'Storytelling: the seeds of children's creativity', *Australian Journal of Early Childhood*, 25(3), pp. 1–5.

Pinar, W., Reynolds, W., Slattery, P. and Taubman, P. 1995, *Understanding Curriculum*, New York, Peter Lang Publishing.

Pratt, M. 1999, 'The importance of infant/toddler interactions', *Young Children*, 54(4), pp. 26–7.

Rayna, S. 2001, 'The very beginnings of togetherness in shared play among young children', *International Journal of Early Years Education*, 9(2), pp. 109–16.

Roe, D. 2001, *Autism Spectrum Disorder and Young Children*, Watson, ACT, Australian Early Childhood Association.

Ryan, S., Oschner, M. and Genishi, C. 2001, Miss Nelson is Missing! Teacher sightings in research on teaching, in S. Grieshaber and G. Cannella, eds, *Embracing Identities in Early Childhood Education: Diversity and Possibilities* (pp. 45–59). Teachers College Press New York.

Shim, S., Herwig, J. and Shelley, M. 2001, 'Preschooler's play behaviours with peers in classroom and playground settings', *Journal of Research in Childhood Education*, 15(2), pp. 149–63.

Sleeter, C. and Grant, C. 1999, *Making Choices for Multicultural Education: Five Approaches to Race, Class and Gender*, third edn, New Jersey, Merrill Prentice Hall.

Chapter 10
Listening

Listen: to take heed, to pay attention (to concentrate on hearing something).

(Collins Dictionary of the English Language, p. 858)

When teachers listen to children, they are, first of all, building a climate of acceptance of the children and their ideas.

(Seefeldt 1980, p. 148)

To listen is not just to hear; it is the active construction of meaning from all the signals—verbal and nonverbal—a speaker is sending.

(Hennings 1992, p. 3; cited in Renck Jalongo 1995, p. 13)

WHAT?

When you listen to someone you pay attention to them. You concentrate on what is said, you note what they are saying and think about it carefully. When staff use listening as a teaching strategy, they try to understand what children are saying and, through doing so, try to better understand them. Lerner et al. (1987) identified six interrelated phases to listening: hearing, focusing on what is heard, identifying what is heard, translating this into meaning, interpreting it and then remembering it. When children are listened to by staff and other children, they feel valued and included. This increases their self-esteem and confidence.

HOW?

Staff can improve their listening skills by:

 making time to listen to children. Children in early childhood centres can spend between 25 and 50 per cent of their time listening to staff (Renck Jalongo 1995). When this occurs, children's learning becomes dominated by adult directions, expectations and thoughts. If staff spend more time listening to the children, the children will be more able to direct their own learning and the staff will have more time to learn from the children

 trying to think carefully about what important things the children are saying to staff and to each other

 waiting a few seconds before responding so the children realise that their comments are taken seriously (Seefeldt 1980)

modelling active listening skills to help children learn to listen to others. Many adults are poor listeners who are '. . . preoccupied, distracted and forgetful nearly 75 per cent of the time' (Renck Jalongo 1995). So if staff want children to become thoughtful and active listeners they will need to guard against such tendencies in themselves

 responding to children's comments with care and thought. For further information on this issue, readers should refer to the ways of developing discussions with children in Chapter 5 and to Chapter 8 about giving children feedback

 acting as a scribe for what children say. Ideas for documenting children's work can be found in Chapter 22.

> A class of six-year-olds have been for an excursion to Science Works (a science museum for children in Melbourne). Their teachers have set aside time for the children to recall their experiences. One teacher is sitting at a table with the children as they draw pictures of the various exhibits and chat about what they have seen. He listens carefully to what they are saying and offers to be a scribe for them.

Sometimes staff don't have sufficient time to listen to what a particular child has to say because they are needed elsewhere in the play area or are in the midst of another conversation. On such occasions, staff can still let children know that they value what they have to say by suggesting they tell staff about it in some other way. Renck Jalongo (1995, pp. 14–15) suggested children could be encouraged to write or draw what they want to say:

> We can still let the children know that we are listening by channelling the child's enthusiasm into other means of self-expression, such as drawing or writing.

When and why?

Goal relevance

Staff need to listen to and understand what children are telling them when they are trying to:

 encourage children to share a thought or an experience. It is important for staff to listen so the children learn that what they say is important to others. They need to know that their thoughts and comments on the world matter

> Jack brings his excitement about a car crash that he's seen to the kindergarten. Arthur, his teacher, allows Jack to tell his story and listens attentively. Later on, Arthur makes sure he gives Jack more time to talk about what he saw.

 help children explain their ideas to others. If staff listen to children, they can learn more about what children understand and thus make their teaching more relevant to the children's growing interests and developmental abilities. Paley (1986, p. 94) suggested that listening is often the best way to learn:

> And I, outsider to three-year-old thinking, am learning to listen at the doll corner doorway for the sounds of reality.

- decide if and when to intervene in children's play. Staff will have a better sense of when children's play needs adult guidance, support or control if they listen carefully to children's exchanges with themselves and with others
- learn about and contribute to the children's language development

> Cathy notices that Mitzu, who is twenty months old, has just begun to join more than one word together. She hears 'me up' and 'shoes on'. This tells Cathy that Mitzu has moved to another level in her language development, and is able to ask for what she wants more easily.

- show children that their play and their ideas are valued (Moyles 1989)

> Dina is talking to her first grade class about how they might use their 'free play' time in the afternoon. 'I saw William making tunnels in the digging patch yesterday; he was channelling the water in three different directions. He has thought about how to do this very carefully, I wonder who would like to work some more on William's project?'

- develop an emergent curriculum based on children's interests and curiosities. If staff are listening carefully to children they will have a strong sense of what children's current interests are and thus be in a strong position to respond to and extend their interests (Jones 1999)

Kylie and Isobel listen to Tristan.

➲ allow children to express their questions, fears and worries after they have experienced a traumatic event. As increasing numbers of young children experience or see traumatic events, such as those associated with the attacks of September 11 2001 in New York and Washington DC, it is important that they have the opportunity to have their questions, fears and worries heard and responded to by adults around them. Listening to children's feelings can validate them and help children learn from each other about fears and feelings (Alat 2002).

Developmental considerations

Young children's learning is strongly influenced by their relationships with staff. The key to maximising babies' and toddlers' learning is '. . . the quality of the attachment relationships with their caregivers . . .' (Hutchins 1995, p. 3). High-quality attachment relationships develop when staff are positive, responsive, respectful and attentive in their interactions with babies and toddlers, and an important ingredient in such interactions is listening. When staff take time to listen to a baby's babbles and coos, they show the baby they care about his efforts to communicate (Harrison 1996; Benson McMullen 1999). Babies need to experience such care to thrive.

Staff can learn about a baby's likes and dislikes by listening to her gurgles, chuckles, coos, grunts, giggles, babbles or cries. Each baby will communicate through a range of sounds and a range of tones within those sounds. For example, some babies grunt when they actively enjoy the effort of stretching their limbs, trying to crawl or pushing themselves up, while other babies might gurgle during such movements. Learning each baby's repertoire of sounds and the meanings of those sounds can help staff make judgements about when that baby needs further support and encouragement. It can also help staff to recognise when a baby is tired, hungry, unwell, excited, frustrated, fascinated or rested. Staff can then judge how best to be with a baby. Sometimes cuddles will be appropriate and at other times new challenges will be more appropriate. What is critical for a baby's well-being is that staff respond to his efforts to communicate his needs and interests. Responsive caregiving is at the heart of best practice with babies and toddlers (Benson McMullen 1999; Thompson 2001).

Listening to toddlers as they struggle to verbally express themselves is also a sign that you care about them. If staff take time to find out what is being expressed, children learn that it is worth sharing their ideas and thoughts with staff. If, however, staff pretend to have heard what was said or give up on what was said, children learn that the adults don't care about what they have to say. At twenty months of age, Jo is learning that his thoughts are important to his caregiver:

> Jo is 'talking' animatedly with his caregiver as she hangs out the bibs. He is playing with the pegs and looking up at the clothes line. Jo uses intonation and patterns that are very like 'real' speech. He uses sentence-like structures. After about one minute of this type of verbalising, he looks expectantly up at his caregiver. The caregiver tries to guess what Jo has been talking about. She uses all the clues available to her, drawing on the immediate environment and her knowledge of Jo. 'Yes, Jo', she responds, 'It is windy today and the clothes are blowing about a lot in the wind'.

However, sometimes it can be hard for staff to hear what toddlers might be trying to tell them. When they are in a rush to express their wishes, their words can be garbled or muddled. On such occasions, staff should ask the child to repeat themselves slowly and listen carefully to what the child says. Slowing a toddler down improves staff's chances of understanding what they are being told. Slowing a toddler's speech is likely to improve the clarity of their key word and will change their tone of voice to a lower, less excited pitch. Changes in '. . . the tone of voice, the rate of the utterance, [and] keywords' (Partington and McCudden 1992, p. 139) can all improve staff's ability to understand what is being said.

Confusion over meaning can arise when toddlers begin to use two- and three-word sentences such as, 'Me toilet', 'Go water' or 'Me bike home'. These sentences generally consist of a noun or verb, or a noun and a verb together, and are known as telegraphic sentences because they rely on a few words to express their meaning. Telegraphic sentences are an important phase in children's expressive language development. However, sometimes a toddler's sentences are so 'telegraphic' that their meaning is unclear. For example, 'Me blocks' could mean, 'I would like to play with the blocks' or it could mean, 'Come and see the block building I have just made'. In such instances, staff can help clarify the meaning by asking a toddler to show them what they want or to take them where they want to go. Staff can also turn a sentence into a question and clarify the intended meaning through a toddler's response. For example, if a toddler says, 'Me toilet', staff could ask, 'Would you like to go to the toilet?' or 'Have you just been to the toilet?'. The toddler's response will probably reveal their intended meaning. Once again, staff should take the time to listen to the toddler's response, rather than give up or assume that they know what was intended. Toddlers need to learn that their communication matters.

Preschoolers' language skills rapidly increase and they constantly use language during the day to express their ideas and feelings to themselves and to others. Children between three and four years of age will speak an average of 15 000 words a day as they practise communicating through speech (Hurlock 1978; Thompson 2001). Staff can learn a great deal about preschool children's social, emotional and cognitive developmental interests and needs by listening to what they say. Listening can, therefore, provide staff with valuable information about how to best support the preschool child's learning across various developmental areas. For example, preschoolers will often talk to themselves for long periods of time when they are concentrating on an activity or when they are involved in imaginative play.

> Hannah plays in a corner of the room that is set up like a home environment. She is playing with her favourite doll, bathing her, dressing and feeding her, and putting her to bed. 'I'm gonna take the towel, yeah, the towel, and rub your head, rub, rub, rub, you gotta rub to make clean . . . not too hard 'cos it hurts, like that, yeah . . . like that. Now, finish, get clothes . . . where put them . . . can't find them . . . nothing here. Stop wriggling, doll. Bad to wriggle. Now, where . . . where is nappy? Up botty, now put on nappy. Oops! Powder first . . . that's right, powder. Sit up now, that's right, good girl, that's good, good girl for mummy, mummy loves you . . . good girl.'

A child's monologues can tell staff a good deal about them. For example, staff listening to the above monologue would have learned that Alisha is familiar with a baby's bathing and dressing routine. She remembers the sequence of the routine and goes through it much as she must have seen an adult go through it. She imitates an adult in her play and talks to the doll much as an adult might talk to a child. She uses language to monitor her play.

Vygotsky referred to this language as 'private speech' and believed that it is important to children's ability to develop new cognitive skills and abilities. More detailed information on the role of private speech in children's cognitive development can be found in Chapter 27.

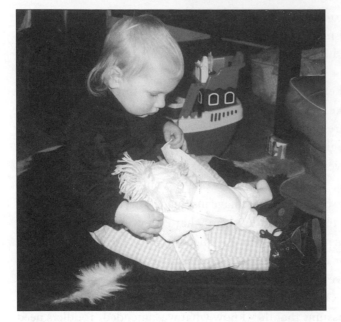

Hannah talks to herself as she undresses a doll.

Listening to children can also provide staff with important information about children's social relationships. Children can use speech to share, negotiate and maintain positive social relationships with each other. They can also use it to demand, command, threaten, exaggerate, boast, tease, tell tales and name-call (Hurlock 1978). By listening to how children use speech, staff can judge how and when to support children in their social relationships and how and when to help children learn positive ways of relating to each other.

Children's ability to tell simple stories is an important pre-reading skill. Storytelling helps children develop an understanding of narrative and helps them build their own language fluency (Phillips 2000). Listening to children's stories encourages them to tell more stories as they learn that staff take their stories seriously. In addition, listening to children's stories can also help teachers assess children's understanding of narrative and their current level of language fluency. Teachers can then target their questions and comments on the story to prompt children to fill the gaps in their narrative and to help children clarify their story so that others can understand it (Soundy and Humadi Genisio 1994). By about the age of five, children can begin to include feelings and reasons for doing things in their stories. Staff can use this development to help build on children's vocabulary for talking about emotions and moral behaviour.

Young children's stories will often be about events in their daily lives. Children will often enthusiastically share their story of what happened the night before when the electricity went off and no-one could remember where the candles were or what dad did when the new dog fouled the carpet. Staff need to listen to these stories with respect and show acceptance of the children's diverse family values and lifestyles. There is much diversity that staff will encounter. Some children will be leading very complex lives living with their dad and his new partner on the weekend and their mum during the week. Other children will have a parent who is not in any permanent relationship but has lots of friends visiting. Still other children will have gay or lesbian parents who may or may not lead a very traditional lifestyle. If children are to share their stories with staff they will need to know that their family lifestyle is accepted and respected. They will learn about staff's attitudes to their family lifestyle by how staff listen to their stories. Staff who raise eyebrows, snicker or ask questions in disbelief when children tell their stories of daily family life will quickly silence such stories. Such silencing means a lost opportunity for assisting children's acquisition of language and pre-reading skills.

Listening to children's comments and questions is an important strategy in building children's interest and sense of wonder in the world about them (McWilliams 1999; Fleer and Cahill 2001). For instance, teachers can support the growth of wonder in children when they listen attentively to children's theories, comments and questions about the world and demonstrate interest and respect for them by commenting and sometimes extending on the child's questions and comments (McWilliams 1999).

EQUITY CONSIDERATIONS

'Race' and culture

As mentioned above, children's expressive language is influenced by their age and stage of development. However, it is also influenced by the context in which they try to express themselves. Children are more likely to want to express themselves in an environment where their ideas are valued and are not subject to bias. They will feel that their ideas are valued when staff take the time to listen to them. Staff need to ensure that they listen for equal time and with equal attention to each child in the group, irrespective of 'race' or cultural background. There is some evidence to suggest that staff distribute their listening time unevenly between children from different cultural and racial backgrounds. Ebbeck (1991) pointed to staff's tendency to spend more time with 'talkative' children than with 'quiet' children. This can result in staff spending less time with children learning ESL than with English-speaking children because many children learning English as a second language (ESL) go through a 'silent period' in which they do not communicate verbally (Clarke 1992). Once children with an ESL background are through their 'silent period', staff should take time to listen to their responses to questions. Partington and McCudden (1992, p. 139) argued that:

> The second language learner needs time to process what is said. It may involve receiving the English, translating it into the first language, arriving at a response and translating it into English and them giving it in a form understood by the teacher.

Staff need to provide time for such processing, translating and replying to occur. When staff wait for a response they are supporting and respecting the child's efforts to learn a second language. As Clarke (1992, p. 19) said: '. . . if staff take the time to listen to children, the children will respond in the same way'. Developing children's listening skills in this way helps the ESL child to develop their second language competence.

The opportunity for children to listen to their own language provides them with a sense that their language is valued. As English is the dominant language spoken in most early childhood centres in Australia, children whose language is other than English may have few opportunities to listen to their first language and, thus, to maintain and enrich their competence in it. Clarke (1992, p. 34) suggested that staff can provide for children's first language to be spoken in the centre in the following ways. By:

- ❯ employing bilingual staff in their centres
- ❯ inviting bilingual high school students to come for work experience
- ❯ encouraging parents to participate in their program
- ❯ organising local community workers to visit.

Children whose first language is not English will clearly benefit from hearing their own language spoken in the early childhood centre, but so will the whole group. Each child can benefit by experiencing the richness and diversity of sounds and meanings from a language other than their own, and staff can take the opportunity to model respect for and enjoyment in diversity of language.

It is also important that staff listen closely to children's comments and conversations with each other so they can be alert to biased or racist comments and respond to them. In particular, it is important that when staff hear biased comments between children they 'validate the feelings of the child who is on the receiving end' (Elswood 1999, p. 63) of any racist or biased comment.

Gender

Staff can learn a lot about children's gender relationships through listening to how children speak to each other. Staff can hear if boys and girls are speaking in ways that show respect for the other or not. They can note if children are using speech pro-socially to share, negotiate and maintain positive social relationships with each other. They can also note who is using speech anti-socially to demand, command, threaten, exaggerate, boast, tease, tell tales and name-call. Noting the gender balance in use of pro-social and anti-social speech gives staff important information about if and how children's play is gender-biased, and can alert them to the need to intervene immediately in children's play to stop or challenge what is happening. For example, a staff member who is listening to a group of boys and a girl playing and hears the boys teasing the girl could immediately intervene to stop the teasing. However, they could also use the experience to plan how to reduce gender bias in the future by, for example, teaching the girl concerned how to stand up to the boys in the future and where to go for support whenever it happens.

It is particularly important to listen to girls and boys when they cross traditional gender boundaries in their play, for example, when girls move into the blocks areas when boys are present or when boys play with dolls when girls are present. In these situations, gender-based teasing, verbal threatening and name-calling between girls and boys is much more likely (Browne and Ross 1991). Girls can also have their ideas and suggestions ignored by boys in these situations. If staff are listening carefully to the play that occurs when girls do cross the gender boundaries in their play then they can actively intervene to ensure that girls are supported to express their ideas and have them heard by their peers (Marshall et al. 1999).

Disability and additional needs

The successful integration of children with disabilities into an early childhood program depends on building positive and respectful attitudes towards people with disabilities. Listening to children's discussions with each other can help staff to assess the extent to which children are developing positive and respectful attitudes towards people with disabilities. Staff need to be alert to the disrespectful ways in which children without disabilities can speak to those with disabilities, including teasing, name-calling or verbally threatening. If this occurs, staff must swiftly counter the effect of such disrespect on the child at whom it is targeted and help the children to understand why such language is unacceptable.

Listening to children's questions about people with disabilities can also help staff to assess how far children have developed positive and respectful attitudes towards people with disabilities. From children's questions, staff can learn about children's understandings of the lifestyle, feelings, needs and interests of people with disabilities and about their misconceptions, fears or prejudices concerning disabilities. Staff can also judge the extent to which children without disabilities feel positively or negatively about people with disabilities. Staff can use this information to plan how to correct and enrich what the children know about disabilities. Questions such as, 'Why won't Sammy climb to the top of the slide by himself?' offer staff opportunities to explain that Sammy's arms and legs are not strong enough for him to climb the slide without help.

REFLECTING ON LISTENING TECHNIQUES

1   Briefly define active listening.
2   What do you think is the major difference between listening and hearing?
3   What might you learn about a three-year-old child's cognitive skills through listening to their private speech as they complete a puzzle?
4   What are the main reasons you might listen to a baby's sounds when they are playing with a mobile above their cot?
5   List three ways you could show a four-year-old child you were interested in their ideas if you did not have the time to listen to them.
6   What are three characteristics that you need to be an effective listener?
7   Record the sounds and movements made by a baby under twelve months of age during a fifteen-minute observation period. How did the baby express pleasure? How did it express displeasure? Would listening to the baby be sufficient to tell you when it needed your attention?
8   Record the monologue of a three-year-old child. What can you learn about the child's developmental interests and needs from this monologue?
9   Observe a small group of five-year-old boys and girls engaged in play with each other. How often did they use language to develop positive social relationships? How often did they use language to develop negative social relationships? Were there any gender differences in the use of pro-social and anti-social speech?
10 Observe a small group session between an early childhood worker and a group of four-year-old children. What factors made it easy and what factors made it difficult for the worker to:
    - make time to listen to children?
    - wait a few seconds before responding?
    - model active listening skills?
    - respond to children's comments with care and thought?

IMPROVING TEACHING IN PRACTICE

1   Videotape the conversations you have with children during several five-minute teaching periods.
2   How well did you:
    - make time to listen to children?
    - wait a few seconds before responding?
    - model active listening skills?
    - respond to children's comments with care and thought?

3   How and how well did you take account of equity considerations as you listened to the children?
4   What are your areas of strength and weakness in listening to promote children's learning?
5   How can you work to improve your listening techniques in practice?

Further reading

Fleer, M. and Cahill, A. 2001, *I Want to Know: Learning About Science*, Watson, ACT, Australian Early Childhood Association [refer to pp. 3–12].

Renck Jalongo, M. 1995, 'Promoting active listening in the classroom', *Childhood Education*, 72(1), pp. 13–18.

Seefeldt, C. 1980, *Teaching Young Children*, New Jersey, Prentice Hall Inc. [refer to pp. 146–59].

References

Alat, K. 2002, 'Traumatic events and children: how early childhood educators can help', *Childhood Education*, 79(1), pp. 1–8.

Benson McMullen, M. 1999, 'Achieving best practices in infant and toddler care and education', *Young Children*, 54(4), pp. 69–77.

Browne, N. and Ross, C. 1991, '"Girls' stuff, boys' stuff": young children talking and playing', in N. Browne, ed., *Science and Technology in the Early Years* (pp. 37–51), Milton Keynes, Open University Press.

Clarke, P. 1992, *English as a 2nd Language in Early Childhood*, Melbourne, FKA Multicultural Resource Centre.

Ebbeck, M. 1991, *Early Childhood Education*, Melbourne, Longman Chesire.

Elswood, R. 1999, 'Really including diversity in early childhood programs', *Young Children*, 54(4), pp. 62–6.

Fleer, M. and Cahill, A. 2001, *I Want to Know: Learning About Science*, Watson, ACT, Australian Early Childhood Association, pp. 3–12.

Harrison, L. 1996, *Planning Appropriate Learning Environments for Children Under Three*, revised edn, Watson, ACT, Australian Early Childhood Association.

Hurlock, E. 1978, *Child Growth and Development*, New Delhi, Tata McGraw Hill Publishing Co.

Hutchins, T. 1995, *Babies Need More than Minding: Planning for Babies and Toddlers in Group Settings*, Watson, ACT, Australian Early Childhood Association.

Jones, E. 1999, 'An emergent curriculum expert offers this afterthought', *Young Children*, 54(4), p. 16.

Lerner, J., Mardell-Czudnowski, C. and Goldenberg, D. 1987, *Special Education for the Early Childhood Years*, second edn, New Jersey, Prentice Hall Inc.

Marshall, N., Robeson, W. and Keefe, N. 1999, 'Gender equity in early childhood education', *Young Children*, 54(4), pp. 9–14.

McWilliams, S. 1999, Fostering wonder in young children, Paper presented at the *Annual Meeting of the National Association for Research in Science Teaching*, Boston, MA, March 28–31, ED 444833.

Moyles, J. 1989, *Just Playing: The Role and Status of Play in Early Childhood Education*, Milton Keynes, Open University Press.

Paley, V. 1986, *Mollie is Three: Growing up in School*, Chicago, University of Chicago Press.

Partington, G. and McCudden, V. 1992, *Ethnicity and Education*, Sydney, Social Science Press.

Phillips, L. 2000, 'Storytelling: the seeds of children's creativity', *Australian Journal of Early Childhood*, 25(3), pp. 1–5.

Renck Jalongo, M. 1995, 'Promoting active listening in the classroom', *Childhood Education*, 72(1), pp. 13–18.

Seefeldt, C. 1980, *Teaching Young Children*, New Jersey, Prentice Hall Inc.

Soundy, C. and Humadi Genisio, M. 1994, 'Asking young children to tell the story', *Childhood Education*, 71(1), pp. 20–3.

Thompson, R.A. 2001, Development in the first years of life, *The Future of Children*, 11(1), 21–33.

Wilkes, G. (ed.) 1979, *Collins Dictionary of the English Language*, Middlesex, Penguin Books.

Chapter 11

Modelling

Model: a representation.

(*Collins Dictionary of the English Language*, p. 947)

The ways that you communicate, solve problems, and relate to others form a powerful model for how children and others . . . will behave. Children tend to do what adults do regardless of what adults say.

(Feeney et al. 1991, p. 15)

Following demonstrations by a model, or (though to a lesser extent) following verbal descriptions of desired behaviour, the learner generally reproduces more or less the entire response pattern . . .

(Bandura and Walters 1963, p. 106)

WHAT?

Modelling is a process through which children learn how to behave by copying (modelling) the behaviour of others. Staff can teach children how to behave 'appropriately' through presenting them with examples (models) of the dispositions, attitudes and values which the adults around them consider to be appropriate behaviour. Modelling occurs when children copy these behaviours.

HOW?

Modelling is a low-intervention teaching technique. Staff do not intervene directly in children's learning but teach by example. For example, if staff want children to share materials with other children then they need to create circumstances in which they can model sharing materials with the children.

    Children may model themselves on the adults around them even when the adults are not deliberately teaching through example. Thus, staff should try to demonstrate only those behaviours that they want children to emulate! The following points offer guidance on how to successfully use modelling as a deliberate teaching technique.

➲ Decide which behaviours, skills and dispositions you want the children to learn. The Shotby child care centre does this at its regular monthly meeting for the staff. There is always an agenda item concerning the behaviours, attitudes and dispositions on which the staff will concentrate with the children for the month.

- ➲ Identify the smaller steps and components involved in achieving these behaviours, attitudes and dispositions (Robison and Schwartz 1982).
- ➲ Analyse each child's ability to '. . . attend, retain, reproduce motorically, and become interested in the learning to be imitated' (Robison and Schwartz 1982, p. 109).
- ➲ Remember that children will watch the verbal and non-verbal actions and reactions of the social models around them.

> Carmel is a teacher who is very alert to the social model she provides. She has strong views about taking care of the environment and being careful about the earth's resources. She has set up recycling areas in the kindergarten and the children and adults are encouraged to sort out any waste material. The centre also has a worm farm with which to recycle food scraps and the children regularly clean this out, putting the worm casts on the garden to fertilise the plants. Carmel takes care to model respect for the environment inside and out.

- ➲ Plan specific occasions which offer opportunities to provide children with a model of the desired skill.
- ➲ Be alert to incidental and unplanned opportunities to model the desired skills.
- ➲ Be prepared to model behaviours over time. Children are more likely to learn through example if they have lots of examples to follow (Robison and Schwartz 1982; Marion 1987).
- ➲ Remember that peers, siblings, adults, popular culture heroes and characters in books and stories can be used to model desired skills (Allen and Hart 1984).
- ➲ Recognise that children are more likely to model a particular behaviour if they see the person modelling it being rewarded for the behaviour (Seefeldt 1980).
- ➲ Recognise that children are more likely to continue to model a particular behaviour if they are rewarded when they display that behaviour (Seefeldt 1980).
- ➲ Remember that children are more likely to model the people whom they regard as powerful and nurturing in their environment (Marion 1987).

Modelling is successful when children incorporate the behaviours the adults (or peers) have modelled into their own behavioural repertoire (Seefeldt 1980).

WHEN AND WHY?

Modelling should be used when staff want children to learn new 'chunks' of social behaviour through observing and imitating the social models around them.

Goal relevance

Modelling can be used to teach verbal and non-verbal skills to children of all ages (Robison and Schwartz 1982). For example, adult role-modelling can be a successful teaching technique when staff want to:

- ➲ extend or enrich children's play (Arthur et al. 1996)

Nikki is keen to enrich imaginative play. She is sitting on the floor with three toddlers. She has provided some dress-ups, lots of hats and a mirror for them to look into. Liam, who is one of the more reticent toddlers, is watching the other children as they try on hats and vests. Nikki puts on a hat and says to Liam, 'Look at me, I've got a hat on'. Liam takes a hat and puts it on.

- ● help children learn to play co-operatively (Feeney et al. 1991; Hintz and Stomfay-Stitz 1999)
- ● help children learn to solve problems. Children who have observed adults solving problems perform better on these tasks than children who have not had this experience (Feeney et al. 1991)
- ● increase children's desire to eat healthy foods (Feeney et al. 1991)

At a child care centre in inner Melbourne, the staff always eat with the children because they can model enjoyment of wholesome food to them.

- ● build children's interest in reading and writing for themselves (Feeney et al. 1991, Gray 1995; Cress 2000)
- ● enhance the development of intimacy and enjoyment in close relationships (Roland and Lawhon 1994)
- ● increase children's pro-social behaviours, such as sharing and being socially competent (Lerner et al. 1987; McCay and Keyes 2001/02)
- ● encourage children to enter dramatic play (Rybczynski and Troy 1995)
- ● promote children's ability to actively listen to others (Renck Jalongo 1995)
- ● encourage children to tell their own stories (Hough et al. 1987)
- ● build socially inclusive classrooms (McCay and Keyes 2001/02).

Angela models actions during creative movement.

Developmental considerations

At all stages of their development, children can imitate adult models. Research by van Kleeck et al. (1996) showed that babies as young as six months of age can learn about thinking from adults who model giving and receiving information. Such modelling included simple behaviours such as answering their own questions, underlining text in a book with a finger when the text is spoken, repeating statements for emphasis and speaking for the baby.

> Quentin is sitting in a large bean bag with two eleven-month-old babies. He is showing them a book and as he looks at each page he points to the pictures, labels them and shows interest in the babies' responses.

However, it is important to remember that children's ability to imitate specific behaviours will be limited by their cognitive, emotional, social and physical ability to reproduce the skills or dispositions they observe. Consider the following example:

> A very young child who had observed an adult express affection to a dog by a multiple set of actions such as patting, kissing and hugging, in that order, copied only one behaviour, the patting action. Having little sense of the intensity of the patting, and limited motor ability to control it, the child hit the dog repeatedly, provoking a snapping reaction from the dog (Robison and Schwartz 1982, p. 109).

According to Cole and Chan (1990), modelling requires the child to have the following abilities:

- to be able to grasp what adults want them to reproduce
- to be able to remember the key elements of what adults want them to reproduce
- to be able to represent what is to be reproduced in symbolic form
- to be able to convert the symbolic information into action.

Consequently, as children grow and develop, their ability to model complex behaviours and skills will also develop.

The child also needs to be motivated to model what adults want them to learn. Children are more motivated to model adult behaviours when they have a close bond with the adult concerned (Roland and Lawhon 1994). However, children will also model the skills and dispositions of children more competent than themselves (Arthur et al. 1996; Allen and Hart 1984). This suggests that mixed-age and mixed-ability groupings can encourage children to 'try' more complex skills.

Access to same-age peers as models can be particularly important for toddlers. Toddlers add to their rapidly expanding repertoire of social and cognitive skills and behaviours through modelling each other (Castle 1990). They try out what other toddlers are doing and, in doing so, solve social and cognitive problems they may not have confronted before. This means that it is very important for staff to provide time, space and opportunity for toddlers to watch and imitate each other.

Teachers who model communication with preschool children have been shown to positively support children's cognitive development (Bowman et al. 2001).

In the early years of schooling children are becoming increasingly competent language users. They have a strong enough understanding of the structure and meaning of language to be able to play with words and sentence structures and create funny alternatives to what should normally be said or written (Arthur et al. 1996). Teachers can build on this tendency to enhance their creative language use through modelling enjoyment in language games and sharing funny words and word games with the children. Modelling was also shown to be an effective component of a literacy program with children in the early years of school when children with and without disabilities were paired to tutor each other in reading. Each member of the pair took on the role of Coach and/or Reader and acted as tutors for each other in learning to read. Teachers used modelling to introduce the whole class to the different roles taken by children in their literacy pairs and to show what these roles looked like in practice (Fuchs et al. 2001). Research has shown that young children learn many early literacy skills and behaviours through modelling and that many early writers have observed their parents regularly engaged in reading and writing activities (Cress 2000). This points to the need for teachers to proactively model literacy behaviours to beginning writers. Modelling can also be effectively used by teachers to help children develop skills in critically choosing books for reading and deciding whether or not a book would be too difficult for them. Research has shown that when teachers modelled these behaviours for children they were more effectively used by the children than when didactic teaching methods were used (Kragler 2000).

EQUITY CONSIDERATIONS

'Race' and culture

A positive self-identity is the basis for confident involvement in the world. Racism can mar the development of a positive self-identity for many black and ethnic minority children. These children develop a positive self-identity partly by having access to positive role models from within their own ethnic and 'racial' group. Perry and Furkawa (1980; cited in Cole and Chan 1990) have shown that models which are similar in 'race' to the child will enhance the acquisition of desired behaviours and dispositions. However, providing positive role models for children from different racial and ethnic backgrounds presents a major challenge for early childhood staff, because the majority of early childhood workers are 'white, female, middle-class people with Western practices, beliefs, values and attitudes' (Fleer 1996, p. 7).

There is clearly a need to work for greater ethnic diversity within the staff group, but there are some other ways in which staff can offer children positive ethnic role models. Adler Matoba explains the reasons for this powerfully within the context of the USA:

> European American teachers, particularly in the Midwest, may view their Asian American students through cultural lenses formed by their own limited experiences with people of color, stereotypes like the 'model minority' . . . and a color-blind perspective, which focuses on overlooking racial differences. (Adler Matoba 2001, p. 151)

Colbung and Glover (1996) discussed the issues within an Australian context and argued that it is extremely important that Indigenous Australian children are exposed to positive Indigenous role models with which to develop a positive self-identity and to counter the effects of racism against Indigenous Australians:

> The availability of cultural role models will, to a large degree, affect children's achievements. Role models show children that they do not have to sacrifice their Aboriginality in order to succeed in mainstream institutions . . . (Colbung and Glover 1996, p. 38).

Staff can introduce Indigenous children to positive Indigenous role models by bringing local Indigenous 'identities' into the centre and by inviting Indigenous performers and artists to visit it. Local Indigenous adults can advise staff how best to do this. Staff can do similar things to offer positive adult role models to children whose ethnic and racial background differs from that of the staff group. However, it is important in this endeavour to avoid doing it only occasionally, that is, tokenisticly.

Children who have prejudicial behaviours and beliefs modelled at home can reject these and so it is important that staff proactively model for all children anti-racist ways of thinking and acting at all times. As Sleeter and Grant (1999, p. 85) explained:

> Teachers who are 'real' with students—who talk honestly with them about real issues—can serve as influential role models and can prod students to think about their beliefs.

Gender

Much of the daily content of early childhood programs provides children with clear representations of how males and females should behave, think and act. Research (for example, Alloway 1995; MacNaughton 1995, 2000) indicates that many of the gender role models which children see in early childhood settings are gender-stereotyped. In addition, many stories, posters, games, puzzles, poems and songs contain mainly male role models. It is, therefore, important that staff include resources in their program that present girls and boys with positive, non-stereotypical female role models. One way to expand the gender role models available to young girls is to invite to the centre women who have jobs from which they have traditionally been excluded, such as firefighting and truck driving.

Female staff can expand girls' involvement in curriculum areas and experiences which they often avoid, such as those traditionally associated with the sciences and mathematics, by modelling an active interest in them. Similarly, male staff can expand boys' involvement in curriculum areas and experiences which they often avoid, such as those traditionally associated with the arts, the caring professions and the world of daily domestic life, by modelling an active interest in them. However, it is important for staff to remember that modelling alone is unlikely to change well-entrenched gender role differences in young children (Sleeter and Grant 1999; MacNaughton 2000). Modelling needs to be combined with a wide range of more proactive teaching techniques to produce changes in gender expectations and forms of participation in the early years.

Similarity in gender between adult models and the child is important, as this has been shown to enhance the child's acquisition of desired behaviours from the adult model (Cole and Chan 1990). The opportunities to do this are likely to be greater when there is a mix of male and female staff in a centre:

At a meeting in an early learning centre in Sydney's southern suburbs, the staff are discussing how they might help boys and girls to experience less gender-stereotyped play.

Albert: 'We have two male teachers and three female teachers at the centre and I can't help but notice that we are all falling thoughtlessly into particular roles. For example, I'm the one who always teaches and supervises the carpentry and Jannette always takes the children for cooking activities.'

Jannette: 'That's because I love cooking and you don't enjoy it much!'

John: 'What about if I do cooking sometimes and perhaps Sally, Dia and Jannette could do some of the more physical activities like the outside block play, gardening and digging? In this way, the children won't get the idea that only men do some things and women others.'

Disability and additional needs

Meeting a child with a disability in an early childhood setting may be the first encounter many able-bodied children have with disability. Adults can provide clear signs to able-bodied children about how to respectfully handle this encounter through modelling respect and acceptance themselves (Winter 1994/95). Crary (1992, pp. 12–14) suggested that staff should model the following behaviours:

- Greet people with disabilities directly and with respect by, for example, making eye contact as staff would with other people. Many people with disabilities report that they can feel invisible because other people speak to whoever they are with rather than directly to them.
- Respect the personal space of people with disabilities by not touching them in ways which would be inappropriate with other people and by not leaning on or touching their special equipment (for example, wheelchairs) unless given permission to do so.
- Allow time for people with disabilities to be independent in their movements or speech, and model patience in waiting for them.

If children with disabilities have learned to see themselves as 'odd' or 'different', staff should provide children with positive role models of living with a disability by, for example, inviting people with disabilities to the centre to talk about their achievements; and by using posters, books, poems and puzzles that include positive models of being a person with a disability. However, staff should

Marg shows Eliza how to use a spade.

ensure that such sessions aren't one-off, tokenistic sessions. (For more information in this area refer to Chapter 3.)

Modelling has been shown to be a very effective way to teach a wide variety of skills, including social skills, to children with a wide range of disabilities (Lowenthal 1996; Fuchs et al 2001; McCay and Keyes 2001/02). Cole and Chan (1990) and McCay and Keyes (2001/02) discussed in detail how modelling may be used to teach social and other skills to children with disabilities. However, modelling alone may not be sufficient to teach children with disabilities social competence. McCay and Keyes (2001/02, p. 77) concluded:

> The key, then becomes providing multiple skill exposure and practice for children with low cognitive functioning, while offering new and varying learning opportunities for children without such disabilities . . . the teacher should actively choose to teach social competence, using his or her professional knowledge of many perspectives to select from a wide repertoire of strategies.

REFLECTING ON MODELLING TECHNIQUES

1   Define modelling.
2   What does research suggest are the keys to using modelling to optimise children's learning?
3   When do you think modelling should be deliberately used in your teaching?
4   Are there any times when you think that the use of modelling is inappropriate with young children?
5   How could modelling be used to promote communicative competence with infants? What sort of modelling could you use to achieve this aim?
6   What things do you think could be successfully taught to toddlers through modelling?
7   What dispositions do you think you could successfully teach through modelling to four-year-old children?
8   List three behaviours that you would like to model with a mixed-age group of children. Identify five ways you could actively model these behaviours to them. Identify five difficulties you could encounter in trying to model these behaviours. How could you overcome these difficulties? Would you need to draw on any other teaching techniques to assist you in this work?
9   List the types of visual aids and props you could collect to provide positive role models for children with disabilities.
10 Choose one storybook you could use with two-year-old children to provide them with a positive role model of being 'black'.
11 Find one poem you could use with four-year-old children to provide a positive role model of girls being adventurous.

IMPROVING TEACHING IN PRACTICE

Visit an early childhood centre and discuss with the adults what behaviours and dispositions they are trying to teach the children through modelling. How are they trying to teach them? To what extent did the staff:

- ❍ decide in advance what they wanted the children to learn?
- ❍ take a logical step-by-step approach to modelling?
- ❍ analyse each child's current level of ability to acquire the desired behaviour?

- show awareness of what children might learn from verbal and non-verbal behaviours being modelled?
- plan specific times to model for the children?
- use incidental opportunities for modelling?
- model over an extended period of time?
- involve other people and resources in the modelling process?
- reward the children when they reproduced the desired behaviour?

Further reading

Cole, P. and Chan, L. 1990, *Methods and Strategies for Special Education*, New Jersey, Prentice Hall Inc. [refer to Chapter 7].

Crary, E. 1992, 'Talking about differences children notice', in B. Neugebauer, ed., *Alike and Different: Exploring our Humanity with Young Children* (pp. 11–15), Washington, National Association for the Education of Young Children.

Kean, J. 1991, 'Socialization of affect display in young children: a review', *Australian Journal of Early Childhood*, 16(2), pp. 15–19.

Marion, M. 1987, *Guidance of Young Children*, second edn, USA, Merrill [refer to pp. 192–5].

Video

Centre Based Infant Care Session 1, Open Training and Education Network, TAFE, NSW, Australia 1992.

Modelling, 2000, Introduction to Visual Arts Series available from Marcom Projects at www.marcom.com.au

References

Adler Matoba, S. 2001, 'Racial and ethnic mirrors: reflections on identity from an Asian American educator', in S. Grieshaber and G. Cannella, eds, *Embracing Identities in Early Childhood Education: Diversity and Possibilities*, pp. 148–57, New York, Teachers' College Press.

Allen, K. and Hart, B. 1984, *The Early Years: Arrangements for Learning*, New Jersey, Prentice Hall Inc.

Alloway, N. 1995, *Foundation Stones: The Construction of Gender in Early Childhood*, Melbourne, Curriculum Corporation.

Arthur, L., Beecher, B., Dockett, S., Farmer, S. and Death, E. 1996, *Programming and Planning in Early Childhood Settings*, second edn, Sydney, Harcourt Brace and Company.

Bandura, A. and Walters, R. 1963, *Social Learning and Personality Development*, New York, Holt, Rinehart and Winston.

Bowman, B., Donovan, M. and Burns, S. 2001, *Eager to Learn: Educating Our Preschoolers*, Washington DC, National Academy Press.

Castle, K. 1990, 'The second year: 12–24 months', in E. Surbeck and M. Kelly, eds, *Personalizing Care with Infants, Toddlers and Families* (pp. 23–32), Wheaton, MD, Association for Childhood Education International.

Colbung, M. and Glover, A. 1996, 'In partnership with Aboriginal children', in M. Fleer, ed., *Conversations about Teaching and Learning in Early Childhood Settings* (pp. 33–40), Canberra, Australian Early Childhood Association.

Cole, P. and Chan, L. 1990, *Methods and Strategies for Special Education*, New Jersey, Prentice Hall Inc.

Crary, E. 1992, 'Talking about differences children notice', in B. Neugebauer, ed., *Alike and Different: Exploring our Humanity with Young Children* (pp. 11–15), Washington, National Association for the Education of Young Children.

Cress, S. 2000, 'A focus on literacy in home day care', *Australian Journal of Early Childhood*, 25(3), pp. 6–11.

Feeney, S., Christensen, D. and Moravcik, E. 1991, *Who am I in the Lives of Children? An Introduction to Teaching Young Children*, fifth edn, New York, Macmillan Publishing Company.

Fleer, M. 1996, 'Talking about teaching and learning', in M. Fleer, ed., *Conversations about Teaching and Learning in Early Childhood Settings* (pp. 1–8), Watson, ACT, Australian Early Childhood Association.

Fuchs, D., Fuchs, L., Al Otaiba, S., Thompson, A., Yen, L., McMaster, K., Svenson, K. and Yang, N. 2001, 'K-Pals: helping kindergartners with reading readiness: teachers and researchers in partnerships', *Teaching Exceptional Children*, Mar/Apr, pp. 76–80.

Gray, L. 1995, 'Taking from books by asking questions', *Journal of Research in Childhood Education*, 10(1), pp. 23–8.

Hintz, B. F. and Stomfay-Stitz, A. 1999, Peace education and conflict resolution through expressive arts in early childhood education and teacher education, Paper presented at the *Annual Conference of the Eastern Educational Research Association*, Hilton Head, SC, February 26, ED433105.

Hough, R., Nurss, J. and Wood, D. 1987, 'Tell me a story: making opportunities for elaborated language in early childhood classrooms', *Young Children*, November, pp. 6–12.

Kragler, S. 2000, 'Choosing books for reading: an analysis for three types of readers', *Journal of Research in Childhood Education*, 14(2), pp. 133–41.

Lerner, J., Mardell-Czudnowski, C. and Goldenberg, D. 1987, *Special Education for the Early Childhood Years*, second edn, New Jersey, Prentice Hall Inc.

Lowenthal, B. 1996, 'Teaching social skills to preschoolers with special needs, *Childhood Education*, 72(3), pp. 137–40.

MacNaughton, G. 1995, 'The gender factor', in B. Creaser and E. Dau, eds, *The Anti-Bias Approach in Early Childhood* (pp. 51–70), Sydney, Harper Educational.

MacNaughton, G. 2000, Rethinking Gender in Early Childhood, Allen & Unwin, Sydney.

Marion, M. 1987, *Guidance of Young Children*, second edn, USA, Merrill.

McCay, L. and Keyes, D. 2001/02, 'Developing social competence in the primary schools', *Childhood Education*, 78(2), pp. 70–78.

Renck Jalongo, A. 1995, 'Promoting active listening in the classroom', *Childhood Education*, 72(1), pp. 13–18.

Robison, H. and Schwartz, S. 1982, *Designing Curriculum for Early Childhood*, Boston, Allyn and Bacon Inc.

Roland, S. and Lawhon, T. 1994, 'How do I love thee: enhancing intimacy in children', *Childhood Education*, 71(1), pp. 38–41.

Rybcyznski, M. and Troy, A. 1995, 'Literacy-enriched play centres: trying them out in "the real world"', *Childhood Education*, 72(1), pp. 7–12.

Seefeldt, C. 1980, *Teaching Young Children*, New Jersey, Prentice Hall Inc.

Sleeter, C. and Grant, C. 1999, *Making Choices for Multicultural Education: Five Approaches to Race, Class and Gender,* third edn, New Jersey, Merrill Prentice Hall.

van Kleeck, A., Imholz Alexander, E., Vigil, A. and Templeton, K. 1996, 'Verbally modeling thinking for infants: middle-class mother's presentation of information structures during book sharing', *Journal of Research in Childhood Education*, 10(2), pp. 101–13.

Wilkes, G. (ed.) 1979, *Collins Dictionary of the English Language*, Middlesex, Penguin Books.

Winter, S. 1994/95, 'Diversity, a program for all children', *Childhood Education*, 71(2), pp. 91–5.

Chapter 12

Positioning people

Position: the place, situation or timing of a person or thing.

(Collins Dictionary of the English Language, p. 1143)

The experienced teacher, even when she is working with one child, will be in a position to observe at a glance what the other children are doing— alert to the total situation.

(Read et al. 1993, p. 101)

One is often in a better position to help a child when one is at the child's level.

(Read et al. 1993, p. 101)

WHAT?

Positioning is the process of placing oneself near other individuals, groups or objects in ways that support children's learning and that maintain children's safety. Careful positioning of people can enrich children's planned and unplanned learning experiences.

HOW?

Staff can best assist children's learning by thinking about several interrelated levels of organisation:

- ➡ overall social organisation of the learning areas
- ➡ daily timetabling of staff–child interactions
- ➡ daily placement of adults
- ➡ safe placement of people
- ➡ placing people for security and for competence
- ➡ positioning staff for meaning-making with children.

Overall social organisation of the learning areas

In placing materials and equipment within the learning environment in ways which facilitate social interaction, staff need to think about the following issues:

- ➡ that there are places for adults and/or children to stand and sit individually and in groups on the floor and on chairs

➲ that equipment is placed within easy reach of the children

➲ that some equipment is accessible only to adults

➲ that children are able to work in groups of different sizes

➲ that there are spaces to encourage individual learning

➲ that placement of staff reflects these considerations.

Daily timetabling of staff–child interactions

Staff need to plan for the placement of children and adults throughout each day. They have many choices about how to do this. Staff can place themselves near a learning experience when it begins to help capture children's interest in that experience. Once a learning experience has begun, staff can join in to maintain children's interest in it and to support their explorations of it. Staff can join a learning experience after some time to extend children's interests and to prompt their exploration of alternative solutions to problems. This array of choices requires staff to consider when timetabling if they will:

➲ sit near a particular child or group of children

➲ place themselves inside or outside of the group

➲ place themselves near a particular learning experience or move about

➲ stand, kneel or sit.

> The Millicent child care centre is in an inner urban area under some housing commission flats. The staff are keen to help the children to develop curiosity and enthusiasm for learning. Each day before the children arrive, the staff have a five-minute meeting to discuss which staff will be where in the room and which will be outside in the playground. In this way, they make sure that they cover all areas and thus ensure that the children are safe and that staff are available to help stimulate children's interest and curiosity.

Daily placement of adults

Staff may have an overall plan for organising their responsibilities during the day, but some daily changes can enrich and extend children's learning. For example, placing a visitor such as a parent or student near where a child is playing can prompt the child's interests and make their play more elaborate. Staff need to think about when and where they will place adults to encourage children's active involvement in the program.

> Lynne, a kindergarten teacher in a country town in Victoria, has spent a lot of time and energy trying to include the parents and members of the community in her program. She has a strong belief that children's learning is enhanced by having adults around who can stimulate curiosity and develop children's learning. She has advertised in the local newspaper for volunteers and she has made personal contact with each family to ask for their time. She keeps a list of extra adults who will be at the kindergarten each day. At the beginning of each session, Lynne talks with each adult and gives them suggestions as to where they should position themselves in relation to the children.

In deciding how to place people, staff should ensure that their decisions create and maintain a safe, secure, interesting and pleasurable learning environment for children and adults. To do this staff need to ensure that:

- children's and staff's health and safety needs are met
- children gain a feeling of security and competence in their learning environment.

Placing people for safety

Staff need to ensure that they can supervise children's learning by placing themselves where they can easily see the children. Staff should always sit in places from where they can easily scan the room on a regular basis. Careful staff positioning is particularly important near high-risk activities, to ensure children's safety while allowing them new and challenging experiences. High-risk activities include those in which:

- there is water in containers on the ground near young children. Babies and toddlers might drown if they land face-down in the water
- there are sharp tools, such as in the digging patch, gardening area, clay modelling, collage or woodworking areas. Children might damage themselves or others through awkward or careless use of these tools
- children might overreach or over-balance and fall—these are part of the new challenges with climbing equipment
- children have access to animals that might sting, bite or scratch them
- children are near heat sources such as stoves and heaters
- children are handling very hot or very cold materials (liquids or solids)
- there are very small items that children could swallow if left unsupervised.

These experiences should only be attempted if close, constant and careful adult supervision can be guaranteed. Staff should also have a clear understanding of the children's particular skills and limitations. Each child's particular physical, emotional, social and cognitive stage of development will create different potential hazards.

Some questions to prompt staff reflection on how to place themselves and others to promote a safe learning environment include:

- Do staff know who will be available when, and to supervise which areas?
- Can staff readily scan the inside and outside play area when sitting?
- Can staff move quickly to all areas they are supervising?
- Are staff positioned near all high-risk activities?
- Have staff assessed children's developmental abilities before offering high-risk activities?

Positioning for security and competence

Children need to feel secure and competent in their daily environment in order to build positive relationships with adults. By sitting near children or alongside them staff can easily promote an atmosphere of warmth and caring through simple gestures such as eye-to-eye contact, cuddles and smiles (Briggs and Potter 1995). Being near children also enables staff to provide them with a sense of security and to easily remind children of the safety rules in the group as necessary. For example, by sitting near children in the sand play area, a staff member can more easily remind children that throwing sand is unacceptable because it can get into other children's eyes.

Staff can use their position to prevent difficulties arising in children's relationships with each other (Read et al. 1993). Sitting or standing between children who are about to interfere with each other, or between whom tension is mounting, may defuse these tensions or threats of intrusion.

Positioning for meaning-making

There is increasing interest in generating early childhood curriculum through the lived experiences of young children and the teacher in their daily classroom life together. Curriculum is generated through teachable moments, responsiveness to individual children's interests and shared decision-making between children and teachers (Burton 2001; Hyun 2001). Central to this approach to curriculum is the capacity of the teacher to actively engage in meaning-making with children. This can only happen if the teacher is positioned within the classroom in ways that make close interaction with children possible. Staff need to consciously plan how they will position themselves in ways that link them with children's activities and learning and enable them to actively engage with children's meaning-making through listening, commenting, questioning and enriching conversations with children.

Some questions to prompt staff reflection on how to place themselves and others to engage proactively with children's meaning-making include:

- ➲ Do staff know who will be available when, and to engage with children in which areas?
- ➲ Will staff be able to have periods of time with individual and small groups of children?
- ➲ Are staff positioned near enough to children to be able to engage in conversation with them?

WHEN AND WHY?

In any early childhood program, decisions about how to position staff will be influenced by the staff's approach to curriculum and by their specific teaching and learning goals for the children.

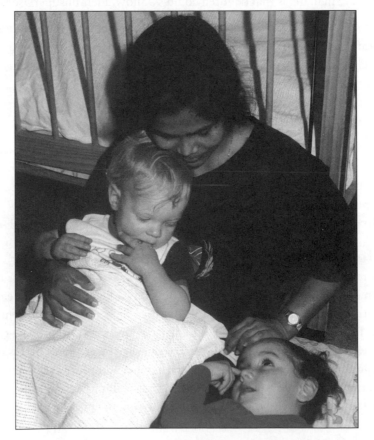

Staying close at sleep time comforts and relaxes children.

Goal relevance

In general, staff can position themselves or others near someone or something to:

● gain and maintain children's attention during a specific learning experience. Staff can gain children's attention more readily when they have eye contact with them (Briggs and Potter 1995), so, when staff want children's attention, they should position themselves so that good eye contact with children is possible. For example, if children are sitting on the floor, staff can move down to their level to achieve this. When organising small group learning, staff need to place themselves so that the children can readily hear and see them

● increase children's concentration on specific experiences. If staff place themselves near children who have trouble concentrating, they can use simple verbal or non-verbal techniques to increase such children's concentration

● extend or enrich a particular experience (Hildebrand 1991). Research has found that when staff play alongside young children, the length and complexity of the children's play increases (Feeney et al. 1991). Lally (1991, p. 13) described how this can happen:

> In one class, the children had been observed making police and fire service vehicles with the large, hollow, wooden block, and had been using these in dramatic play. They were using small, rectangular blocks as 'walkie talkie' radios. The teacher, remembering that she had two unwanted, broken pocket radios at home, brought these into school the next day and added them to the block play areas. These added a new dimension to the play as the children learned where the on/off switch was, how to change the frequency and how to put the aerial up and down.

● encourage children's participation in a specific experience. For example, including a child's favourite adult to a specific area may encourage a reluctant child to participate in a new experience. Similarly, placing a person from a child's own cultural background may encourage them to explore experiences they have avoided.

Developmental considerations

Positioning adults to encourage interactions between children of mixed abilities can have positive effects on children's learning. Bennett and Cass (1988; cited in Edwards and Knight 1994) found that placing two children of 'higher' ability in the same group as a child of 'lower' ability enhanced the learning of the 'lower' ability child. Adding another child of 'lower' ability to the group enhanced the learning of all children in the group. This suggests that placing children of mixed ages and/or mixed abilities in small groups could enhance children's learning. For example, placing toddlers and babies or toddlers and preschoolers in small groups could enhance each child's skill development.

Babies benefit from much close and caring attention from adults. By placing comfortable adult chairs in areas where babies will be, staff can create space in which babies, other children and adults can sit quietly and comfortably together, can cuddle and be involved in playful games with each other. Pillows, bean-bags and soft-carpeted surfaces can make it more likely that adults will be comfortable placing themselves with babies on the floor and can make the floor a comfortable and safe space from which babies can explore the world around them.

Babies also need responsive and close communication with adults to grow emotionally strong and learn how to communicate their needs to others. They need adults who can 'tune into the infant's emotional signals and actively try to understand them' (Fleer and Linke 2002, p. 6). To do this, adults need to be positioned near enough to babies to pick up on their cries, noises, movements and expressions that tell others how a baby is feeling. Finding time to hold babies, sit them on your lap and be positioned so you can see baby and they can see a you is critical to building 'responsive communication with infants' (Fleer and Linke 2002, p. 7).

Toddlers sometimes find sharing difficult and so it can be useful for staff to position themselves near toddlers who are practising sharing and co-operation. Such positioning enables staff to quickly add another toy to the experience so that each toddler has their own, or to avoid conflict by simple redirection.

Careful positioning of adults can create a safe learning environment. Toddlers often 'outdistance their judgment, and they might tumble down a flight of stairs, run into the street or touch a hot stove' (Balaban 1990, p. 35). Adults need to be close enough to toddlers to guard against accidents, yet far enough away to enable toddlers to feel independent in exploring the world about them.

Preschoolers are extremely mobile, often social and highly inquisitive people who can often enter social and physical situations without the skills with which to engage in them safely and enjoyably. It is, therefore, important that staff are vigilant in supervising all areas of preschoolers' activity. In addition, preschoolers are just beginning to form complex and changing friendships and adults need to position themselves far enough away from small groups of children to allow them independence and social exploration, but close enough to ensure fair play and to ensure that difficulties are resolved readily. With each age group this is a balancing act in which experience with a particular child or group of children will often guide how best to reach the balance.

Toddlers play in the sandpit with a staff member nearby.

Children in the early years of school are able to work independently of adults for considerable periods of time. Many teachers draw on this ability to organise small group project work. While children learn lots through peer interactions in small group projects they also benefit considerably from adult involvement. Children's acquisition of literacy and numeracy skills is greatly enhanced when they can talk with teachers about their learning (Hass Dyson and Genishi 1993; Moyles 1989). This is particularly important when children are using electronic media to support their acquisition of literacy and numeracy. Staff need to strongly supervise children's use of new programs and be available for ongoing mediation of their use. The higher order literacy and numeracy skills that can be developed via computer programs are most likely to develop when staff support children's learning as they use the programs (Clements and Nastasi 1993). Staff alert to the learning potential that arises from children talking about how and what they are learning need to maximise their opportunities for such talk with children.

For all children, but especially young children, sharing interactions with adults in which adults are attentive to the interests and expressions of a child is important. Positioning teachers so that episodes of 'joint attention' (for example, Smith 1999) are possible is important for many aspects of a child's growth and well-being, including their emotional well-being and the successful acquisition of language. Smith (1999) studied joint attention episodes in New Zealand early childhood centres and concluded that 'about a third of the children in the study (35%) did not experience any joint attention episodes with caregivers' (p. 94). This is a reminder of the importance of actively planning where and how teachers are positioned within a room so that they can actively create and participate in moments of shared attention with young children.

EQUITY CONSIDERATIONS

'Race' and culture

People have different levels of comfort about what is an acceptable physical distance between one person and another. Staff who work with children and adults from a different cultural background to their own should familiarise themselves with each person's personal space comfort zones. Staff can demonstrate respect for others by taking note of each person's comfort zone and using it in their daily interactions with children and other adults.

Colbung and Glover (1996) believed that many Aboriginal children regard eye contact for any extended period of time as intrusive and threatening. They suggested that non-Aboriginal staff can build and maintain positive relationships with Aboriginal children by positioning themselves next to them so that they can speak to each other on equal terms.

Bilingual children need to be able to play alongside other children without always having to use language to interact (Arthur 1995). Jenny van Oosten (1988) found that music and movement experiences, where the verbal component of the experience is minimal, allow positively for such interactions between English-speaking and non-English-speaking children.

Gender

Adults' position in the early childhood centre gives children strong messages about what and who the adults value. For example, some adults who work with toddlers position themselves more actively alongside boys who are building with blocks than they do when girls build with blocks (Leipzig 1992). Also, adults' positions influence children's play choices. Girls are more likely to become involved in activities traditionally associated with boys if a female staff member is nearby; and boys are more likely to become involved in activities traditionally associated with girls if a male staff member is nearby (Browne and Ross 1991). Staff can use this knowledge to encourage boys and girls to explore areas of the program which they have avoided.

Staff should consider placing children in girls-only and boys-only groups sometimes. Girls perform less well when they are involved in discussion and problem-solving sessions which are mixed gender than when the sessions are individual or girls-only (Parkin 1991). Placing girls and boys in separate groups can also lead them to appreciate the accomplishments of the other group. Epstein (1995) found that girls-only building times changed some boys' opinions of the girls' ability to build. As one boy said:

> I used to think girls don't do bricks. Then we made a girls' time for bricks. They made really good houses, specially Clare. Now I like to play with Clare in the bricks. We make lots of good buildings (Epstein 1995, p. 65).

Disability and additional needs

Staff should monitor their position in relation to children with additional needs in the group to ensure that they do not 'hover over' children with disabilities as they struggle, as all children do, to become independent. These children should have the opportunity to build the skills that will enable them to become independent learners (Palmer 1995), but staff should be nearby to help when needed. Close proximity will make it easier to offer verbal and physical support to children.

As mentioned above, adults' positioning in an early childhood centre gives strong messages to children about who and what the adults value. Staff can use this knowledge to actively model enjoyment in the acceptance of children with disabilities. They can ensure that they regularly work alongside children with disabilities in activities that show adult and child positively responding to each other. Staff can also use this knowledge to give children messages that they trust children with disabilities to be in charge of their own learning.

REFLECTING ON POSITIONING TECHNIQUES

1   Define positioning.
2   Robison and Schwartz (1982) believed that there were five main teaching roles for early childhood staff. These were:
    ➲   nurturer—this involves offering children positive support and encouragement
    ➲   reinforcer—this involves ensuring that desired forms of behaviour increase and undesired forms decrease
    ➲   information giver—this involves telling children about particular facts or ideas
    ➲   challenger—this involves creating novel and puzzling environments for children
    ➲   tutor—this involves actively instructing a child how to do something.

    To what extent do you think that positioning can be used to assist you in each of these roles?
3   Visit an early childhood centre. Sketch the inside and outside learning areas. Note the strategic places to position yourself to ensure safe and wide supervision of children's learning. Note any areas that are potentially hazardous for children's learning.

IMPROVING TEACHING IN PRACTICE

1   Record the different ways in which you positioned yourself in relation to children and staff during several half-hour periods during the day. Note how long you stayed in each place and why you moved from one position to another.

2   How often did you use positioning to:
   - ➧ gain and maintain children's attention during a specific learning experience?
   - ➧ increase children's concentration on specific experiences?
   - ➧ ensure safe supervision of children's learning?
   - ➧ extend or enrich a particular experience?
   - ➧ encourage children's participation in a specific experience?
   - ➧ encourage social interaction between children?

3   How and how well did you take account of developmental considerations when positioning yourself?

4   How and how well did you take account of equity and anti-bias considerations when positioning yourself?

Further reading

Briggs, F. and Potter, G. 1995, *Teaching Children in the First Three Years of School*, second edn, Sydney, Longman [refer to Chapters 7 and 8].

Fleer, M. and Linke, P. 2002, *Babies: good beginnings last for ever*, Watson, ACT, Australian Early Childhood Association.

Gandini, L. 1994, 'Educational and caring spaces', in C. Edwards, L. Gandini and G. Foreman, eds, *The Hundred Languages of Children: The Reggio Emilia Approach to Early Childhood Education* (pp. 135–50), New Jersey, Ablex Publishing Corporation.

Read, K., Gardner, P. and Mahler, B. 1993, *Early Childhood Programs: Human Relationships and Learning*, Fort Worth, TX, Holt, Rinehart and Winston Inc. [refer to pp. 101–3].

Video

Teacher Child Interaction, Early Childhood Training Series, Magna Systems, 1995/2002, available from Marcom Projects at www.marcom.com.au

Exploring and learning, Curriculum for Infants and Toddlers Series, Magna Systems, 2002, available from Marcom Projects at www.marcom.com.au

References

Arthur, L. 1995, 'Linguistic diversity', in B. Creaser and E. Dau, eds, *The Anti-Bias Approach in Early Childhood* (pp. 85–113), Sydney, Harper Educational.

Balaban, N. 1990, 'Toddlers: 24 to 36 months', in E. Surbeck and M. Kelly (eds.) *Personalizing Care with Infants, Toddlers and Families* (pp. 33–40), Wheaton, MD, Association for Childhood Education International.

Briggs, F. and Potter, G. 1995, *Teaching Children in the First Three Years of School*, second edn, Sydney, Longman.

Browne, N. and Ross, C. 1991, '"Girls' stuff, boys' stuff": young children talking and playing', in N. Browne, ed., *Science and Technology in the Early Years* (pp. 37–51), Milton Keynes, Open University Press.

Burton, L. 2001, Children's mathematical narratives as learning stories, Keynote address presented at the *European Conference on Quality in Early Childhood Education (EECERA)*, Alkmaar, Netherlands, 29 August–1 September, ED462135.

Clements, D. and Nastasi, B. 1993, 'Electronic media and early childhood education', in B. Spodek, ed., *Handbook of Research on Early Childhood Education* (pp. 251–75), New York, Macmillan Publishing Company.

Colbung, M. and Glover, A. 1996, 'In partnership with Aboriginal children', in M. Fleer, ed., *Conversations about Teaching and Learning in Early Childhood Settings* (pp. 33–40), Canberra, Australian Early Childhood Association.

Edwards, A. and Knight, P. 1994, *Effective Early Years Education: Teaching Young Children*, Milton Keynes, Open University Press.

Epstein, D. 1995, '"Girls don't do bricks": gender and sexuality in the primary classroom', in J. and I. Siraj-Blatchford, eds, *Educating the Whole Child: Cross-Curriculum Skills, Themes and Dimensions* (pp. 56–69), Milton Keynes, Open University Press.

Feeney, S., Christensen, D. and Moravcik, E. 1991, *Who Am I in the Lives of Young Children? An Introduction to Teaching Young Children*, New York, Merrill.

Fleer, M. and Linke, P. 2002, *Babies: good beginnings last for ever*, Watson, ACT, Australian Early Childhood Association.

Hass Dyson, A. and Genishi, C. 1993, 'Visions of children as language users: language and language education in early childhood', in B. Spodek, ed., *Handbook of Research on the Education of Young Children* (pp. 122–36), New York, Macmillan Publishing Company.

Hildebrand, V. 1991, *Introduction to Early Childhood Education*, fifth edn, New York, Macmillan Publishing Company.

Hyun, E. 2001, Cultural complexity that affects young children's contemporary growth, change and learning, Paper presented at the *Annual Meeting of the Educational Research Association*, Seattle, WA, April 10–14, ED451941.

Lally, M. 1991, *The Nursery Teacher in Action*, London, Paul Chapman Publishing.

Leipzig, J. 1992, 'Helping whole children grow: non-sexist childrearing for infants and toddlers', in B. Neugebauer, ed., *Alike and Different: Exploring our Humanity with Young Children* (pp. 32–41), Washington, National Association for the Education of Young Children.

Moyles, J. 1989, *Just Playing: The Role and Status of Play in Early Childhood Education*, Milton Keynes, Open University Press.

Palmer, A. 1995, 'Responding to special needs', in B. Creaser and E. Dau, eds, *The Anti-Bias Approach in Early Childhood* (pp. 71–84), Sydney, Harper Educational.

Parkin, R. 1991, 'Fair play: children's mathematical experiences in the infant classroom', in N. Browne, ed., *Science and Technology in the Early Years* (pp. 52–64), Milton Keynes, Open University Press.

Read, K., Gardner, P. and Mahler, B. 1993, *Early Childhood Programs: Human Relationships and Learning*, ninth edn, Forth Worth, TX, Holt, Rinehart and Winston Inc.

Robison, H. and Schwartz, S. 1982, *Designing Curriculum for Early Childhood*, Boston, Allyn and Bacon Inc.

Smith, A. 1999, 'Quality care and joint attention', *International Journal of Early Years Education*, 7(1), pp. 85–98.

van Oosten, J. 1988, 'Integrating Music in the Programme', *Resource*, 56, July, no page specified.

Wilkes, G. (ed.) 1979, *Collins Dictionary of the English Language*, Middlesex, Penguin Books.

Chapter 13

Questioning

Question: a form of words addressed to a person in order to elicit information or evoke a response.

(Collins Dictionary of the English Language, p. 1197)

. . . the art of questioning remains an important teaching technique, and many rules laid down in method books of the last century are still useful.
(Hughes and Hughes 1937, p. 392)

It takes a great deal of reflection, comprehension and synthesis to ask an insightful question.

(Wing 1992, p. 81)

WHAT?

A question is 'a sentence worded or expressed to seek information' (Allen 1990, p. 981). When we ask questions about someone or something, we are trying to find out about them or it. We use questions to gain new information, to increase our understanding of something or to compare our own understandings with other people's. Learning to ask questions that prompt children's learning takes time (Sook Lim and Cole 2002).

Staff can use two main types of questions to gain information from children: open questions and closed questions. Each type of question makes different demands on children's cognitive skills, their language skills and their need to go beyond what they already know.

Open questions assume that there is no right or wrong answer. There are many possible answers to an open question—there are many 'openings' for the person answering the question to express what they know, think, feel or believe. Open questions are often used to find out how others are thinking about and making sense of the social and natural world about them. For example, they can encourage children to hypothesise about how the natural world works or to create new story-lines in their imaginative play, or to predict outcomes around specific events. Seefeldt (1980, p. 150) called open questions, 'thought questions'.

Open questions generally inquire into the child's thought processes and require the child to share their theories, understandings, imaginings and feelings with adults or other children. They can be used to interest the child in an event, person or object, and to provoke thought and puzzlement over it. They also encourage the growth of children's problem-solving skills (Klein et al. 2000). Here are some illustrations:

Sharing theories and understandings
'How do you think it works?'; 'Is this part important? Why?'; 'How could we find out more about it?'; 'Why do you think Sulu did that?'.

Sharing feelings
'How did it make you feel when Craig knocked over your blocks?'; 'How do you feel when Sarah is crying?'.

Sharing imaginings and provoking thoughts
'What do you think would happen if . . . ?'; 'How could we end the story differently?'; 'What would we call an animal that was half elephant and half cat?'.

A closed question limits the answer that is possible to give—it 'closes off' the options a person has in answering it. Often, a closed question is a request for factual information and the answer to it is clear and known to the questioner. Closed questions often require only a short answer, so they can be used to find out what a person knows about something or what they recall of a particular event. In early childhood settings, closed questions can be used to find out if children know the names of particular animals or what the rules of the centre are.

Closed questions generally require children to recall what they have been told or experienced. Here are some examples:

Recalling facts
'What is your cat's name?'; 'Do you have a brother?'; 'How many cups are on the table?'; 'What colour are your eyes?'.

Recalling experiences
'What was the name of our visitor yesterday?'; 'What did you do after milk and fruit today?'; 'Which colour swing did you play on today, Kwong?'.

HOW?

As with any teaching technique, questioning will be most effective if staff have established a positive relationship with children. From this base, staff can become skilful questioners of children by:

- asking children how, when, where, what or why and ensuring that their questions have a simple and direct sentence structure. The younger the child, the more important this becomes. Young children will find it easier to follow a direct question such as, 'What is the name of your brother?' than an indirect questions such as, 'The name of your brother is . . . ?'

> William has just arrived from America and joined the second grade class. The teacher, by helping William to settle into his new class, is careful to include him in the group at 'sharing time' by asking him questions that he is able to answer easily: 'Do you have any brothers and sisters? Did you fly to Australia or did you come by sea?'

- using short sentences. Young children are more likely to readily comprehend these than long, wordy sentences, and they are more effective in arousing children's interest (Hogg and Foster 1973)

- asking one question at a time. Asking two or more questions at once can confuse young children

> At lunchtime Anna is careful to ask the toddlers one question at a time about their food preferences: 'Would you like some rice? Shall I give you some peas?'

- focusing questions on a single task, thought or event. Young children can be confused by 'double-barrelled' questions (Turney 1985) such as, 'How many meals do you have a day and what do we call the last meal of the day?'. 'Double-barrelled' questions should be divided in two and the second should only be asked once the child has responded to the first
- asking questions in a logical order to avoid misunderstandings and confusion (Briggs and Potter 1995)
- asking questions that require some definite information or opinion from the children. Avoid questions that merely require a 'yes' or 'no' answer. Children find such closed questions boring and quickly learn to ignore them. In addition, if children have language experiences that have clear purposes, they are more likely to become positively involved in formal reading (Stone 1996)

> Naomi, a child care worker, noticed that Joshua (who was two years old) became silent and withdrawn when his mother came to collect him at the end of the day. On closer observation, she heard on several occasions that Joshua's mother was bombarding him with closed questions such as, 'What colour are your shoes?; How many fingers have you got?; How many children are in the room?; What colour are the doll's eyes?; What did you bring mummy today?'.
>
> Naomi explained to Joshua's mother that he was tired at the end of the day and gave her some suggestions as to how to interact with Joshua when she picked him up from the child care centre. Joshua's mother took Naomi's advice and soon Joshua was interacting animatedly with his mother.

- using questions prudently, avoiding overreliance on them as a teaching technique. Tizard and Hughes (1984) found that early childhood staff used questioning as a major teaching technique with young children and this was a dominant form of conversation in the centre. An over-use of questioning to promote children's learning can be ineffective and can create a very intense atmosphere in early childhood settings (Laishley 1983)
- limiting the amount of 'whole group' questioning. Questioning children to promote learning is most effective when it is done in small groups or in individual sessions that are specially planned and involve careful use of questions (Laishley 1983)
- allowing children time to answer questions. Some teachers tend to wait longer for children whom they believe to be more capable of answering questions than they do for those they believe to be less capable (McAllister 1990). This can reinforce some children's sense that their ideas and their abilities are valued less than other children's
- responding to children's answers with interest and warmth, as this shows children that their answers are valued. Thus they will be more likely to take an interest in the questions that follow or questions that others ask in the future (Hildebrand 1991)

> ➲ using prompting techniques to encourage children's thinking and perseverance. For example, rephrasing or simplifying the question or summarising what the children have said to date can prompt children to respond further to the questions (Turney 1985).

To summarise, the following rules should be observed when questioning: ask meaningful questions which are simple and direct; ask how, when, where, what and why, and use short sentences. Ask one question at a time, be logical, limit group questions and allow time for answers. Respond warmly and prompt children to encourage perseverance, and use questioning prudently.

Turney (1985) argued that there are four questioning techniques that should be avoided:

➲ repeating the same question until children answer it
➲ repeating children's answers
➲ answering one's own questions
➲ encouraging chorus answers.

Each reduces the effectiveness of questioning as a teaching technique because it can lead to children losing interest in what is being said and ignoring questions from staff on future occasions.

When and why?

Goal relevance

Questioning is such a valuable and pervasive teaching technique that it is relevant to most learning experiences for young children. However, research (for example, Turney 1985; Tizard and Hughes 1984) has indicated that teachers tend to use questioning for the very limited purposes of checking:

➲ what facts children know and, therefore, what they need to be taught. For example, do children know their colours, the correct names for animals or road safety rules?

➲ what children have remembered of what they have been taught. For example, do they remember how to count to ten or what the words of a particular song are?

Cazden (1986) believed that there are three main reasons why staff ask children 'closed' questions, that is, those to which there is a right and a wrong answer. First, such questions can assist the flow of a discussion; second, they can help children learn specific facts; and third, they can help staff assess what children do and don't know. However, 'closed' questions can also help children to feel positive about what they know by learning that it is possible and sometimes easy to 'get it right'. Research (Tizard and Hughes 1984; Makin 1996) has shown that early childhood staff often use 'closed' questions about the here and now to assess what children do and don't know. However, that research has shown that this was a very ineffective teaching technique as the children often became confused in trying to 'guess' the answer the staff member wanted, or they became silent. The children also became bored with simple, obvious questions about the here and now, such as, 'What colour is the fire engine in this picture?' or 'How many ounces of flour did we put in the cake?'.

Skilful questioning can effectively promote children's learning rather than merely check what they know by building on children's skills, knowledge and dispositions. Skilful questioning can, for example:

➲ direct children's attention to a particular issue, event or phenomenon

Carla is keen for the six-year-old children in her class to learn how to observe differences between several rabbits they have in the classroom. Carla is encouraging them to look carefully at the physical properties of the animal and uses questions to direct their attention to some of the key differences between the rabbits.

'Can you see the length of the fur? What colour is it? Can you see the different shapes of their ears? What words could you use to talk about the differences?'

- excite children's interest and curiosity about events, information or feelings
- help children reflect on information, feelings or events
- involve children in active learning through discussion
- identify children's difficulties in understanding
- encourage children to question themselves, others and their social and natural environment
- involve children in using a variety of cognitive abilities
- extend and enrich children's imaginative and socio-dramatic competencies
- develop children's curiosity and wonderment
- extend children's communication and language skills, including their ability to create their own stories
- encourage children to empathise with other children's feelings.

Stephanie is a kindergarten teacher who uses questions to support the development of empathy between children. She is helping her small group to understand how Solonge (a new child) feels. She asks 'open' questions:

'How would you feel if you went to a new kindergarten and you didn't know any of the other children? How can we all help Solonge to feel comfortable about being here?'

The following discussion provides staff with some pointers on how to vary their questioning and thus the ways in which children engage with and learn from an experience. For example, it shows how staff can use one style of questioning to help children learn through looking and another for helping children learn through reflection.

DIRECT ATTENTION TO A PARTICULAR ISSUE, EVENT OR PHENOMENON

One of the easiest ways to direct young children's attention to something is to ask them a question about it. Questions should be short and simple, and should be asked in a tone of voice that conveys the questioner's own interest in the subject. For example: 'Why is the fire engine in such a hurry?'; 'How did Lee get the dolls inside his block building?'; 'Do you know what I've found?'; 'Why have all the daffodils fallen over?'.

EXCITE INTEREST AND CURIOSITY ABOUT EVENTS, INFORMATION OR FEELINGS

Questioning is an important technique through which to excite children's interest in something and, thus, to initiate their learning about it. A learning experience which begins with a question is valuable because it invites the children to discover something for themselves (Hogg and Foster 1973). Staff can also use questions to sustain interest in a particular learning experience. For example,

'Sam, can you guess what happens next?'; 'Tilly, how are you going to decorate the cake?'; 'Joshua, where could we find some clean clothes for the baby?'; 'Babette, what else could we use to help us fight the fire?'.

HELP CHILDREN REFLECT ON INFORMATION, FEELINGS OR EVENTS

Reflection is the process of thinking about something. It involves taking time to ponder. Reflection is an important part of the process of making sense of our daily world and of building a sense of what we understand about it. Questions that encourage children to reflect on what they know need not always require answers: staff may use them to help children begin to reflect on what they have been learning. Children can be prompted to reflect by being asked to think about what they have learned or what they think they know about something. Such questions are useful when children assert that something is true. For example: 'How do you know that all cats meow?'; 'Is there anything else you need to have before you build your hospital?'; 'Do you know what astronauts do when they go to the moon?'.

INVOLVE CHILDREN ACTIVELY IN LEARNING THROUGH DISCUSSION

Learning is a highly active process in which children seek to make sense of their world and become competent in it across all domains of development: social, emotional, cognitive, communicative and physical. High-quality discussions—that is, those in which adults ask children leading questions about their experiences—prompt children to learn at a higher level than they might otherwise have done (Abbott and Rodger 1994).

ENCOURAGE CHILDREN TO QUESTION THEMSELVES, OTHERS AND THEIR SOCIAL AND NATURAL ENVIRONMENT

Raising questions with children about the natural world can be an effective way to involve them in scientific learning. Scientific inquiry asks 'How?' about a variety of 'happenings' in the natural world and Beaty (1996, p. 117) likened scientific inquiry to a 'treasure hunt' in which children and staff can search for the answers to an endless list of topics about it. In such a 'treasure hunt', the process of raising and exploring questions is important, not finding the right answer. Beaty (1996) suggested that in early childhood settings, scientific inquiry involves six steps:

- ➋ finding and stating a question that staff or children want to answer
- ➋ guessing possible answers
- ➋ checking if the guesses are right (experimenting)
- ➋ looking at what happens when you check if the guesses are right
- ➋ discussing what happened and if the guesses are right
- ➋ recording what staff or children did and what happened when they did it.

Questions are the starting point for staff who want to teach children the scientific way of finding out about the world or to teach them particular scientific 'facts'. Questions that could begin a 'scientific treasure hunt' with the children include:

- ➋ 'Do boats made of paper float in water?'
- ➋ 'How do you make a kite fly?'
- ➋ 'Why do worms have bands in the middle?'

- 'How do birds build their nests?'
- 'Why do cars stop when they don't have any petrol?'
- 'How does the torch work?'
- 'Why do we hiccup?'

INVOLVE CHILDREN IN USING A VARIETY OF COGNITIVE ABILITIES

Questions can be used to actively promote children's thinking and to develop a broad range of cognitive skills. They can encourage children to:

- organise, use and evaluate information
- articulate their reasoning
- co-construct knowledge with others (see Chapter 19)
- explore creative and novel ideas.

Questions vary considerably in the intellectual operations they demand of the child and some types of questions are better than others in assisting children's cognitive development. Davis and Tinsley (1986) believed that the following types of questions positively assist the development of a child's higher order thinking skills:

- Interpretative questions require the child to describe the relationships between particular types of information—to interpret how one thing relates to another.

  For example: 'What happened when we added soap to the water?'; 'How did you make the slippery material stay on the paper?'; 'Why did Sally close the windows in the play-room when it rained?'.

- Translation questions require the child to change information from one form to another (for example, visual information in a picture can be changed to a three-dimensional representation of it or to a verbal description). The child needs to translate understandings from one form of representation to another.

  For example: 'Can you draw a picture of your block building?'; 'Can you build a model of the car you just have just painted?'; 'Can you tell me how feeling happy looks?'.

- Application questions require the child to use knowledge and skills to solve a real-life problem. The child has to apply her understandings or skills.

  For example: 'How can we use the blocks to make the bed big enough for Sam?'; 'What other tools could we use to make holes in the paper?'; 'What musical instruments could we use to make a sound like thunder?'.

- Synthesising questions require the child to combine a variety of knowledge and skills in order to wonder about or create a solution to problems they might not have encountered before. Children have to synthesise (combine) what they know to solve a problem.

  For example: 'We have a new child, Jansen, starting at the centre next week who cannot hear very well. How could we make Jansen feel welcome?'; 'How could we make sure that everyone has a fair go at playing with our new water-wheel?'; 'What could we do to invite all the parents to our end-of-year party?'.

- Evaluative questions require the child to make judgements about what should happen, what might work and what could be done differently.

  For example: 'Why do you think the bridge fell down?'; 'How do you know if Sarah's happy with playing in her tent?'; 'What do you think we could do next time to make sure everyone has a piece of pineapple?'; 'Why do you think that we can't dig deep enough to find the treasure?'.

Children are more likely to attend to such questions when they match their level of cognitive competence. When questions are too complex, children lose interest and ignore teachers' requests (Crahay and Delhaxhe 1991).

EXTEND AND ENRICH CHILDREN'S IMAGINATIVE AND SOCIO-DRAMATIC COMPETENCIES

There are many different ways to encourage children's imagination, and questioning is important in several of them. Questions can prompt children to create new storylines for their socio-dramatic play and to practise their own story-telling skills. For example, introducing the children to props such as puppets, dolls or pictures and then inviting them to tell a story based on those props is a simple and effective way to encourage them to develop their imaginations. Soundy and Humadi Genisio (1994, p. 21) believed that once a prop has been introduced, simple follow-up questions would often initiate children's stories:

> . . . the teacher could begin by displaying a skunk puppet and suggesting the class make up a story about another uninvited visitor to the campsite. Two or three follow-up questions could help initiate the story-telling: 'What name shall we give the skunk?', 'What kind of trouble might this skunk create?' and 'What do you think scares a skunk?'.

Questions can also challenge children to imagine beyond what they know and play around with the fantastic. Children can be asked to imagine new words, to create new animals or to think in new ways about everyday events. For example: 'What would a name be for an animal that is part cockatoo and part kangaroo?'; 'How might a rainbow sound?'; 'What might the movement of butterfly wings look like on paper?'; 'What could be a different ending for this story?'; 'What would we call someone who lived on the moon?'.

Questions can encourage children to have fun playing with sounds, movements, words, ideas and events, and can also encourage them to create new ways of thinking about them. Questions can also encourage children to tell their own stories and to build their story-telling skills (Hough et al. 1987).

DEVELOP DISPOSITIONS OF CURIOSITY AND WONDERMENT

Katz (1989) argued that to be curious and full of wonder is the key to successful learning. Questioning is an important process through which staff can convey their own sense of curiosity and wonderment about the world to children and can encourage children to be curious about the world around them. Curiosity and wonderment can be fostered by asking children:

 how to find out more about things that interest them
 how and why things work
 how they can make things happen
 how they can make their thoughts visible to others.

Questions that invite wonder need to invoke a sense of 'paradox or puzzlement, not knowing' (McWilliams 1999, p. 9). Such questions include:

'How does it move?'

➡ Why is this so?

➡ How is this so?

➡ I wonder what would happen if . . . what do you think?

Some examples of questions that children generated when a teacher asked them to wonder about the moon included:

➡ . . . is the moon made of cheese?

➡ . . . if you touch the moon will it move?

➡ . . . is the moon bumpy? (McWilliams 1999, p. 9)

EXTEND CHILDREN'S COMMUNICATION AND LANGUAGE SKILLS

In the first few years of life, children's language and communication skills are building rapidly. Modelling good questioning styles and using questions to build conversational patterns with children of all ages are important to the development of these skills in young children. 'Open' questions that require the children to think carefully can develop more complex language-use in children from three years of age, can encourage them to form sentences and to ask questions of each other and of adults, and can help them to become confident when responding to questions from others (Beaty 1996).

ENCOURAGE CHILDREN TO EMPATHISE WITH OTHER CHILDREN'S FEELINGS

The success of children's learning is influenced by its social and emotional context (Abbott and Rodger 1994). Questioning can be an important technique through which to build positive relationships between peers and thus to develop a supportive and co-operative learning environment. From two to three years of age, children can talk about their relationships with other children (Browne and France 1986). Staff can help them to empathise with others' feelings by asking children to think about the consequences for others of their or somebody else's actions. Questions commonly used in this process include: 'How do you think that made Shona feel?'; 'What could we do to make Gerald feel happier?'; 'How do you feel when someone hurts you? Do you think Marci feels that way too?'. Staff can also use questions to encourage children to think about how to be kind and fair to others. For example: 'What do you think "kindness" means?'; 'How would you know if someone was being fair to you?'; 'Do they think that kindness is a good thing?' (Smith 1982).

Developmental considerations

From an early age, children use questions as an important way to communicate with each other and with adults. Therefore, adults should use questioning to promote learning through dialogue with children. Young children's communicative and cognitive competence clearly influence the nature and type of questions that adults can usefully ask them. As a general guideline, the younger the child, the simpler, more concrete and more focused on the here and now the question should be. For example, asking toddlers about a cat they have just seen is more likely to generate responses than asking them why cats are called cats.

Staff can judge the likely influence of children's developmental competence on the type of questions they ask by observing the questions asked by children of differing ages or stages. Staff can then use this knowledge to 'pitch' their questions at appropriate levels. For example:

- Pre-verbal children ask questions using body language such as pointing or gesturing, or using a particular intonation. Verbalising such questions plays an important role in developing their communicative competence.
- Children under two use single words to ask questions. They can, therefore, understand simple questions adults ask of them.
- Children as young as two use questions to gain information with which to make sense of their world. Often these questions are very concrete about the here and now. Therefore, questions about the here and now are likely to interest children at this age.
- Children between two and five are extremely persistent questioners, one of their favourite questions being 'Why?'. More complex questions about how and why things happen can be introduced at this stage.

Children's age and stage of development provide a guide for the staff's nature and style of questioning, but staff should 'experiment' with asking children of all ages a variety of concrete and abstract questions. Research and experience shows that from a very early age, children are capable of reflecting on and answering quite abstract questions about the past, present and future. Some two-year-olds may be quite fascinated by a question about why cats are called cats, and many four-year-olds need and enjoy questions about the immediate, concrete, here and now. Such questions can often lead children to give quite complex and abstract answers. Staff will not know what questions children can answer until they ask them, as in the following conversation between an adult and a four-year-old child:

'How full is it?'

Adult: 'I've noticed that you are often the only girl playing with the boys. Why is that Chloe?'

   Chloe: 'Well, you see, it's like this. In all the movies, there's only one girl playing with the boys. That's why.'

The 'movies' to which Chloe referred included *Ninja Turtles* and *Ghostbusters*. At four years of age, Chloe had made a very complex and sophisticated observation about sexism within the media and had used this observation to make sense of her own and her peer group's play patterns.

By using language that is more complex than the language stage a child has reached, adults can help the child move to more complex involvement in the use and understanding of language (Bruner 1983; cited in Brewer 1992).

Questions are also an effective way to build the literacy skills of children in their early years of schooling. By about seven years of age children can answer questions about meanings in written and spoken language, and can begin to question the structure of their own written and spoken language (Roop 1990).

Staff can use questions to encourage children in the early years of schooling to reflect on their own language use and to help them understand that they can improve their writing skills through such reflection. Roop (1990, p. 283) suggested questions such as the following are useful to promote such reflection:

Does this sentence make sense? Does this part move the story forward? Is this really the way my character would react . . . Can I shorten this paragraph and say the same thing in a better way?

Children's reading skills can be enhanced through the use of questions. Beck and McKeown (2001, p. 14) described a read-aloud program with children in the early years of school that used two types of questions that can be used to help children construct meaning from texts during reading aloud sessions. They were:

Initial questions. Interspersed open questions require children to describe and explain text ideas, rather than recall and retrieve words from text.

Follow-up questions. Questions scaffold students' thinking by using their initial responses to form questions that encourage elaboration and development of initial ideas.

Questions can also be an important part of building children's metacognitive skills as they make sense of the sense world around them. Staff can alert children to their own ways of thinking through using questions that guide them to 'imagine, think, verbalize and reflect' (Doverborg and Pramling Samuelsson 1999, p. 100).

EQUITY CONSIDERATIONS

'Race' and culture

Most questions require answers and in Anglo-Australian culture there is a strong sense of turn-taking associated with questioning—one person asks a question and then waits for an answer. However, staff in multicultural settings should remember that each culture has its own rules associated with social discourse and turn-taking, and that these can lead to 'different speakers being accused of rudeness, even though they are operating within a set of culturally accepted rules: but they are the rules of another culture' (Partington and McCudden 1992, p. 221). To avoid misunderstandings, it is important for Anglo-Australian staff to familiarise themselves with the patterns of social discourse used by children in their group who have cultural backgrounds different from their own.

Aboriginal children may have learned within their communities that periods of silence in conversations are quite acceptable and they may decide to remain silent or to ignore questions (Colbung and Glover 1996). This does not mean they do not know the answers to the questions posed or are being disrespectful. Silence can also be seen as a polite and non-offensive way of responding to a question when an Aboriginal child believes the answer may offend the questioner (Partington and McCudden 1992). Therefore, non-Aboriginal staff should not rely strongly on questioning to explore the understandings, feelings and imaginings of Aboriginal children.

Silence also plays an important social role in the language interactions of many people from a variety of Asian backgrounds. Lynch and Hanson (1992, p. 233) explained:

On the one hand, maintaining silence in a conversation may serve as an expression of interest and respect. On the other hand, if silence follows consistent verbal responses . . . it may indicate disagreement or negative reactions such as anger . . .

It is, therefore, very important that early childhood staff develop an awareness of and sensitivity to how the children in their care may respond to questions. They should avoid simplistic, stereotyped understandings about how 'Asians', 'Aborigines' or any other group of children respond to questions. There are differences both within and between cultures. Staff can learn about these by drawing on the advice and expertise of staff in relevant advice agencies in their state. Please refer to the Appendix for details.

Early childhood staff also need to reflect carefully on the type of questions they ask children from differing ethnic and racial backgrounds. Brophy and Good (1987; cited in Partington and McCudden 1992) reported that the questioning styles of Anglo-Australian teachers in ethnically diverse classrooms are of some concern. Teachers tended to wait less time for children from ethnic minority backgrounds and children from Aboriginal backgrounds to answer questions, called on these children less to respond to questions, and asked them easier questions. These findings related to older children, but they are an important reminder to staff in early childhood settings to think carefully about how they question children in ethnically and racially diverse groups.

A structured conversation with young children can be an effective tool to gain an understanding of what children do and do not understand about the diversity in the world around them and what their attitudes to 'racial' and ethnic diversity are. To build positive attitudes towards racial and ethnic diversity, questions should help children to restructure their understandings of diversity, rather than just describe what they know (Bernstein et al. 2000). It is also important to allow children's questions to surface during discussions about diversity.

Gender

Boys and girls can respond quite differently to questions that encourage them to solve problems. Often, girls will be more interested in solving scientific and technical problems if they are placed in a social context (Beat 1991). For example, staff could more effectively ask girls to think about how fires are put out if they develop a story about some imaginary people whose house is on fire and then ask the girls how they might put it out.

From as early as two years of age, many boys and many girls begin to decide in traditional, gender-stereotypical ways about where to play, what to play with and how to play with each other, and these choices solidify as the children develop (MacNaughton 1995). Questioning can help children to think about how they might make less gender-stereotyped choices in their play. For example, Epstein (1995) described a discussion circle in which she asked boys to explain why they were excluding girls from block play and asked the girls to explain why they wanted to play in block play. She used this as a basis from which to develop some 'rules' about 'fair' play in the block area.

Leipzig (1992) found that early childhood staff interrupt infants' and toddlers' explorations more frequently if they are girls than if they are boys. Leipzig (1992) suggested that this may make girls feel less able to complete tasks by themselves than boys. As staff question girls about what they are doing, they should think carefully about this and hence, about the timing of their questions. Staff should consider refraining from questioning a girl if this might enable her to complete a task by herself.

Disability and additional needs

When staff question children with additional needs they should take into account individual children's particular developmental levels and abilities, as they do with all children, and adjust their questioning accordingly. In addition, staff may need to specifically modify their questioning techniques to take account of a child's specific disability. For example, as staff speak to children with hearing impairments, they may need to stand face-to-face with them.

Asking children with disabilities if they need and want staff's help to do things is an important way in which staff can show respect for these children (Crary 1992). If children can understand and respond to questions, staff should ask them if they would like help, rather than automatically assuming that they would. Helping the children without asking them first 'tells' them that staff do not believe they are capable of doing things for themselves and that they have no rights to decide for themselves when help is appropriate.

Asking questions that children might have about children with disabilities in the group is an important technique for helping children feel comfortable about diversity (Crary 1992). It provides staff with an avenue through which to clarify children's misconceptions and answer any fears or concerns they may have.

REFLECTING ON QUESTIONING TECHNIQUES

1. Define questioning.
2. What does research suggest are the keys to using questioning to optimise children's learning?
3. When do you think closed questions should be used in your teaching?
4. Are there any times when you think that the use of open questions is inappropriate with young children?
5. 'A questions curriculum empowers both teachers and students' (Wing 1992, p. 81). To what extent do you agree with Wing? Why? Why not?
6. How could questions be used to promote communicative competence with infants? What sort of questions could you use to achieve this aim?
7. What things do you think toddlers would enjoy having questions asked about?
8. What are the most interesting questions you have heard adults ask four-year-old children?
9. What do you know about the role of questions in cultures different to your own?
10. What differences have you noticed in how boys and girls respond to questions?
11. How could you use questions to promote self-esteem for children with disabilities?
12. Imagine you were working with a group of three-year-olds who were visiting a city farm. Try and develop at least two questions that would achieve the following aims:
    - direct attention to a particular issue, event or phenomenon
    - excite interest and curiosity about events, information or feelings
    - help children to reflect on information, feelings or events
    - involve children actively in learning through discussion
    - encourage children to become questioners of themselves, others and their social and natural environment
    - involve children in using a variety of cognitive abilities
    - extend and enrich children's imaginative and socio-dramatic competencies
    - encourage children to develop dispositions of curiosity and wonderment
    - extend children's communication and language skills
    - encourage children to empathise with other children's feelings.
13. Questions that develop higher order thinking skills in young children need to help them interpret, translate, apply, synthesise and evaluate information. Develop a plan for a learning experience for four- to five-year-old children in which you have examples of questions that achieve each of the above aims.
14. Imagine you are working in a mixed group of two- to five-year-old children. One of the five-year-old children has brought their pet turtle to the centre to share with the other children.

Would you use closed or open questions to provoke and enrich the group's interest in the turtle? Write some examples of the questions you might use to assist the development of children's creativity and imagination as they learn about the turtle.

IMPROVING TEACHING IN PRACTICE

1 Record (using a tape-recorder or written notes) the questions you ask children during several half-hour teaching periods.

2 What is your current style of questioning?
- ❯ What balance did you have between open and closed questions?
- ❯ Was your use of open and closed questions appropriate?
- ❯ How repetitive was your questioning?
- ❯ How did children respond to your questioning?
- ❯ Did your questioning encourage children to expand their understandings of the world about them?

3 How and how well did you take account of:
- ❯ developmental considerations?
- ❯ equity and anti-bias considerations of culture, 'race', gender and disability?

4 What are your areas of strength and weakness in using questions to promote children's learning?

5 How can you work to improve your questioning techniques in practice?

Further reading

Briggs, F. and Potter, G. 1995, *Teaching Children in the First Three Years of School*, second edn, Sydney, Longman [refer to pp. 268–73].

Fleer, M. and Cahill, A. 2001, *I Want to Know: Learning About Science*, Watson, ACT, Australian Early Childhood Association [refer to pp. 3–12].

Heausler Adams, N. 1994, Ask, don't tell, Paper presented at the *Annual Conference of the Association for Childhood Education International*, ED 372867.

Paley, V. 1990, *The Boy Who Wanted to be a Helicopter*, Cambridge, MA, Harvard University Press [refer to pp. 151–63].

Wasserman, S. 1991, 'The art of the question', *Childhood Education*, 67(4), pp. 257–9.

Wing, L. 1992, 'The interesting questions approach to learning', *Childhood Education*, 69(2), pp. 78–85.

Video

Anti-Bias Curriculum, Pacific Oaks College, Extension Services, 714 West California Bvd, Pasadena, California, USA.

Getting in Tune: Creating Nurturing Relationships with Infants and Toddlers, California Department of Education, Child Care Video Magazine, 1990.

Growing minds, Detroit Educational Television Foundation, 1997.

Respectfully Yours: Identifying Quality Child Care for Infants and Toddlers, Roger Neugebauer Publications, Child Care Information Exchange, 1988.

CD-ROM

Equity Adventures in Early Childhood, MacNaughton, G., Campbell, S., Smith, K. and Lawrence, H. 2002, Centre for Equity and Innovation in Early Childhood, University of Melbourne, Australia, [Strand on stories].

Websites—extending learning online

http://www.edfac.unimelb.edu.au/LED/CEIEC/

References

Abbott, L. and Rodger, R. 1994, *Quality Education in the Early Years*, Milton Keynes, Open University Press.

Allen, R. (ed.) 1990, *The Concise Oxford Dictionary of Current English*, Oxford, Clarendon Press.

Beat, K. 1991, 'Design it, build it, use it: girls and construction kits', in N. Browne, ed., *Science and Technology in the Early Years* (pp. 77–90), Milton Keynes, Open University Press.

Beaty, J. 1996, *Skills for Preschool Teachers*, fifth edn, New Jersey, Prentice Hall Inc.

Beck, I. and McKeown, M. 2001, Text talk: capturing the benefits of read-aloud experiences for young children, *The Reading Teacher*, 55(1), pp. 10–20.

Bernstein, J., Schindler Zimmerman, T., Werner-Wilson, R. and Vosburg, J. 2000, 'Preschool children's classification skills and a multicultural education intervention to promote acceptance of cultural diversity', *Journal of Research in Childhood Education*, 14(2), pp. 181–92.

Brewer, J. 1992, *Introduction to Early Childhood Education: Preschool through Primary Grades*, Boston, Allyn and Bacon.

Briggs, F. and Potter, G. 1995, *Teaching Children in the First Three Years of School*, second edn, Sydney, Longman.

Browne, N. and France, P. 1986, *Untying the Apron Strings: Anti-sexist Provision for the Under Fives*, Milton Keynes, Open University Press.

Cazden, C. 1986, 'Classroom Discourse', in M. Wittrock, ed., *Handbook of Research on Teaching* (pp. 432–63), London, Macmillan.

Colbung, M. and Glover, A. 1996, 'In partnership with Aboriginal children', in M. Fleer, ed., *Conversations about Teaching and Learning in Early Childhood Settings* (pp. 33–40), Canberra, Australian Early Childhood Association.

Crahay, M. and Delhaxhe, A. 1991, 'How do preschool teachers' requests influence children's behaviours', *Teaching and Teacher Education*, 7(3), pp. 221–39.

Crary, E. 1992, 'Talking about differences children notice', in B. Neugebauer, ed., *Alike and Different: Exploring our Humanity with Young Children* (pp. 11–15), Washington, National Association for the Education of Young Children.

Davis, O. and Tinsley, D. 1986, 'Cognitive objectives revealed by classroom questions asked by social studies student teachers', in M. Hammersley, ed., *Case Studies in Classroom Research* (pp. 63–9), Milton Keynes, Open University Press.

Doverborg, E. and Pramling Samuelsson, I. 1999, 'Apple cutting and creativity as a mathematical beginning', *Kindergarten Education: Theory, Research and Practice*, 4(2), pp. 87–103.

Epstein, D. 1995, 'Girls don't do bricks', in J. and I. Siraj-Blatchford, eds, *Educating the Whole Child: Cross-curricula Skills, Themes and Dimensions* (pp. 56–69), Milton Keynes, Open University Press.

Hildebrand, V. 1991, *Introduction to Early Childhood Education*, 5th edn, New York, Macmillan Publishing Company.

Hogg, A. and Foster, J. 1973, *Understanding Teaching Procedures*, Sydney, Cassell Australia.

Hough, R., Nurss, J. and Wood, D. 1987, 'Tell me a story: making opportunities for elaborated language in early childhood classrooms', *Young Children*, November, pp. 6–12.

Hughes, A. and Hughes, E. 1937, *Learning and Teaching: An Introduction to Psychology and Education*, London, Longmans.

Katz, L. 1989, 'Children as learners: a developmental approach', in *Weaving Webs: A Collaborative Approach to Teaching and Learning in the Early Childhood Curriculum*, Melbourne, Australia, 11–13 July.

Klein, E. R., Hammrich, P., Bloom, S. and Ragins, A. 2000, Language development and science inquiry: a child-initiated and teacher-facilitated program, Paper presented at the *Annual Meeting of the American Education Research Association*, New Orleans, April, ED 440756.

Laishley, J. 1983, *Working with Young Children: Encouraging their Development and Dealing with Problems*, London, Edward Arnold.

Leipzig, J. 1992, 'Helping whole children grow: non-sexist childrearing for infants and toddlers', in B. Neugebauer, ed., *Alike and Different: Exploring our Humanity with Young Children* (pp. 32–41), Washington, National Association for the Education of Young Children.

Lynch, E. and Hanson, M. 1992, *Developing Cross-Cultural Competence*, Baltimore, Paul H. Brookes.

MacNaughton, G. 1995, 'The Gender Factor', in B. Creaser and E. Dau, eds, *The Anti-bias Approach in Early Childhood* (pp. 51–70), Sydney, Harper Educational.

Makin, L. 1996, 'Play and language profiles and scales', in M. Fleer, ed., *Play through the profiles: Profiles through play* (pp. 68–84), Watson, ACT, Australian Early Childhood Association.

McAllister, E. 1990, 'Anatomy of a crushed spirit', *Childhood Education*, 66(4), pp. 204–5.

McWilliams, S. 1999, Fostering wonder in young children, Paper presented at the *Annual Meeting of the National Association for Research in Science Teaching*, Boston, MA, March 28–31, ED 444833.

Partington, G. and McCudden, V. 1992, *Ethnicity and Education*, Sydney, Social Science Press.

Roop, P. 1990, 'The magic of writing: how a writer teaches writing', *Childhood Education*, 66(5), pp. 281–4.

Seefeldt. C. 1980, *Teaching Young Children*, New York, Prentice Hall.

Smith, C. 1982, *Promoting the Social Development of Young Children*, Kansas, Mayfield Publishing Company.

Sook Lim, Y. and Cole, K. 2002, 'Facilitating first language development in Korean children through parent training in picture book interactions', *Bilingual Research Journal*, 26(2), pp. 213–227.

Soundy, C. and Humadi Genisio, M. 1994, 'Asking young children to tell the story', *Childhood Education*, 71(1), pp. 20–3.

Stone, S. 1996, 'Promoting literacy through centers', *Childhood Education*, 72(4), pp. 240–1.

Tizard, B. and Hughes, M. 1984, *Young Children Learning: Talking and Thinking at Home and at School*, London, Fontana.

Turney, C. 1985, *Anatomy of Teaching*, Sydney, Novak Publishing.

Wilkes, G. (ed.) 1979, *Collins Dictionary of the English Language*, Middlesex, Penguin Books.

Wing, L. 1992, 'The interesting questions approach to learning', *Childhood Education*, 69(2), pp. 78–85.

Chapter 14

Reading

Read: to comprehend the meaning of (something written or printed) by looking at and interpreting the written or printed characters.

(*Collins Dictionary of the English Language*, p. 1215)

Reading is an act of thinking and understanding, and learning to read is a constructive problem-solving process.

(Spodek and Saracho 1994, p. 337)

When we read to . . . [children] . . . we expose them to the beauty of the literary language and a wider variety of language forms than they hear in other situations.

(Robison and Schwartz 1982, p. 245)

WHAT?

Reading is the recognition and interpretation of the meaning(s) of a printed word or symbol and of groups of words or symbols. Reading is about making meaning(s) from print. When we read a road sign we recognise the word or symbol on the sign and then try to interpret its meaning(s). When we read books we recognise groups of printed words and images in the book and then try to interpret their meaning(s). We need to read for many reasons. Reading enables us to do diverse things, such as follow signs, find out a person's name, order food in a restaurant, pass exams and experience stories. We read to gain information and for enjoyment. Reading to someone involves us speaking the written word, the other person hearing the sounds we make and then interpreting them. Therefore, as we read or are read to, we are involved in a process of constructing meaning from printed words or symbols.

As a teaching technique, reading to or with children is used to help them to construct meanings about the world around them. For the purposes of this chapter we will focus on reading for enjoyment. Reading books and stories is one of the most common ways in which early childhood staff read to or with children, because it is often a very pleasurable experience for those involved.

The story method of reading is really a form of word and picture play and is an immediately pleasurable activity for children and adults alike (Moyles 1989, p. 52).

This chapter will focus on how reading to or with children can support their learning.

HOW?

There are strong opinions in the early childhood field about the best way to read books to or with young children. Staff will need to develop their own list of dos and don'ts, but the following suggestions can provide a starting point for reflecting on how best to share books with children. Read et al. (1993) argue that when choosing books to share with children, staff should ensure that the books:

 are in good repair. There should be no torn or missing pages and the covers should be intact. This helps children to respect and care for books

 match the children's interests

 do not frighten the children

 are read to children in a clear voice and are read in ways that enable the children to readily see any pictures related to the words being read.

Nasta reads with the children.

When staff read to children they should think about the children's comfort. Children concentrate best when they are comfortable. They may be comfortable sitting on an adult's knee, cuddling up by someone in a big, soft chair or resting against large, soft floor cushions. Choosing a relaxed and comfortable environment for reading will help both adults and children to feel more relaxed and comfortable.

> Sandy, a Grade 2 teacher, regularly takes the children outside to read under the large gum tree in the yard. They take a rug from the classroom so that they can be comfortable. The children sit and lie on the rug as they become engrossed in the stories which Sandy reads.

When staff show enthusiasm for reading and enjoyment in using books for fun and learning, children will develop a love of books and reading. When thinking about how children can get the most from being read to, staff may find that the following research findings act as useful pointers:

- Speaking clearly and stressing important words helps children to learn their meaning (Moyles 1989).
- Re-reading stories which children enjoy helps them to revisit new words and ideas and to learn their meaning (Moyles 1989). It also helps children with early literacy skills as they '. . . acquire an understanding of the functions of print, of how print is used, and of what people are doing when they are reading' (Spodek and Saracho 1994, p. 352).
- Allowing children opportunities to ask questions about what is being read to them and hearing answers helps children's understandings and knowledge to grow (Soundy 1993). It can also help children to develop critical thinking skills (Lehr 1990).
- Engaging in conversation with the children about the story encourages them to share their own observations about it and to develop their own interpretations. This can increase children's interest in a story and their understanding of narrative, particularly if they have not been read to prior to arrival in an early childhood program (Dombey 1994).
- Retelling stories with props can increase children's understandings of words, plots and characters (Soundy 1993).

WHEN AND WHY?

Goal relevance

Reading can enhance children's learning in many ways. It is particularly helpful in achieving the following goals:

- Developing a sense of wonder in children. Children's sense of wonderment in the world is encouraged when adults read stories to them with enthusiasm and excitement (Haiman 1991).
- Developing children's language skills. Reading stories to children can help them to learn the meanings of words as they hear words being used in a variety of ways (Moyles 1989; Sook Lim and Cole 2002). Stories about feelings, thoughts and values help children develop meta-cognitive language, that is, language through which they can talk about what they know, how they think and what they remember. Fairy stories seem to be particularly rich in ideas that develop meta-cognitive language (Hinchcliffe 1996).
- Supporting children's early literacy development by reading stories to children and reading with children using a variety of print materials (for example, books, newspapers and signs). Children who have been read to early in their life learn to read at an early age (McCarthy 1995).
- Increasing children's understanding of narrative forms. Reading stories to children can help them to understand that experiences have beginnings, middles and endings (a narrative form). This helps children to recall key ideas and events in stories and in their own lives (Lehr 1990; Beck and McKeown 2002).
- Building children's early mathematical vocabulary and concepts such as size, shape and length. Reading to children stories about size or shape can help them to learn mathematical

language and reinforce concepts being explored through other more concrete experiences. However, Hawthorne (1992, p. 8) cautioned that the '. . . mathematical focus should emerge naturally from the book, not be imposed upon it'.

- Stimulating children's thinking and concept development. Reading to children stories that are humorous and that use '. . . exaggeration and physical incongruity' (Klein 1992, p. 215) helps children to think about everyday events and concepts.

- Reducing children's stress and distress. Reading to children stories about the events and experiences that cause stress in their daily lives, such as nightmares and separating from their parents, can help children to cope with these events. If the stories are humorous, the laughter they generate helps the children to relax (Klein 1992).

Developmental considerations

Once babies are able to sit on an adult's lap, they will enjoy looking at simple picture books and listening to staff reading to them (Department of Human Services 1996). This experience helps babies to associate sound symbols (words) with images. The ability to use symbols such as words to think and to understand is an important part of becoming competent at using language. Reading to babies also helps a sense of sharing and closeness to develop between the baby and the adult. It provides an opportunity for one-to-one communication and a time to enjoy each other's company.

> In the corner of the babies' room is a large arm chair in which the staff can sit comfortably holding the children as they look at books. Each day, time is set aside for this to happen. The staff enjoy this quiet time with the babies and use it as an opportunity to relax with them.

Toddlers have an amazing interest in themselves and in the everyday objects in their world. They can become fascinated by a new spoon as readily as by their reflection in a mirror. Consequently, they are most likely to be interested in stories about toddlers and the everyday events and objects that they are exploring. Toddlers face lots of challenges in learning to walk, dress, run, eat and toilet, and they like humorous stories based on these experiences. As Klein (1992, p. 214) suggested:

> Laughing at the character's funny mistakes, children feel a sense of accomplishment because they are able to do these simple tasks.

Nichols and Sears (1987) suggested that stories to be read to toddlers should:

- have simple plots
- be based on events and experiences with which the toddlers are familiar
- have a small number of characters
- have some repetition in what the characters do or say
- be read enthusiastically by the adult.

Even taking these factors into account cannot guarantee a toddler's interest in a story or book, as toddlers have an 'unpredictable attention span' (Stonehouse 1988, p. 8). Sometimes they will be happy to read the same story repeatedly for long periods of time. Sometimes they will lose interest in a story that has been a favourite. Sometimes they will want to listen to stories being read and sometimes they won't. Reading to toddlers in small, informal groups allows individual toddlers to come, stay and go as their interest dictates, and creates story times which both children and staff find relaxed and enjoyable.

Babies and toddlers need stories read to them that:

 help them to acquire their first language (Cook and Porter 1996)

 have positive images of people from different cultural and racial backgrounds involved in everyday tasks (Cook and Porter 1996).

Preschool children can make connections between the stories they hear, real-life events and their own personal lives. This happens most when they identify with the central character in a story (Lehr 1990). Staff can use this ability to help teach children specific ideas and concepts:

. . . when one of the children . . . heard a story about a lost giraffe, the mother used the story as an opportunity to underscore the value of not wandering off. The child responded by recalling a time that he had gotten lost (Lehr 1990 p. 39).

Preschool children's emergent literacy skills can also be supported through staff reading other forms of print to them. These forms can include lists of favourite toys or songs, labels on toys, signs around the centre, and stories that the children tell (Sumison 1991). Reading each form of print to children helps them to associate meaning with printed words and symbols, and helps them to learn that reading can be used for many purposes. An environment which features a rich variety of forms of print and in which adults explain the meanings within the print will help children to 'learn a great deal about the processes involved in reading and writing' (Sumison 1991, p. 16). Such indirect teaching supports children's own reading skills much more effectively than direct reading tuition (Willert and Kamii 1985).

Reading to preschool children who are bilingual strongly supports their development of oral language, increasing how long they speak for, how often they speak and the range of words they use when they speak (Sook Lim and Cole 2002).

In the early years of schooling, children are developing the ability to write about their own lives for themselves. Reading stories to children that are personally meaningful helps support and sustain their interest in their own writing (Quintero and Rummel 1996). Stories about things they do in their local community, places they visit outside their community and the daily events that make up their lives in school are all a good source of inspiration for the children's own writing. Through having such stories read to them they learn that people's daily lives, including their own, are worthy of writing about. In using story-reading to support young children's language comprehension and vocabulary development it is important that 'a teacher intersperses reading with open questions and discussion, and follows each story with explicit attention to vocabulary' (Beck and McKeown 2001, p. 18). Beck and McKeown discuss the need for teachers to focus, monitor and scaffold children's language learning during story-reading sessions.

Shared reading activities can also help develop young children's oral language skills and other emergent literacy skills such as listening comprehension and the development of vocabulary. For instance, a study of ninety-five children from low-income families considered to be at risk showed that nineteen 10–15 minute sessions of shared reading activities significantly increased oral language and emergent literacy skills for these children (Lonigan et al. 1999).

Beck and McKeown (2001) detailed the criteria they used to choose books that supported children's capacity to construct meaning in the early years of school. Such books needed to:

Kim and the children enjoy a story.

- ❯ be intellectually challenging in that they required children to explore ideas and to use language to explain the ideas that were in the text
- ❯ be more reliant on language than image to convey meaning
- ❯ have a structure that was event based.

EQUITY CONSIDERATIONS

As mentioned above, preschool children most readily connect the stories they hear with real-life events and their own personal lives when they identify with the central character in a story (Lehr 1990). Children identify with characters who are like themselves, characters who share their lifestyle, their cultural and racial background, their gender and their ability levels. For this reason, it is very important that staff read to children stories that represent who the children are in all their diversity. Stories should present them with a diverse range of characters from a diverse range of backgrounds who are powerful and competent and who feel like 'real' people.

Some specific points to consider when choosing stories to reflect children's racial, cultural, gender and ability interests are detailed below.

'Race' and culture

When choosing a book with which to challenge traditional racial and cultural stereotypes, staff need to be alert to the following elements:

- ❯ Physical features. Are the skin tones and facial features of people from black and ethnic minority backgrounds portrayed accurately? Are colours lifelike or are black people a grey colour? Do black and ethnic minority people look like white people that have been coloured in as an afterthought? Do black and ethnic minority characters appear identical in appearance, with one variety of hair, skin tone and similar facial features?

➲ Setting. Are black and ethnic minority characters shown in a variety of settings? Books in which black and ethnic minority characters are mainly in less affluent settings reinforce the idea that all black and ethnic minority people are poor and to be pitied. In Australia, it is especially important to show Aboriginal people in a variety of rural and urban settings. Books in which Aboriginal people appear only in tribal, rural settings reinforce the stereotype that all Aborigines still live traditional lifestyles. Are the stories set in Australia? It is important that children from black and ethnic minority backgrounds have stories about their own lives and lifestyles here in Australia.

➲ Characters. Are all the characters in the book decision-making and self-respecting? Do black and ethnic minority characters have the power to decide what happens to them and others? Do black and ethnic minority characters get involved in a wide variety of tasks and activities, including everyday tasks? Books in which black and ethnic minority characters are mainly involved in special celebrations or events reinforce the idea that their lifestyle is different and exotic.

➲ Language. Is the language respectful of all groups of people? Is offensive language avoided? Is dialect used in ways which demean or caricature a character?

➲ Storylines. Are there storylines in which black and ethnic minority children can identify with self-confident characters who have interesting and exciting adventures? Are there storylines in which black and ethnic minority children can identify with characters who are caring and who desire to co-operate with other people? Do the storylines reinforce feelings of superiority which white children may have? Do storylines show black and white people working and living together co-operatively?

Gender

When choosing a book with which to challenge traditional gender-role stereotypes, staff need to be alert to the following elements:

➲ Clothing. Do women, girls, men and boys wear lots of different sorts of clothes? Books in which women appear dressed in pretty, frilly, pink dresses reinforce the idea that women's and girls' clothing should always be feminine rather than functional and that women's and girls' clothing is for looking good in, rather than for doing active things in. Books in which men are always dressed in sombre colours and work clothes reinforce the ideas that men's and boys' clothing should always be functional.

➲ Setting. Do women, girls, men and boys appear in a variety of settings? Books in which women and girls appear mainly in indoor, domestic settings reinforce the idea that this is their main area of responsibility and competence. Books in which men and boys appear mainly in outdoor, adventure and work settings reinforce the idea that this is their main area of responsibility and competence.

➲ Characters. Are all the characters in the book decision-making and self-respecting? Do women and girls have the power to decide what happens to themselves and others? Are women, girls, men and boys involved in a wide variety of tasks and activities? Books in which women and girls are shown mainly involved in indoor domestic tasks reinforce the idea that this is their main area of responsibility and competence. Books in which men and boys are mainly involved in outdoor, adventure and work tasks reinforce the idea that this is their main area of responsibility and competence.

➜ Language. Is gender-inclusive language used to describe objects, animals and jobs? Books in which all objects and animals are described by the male pronouns (he and him) reinforce the idea that the male is the most important gender in our society. Books in which only the cute, soft, cuddly, silly or gentle objects and animals are described by the female pronouns (she and her) reinforce the idea that the female is the more vulnerable and less serious gender in our society. Books in which all occupations are described by the male gender, such as 'policeman' or 'postman' reinforce the idea that these jobs are best done and only done by men.

➜ Storylines. Are there storylines in which girls can identify with self-confident characters who have interesting and exciting adventures? Are there storylines in which boys can identify with characters who are caring and who have a desire to co-operate with other people?

Choosing the right book is only half the battle. Davies (1989) showed that boys and girls will often resist storylines that challenge their own gender stereotypes and can read non-traditional storylines in very traditional ways. Staff need to deconstruct (see Chapter 21) children's gender role stereotypes as part of the process of reading stories to and with them.

Disability and additional needs

Books offer lots of opportunities to present positive images and ideas about the interests and abilities of children with disabilities. Books convey very powerful messages about people and about the ways in which they are or aren't valued. Staff working within an anti-discriminatory approach to disability should read children stories in which the heroine has a disability and in which a disability is not presented as an overwhelming handicap. Staff should avoid books containing negative messages about disabilities. Several children's books contain powerful negative images of people with disabilities and present people with disabilities as naughty or frightening, for example, the nasty one-handed pirate, Captain Hook. The following checklist can help early childhood practitioners to use an anti-discriminatory perspective to critically evaluate the disability content of books:

➜ Faces. Are people with disabilities portrayed in ways that show they have lots of different emotions? Books in which people with disabilities are portrayed in ways which invoke sadness or pity reinforce the idea that people with disabilities should be pitied.

➜ Setting. Do people with disabilities appear in a variety of settings and surroundings? Books in which they appear mainly in settings reflecting able-bodied people's needs reinforce the view that people with disabilities don't require special adaptations to be made to their environment. Books in which people with disabilities are in a variety of indoor, outdoor, adventure and work situations reinforce the idea that they can be independent and competent in a variety of settings.

➜ Characters. Are all the characters with disabilities in the book decision-making and self-respecting? Do people with disabilities have the power to decide what happens to them and others? Do people with disabilities get involved in a wide variety of tasks and activities? Books in which people with disabilities are shown as passive and mainly dependent on able-bodied people reinforce the idea that people with disabilities cannot do things for themselves. Do people with disabilities have distinct characters or are they portrayed just in terms of their disability?

❍ Language. Is the disability of a character accurately described? Are the characters presented through stereotypical images? Are there value-laden terms such as 'Stand on your own two feet' and 'As blind as a bat'?

❍ Storylines. Are there storylines in which children with disabilities can identify with self-confident characters who have interesting and exciting adventures? Are children with disabilities the heroes and heroines? Are there storylines in which children with disabilities can identify with characters who are caring and who have a desire to co-operate with other people? What does the storyline say about relations between people with disabilities and people without disabilities?

REFLECTING ON READING TECHNIQUES

1   Briefly define reading.
2   Find three books that you could read to toddlers to support their exploration of the natural world around them.
3   Find four books that you could read to preschoolers to support their mathematical learning in relation to classifying and comparing size, shape and number.
4   Review three humorous books written for very young children. To what extent do you think they would help stimulate children's thinking about the world about them? In what ways could they do this?
5   Collect your five favourite books for young children. Use the equity and anti-bias checklists above to review the books. How and how well did your favourite books support equity and diversity considerations?
6   Watch a story-reading session on a children's television program. How and how well did the presenter use voice to interest children in the story?
7   Observe an early childhood staff member reading a book to a group of children. How and how well did the staff member:

❍   stress clearly important words?
❍   allow children opportunities to ask questions about what was being read to them?
❍   engage in conversation with the children about the story?

8   Observe a group of toddlers listening to a story being read. Did the story:

❍   have a simple storyline that drew on everyday events and experiences that were of interest to them?
❍   have one or two key characters that helped toddlers remain focused on the main events within the story?
❍   have characters that used repetitive actions or words that helped toddlers predict outcomes and follow the main storyline?

IMPROVING TEACHING IN PRACTICE

1   Record (using a tape-recorder or written notes) yourself reading a story to a small group of preschool children, a baby and a toddler.

2 How and how well did you:
- ➋ choose a developmentally appropriate story?
- ➋ use your voice to gain children's interest and attention?
- ➋ acknowledge children's questions about the story?
- ➋ talk with the children about the story?

3 What are your strengths and weaknesses in reading to young children?

4 How can you improve your reading techniques?

Further reading

Beck, I. and McKeown, M. 2001, 'Text talk: capturing the benefits of read-aloud experiences for young children', *The Reading Teacher*, 55(1), pp. 10–20.

Beck, J. and McKeown, M. 2002. *Bringing words to life: robust vocabulary instruction*, New York, Guilford Press.

Conlin, A. 1992, 'Giving Mrs. Jones a hand: making group storytime more pleasurable and meaningful for young children', *Young Children*, 47(3), pp. 14–18.

Klein, A. 1992, 'Storybook humor and early development', *Childhood Education*, 68(4), pp. 213–17.

Matthews, S. 1993, 'Growing readers: what to look for in children's books', *Australian Early Childhood Association Resource Book Series*, (1), pp. 1–16.

Nichols, J. and Sears, L. 1987, *Storytimes for Two-Year-Olds*, Chicago and London, American Library Association.

Read, K., Gardner, P. and Mahler, B. 1993, *Early Childhood Programs: Human Relationships and Learning*, ninth edn, Forth Worth, TX, Holt, Rinehart and Winston Inc. [refer to pp. 318–24].

Soundy, C. 1993, 'Let the story begin! Open the box and set out the props', *Childhood Education*, 69(3), pp. 146–9.

The Australian journal *Every Child* and the USA journal *Childhood Education* each have a regular section which describes and reviews books for young children. They are an excellent resource for ideas about appropriate books to read to and with young children.

Video

Building Early Literacy Competencies in Early Childhood, Educational Media, Australia, 2000.

Teacher strategies and assessment, produced by General Learning video for Magna Systems, 2001.

References

Cook, C. and Porter, C. 1996, *Babies and Toddlers: Considering Multicultural Perspectives*, Melbourne, FKA Multicultural Resource Centre.

Davies, B. 1989, *Frogs and Snails and Feminist Tales: Preschool Children and Gender*, Sydney, Allen & Unwin.

Department of Human Services (DHS) 1996, *Babies, Toddlers and Two Year Olds: A Curriculum Resource for Developing Child-Centred Programs for Children Under Three*, Melbourne, Government of Victoria.

Dombey, H. 1994, 'Narrative in the nursery class', *International Journal of Early Years Education*, 2(3), pp. 38–53.

Haiman, P. 1991, 'Developing a sense of wonder in children', *Young Children*, 46(6), pp. 52–3.

Hawthorne, W. 1992, 'Young children and mathematics', *Australian Early Childhood Resource Booklets* (1).

Hinchcliffe, V. 1996, 'Fairy stories and children's developing theories of the mind', *International Journal of Early Years Education*, 4(1), pp. 35–46.

Klein, A. 1992, 'Storybook humor and early development', *Childhood Education*, 68(4), pp. 213–17.

Lehr, S. 1990, 'Literature and the construction of meaning: the preschool child's developing sense of theme', *Journal of Research in Childhood Education*, 5(1), pp. 37–46.

Lonigan, C., Anthony, J., Bloomfield, C., Dyer, S. and Samwel, C. 1999, 'Effects of two shared reading interventions on emergent literacy skills of at-risk preschoolers', *Journal of Early Intervention*, 22(4), pp. 306–22.

McCarthy, R. 1995, 'The importance of storybook reading to emergent literacy: a review of the research', *ED396235*.

Moyles, J. 1989, *Just Playing: The Role and Status of Play in Early Childhood Education*, Milton Keynes, Open University Press.

Nichols, J. and Sears, L. 1987, *Storytimes for Two-Year-Olds*, Chicago and London, American Library Association.

Quintero, E. and Rummel, M. 1996, 'Something to say: voice in the classroom', *Childhood Education*, 72(3), pp. 146–51.

Read, K., Gardner, P. and Mahler, B. 1993, *Early Childhood Programs: Human Relationships and Learning*, ninth edn, Forth Worth, TX, Holt, Rinehart and Winston Inc.

Robison, H. and Schwartz, S. 1982, *Designing Curriculum for Early Childhood*, Boston, Allyn and Bacon Inc.

Sook Lim, Y. and Cole, K. 2002, 'Facilitating first language development in young Korean children through parent training in picture book interactions', *Bilingual Research Journal*, 26(2), pp. 213–27.

Soundy, C. 1993, 'Let the story begin! Open the box and set out the props', *Childhood Education*, 69(3), pp. 146–9.

Spodek, B. and Saracho, O. 1994, *Right from the Start: Teaching Children Ages Three to Eight*, Boston, Allyn and Bacon.

Stonehouse, A. 1988, 'Characteristics of toddlers', in A. Stonehouse, ed., *Trusting Toddlers: Programming for One to Three Year Olds in Child Care Centres* (pp. 1–13), Watson, ACT, Australian Early Childhood Association.

Sumison, J. 1991, 'Playing with print', *Australian Early Childhood Association Resource Book Series* (4), pp. 1–16.

Wilkes, G. (ed.) 1979, *Collins Dictionary of the English Language*, Middlesex, Penguin Books.

Willert, M. and Kamii, C. 1985, 'Reading in kindergarten: direct vs indirect teaching', *Young Children* May, pp. 3–8.

Chapter 15

Recalling

Recall: to bring back, to recollect, to remember.

(*Collins Dictionary of the English Language*, p. 1218)

Remember: to become aware of something (forgotten), to bring back to one's consciousness, to recall.

(*Collins Dictionary of the English Language*, p. 1234)

Recalling and remembering involve making associations. Children enjoy recalling what they did once or what they saw when they were on a walk or a trip.

(Read et al. 1993, p. 305)

Purpose is a most important factor in determining what we recall.

(Hughes and Hughes 1937, p. 164)

WHAT?

To recall something is to recollect or to remember it. We can recall sights, sounds, images, texts, people, fragrances and textures. The ability to recall something relies on our ability to bring things back into our memory that we have known or experienced in the past. We cannot recall things that we have not known or experienced or that we have not remembered. For example, we can only recall the fragrance of a rose if we have had the experience of smelling a rose and have remembered the fragrance we smelled. Hence, experience and memory are each critical to our ability to recall.

The ability to recall is critical to many facets of learning; we can only effectively learn spoken language if we can accurately recall which words are used to describe which objects. To know that the word 'dog' is associated with a particular animal requires the ability to recall the word and associate it with the animal. Learning language involves constantly recalling such associations. Similarly, the ability to recall is central to the ability to solve problems. If a child wants to build a block building that looks like the fire station near his home, then part of solving the problem of how to do this will involve the child recalling what the fire station looks like.

Grade 1 children are recalling their visit to a supermarket. Their teacher asks each one to recall what they saw there. For example, the number of aisles, the position of the checkout counters and how the food was presented.

HOW?

Several factors influence children's ability to recall things, including:

➲ the relevance of what is being recalled to their own goals. Children are more likely to recall something if it is relevant to what they are doing or what they want to do (Arthur et al. 1996)

➲ their level of interest in what is being recalled. Children are more likely to recall something to which they have paid close attention (Arthur et al. 1996)

➲ their feelings about what is being recalled. Children are more likely to recall something that they enjoyed (Read et al. 1993)

➲ their attention to what is being recalled. Children are more likely to recall something which they paid close attention to when first experiencing it. Memory games and sorting-and-matching games are good ways to develop children's skills in noticing detail:

The teacher may introduce games that depend on paying attention and remembering, such as a game where the child first looks carefully at objects placed in front of her, then closes her eyes while one of these are removed and, when she looks again, tries to remember the missing object (Read et al. 1993).

➲ their capacity to put their ideas into words or images. Like adults, children cannot always find the right words or images to express their ideas and memories (Moyles 1989). The fact that a child cannot verbally or pictorially recall an event or an idea does not necessarily mean that they do not have an accurate mental picture of it

➲ their level of familiarity with what is being recalled. The more concrete and familiar the experience the more likely it is that children will recall it with ease and interest (Denham 1991)

➲ the time between the original experience, event or person being recalled and its recollection

➲ an adult's involvement in their play. Children are more likely to recall what they did in their play when an adult is involved as a 'parallel player' (Moyles 1989, p. 141).

Staff need to be alert to the influence which each of these factors can have on children's ability to recall. Children's success in recalling will be maximised if they are asked to recall in the following circumstances:

➲ When it will help them to meet their own goals. For example, if children want to reproduce something they have done before, such as building a cubby house, the staff member might say, 'Remember the cubby you built last week under the climbing frame. You used the blankets and the corrugated fibreglass sheet for the roof.'

➲ When they have a high level of interest in what they are being asked to recall. For example, if a child was very interested in a current project, such as dinosaurs, they will probably recall details of each different dinosaur.

➲ When they enjoyed what they are being asked to recall. For example, if they have enjoyed an excursion to the zoo, they will probably recall each animal they saw there.

➔ When they can remember what they are being asked to recall. For example, a staff member may invite toddlers to recall what they played with outside the previous day.

➔ When they are reasonably familiar with what they are being asked to recall. For example, a staff member may ask a group of three-year-olds, 'What do we do after pack-up time?', knowing that the children are familiar enough with the routines to be able to answer correctly.

➔ When what they are being asked to recall occurred relatively recently. For example, a staff member who is helping a four-year-old child to use a complicated construction toy might ask, 'How did you get the other one to stay in? That's right—you twisted it.'

Children's ability to recall can also be enhanced by staff talking about the process of recalling.

By talking about how we remember, what helps to remind us, and how often we forget, children's awareness of memory strategies can be increased (Arthur et al. 1996, p. 89).

Other techniques staff can use to help children practise their verbal recall skills include rehearsing information with children, playing memory games and sorting-and-matching games, and elaborating on what is to be recalled through singing songs or telling a story about it (Arthur et al. 1996). Children can be encouraged to practise their non-verbal recall skills through making pictures, posters and models of events and experiences that are meaningful to them. For example, after an excursion to the zoo, staff could sing songs about the animals and make a poster of them to help the children remember them.

Questions which are 'open' and process-oriented (see Chapter 13) can effectively encourage children's recall (Schwartz 1996). Some examples of such questions are:

➔ 'What happened when you tried that?'
➔ 'How did that happen?'
➔ 'What do you remember about . . . ?'
➔ 'How did that work?'

Using Bloom's taxonomy of thinking, researchers (Klein et al. 2000) exploring children's scientific literacy skills in the early years of schooling used the following questions to invite children to recall specific science demonstrations in the classroom. They offer some simple starters for engaging children in recall. They were:

➔ Tell what—for example, what happened when we . . . ?
➔ Tell when—for example, when did X happen?
➔ Tell where—for example, where were you when it happened?
➔ Tell who or whose—whose actions made it happen?
➔ Tell which—which X made it happen?
➔ Tell how—how did it happen?
➔ Tell how many—how many times did it happen?

WHEN AND WHY?

Goal relevance

Children's ability to recall is associated with their abilities to remember and to attend. Their ability to recall helps them to solve problems (Read et al. 1993) and is central to their ability to process information (Arthur et al. 1996). Specifically, asking children to recall things can help them to:

Kylie writes on Sam's painting as he recalls the excursion.

- ➔ reinforce their ideas, concepts and knowledge
- ➔ review their own learning
- ➔ express their understandings
- ➔ practise sharing ideas and information with other people
- ➔ document their work. Recollection is an important part of the process of developing, running and documenting projects based on the Reggio Emilia multi-symbolic approach to children's learning. Forman et al. (1994, p. 235) explained the role of recollection in the 'City in the Snow' project at the Marks Meadow Elementary School in Massachusetts, New England:

> Children discuss the recollections of snow, how it changes the playground, how it affects walking, what you can do in the snow, and how the city handles huge quantities of snow . . .

> From this discussion, children developed some initial drawings of snow scenes, simulated a snowfall and eventually moved to a point of drawing clouds and machines that make snow. Children's ability to recall snow was the foundation for all that emerged throughout the project. (Additional information about the role of recall in documentation of children's learning and about the Reggio Emilia schools can be found in Chapters 22 and 29.)

- ➔ report their experiments to others. Recalling is a particularly important part of how children learn scientific thinking and processes (Fleer and Leslie 1992)
- ➔ develop their concentration skills and memory skills (Seifert 1993).

Developmental considerations

The ability to recall is related to the ability to remember. Therefore, fostering children's skills in recalling is an important part of fostering their memory skills. However, practising recalling with young children will not immediately lead to obvious gains in their learning. Research into children's cognition suggests that children need to practise cognitive skills such as recalling for some time before it positively benefits their learning (Seifert 1993).

Babies' abilities to remember events and objects can be developed through simple games in which they can practise their recalling skills. Games such as peek-a-boo and jack-in-the box encourage listening and watching, and involve clear sight and sound pictures that help babies practise their recall skills. Toddlers' abilities to remember events and objects can be developed through find-and-seek games and through simple guessing games. As children become more able to remember several events or objects at once, the games can become more elaborate. For example, a ball may be hidden where the child has looked for it before, then it may be hidden in a place where the toddler has not looked yet. Verbal clues may be given at first to help the child to remember.

Developing children's abilities to recall lays the foundation for encouraging them to transfer information from their short-term to their long-term memory. This cognitive technique is an important component in children's learning across all developmental domains (Seifert 1993). However, children's ability to recall will be influenced by their ability to represent ideas and images to others. Toddlers are increasingly able to express themselves through language, but they are also likely to rely on non-verbal ways of recalling an experience such as painting or drawing it. When toddlers recall experiences in this way they are more likely to represent the experience on paper through movement and gesture than pictorially, as Fasoli (1988, p. 60) explained:

> An example of this would be a child zooming the crayon all over the page as a way to represent a car.

Staff can encourage toddlers to build their capacity to recall in non-verbal as well as verbal ways. A toddler who has just seen a cat run up a tree is very keen to tell other children about it but will have difficulty recalling the event verbally. Staff could encourage the child to recall the event through drawing it for others. Encouraging children to experiment with diverse ways of representing their experiences provides an important foundation for learning how to use mathematical symbols such as numbers (Hawthorne 1992).

Research shows that toddlers can also be encouraged to recall events that happened some time ago. For instance:

> Two-year-olds can often remember the locations of novel objects seen only once, many months earlier, for example, the drawer where a rarely visited grandparent kept a deck of cards on a previous visit (Seifert 1993, p. 12).

Three-year-olds have some difficulty recalling a belief they held once they learn that their belief is false. They quickly replace their false belief with their new understandings and can accurately recall this (Freeman 1995).

As early literacy skills depend on a child's memory, staff can support the growth of early literacy in preschool children by encouraging them to recall events and experiences.

Preschool children tend to recall events and experiences more easily when they have *talked with* an adult about them as they are occurring than when the adult *talks to* the child about the event (Seifert 1993). In other words, when preschool children have conversations with adults during experiences, they are more likely to recall the experiences later. This likelihood is increased if adults reminisce during these conversations about past experiences that are connected in some way to the current experience. Staff can begin these conversations with phrases like, 'Do you remember when . . . ?'. Research has shown that preschoolers' ability to recall a museum experience was helped by adults talking with them about related experiences the children had had (Seifert 1993).

For instance, the children were more able to recall a visit to a museum when the adults talked about a visit to the zoo in which children had seen the same animals as those in the museum.

Preschool children are also more likely to be able to recall when they have had lots of practice at recalling. Practice builds children's capacity to recall.

Children in the early years of school are often able to recall events in great detail because of their increasing memory capacity and their increasing ability to develop strategies which help them to remember, such as rehearsing information, developing a story about what has happened, asking people to remind them about what they want to remember and writing things that they want to remember (Arthur et al. 1996). Talking with the children about how they have tried to remember things and what strategies have been successful helps to build their recalling skills.

Recall can be used to increase teacher understanding of children's scientific literacy and problem-solving skills in children in the early years of schooling. A stepped process where the teacher asks a child to recall factual information about science demonstrations, comment on what has changed, make generalisations, analyse and make judgements about what has happened provides teachers with insights into children's scientific understandings (Klein et al. 2000).

EQUITY CONSIDERATIONS

'Race' and culture

Empathy is an important foundation on which to build a positive attitude towards racial and cultural diversity with young children (Whaley and Swadener 1990). Empathy enables children to '. . . sustain stable and meaningful relationships . . .' with people from a diverse range of backgrounds (Brown 1995, p. 14) and to understand that racism is hurtful.

Children who develop empathy can respond to other people's emotions (Strayer 1986), but to respond to other people's emotions, children need to accurately recognise a range of human emotions. For instance, children need to be able to recognise feelings of hurt if they are to empathise with someone who has been hurt by a racist comment or image and to respond with concern. Children learn to accurately recognise other people's emotions by expressing and experiencing a broad range of emotions in themselves and in others (Whaley and Swadener 1990). However, they also need to be able to name and remember these feelings if they are to develop empathy (Strayer 1986). Staff need to provide children with names or labels for their emotions and encourage the children to remember these labels if empathy is to grow.

Recalling can help staff in this process. Children are able to recall events and experiences more easily when they have talked with an adult during an experience or event (Seifert 1993). Hence, talking with children about their own feelings and the feelings of others will help children to recall the labels for those feelings more readily. If these conversations with children involve reminiscences about their own feelings, their capacity for accurately naming them should be enhanced. Staff could, therefore, begin conversations about feelings with phrases like, 'Do you remember how sad you felt when you lost your pink teddy bear? Well, that's a little like Nathan feels now.' Preschool children are able to recall their emotional reactions to events as well as the events themselves very accurately (Liwag and Stein 1995).

However, it is equally important to explain to the children why someone is unhappy so that they learn that negative comments about physical appearance and lifestyle can hurt. In the previous example it would be important to add, 'Nathan is very sad because Kelly said his skin looks yucky'.

Gender

There is evidence that girls' ability to learn mathematics may be inhibited by the fact that they have '. . . less well-developed three-dimensional, spatial visualisation skills than boys . . .' (Hawthorne 1992, p. 13). Girls may not fully develop these skills because boys dominate activities such as block-building and climbing that provide concrete experiences of three-dimensionality (Askew and Ross 1988). Staff can help to maximise girls' chances of developing their three-dimensional, spatial visu-alisation skills by providing girls with access to a variety of concrete, three-dimensional experiences. When girls have access to these experiences, their skills can be improved by encouraging them to recall three-dimensional objects such as buildings. Staff can help girls to recall three-dimensional objects visually through encouraging them to make models or draw pictures of them and to recall these objects verbally through dialogue.

Disability and additional needs

Developing empathy is an important part of building positive and accepting relationships between children with different abilities. The majority of able-bodied children may have their first close experience of a child with a disability in an early childhood setting. Early in this experience, the able-bodied children and the child with a disability may be curious or fearful about each other. Staff can use recall to help build empathetic relationships between the children at this early stage in their relationships with each other.

This is particularly important when a child with a disability is introduced into a settled group of children. Staff can help children to think about how they might make friends with their new group member by talking about how it feels to have friends and people who like them and how it feels when no-one plays with them. Children can be encouraged to recall moments when they were new in the centre and didn't know people and to recall the moments when they knew they had friends. Such recalling can act as a basis for talking about how they might make friends with their new group member. Staff will need to help children think of non-verbal ways of showing that they would like to be friends with a new group member with language and communication disabilities (Brown 1995).

REFLECTING ON RECALLING TECHNIQUES

1 Briefly define recalling.
2 What do you think is the relationship between remembering and recalling?
3 List 10 ways of using recalling to support children's learning. Would each of these processes be suitable for use with babies?
4 To what extent do you agree with the statement that 'Purpose is a most important factor in determining what we recall' (Hughes and Hughes 1937, p. 164)?
5 What factors influence your own ability to recall experiences, events and people? How many of these factors could influence a preschooler's ability to recall experiences, events and people?
6 Paying attention to an experience is an important factor in successfully recalling the experience. Design two games you could play with toddlers that require them to pay attention to something and then to recall it.
7 What changes would be needed to make these games suitable for preschoolers?
8 How could you use recall to help a toddler new to your group to learn the daily routine of the centre? Would recall be the most appropriate technique to use? Why? Why not?

9   Observe a small group discussion between an adult and a group of four-year-old children. How was recall used to promote children's learning?

Improving teaching in practice

1   Videotape the teaching interactions you have with children during several five-minute teaching periods.

2   How and how well did you use recall to support children's learning? Did you ask children to recall when:

- ➲   you wanted to support them in achieving their own goals?
- ➲   they were clearly interested in what was being talked about?
- ➲   you knew they had enjoyed and were still interested in a specific experience, event or person?
- ➲   you knew they had some recent memories of note?

3   What are your areas of strength and weakness in using recall as a teaching technique to promote children's learning?

4   How can you improve your recall techniques in practice?

Further reading

Catron, C. and Allen, J. 1993, *Early Childhood Curriculum*, New York, Macmillan Publishing Company [refer to pp. 231–5 for games to promote children's recall skills].

Denham, S. 1991, 'Teaching thinking skills: The "what" and the "how" of young children's thinking', *Early Childhood Development and Care*, 71, pp. 35–44.

Read, K., Gardner, P. and Mahler, B. 1993, *Early Childhood Programs: Human Relationships and Learning*, ninth edn, Forth Worth, TX, Holt, Rinehart and Winston Inc. [refer to pp. 303–6].

Video

Mia Mia: A New Vision for Day Care. Part 1. The Program for 2- to 5-year-olds, Summerhill Films for the Institute of Early Childhood, Macquarie University, North Ryde, Australia, 1995.

Thinking through Play: a resource for an event based approach to teaching, School of Early Childhood, Queensland University of Technology, Brisbane, Australia, 1995.

References

Arthur, L., Beecher, B., Dockett, S., Farmer, S. and Death, E. 1996, *Programming and Planning in Early Childhood Settings*, second edn, Sydney, Harcourt Brace and Company.

Askew, S. and Ross, C. 1988, *Boys Don't Cry*, Milton Keynes, Open University Press.

Brown, B. 1995, *All Our Children: A Guide for Those Who Care*, 3rd edn, London, British Broadcasting Commission Education.

Denham, S. 1991, 'Teaching thinking skills: The "what" and the "how" of young children's thinking', *Early Childhood Development and Care*, 71, pp. 35–44.

Fasoli, L. 1988, 'Nurturing creativity', in A. Stonehouse, ed., *Trusting Toddlers: Programming for One to Three Year Olds in Child Care Centres* (pp. 54–64), Watson, ACT, Australian Early Childhood Association.

Fleer, M. and Leslie, C. 1992, 'The light side of darkness: helping children to understand the concept of "light and colour"', *Australian Early Childhood Resource Booklets* (4).

Forman, G., Lee, M., Wrisley, L. and Langley, J. 1994, 'The city in the snow: applying the multisymbolic approach in Massachusetts', in C. Edwards, L. Gandini and G. Forman, eds, *The Hundred Languages of Children: The Reggio Emilia Approach to Early Childhood Education* (pp. 233–50), New Jersey, Ablex.

Freeman, N. 1995, 'Cued-recall approach to three-year-olds' memory for an honest mistake', *Journal of Experimental Child Psychology*, 60(1), pp. 102–15.

Hawthorne, W. 1992, 'Young children and mathematics', *Australian Early Childhood Resource Booklets* (1).

Hughes, A. and Hughes, E. 1937, *Learning and Teaching: An Introduction to Psychology and Education*, London, Longmans.

Klein, E. R., Hammrich, P., Bloom, S. and Ragins, A. 2000, Language development and science inquiry: a child-initiated and teacher-facilitated program, Paper presented at the *Annual Meeting of the American Education Research Association*, New Orleans, April, ED 440756.

Liwag, M. and Stein, N. 1995, 'Children's memory for emotional events: the importance of emotion-related retrieval cues', *Journal of Experimental Child Psychology*, 60(1), pp. 2–31.

Moyles, J. 1989, *Just Playing: The Role and Status of Play in Early Childhood Education*, Milton Keynes, Open University Press.

Read, K., Gardner, P. and Mahler, B. 1993, *Early Childhood Programs: Human Relationships and Learning*, ninth edn, Forth Worth, TX, Holt, Rinehart and Winston Inc.

Schwartz, S. 1996, 'Hidden messages in teacher talk: praise and empowerment', *Teaching Children Mathematics* (March), pp. 396–401.

Seifert, K. 1993, 'Cognitive development and early childhood education', in B. Spodek, ed., *Handbook of Research on the Education of Young Children* (pp. 9–23), New York, Macmillan Publishing Company.

Strayer, J. 1986, 'Current research in affective development', *Journal of Children in Contemporary Society*, 17(4), pp. 27–55.

Whaley, K. and Swadener, B. 1990, 'Multicultural education in infant and toddler settings', *Childhood Education*, 66(4), pp. 238–40.

Wilkes, G. (ed.) 1979, *Collins Dictionary of the English Language*, Middlesex, Penguin Books.

Chapter 16

Singing

Sing: to produce or articulate (sounds, words, etc.) with definite and usually specific musical intonation.

(Collins Dictionary of the English Language, p. 1358)

Singing can be a powerful tool for letting a baby know that you care, that you understand her feelings or his needs.

(Honig 1995, p. 73)

Singing around the piano may be fun, but it does not take the place of singing in connection with activities.

(Read et al. 1993, p. 339)

WHAT?

When people sing, they use their voice to make musical sounds. People may sing songs or chants for a number of reasons. As a teaching technique, staff may sing songs or chants with or for children to enhance their learning across all developmental domains. Children's learning may be enhanced by singing during formal small and large group times and during informal moments throughout the day.

HOW?

Singing comes more easily to some people than to others. Honig (1995) suggested that staff who find singing difficult could:

- ➲ focus on singing very simple songs which they put to the melody of nursery rhymes with which they are familiar
- ➲ listen to lots of children's music and sing along in private till they feel they can manage without the record or tape.

Irrespective of staff's singing competence, the following suggestions should help to maximise children's learning through singing:

- children are more likely to sing when they are having fun and are able to move in rhythm to the singing (Read et al. 1993). Janet often combines song with movement:

It is a windy day and Janet, a teacher of a prep grade, is outside with the children. She watches the children as they run around and begins to sing a 'windy day' song with them. She then extends this song into verses about what the wind can do. The children translate each verse into different movements. They move to show how they can blow, be tossed about, swirl around and land on the ground.

- the more that adults show enjoyment in singing, the more that children are likely to join in (Spodek and Saracho 1994).

- many of the songs that children make up and sing to themselves are low-pitched and in a minor key. Singing similarly pitched songs with the children will make singing fun rather than challenging (Read et al. 1993).

- young children love songs about, '. . . animals, themselves or their friends, and some nonsense rhymes and jingles . . .' (Brewer 1992, p. 332).

Singing together.

WHEN AND WHY?

Goal relevance

Singing can enhance children's learning in many ways. It can be particularly helpful when staff wish to:

- help children to learn daily routines (Honig 1995). For instance, a song may be used to cue children into pack-up time

➲ encourage children's own singing efforts. Respecting and celebrating children's singing through singing with them will encourage them to use singing as a form of self-expression (Barrett 1993). For instance, a staff member may pick up on a song that a child is singing and extend it or repeat it

➲ familiarise children with basic musical concepts such as melody, rhythm, tempo, pitch and tone (Robison and Schwartz 1982)

➲ improve children's listening skills (Clarke 1992)

➲ provide opportunities for children to solve problems by thinking about actions they can do to songs or by thinking about new words they could sing to a familiar tune (Brewer 1992)

➲ support children's acquisition of language. Singing simple songs in which the words of the song match the children's actions helps them to learn the meaning of words. This can be a particularly effective way to build toddlers' language competence (Olsson 1988) and to help with the acquisition of English as a second language (Clarke 1992)

➲ '. . . awaken a love of poetry and imagery . . .' (Honig 1995)

➲ help children experience fun and develop a sense of humour (Honig 1995). For instance, a staff member may sing some new, funny words to a familiar tune

➲ help children to reveal and express their feelings and understandings (Barrett 1993).

Ann, Chris and Anouk each incorporate singing into their program on a regular basis:

> Ann, a child care worker in the three-year-old group, always uses singing when there is a transition time, for instance; at pack-up time, at lunchtime and at going outside time.
>
> Chris loves to make up songs about the children and their activities. At the end of each kindergarten session he sings a song to the children about what he has seen them doing during the morning or the afternoon. Sometimes Chris uses tunes that the children already know and sometimes he invents new tunes.
>
> Anouk sings simple repetitive songs to her group of one-year-old children. As they play outside, she sings about what the children are doing. For instance, she sings to Sarah in the sand pit, 'digging, digging, in the sand,' or to Tran on the swing, 'Tran is swinging, swinging, swinging'.

There is research evidence to suggest that musical activities, including singing, can support the learning of children who 'find it difficult to learn from a strictly verbal presentation' (Strickland 2001/02, p. 103), but that it is important that the music selected is enjoyed by those children.

Developmental considerations

Research shows that babies can and do respond to different types of music from the moment they are born and that they can be calmed, excited or distressed by the music around them (Craig Pery 1993). In general, very young babies (under four months of age) tend to find quiet, gentle music calming and lively music exciting. Singing soft, gentle songs such as lullabies can be a very effective way to soothe and calm babies in moments of stress (for example, when separating from a parent) or in preparation for rest times. Some lullabies recommended by Honig (1995) are:

➲ 'Rock-a-Bye Baby in the Tree Top'

➲ 'All the Pretty Little Horses' (sometimes known as 'Hush-A-Bye Baby')

➡ 'Summertime'

➡ 'Sleep, Sleep My Beautiful Little Son'

➡ 'Mockingbird' (sometimes known as 'Hush, Little Baby')

➡ 'Morningtown Ride'.

Working with babies and toddlers involves lots of daily care routines such as rest times, nappy changing times and meal times. Each of these can be made more enjoyable and enriching for children through songs. Simple songs and chants can help to quieten the children, can provide something for them to focus on other than the routine itself and can help them to feel cared for (Honig 1995; Linke and Fleer 2002). These songs and chants can be made up by the staff as the moment occurs. They can be about mundane things. The more that staff practise these small songs, the easier it will become to sing them. Singing to babies and playing rhyming games with them can also support emergent literacy skills and knowledge (Cress 2000) through enhancing their language development and their sense of connection between language and actions.

> Toddlers have reached the stage in their musical development where they can 'dance' to music and enjoy doing so. Action songs, such as 'Hokey Pokey', are likely to interest toddlers at this stage of their development.
>
> The toddler now attempts to 'dance' to music by bending his [her] knees in a bounding motion, turning circles, swaying, swinging his [her] arms, and nodding his [her] head. He [she] especially likes a marked rhythm, so band music, nursery songs, or catchy TV jingles may be favorites. (Bayless and Ramsey 1991; cited in Brewer 1992, p. 336)

With this in mind, staff can increase toddlers' enjoyment of song by providing lots of space and opportunities for 'dancing' to song. Toddlers love it when the staff join in with their dancing.

Preschoolers increasingly enjoy using song to express their ideas. They can make up their own songs or use familiar songs to accompany their play (Brewer 1992). Staff can encourage these developments through singing with the children. During their preschool years, children's interest in and understanding of song lyrics increases and staff can use this as an opportunity to expand children's vocabulary and introduce them to new ideas. Children are not only able to understand song but also to produce their own if they are afforded the opportunity to do so. Encouraging children to produce their own songs acknowledges that they have the capacity to be music-makers and offers the staff opportunity to scaffold this music-making (Whiteman 2001).

Song and chant are particularly powerful ways to introduce children to the alphabet. Songs and chants that are fun and that emphasise the sounds and names of letters help children remember the alphabet (Reutzel 1992). Children in the early years of school will enjoy puns and humour in their songs, and the more they enjoy the songs the more effective the learning will be. The television program 'Sesame Street' has used this knowledge to good effect! Songs can also be helpful in introducing children to new languages and, alongside other methods, enhance their learning of a new language (Omari 2001).

EQUITY CONSIDERATIONS

'Race' and culture

Song is an important means of expression in many cultures. It can be a way to share joys and sadnesses. It can also be a way to record the history of a cultural group and to share that history with others. Many cultures have a rich and diverse bank of songs known by different groups who use them for a wide variety of purposes.

Children's enjoyment of specific music grows through regular exposure to it. Their enjoyment also grows when it is music that is enjoyed by the adults about them (Craig Peery 1993). So, if staff regularly share with children the songs they enjoy from a diverse range of cultures, they can develop children's enjoyment in and respect for them. If children enjoy songs from a diverse range of cultures they can:

- ➲ learn about similarities and differences within and between different cultural groups (Spodek and Saracho 1994)
- ➲ discover cultural diversity. Learning about music from different cultures can be an enjoyable and effective way to learn about cultural diversity. Children often enjoy the folk songs and the work songs of different cultures because of their repetitive lyrics and strong rhythms (Ramsey 1987)
- ➲ share their own cultural heritage with others (Clarke 1992). Children can help to teach songs from their own culture to other children in the group. This helps enrich the group's musical repertoire and children build a sense of worth from contributing to this repertoire
- ➲ learn a second language. Simple songs with repetitive lyrics can help children to learn to say 'Hello', 'Good-bye', 'Welcome', etc. in their local community languages. Songs can also help children to learn English as a second language. Simple songs can help them to participate on '. . . an equal footing in the group with native speakers . . .' (van Oosten 1996, p. 3).

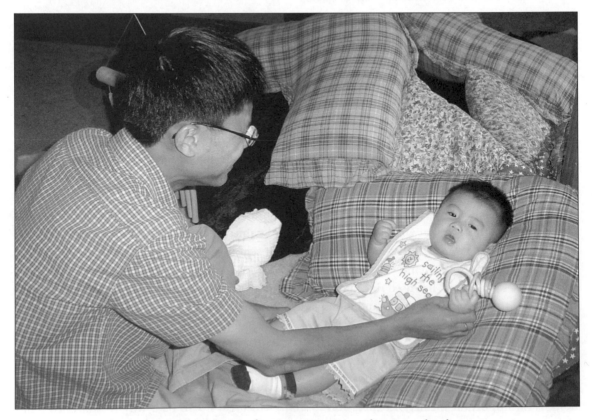

Showing enjoyment in vocalisations encourages language development.

Acceptance of and respect for cultural diversity can increase when staff share songs that:

 represent the languages and lifestyles of all the children in the group. Babies learn their first language through being constantly surrounded by its sounds (Garcia 1993). Their first language acquisition will best be supported by being able to listen to and communicate with staff who share their first language. When staff do not share a baby's first language, they can help to support language acquisition by learning simple songs and lullabies in the baby's first language. This not only supports that specific baby's language acquisition but also enriches the diversity of languages available to all babies in the centre

 increase children's awareness of cultural diversity within the wider community. When children spend time in primarily mono-cultural groups, staff should make a special effort to familiarise them with the multicultural nature of Australian society. Songs can be a fun part of this process

 reflect the songs and chants that are sung by people from particular cultural groups (Dermon-Sparks et al. 1989). This prevents the children learning stereotyped ideas about what is sung within a particular cultural group. For instance, not all Spanish people will necessarily sing 'La Bamba'!

 draw on the diversity of song within a culture. Children can enjoy and learn from all song genres in a culture, including traditional, contemporary, folk and classical genres of song and chant

 encourage empathy and identification with people from diverse cultural backgrounds (Ramsey 1987). Songs about people's joys and sadnesses can help children to empathise with others

 counter stereotypes. Song lyrics should not make fun of or demean a particular cultural group or present them as frightening or silly. For instance, the song, 'We are Siamese' from the musical, *The King and I* presents Siamese (now Thai) people as silly. The song, 'Ten Little Indians' reinforces the stereotype that Native Americans all have bows and arrows and live in tepees

 are integrated in a consistent and meaningful way in the life of the centre. Children will learn to enjoy and respect diversity when it is a daily part of their lives. Learning only one song from a culture for a special occasion is tokenistic.

Staff can also teach children songs that '. . . encourage differences, acceptance, and cooperation'. (York 1991, p. 60). For example, 'What is your name? My name's Amy', or 'I wonder what your name is. I really ought to know. My name is Amy, hello, hello', etc.

Gender

The songs selected for use with preschool children should be so much fun to sing that it's okay that there's a message in there. (Neugebauer 1992, p. 64)

If children enjoy songs, they are more likely to learn the messages contained within them, including messages of gender equality. They can:

 learn about similarities and differences within and between men and women, boys and girls. Preschool children often have very gender-stereotyped views about men's and women's range of feelings and behaviours (Alloway 1995). They can find it hard to believe that women can carry heavy weights, can be adventurous, can be leaders and can do jobs traditionally done by men. They can also find it hard to believe that men can be caring and gentle, can change nappies and do the dishes and can do jobs traditionally done by women. Staff can challenge children's gender stereotypes by sharing songs with the children that celebrate the non-traditional ways of being male and female. Staff may need to make up songs and rhymes if they can't find any

- discover gender diversity. Many songs and rhymes for young children are very sexist. They tell of girls (Polly) putting kettles on and boys (Johnny) working with hammers. One way to increase children's awareness of gender role diversity is to substitute boy's/girl's names in the songs and rhymes. 'Polly put the kettle on' can become, 'Johnny put the kettle on'; and 'Johnny works with one hammer' can become 'Polly works with one hammer'. If the children are familiar with the song, they will often tell staff that they have got the words 'wrong'. Staff can use this assertion as a way of talking to the children about gender stereotypes and of begining to deconstruct gender stereotypes with the children. (For further information on this, refer to Chapter 21)
- share their achievements with others. Staff can make up songs to sing to the children about the things they do each day that challenge traditional gender stereotypes. Singing about 'The big block building the girls made', or 'How the boys helped with tidying up the home-corner' can help to celebrate gender-role diversity in the group. However, staff need to be alert to the possibility that many girls may be less confident than many boys about singing about their achievements. Boys tend to be louder and more confident in mixed gender groups than girls
- learn new concepts. Song can be a fun way to introduce children to a variety of prenumber concepts. Songs such as 'Five Little Ducks' help children to learn to count to five, to subtract and to count backwards. There is some evidence that structured music programs might be a particularly effective way to teach prenumber concepts to girls:

> . . . a formal Kodaly program can increase a preschooler's understanding of prenumber concepts of comparison, order, classification, and pattern—but only for girls. (Craig Peery 1993, p. 214)

If song is to increase children's acceptance of and respect for gender diversity, staff need to ensure that their songs and chants:

- represent the gender styles of all the children in the group
- increase children's awareness of gender role diversity within the wider community
- encourage empathy and identification between diverse gender styles
- counter stereotypes. The lyrics in songs should not make fun of a particular gender or make it seem frightening or silly.

However, staff need to be alert to the fact that preschool children will often resist messages that challenge their gender-role stereotypes (Davies 1989). To challenge children's gender-stereotyped beliefs, staff need to do more than change a few words in a few songs. They need to combine this work with an ongoing program in which they use a variety of techniques such as questioning, deconstruction and empowerment to help children grow free of the ways in which gender stereotyping restricts their development.

Disability and additional needs

Using music to encourage children to listen to and interact with others can help them to empathise with others (Craig Peery 1993). Empathy between children of diverse needs and abilities can be supported when songs help children:

 learn about similarities and differences within and between people of varying abilities. Children can be introduced to the idea that different people's bodies work in different ways via song. Singing songs about the different ways we can move our bodies, such as crawling, waving, walking, etc., can be an easy place to start. These songs can help children to think about the similarities and differences between how people with mobility and motor disabilities move their bodies and how people without those disabilities move theirs.

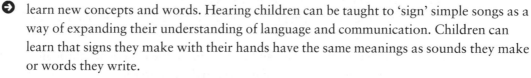 share their achievements with others. Staff can make up songs to sing to the children about the special things they do each day. This can encourage the children to make up their own songs to celebrate their own achievements and those of their friends.

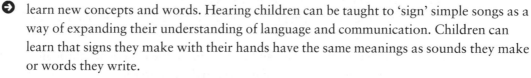 learn new concepts and words. Hearing children can be taught to 'sign' simple songs as a way of expanding their understanding of language and communication. Children can learn that signs they make with their hands have the same meanings as sounds they make or words they write.

Songs should not reinforce the continued invisibility or inaudibility of people with disabilities. Simple changes to the words of familiar and oft-used songs can help in this process. Such changes include:

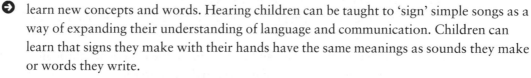 Changing 'The Wheels of the Bus' to 'The Wheels of the Wheelchair' when a child with a wheelchair is in the group

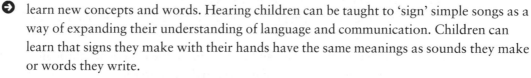 Changing the 'finger' play, 'Ten Little Fingers' to 'Two Big Arms' when a child with an arm with no fingers is in the group.

If song is to increase acceptance of and respect for people of diverse abilities, staff need to choose songs that:

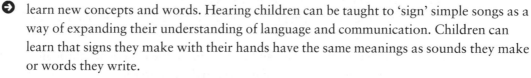 represent the abilities of all the children in the group. Songs about all the children's bodies and experiences need to be included

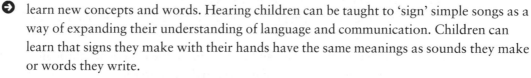 increase children's awareness of people with diverse abilities within the wider community. Songs that celebrate the skills and abilities of people with disabilities need to be included

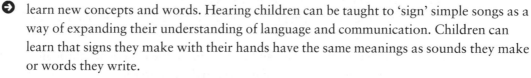 encourage empathy and identification between people with diverse abilities

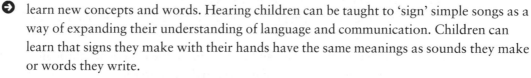 counter stereotypes. The lyrics in songs should not make fun of a particular disability or additional need a child has, or make the child seem frightening or silly.

REFLECTING ON SINGING TECHNIQUES

1 Briefly define singing.
2 How could singing be used to help toddlers learn how to wash their hands after toileting? What would be the pros and cons of using singing to achieve this aim?
3 Find three simple songs you could use to help introduce new vocabulary to a three-year-old child just beginning to learn English as a second language.

4 Find three simple songs you could use to help children improve their memory skills.

5 Make up a simple song you could use to help children learn about taking turns.

6 Write down the words of five of your favourite songs for children. Would your songs need adapting in any way to make them more inclusive of gender or disability? To what extent would the songs extend children's awareness of songs from a diverse range of cultures?

7 View an episode of 'Sesame Street'. How was singing used to assist children's learning?

8 Which of the songs and rhymes used in the program would be suitable to sing to a group of toddlers? Why?

9 How and how well do the singers on 'Sesame Street':
   - ❯ encourage children to have fun by moving in rhythm to what they are singing?
   - ❯ show enjoyment in singing?
   - ❯ sing to children in a low-pitched minor key?
   - ❯ sing about subjects children enjoy such as themselves, their friends or familiar events?

IMPROVING TEACHING IN PRACTICE

1 Record (using a tape-recorder or written notes) several occasions during which you used singing as an incidental teaching technique.

2 How and how well did you encourage fun and enjoyment in the experience through modelling enjoyment and choosing songs and actions of interest to the children?

3 What are your areas of strength and weakness in using singing as a teaching technique to promote children's learning?

4 How can you work to improve your singing techniques in practice?

Further reading and resources

Baker, B. 1993, 'Strengthening language experiences for children through fingerplays', *ED360094*.

Brewer, J. 1992, *Introduction to Early Childhood Education: Preschool through Primary Grades*, Boston, Allyn and Bacon [refer to pp. 330–4].

Clarke, P. 1992, *English as a Second Language in Early Childhood*, Melbourne, FKA Multicultural Resource Centre [refer to pp. 39–41].

Craig Peery, J. 1993, 'Music in early childhood education', in B. Spodek, ed., *Handbook of Research on the Education of Young Children* (pp. 207–24), New York, Macmillan.

Halford, M. 1988, 'A music programme for 2's to 3's', *Resource* (56).

Honig, A. 1995, 'Singing with infants and toddlers', *Young Children* (July), pp. 72–8.

Read, K., Gardner, P. and Mahler, B. 1993, *Early Childhood Programs: Human Relationships and Learning*, ninth edn, Forth Worth, TX, Holt, Rinehart and Winston Inc. [refer pp. 339–40].

White, P., Sergeant, D. and Welch, G. 1996, 'Some observations on the singing development of five-year-olds', *Early Childhood Development and Care*, 118, pp. 27–34.

van Oosten, J. 1988, 'Integrating music in the programme', *Resource* (56).

Websites—extending learning online

http://www.library.unsw.edu.au/~thesis/adt-NUN/public/adt-NUN20010703.094806/

References

Alloway, N. 1995, *Foundation Stones: The Construction of Gender in Early Childhood*, Melbourne, Curriculum Corporation.

Barrett, M. 1993, 'Music in the early childhood classroom: an expressive medium', *Australian Journal of Early Childhood*, 18(1), pp. 23–8.

Brewer, J. 1992, *Introduction to Early Childhood Education: Preschool through Primary Grades*, Boston, Allyn and Bacon.

Clarke, P. 1992, *English as a Second Language in Early Childhood*, Melbourne, FKA Multicultural Resource Centre.

Craig Peery, J. 1993, 'Music in early childhood education', in B. Spodek, ed., *Handbook of Research on the Education of Young Children* (pp. 207–24), New York, Macmillan.

Cress, S. 2000, 'A focus on literacy in home day care', *Australian Journal of Early Childhood*, 25(3), pp. 6–12.

Davies, B. 1989, *Frogs and Snails and Feminist Tales: Preschool Children and Gender*, Sydney, Allen & Unwin.

Dermon-Sparks, L. and the Anti-Bias Task Force 1989, *The Anti-Bias Curriculum*, Washington DC, National Association for the Education of Young Children.

Garcia, E. 1993, 'The education of linguistically and culturally diverse children', in B. Spodek, ed., *Handbook of Research on the Education of Young Children* (pp. 372–84), New York, Macmillan.

Honig, A. 1995, 'Singing with infants and toddlers', *Young Children* (July), pp. 72–8.

Linke, P. and Fleer, M. 2002, *Babies: Good Beginnings Last Forever*, Watson, ACT, Australian Early Childhood Association.

Neugebauer, B. (ed.). 1992, *Alike and Different: Exploring our Humanity with Young Children*, Washington DC, National Association for the Education of Young Children.

Olsson, B. 1988, 'Experiences for toddlers: some practical suggestions', in A. Stonehouse, ed., *Trusting Toddlers: Programming for One- to Three-Year-Olds in Child Care Centres* (pp. 132–9), Watson, ACT, Australian Early Childhood Association.

Omari, D. 2001, A comparison of foreign language teaching methods: total physical response versus song/chants with kindergarteners, ED461987.

Ramsey, P. 1987, *Teaching and Learning in a Diverse World: Multicultural Education for Young Children*, Columbia, Teachers' College Press.

Read, K., Gardner, P. and Mahler, B. 1993, *Early Childhood Programs: Human Relationships and Learning*, ninth edn, Forth Worth, TX, Holt, Rinehart and Winston Inc.

Robison, H. and Schwartz, S. 1982, *Designing Curriculum for Early Childhood*, Boston, Allyn and Bacon Inc.

Reutzel, R. 1992, 'Breaking the letter-a-week tradition', *Childhood Education*, 69(1), pp. 20–3.

Spodek, B. and Saracho, O. 1994, *Right from the Start: Teaching Children Ages Three to Eight*, Boston, Allyn and Bacon.

Strickland, S. 2001/02, 'Music and the brain in childhood development', *Childhood Education*, 78(2), pp. 100–03.

van Oosten, J. 1996, 'Integrating music in the programme, *Resource* (56).

Whiteman, P. 2001, 'How the bananas got their pyjamas: a study of the metamorphosis of preschoolers' spontaneous singing as viewed through Vygotsky's Zone of Proximal Development'.

Wilkes, G. (ed.) 1979, *Collins Dictionary of the English Language*, Middlesex, Penguin Books.

York, S. 1991, *Roots and Wings: Affirming Culture in Early Childhood Programs*, Minnesota, Toys'n Things Press.

Chapter 17

Suggesting

Suggest: to put forward (an idea, plan etc.) for consideration.

(Collins Dictionary of the English Language, p. 1453)

Most of the other teaching strategies teachers use also serve as suggestions to children.

(Allen and Hart 1984, p. 259)

The suggestibility of children gives teachers great power, and the use of suggestion in the classroom entails a great responsibility . . .

(Hughes and Hughes 1937, p. 366)

WHAT?

A suggestion is an offer of advice, ideas and recommendations about what you can do next. When people make suggestions they generally believe there is a better, more interesting or more effective way to do things.

Staff use suggestion as a teaching technique when they believe that the children's learning will benefit. When staff use suggestion they are allowing the children to choose whether or not to follow their advice, ideas or recommendations. It is optional for the children to follow staff advice or not. For example, 'Rowan, you could use the green blanket in the home corner for your tent', is a suggestion. Rowan can decide whether to use the green blanket or not.

As children can ignore or modify suggestions, staff should only offer suggestions when they are prepared to have them ignored or modified by the children. If staff need or want the children to follow their advice, ideas or recommendations then they should tell (refer to Chapter 18) the children what is to be done rather than make a suggestion. To illustrate this using the previous example: if the staff member wanted Rowan to use the green blanket because it was the only blanket she was prepared to have Rowan use, then Rowan should have been told this—'Rowan, if you want to use a blanket for your tent you will need to use the green blanket in the home corner. It is the only blanket we can wash easily if it gets dirty.'

HOW?

Allen and Hart (1984) believe that most teaching techniques act as a form of suggestion. By way of illustration, questions about what a child intends to do next can act as a suggestion. They can prompt the child to test out a new idea. Questions such as 'Have you thought about doing it this way?', 'Have you tried using the bigger trolley to carry the blocks?' or 'Do you think it would be easier if one person pushed and the other person pulled?' can all suggest alternative ways of approaching a task to a child. Verbal feedback can also act as a suggestion. When staff provide a child with feedback about her current actions the child can be prompted to try an alternative way of doing things. Comments such as: 'Have you thought about . . .' or 'I wonder what would happen if . . .' can also suggest to a child alternative ways of approaching a task.

Many suggestions will start with phrases such as:

- ❥ 'You could try it this way . . .'
- ❥ 'If you do this . . . then . . . x might happen'
- ❥ 'Why don't you try this?'
- ❥ 'How about we try it this way?'
- ❥ 'It might help if you did that . . .'
- ❥ 'Try doing this . . .'
- ❥ 'This might help . . .'
- ❥ 'Maybe you could try this . . .'

While children may choose to ignore staff's suggestions, the following guidance will reduce this possibility.

- ❥ Suggestions are more likely to be followed if they are positive. Positive suggestions tell the child what they might do, rather than what they should not do. The suggestion sounds

Jenny suggests ways to use the climbing equipment.

constructive rather than negative and restricting (Read et al. 1993). For example, 'If you walk while you're holding that jug of juice it will not spill'.

- ❯ Suggestions can be direct or indirect (Allen and Hart 1984). Direct suggestions might start with 'Let's try it this way'. Less direct suggestions might start with 'What would happen if you did it a different way?'. The more direct the suggestion, the more likely it is that the children will follow it. Refer to Chapter 13 for more information on open-ended questioning with children.
- ❯ The younger the child the more specific and direct the suggestions need to be.
- ❯ Avoid flooding children with more than one suggestion at a time.
- ❯ Allow children time to test suggestions out in practice.
- ❯ Accept that children may not use your suggestions. If they do not have a choice about what to do next, make it clear that you are not suggesting what to do but telling them what to do.
- ❯ Keep suggestions personal to the child and specific to their needs.

Staff can also use gestures as a form of suggestion or as a way to strengthen their verbal suggestions as they can orient children to the most salient features of the suggestion (Roth 2001).

WHEN AND WHY?

Goal relevance
Suggestions can be used to enhance many areas of children's learning including the following:

- ❯ To prompt children to make an independent discovery by trying out a new method or approach to a problem they are encountering. Children are more thoughtful when staff make suggestions about how to use objects in science programs, such as magnets (Howe 1993). Suggestions can also help build mathematical knowledge. Staff can help children build generalisations by suggesting they revisit experiences (Schwartz 1996). For example, 'Perhaps if you want to make another road of the same length you may need to find five more blocks this long. I wonder if it would work if you did that?'.
- ❯ To increase children's perseverance and to reduce their frustration with a task they are finding difficult. A suggestion about what shape puzzle piece to look for might help a child maintain interest in a puzzle that the child is finding difficult to complete.
- ❯ To redirect children's attention from one task to another. Suggesting that a child play with a toy or get involved in an experience similar to the one they are in can help redirect children's attention (Read et al. 1993). For example, 'You might want to take that dolly over to the basin and wash her'. If this is accompanied by gestures that reinforce where the basin is it will strengthen the suggestion (Roth 2001).
- ❯ To direct children's attention to the salient features of a particular problem, for example, 'Take a good look at this machine, can you notice the wheels and the cogs?'.
- ❯ To enrich children's storylines in dramatic play. Staff interaction with children here can increase the children's interest in this form of play if staff suggestions extend rather than redirect the play (Dempsey and Frost 1993).
- ❯ To help children resolve a social dispute (Brewer 1992). When children both want the same toy, staff can suggest ways that each can have a turn. Children can then work through how to solve their own dispute.

To help children relax. For example, staff can help children relax through teaching them to take slow, deep breaths. To do this staff can suggest different ways of slowing down their breathing and taking deeper breaths. According to Roe (1996, p. 8), the following suggestions help: '. . . suggesting children puff their breath in and out like a train, suggesting children try to breathe like an elephant who is asleep and suggesting children pretend to be a fish and breathe with their mouth open'.

Developmental considerations

Staff need to adapt their suggestions to the children's level of language development and thought, moving from more to less direct suggestions as they get older.

Suggestion is a verbal teaching technique. As such, it is most appropriately used with children once they have the language competence to understand what is being suggested. However, talking with babies in their pre-verbal stage is an important way in which they learn about how language works (Hass Dyson and Genishi 1993). Staff can find it difficult to find things to talk about with babies. Suggestions can often be a good starting point to a conversation with a baby. When staff combine actions with conversation phrases such as: 'How about we try it this way?', 'Try doing this . . .', 'This might help . . .' or 'Maybe you could try this . . .' can help babies learn that words and actions have some correspondence. As staff wait for a baby's response to their physical and verbal suggestion they are helping babies learn about the pattern of two-way communication—speech and or action by one person, and the expected response by another.

Toddlers often have a strong interest in the sounds made by musical instruments and in how those sounds are made (Craig Peery 1993). Providing toddlers with lots of opportunities to experiment with different ways of using musical instruments can help develop their problem-solving skills. They encounter the problems such as how to make sounds louder and softer, how to use their hands or mouth to make sounds, and how to stop sounds once they begin. Staff suggestions about how to use novel objects (such as musical instruments) can help children become more thoughtful about how to solve the problems they encounter (Howe 1993).

> A staff member at the Emu Children's Centre collected old pots and pans from opportunity shops, and also collected a series of wooden spoons. She put these on the floor for the toddlers in her group to experiment with. She modelled different ways to bang the pots: 'Inside makes a different sound from outside'; 'The lids make yet another sound when you bang them'. She then allowed the toddlers to experiment with making different sounds.

Toddlers can often find it difficult to resolve their own disputes over who should play with a particular toy or whose turn it is. Staff can help toddlers gain the social knowledge they need to resolve their own disputes through direct suggestion, for example, by suggesting another toy that a toddler might play with while he awaits a turn with the desired toy. Specific direct suggestions that are accompanied by demonstration are the ones most likely to be followed by toddlers (Brewer 1992). However, toddlers may not always instantly respond to a suggestion. It is important to give them time to process the suggestion that has been made and to try again if they don't follow it successfully first time around (Schreiber 1999).

Preschoolers are beginning to be able to empathise with each other's feelings and so they are often able to successfully negotiate a conclusion to their own disputes (Ladd and Coleman 1993).

However, sometimes their negotiations 'get stuck'. Staff can use these occasions to help build preschoolers' capacity for fair dispute resolution by suggesting ways forward. Questions can often form the basis of this process:

> A dispute over who should use the computer next is occurring between two four-year-olds. They seem unable to come to any resolution so the teacher intervenes saying, 'You don't seem to be able to solve this problem. Would your problem be solved if we tossed a coin to see who should go next? Would that be fair?'.

The older the child the less specific and less direct the suggestions need to be. Staff can use broad suggestions in the form of comments or questions to help expand older children's use of writing as a method of communication. Staff can suggest different ways and different occasions that children can use writing to communicate with others including:

- ➲ letters and thank you notes to each other, to visitors who contribute to classroom life and to people involved in places they might visit (Amos Hatch 1991)
- ➲ letters or email notes to ask other people for information
- ➲ letters or notices to tell people about what is happening in their classroom
- ➲ letters to newspapers or public figures to express their reactions to current events.

Children's writing skills can also be supported through the use of journals or folders. As staff read these they can make suggestions about how a story might evolve or where a child might go to next in their writing. Comments or questions that act as suggestions in these instances show the children that their writing is being taken seriously and is being valued (Amos Hatch 1991).

Sometimes suggestions can be very helpful for primary school children. For instance, when they are attempting to resolve conflicts outside of the classroom. If staff suggest specific games that children can play that are acceptable it can help children to 'work things out during recess' (McDermott 1999, p. 82). It may be necessary when there are difficulties between children at recess time to be with them as they begin their games and make specific suggestions about how to progress them until children can successfully play the game themselves (McDermott 1999).

For children of all ages there is evidence that children's gestures offer an important insight into their levels of cognitive competence on difficult tasks. Research indicates that 'gestures provide cognitive support when children attempt to talk about difficult tasks' (Roth 2001, p. 373). For some children gestures also provide a more accurate sense of what they are understanding than do their words. Some children can 'gesturally express correct conceptual understanding, whereas their speech still expresses incorrect conceptual understanding' (Roth 2001, p. 373). If teachers are alert to these phenomena then they can target their suggestions about how to complete difficult tasks or understand new concepts more precisely.

EQUITY CONSIDERATIONS

'Race' and culture

Young children can act and think in racially prejudiced ways by the time they are preschoolers (Ramsey 1987). They can also act and think in anti-discriminatory ways and learn to stand up against unfairness towards themselves and others (Dermon-Sparks 1992). However, young children need considerable staff support to stand up for themselves and for others when they encounter racial prejudice. With support they can learn how to stop racial name-calling and teasing between children.

Staff can use suggestion to support children's attempts to stand up against unfairness in several ways. They can suggest ways for children to let other people know that they are upset. This might involve suggesting some words the children can use to tell others that they feel angry or hurt. It also involves teaching children how to ensure that others know they mean what they say. Staff can offer suggestions about this. For example, staff can suggest that the children speak more loudly or use a stronger voice when they want others to know that they mean their words (Dermon-Sparks et al. 1989). With practical suggestions and encouragement children can learn to '. . . become tolerant, understanding, and compassionate by the time they are five . . .' (Dermon-Sparks 1992, p. 3). This tolerance can then be consolidated in the early years of schooling by staff suggesting new words and new ways children can express their feelings of hurt to others. This might include writing them a note, telling a story about their feelings to other children or composing a song to share with the group.

Gender

Children's dramatic play is influenced by the gender mix of the playgroups. Boys tend to dominate the choice of storyline in mixed-gender groups (Pelligrini and Boyd 1993). The storylines the boys choose often give them a powerful leadership role and the girls a passive and submissive role (MacNaughton 1995). Staff can help create greater gender equity in mixed-gender playgroups by suggesting alternative storylines in which girls and boys can alternate and share decision-making and leadership. Lots of domestic, rural and adventure storylines lend themselves to this. For example, introducing the idea of co-pilots in spacecraft, shared child care at home or rounding up sheep means that more than one child can experience taking control of the spacecraft, the child (and the play) or the sheep. Staff can suggest to children the advantages of sharing, such as being able to rest when they're tired and to call on help in emergencies (MacNaughton 1995).

As children are likely to be less familiar with these storylines, staff may need to take an active role initially in 'play tutoring'.

> . . . Play tutoring for a given type of play produces increases in both the incidence and quality of that play type (Dempsey and Frost 1993, p. 311).

Play tutoring involves staying with the children as they play and providing direct and indirect suggestions about how the play might proceed, and how differences of opinion might be resolved. If children were 'rounding up the sheep' staff could make suggestions about how many dogs might be needed, what to use to build the sheep pens, who might be in control of the gate, who might be in control of the dogs, or how a ute might be able to help. As staff make suggestions it is important they try to ensure that girls have active, leadership roles in the play and that all the fun jobs are not done by the boys—staff would need to guard against the girls being the sheep and the boys being the dogs, gatekeeper and the ute driver.

Disability and additional needs

Toddlers are very curious about the physical differences and similarities between people. When toddlers first notice and think about these differences, staff have a chance to help them learn to enjoy and value people's diversity.

For this to occur staff need to provide toddlers with active support for understanding physical differences and similarities between the people they see around them. Simple feedback (refer to Chapter 8) about what they have seen provides critical support. The opportunity to read stories about people's diversity and to play with dolls that reflect different abilities and disabilities all help in this process. However, despite staff's best efforts toddlers may feel fearful and uncomfortable when confronted by disability. If this occurs, staff can combine doll play with suggestions to help toddlers feel more comfortable with physical disability:

> Invite the child to play with you—you choose the 'different-looking' doll, and the child chooses his doll . . . suggest a way for the two dolls to be together . . . and for the child to play with your doll (Dermon-Sparks et al. 1989, p. 26).

This play can continue on several different occasions until the child feels comfortable with the diversity.

REFLECTING ON SUGGESTING TECHNIQUES

1 Briefly define suggesting.
2 What is the difference between direct and indirect suggestion? Provide an example of each.
3 Which of the following suggestions are direct and which are indirect?
   - 'You could have a go at doing this . . .'
   - 'If you try this . . . then it might work better'
   - 'Why don't you put this one here?'
   - 'How about we see what happens when . . . ?'
   - 'It might be easier if you did that . . .'
   - 'Try pushing like this . . .'
   - 'This tool might be more useful . . .'
   - 'Maybe you could take another approach . . .'

4 List 10 ways of using suggesting to support children's learning in a mixed-age group setting. Would each of these processes be suitable for use with babies?
5 To what extent do you agree with the statement that 'Most of the other teaching strategies teachers use also serve as suggestions to children' (Allen and Hart 1984, p. 259)? Provide examples of how each of the following techniques could act as a suggestion: recalling, reading, singing, describing, demonstrating and modelling.
6 Observe staff working with toddlers. How and how well did they use suggestion to help toddlers learn the daily routine of the centre? Was suggestion the most appropriate technique to use? Why? Why not?
7 Observe a group discussion between an adult and a group of four-year-old children. How was suggestion used to promote children's learning?
8 Observe a dispute between a group of three- to five-year-old children. How could adult suggestion be used to help children resolve the dispute?

IMPROVING TEACHING IN PRACTICE

1 Videotape the teaching interactions you have with children during several five-minute teaching periods.
2 How and how well did you use suggestion to support children's learning? Did you:

- tend to use direct or indirect suggestions?
- adjust the specificity of your suggestions according to the children's age?
- pace your suggestions so that children could absorb what was being said and test them out for themselves?
- allow children to reject or ignore your suggestions?
- ensure your suggestions were relevant to each child's particular needs?

3 What are your areas of strength and weakness in using suggestion as a teaching technique to promote children's learning?

4 How can you improve your suggestion techniques in practice?

Further reading
Read, K., Gardner, P. and Mahler, B. 1993, *Early Childhood Programs: Human Relationships and Learning*, ninth edn, Forth Worth, TX, Holt, Rinehart and Winston Inc. [refer to pp. 89–99].

Video
Supporting Children's Active Learning: Teaching Strategies for Diverse Settings, The High Scope Press, 1992.

References
Allen, K. and Hart, B. 1984, *The Early Years: Arrangements for Learning*, New Jersey, Prentice Hall Inc.

Amos Hatch, J. 1991, 'Developing writers in the intermediate grades', *Childhood Education*, 68(2), pp. 76–80.

Brewer, J. 1992, *Introduction to Early Childhood Education: Preschool through Primary Grades*, Boston, Allyn and Bacon.

Craig Peery, J. 1993, 'Music in early childhood education', in B. Spodek, ed., *Handbook of Research on the Education of Young Children* (pp. 207–24), New York, Macmillan.

Dempsey, J. and Frost, J. 1993, 'Play environments in early childhood education', in B. Spodek, ed., *Handbook of Research on the Education of Young Children* (pp. 306–21), New York, Macmillan Publishing Company.

Dermon-Sparkes, L. 1992, '"It isn't fair!". Antibias curriculum for young children', in B. Neugebauer, ed., *Alike and Different: Exploring our Humanity with Young Children* (pp. 2–10), Washington DC, National Association for the Education of Young Children.

Dermon-Sparks, L. and the Anti-Bias Task Force 1989, *The Anti-Bias Curriculum*, Washington DC, National Association for the Education of Young Children.

Hass Dyson, A. and Genishi, C. 1993, 'Visions of children as language users: language and language education in early childhood', in B. Spodek, ed., *Handbook of Research on the Education of Young Children* (pp. 122–36), New York, Macmillan Publishing Company.

Howe, A. 1993, 'Science in Early Childhood Education', in B. Spodek, ed., *Handbook of Research on the Education of Young Children* (pp. 225–35), New York, Macmillan.

Hughes, A. and Hughes, E. 1937, *Learning and Teaching: An Introduction to Psychology and Education*, London, Longmans.

Ladd, G. and Coleman, C. 1993, 'Young children's peer relationships: forms, features and functions', in B. Spodek, ed., *Handbook of Research on the Education of Young Children* (pp. 57–76), New York, Macmillan Publishing Company.

MacNaughton, G. 1995, 'The Power of Mum: Gender and Power at Play', *Australian Early Childhood Resource Book Series*, 2(2), pp. 1–14.

McDermott, K. 1999, 'Helping primary school children work things out during recess', *Young Children*, 54(4), pp. 82–4.

Pelligrini, A. and Body, B. 1993, 'The role of play in early childhood development and education: issues in definition and function', in B. Spodek, ed., *Handbook of Research on the Education of Young Children* (pp. 105–21), New York, Macmillan Publishing Company.

Ramsey, P. 1987, *Teaching and Learning in a Diverse World: Multicultural Education for Young Children*, Columbia, Teachers' College Press.

Read, K., Gardner, P. and Mahler, B. 1993, *Early Childhood Programs: Human Relationships and Learning*, ninth edn, Forth Worth, TX, Holt, Rinehart and Winston Inc. pp. 89–99

Roe, D. 1996, 'Young children and stress: how can we help?', *Australian Early Childhood Association Resource Book Series*, 3(4), pp. 1–14.

Roth, M. W. 2001, 'Gestures: their role in teaching and learning', *Review of Educational Research*, 71(3), pp. 365–92.

Schreiber, M. 1999, Time out for toddlers: is our goal punishment or education?, *Young Children*, 54(4), pp. 22–6.

Schwartz, S. 1996, 'Hidden messages in teacher talk: praise and empowerment', *Teaching Children Mathematics*, March, pp. 396–401.

Wilkes, G. (ed.) 1979, *Collins Dictionary of the English Language*, Middlesex, Penguin Books.

Chapter 18

Telling and instructing

Instruct: to direct to do something, to teach (someone) how to do (something).

(*Collins Dictionary of the English Language*, p. 758)

Tell: to let know or notify, to order or instruct.

(*Collins Dictionary of the English Language*, p. 1494)

Certainly telling is a conventional way of dispensing wisdom and knowledge; it fits the dictionary definition of teaching.

(Seefeldt 1980, p. 146)

We tell so that children can hear, but we do not always tell so that they can understand . . .

(Hughes and Hughes 1937, p. 368)

WHAT?

When you tell a person something you describe it or provide some verbal account of what is happening or should happen. Telling children is an important and, as Seefeldt (1980) suggests, conventional teaching technique in which someone with information or knowledge (often the adult) passes that information on to someone (often the child) who does not have it. It is often associated with 'chalk and talk' approaches to teaching, and associated with direct instruction of children. Staff can tell children about ideas, opinions, concepts and reasons for doing things (Turney 1985), or tell children to do things (instructing). Instruction is, therefore, a very specific form of telling. When you instruct someone you tell them how to do something.

HOW?

Telling children about things and telling children to do things is one way of providing them with the information staff want them to have.

While telling can be an effective way to teach young children, it needs to be used with care for the following reasons:

 Telling is a one-way form of communication that allows very little opportunity for children's participation (Seefeldt 1980). If used too often children may become passive learners, quickly bored and disinterested in listening to adults.

➲ Telling relies on symbolic thought and as such is easily misunderstood by children (Seefeldt 1980). It can be most effective when it is accompanied by actions and/or objects; when simple, clear sentences are used; and when children are familiar with the words being used.

➲ Telling children how to behave socially (for example, to always share) is unlikely to be a successful teaching technique unless you also model this behaviour yourself (Hendrick 1990).

➲ Telling assumes that the teacher should be the one to decide what children need to know about, and that accumulating facts and information is in and of itself educational (Spodek and Saracho 1994). However, there are alternative views of education that assume that most learning is child-directed rather than adult-directed and that passively '. . . receiving information is not enough to create knowledge' (Spodek and Saracho 1994, p. 17).

Telling is often necessary when staff want to establish rules:

> The teacher in Grade 1 at the Merrivale Primary School tells the children the rules about playground behaviour: children must play fairly, they must not hurt each other, they must wear hats on sunny days and they must put any rubbish they have in the nearby bins. She states the rules in clear unambiguous terms so that the children are all clear on how to behave when they go out to play.

However, telling children the rules of a centre is often not sufficient by itself:

> Gabrielle, a new graduate working in a kindergarten in the outer western suburbs of Adelaide, has brought a problem to the local kindergarten teachers' group for discussion.
>
> Gabrielle: 'My problem is that the children fight all the time and won't share the equipment, especially outside. I seem to spend my time "putting out fires", going from one dispute to the next and sorting out the children's arguments. What techniques can I use other than telling them what to do and acting as a referee?'
>
> Carlene: 'At the beginning of the year I make all the rules clear to the children. I tell them what the rules are and then I remind them again and again. I mean rules like—walking inside, only four people at the clay table, keep the sand in the sandpit—and I also mean rules of behaviour towards others; that is, sharing, not taking others' equipment, using voices not fists and so on. When the children do something that doesn't fit in with the rules I remind them and help them. If two children are fighting over a wheelbarrow outside, I'll remind them that sharing outside is desirable, and that they need to work this out verbally. At the beginning of the year they don't know how to do this, so I model for them and give them suggestions and techniques for working out turn-taking. They soon get the hang of it and after a few weeks they start to use words instead of physically fighting.'
>
> Gabrielle: 'Is it too late for me to do this? I can see they've got into the habit of me telling them what to do.'
>
> Carlene: 'You should start right away! It's never to late to learn!'

In the case that staff do decide that telling children about or to do something (instructing) will support children's learning, Turney (1985) advises staff to:

➲ use clear, uncluttered language that avoids words that may be unfamiliar to the children

➲ give children practical examples to illustrate the points being made

❍ emphasise the key points or items through tone of voice and gesture

❍ gain feedback from the children to ensure that they've understood what's been said.

Research suggests that young children are more likely to learn to do things through story-telling than through direct instruction. As Seifert (1993, p. 14) explains:

They may learn to zipper jackets more easily if the task is represented as a story ('A bird flying out of its nest').

According to Seifert (1993) research also suggests that story-telling can be successfully used to help children learn to remember things before they can communicate with language. Story-telling is a very special form of telling children about things and it is very different to story-reading.

Story-telling depends on the *spoken word* to connect a story-teller and listener so that a story is created in the imagination.

Story-reading depends on a *focus on print* (words and/or illustrations) for the understanding and appreciation of a story (Smyth 1996, p. 2).

According to Smyth (1996), successful storytelling with young children involves:

❍ telling stories that have a clear theme. Themes that work well are those that derive from the children's own experiences and do not confuse or frighten them

❍ telling stories that move along quickly and have a plot and a sequence

❍ telling stories in which staff have enjoyment and interest

❍ telling stories in settings where children will not be distracted by light, noise and other children.

WHEN AND WHY?

Goal relevance

Sometimes it is important for children to learn something by being told about it rather than discovering it for themselves. Giving children information rather than waiting for them to discover it for themselves is particularly relevant when:

❍ children need to know something to be safe. For example, children need to know about road rules, rules about how to use hammers and rules about using matches. They may need to be told: 'You stop when traffic lights are red'; 'You never put your thumb under a hammer'; 'Hot water will burn you if you touch it'; 'It is dangerous to cross the road without an adult'

❍ it would be difficult for children to find something out for themselves. For example, when children cannot find out the name of an object or person without being told, or when children need to know about social rules and conventions reading from left to right in English, or not to masturbate in public

❍ children may experience considerable frustration or embarrassment trying to discover something for themselves. For example, where the toilet is

❍ children may need direct instruction in how to use a new tool or gain a new skill to help with their independence. For example, if a new tool, such as a drill, is introduced into the woodworking area, the children must be instructed on how to use it.

Developmental considerations

Although telling is a verbal teaching technique it can be used with pre-verbal babies to promote their cognitive and language learning. This is because babies enjoy listening to the human voice. Research shows that newborn babies find listening to the human voice preferable to sounds such as music, and babies by six weeks of age find looking at faces that are speaking preferable to those that are not speaking (Hass Dyson and Genishi 1993).

One way in which staff can capitalise on the interest babies have in the human voice is by telling them simple stories about daily events. Staff can tell babies about what is happening around them, what might happen to them and what has happened previously. For example, a caregiver may say to a baby, 'I'm going to change your nappy now, then we're going to have lunch. You're going to sit in your special chair, your blue chair, remember? the one you sat in yesterday.'

This simple story-telling provides opportunities for babies to:

- ➲ react and respond to sounds
- ➲ begin to learn basic language concepts
- ➲ listen to speech
- ➲ attach meaning to speech
- ➲ learn to recognise verbal sequences
- ➲ begin to visualise the meanings of sounds
- ➲ associate sound with actions and events.

The opportunity to practise these skills and gain these meanings helps the child learn to become:

> . . . a participant in a community dialogue, toward the 'acquisition of shared meaning' through the use of gestures and sounds (Nelson 1985, cited in Hass Dyson and Genishi 1993, p. 124)

Such participation is the key for a child to become a competent member of a social group, and the precursor of oral and written literacy.

By two years of age, children are able to use words and simple sentences to communicate their ideas and needs to other people, and they are able to follow simple adult instructions. It is, therefore, possible for toddlers to learn how to do things through being told how or being told about them. However, toddlers are very active people who most enjoy learning about the world though their own exploration of it (Castle 1990). They often like to move rapidly from one new adventure to another and spend much of their time trying out solutions to the many problems they encounter. They want to know how to make things happen. How to make a block balance on another block, how to turn a tap off or how to make a sandcastle may be just some of the problems faced by a toddler who is busy exploring their world. Telling a toddler how to do these things will generally be inappropriate. The point for toddlers is to discover this for themselves. Telling is probably only useful when:

- ➲ they need to be told how to do something for safety reasons—showing a toddler how to do something is as important as telling them how to do it. A simple, 'Let's do it this way . . .' accompanied by a demonstration will give the words more meaning
- ➲ they have asked to be told the name of something or someone. Toddlers often communicate in simple sentences that rely on nouns and verbs to convey meaning. Telling

toddlers the name of things or actions when they show an interest in them or when they ask, 'What's that?' helps expand their vocabulary and shows that you are taking their questions seriously

➡ they are experiencing considerable frustration trying to discover something for themselves. Toddlers' enthusiasm for exploration and finding out how things work is often not matched by their physical and cognitive problem-solving abilities. This can create considerable frustration. If they are trying to find out how to make one block balance on another and they cannot figure it out, it can be frustrating. Staff can reduce the frustration toddlers feel by telling them how to do it. However, as indicated above, showing a toddler how to do something can be as important as telling them how to do it. Once again, a simple, 'Let's try it this way . . .' accompanied by a demonstration will give the words more meaning.

Narelle is sitting on the floor with Lorenzo as he plays with the Duplo. He is having trouble putting the small person on to the long block. Narelle says: 'Put it on top, Lorenzo'. She then demonstrates for him how the person fits on the top of the block.

Toddlers begin to tell their own stories and follow simple adult stories. Staff can use these emerging abilities to support many aspects of toddlers' learning through storytelling. This form of telling can be far more meaningful than simple instructions. Research indicates that narrative (stories) and metaphor are often better understood by young children than direct instruction (Seifert 1993). Telling toddlers stories about things that have happened to them can be a very powerful way of helping them learn from their own experiences. As Smyth (1996, p. 4) argues:

When we put the familiar into story form we offer a new interpretation—we help children to structure the events of their own lives.

Preschoolers begin to use language to talk with other children, express their feelings, think about why and how things work, and to share their experiences with others. They are also increasingly asking questions about how the world works and why. The question, 'Why?' is one of their most frequently asked questions (Arthur et al. 1996). If staff know the answer to the question, 'Why?' they can tell preschoolers the answer. However, telling them the answers may not help their learning. Children may quickly forget the answer or become dependent on adults to answer their questions. Staff can encourage children to seek the answers for themselves through open-ended questioning (Chapter 13), problem-solving (Chapter 25) and empowering (Chapter 23). This will help children become independent learners.

Children's mathematical understandings in the early years of schooling grow when they have lots of opportunities to '. . . reinvent it through their own daily explorations and with number games . . .' (Perlmutter et al. 1993, p. 21). These explorations and games are likely to lead to more complex, detailed and creative mathematical understandings when children receive general rather than specific instructions about how to proceed. General instructions to children of this age from teachers encourages critical thinking and problem-solving, while more specific and detailed teacher instruction encourages the search for the right answer (Perlmutter et al. 1993).

Children telling stories to each other can also support struggling readers and the development of co-operative learning skills for children in the early years of school. Hintz and Stomfay-Stitz

(1999) described a program in which an early years teacher in Toronto integrated children's story-telling into a Peacemaking program, and in doing so children who had been struggling with reading improved their reading skills considerably. Children were invited to choose their favourite books and then in small groups they told the stories to each other:

> In the beginning, her voice was the loudest, and children joined it in their own pace. She enabled her students to progress by providing a 'safety net' of strategies learned through Peacemaking, such as avoiding derogatory remarks or laughing at those whose pace was slower (Hintz and Stomfay-Stitz 1999, p. 5)

EQUITY CONSIDERATIONS

'Race' and culture

As indicated earlier in this chapter, staff may need to tell children things to keep them physically safe. However, children also need to feel emotionally safe. Prejudice and racism can make early childhood settings emotionally unsafe for children from black and ethnic minority backgrounds. Comments such as, 'My mum hates darkies and so do I!' will be very hurtful to a black child and will make the centre feel unsafe. Children need to know that staff have rules about treating each other fairly and with respect. They will not know about these rules unless they are told and reminded about them.

Telling is also an appropriate technique for giving children information that is important to have but difficult to find for themselves. For example, by three years of age children are aware of differences in skin colour and they become interested in how and why such differences occur. It is difficult for young children to discover the answer as to why these differences exist for themselves. Yet it is important that they have an accurate answer as this prevents misunderstandings developing. Children can think differences exist because people with light skin tones wash themselves harder than people with dark skin tones or because people with dark skin tones eat lots of chocolate.

To find the answer to how and why skin tones differ, children will need to be told the answer in ways that they can understand:

> We get our skin colour in three different ways: from our parents and from relatives who lived long ago, called ancestors; from the sun; and from something called melanin . . . You can't see the tiny melanin grains but everyone has melanin in their skin. If you have dark skin, the melanin in your body is very active. If you have light skin, the melanin in your body is not very busy (Kissinger 1994, pp. 11–13).

Children may also need to be told how to use a tool or implement from a culture different to their own. If staff are adding cooking implements from a particular culture into the program it is important that children are told the correct name and correct use of the implements. Once again, this helps avoid misunderstandings that could be offensive or hurtful to other children and adults in the group.

Gender

Telling is also an appropriate technique for giving children information about gender differences between people. For example, by three years of age children are aware of differences in gender and they become interested in how and why such differences occur. They might become interested in why boys have penises and where girls' penises are. As with differences in skin tone, it is difficult for young children to discover the answer as to why these differences exist for themselves. It is also equally important that they have an accurate answer to prevent misunderstandings. The following conversation highlights how three-year-old children can misunderstand anatomical differences between males and females, and how telling children the facts can overcome such misunderstandings.

> . . . 'My mom doesn't have a penis; she has hair'. The teacher, overhearing the remarks, comments also matter-of-factly, 'Yes, and she has a vagina too. Women have vaginas, men have penises. That's what makes them a woman or a man (Dermon-Sparks et al. 1989, p. 50).

Understanding that it is anatomical differences that makes us male and female helps children learn that what you do doesn't change your biological sex. You will still be a girl if you wear trousers or play with the trucks and you will still be a boy if you wear a skirt and play with dolls. This understanding helps children to begin to think critically about gender stereotypes. They can learn that having or not having a penis should not make any difference to your ability to climb, use blocks, dress up in 'sparkly' clothes or play with dolls.

Disability and additional needs

Children without disabilities are often curious about children with visible disabilities. They might ask questions about why a child has a particular prosthesis, if it hurts or not and what they can or cannot do with the prosthesis. Once again, letting children find their own answers to such questions allows misconceptions to develop. Misconceptions and misunderstandings are the basis for prejudice towards people with disabilities. Misconceptions can be avoided by staff telling children the answers to their questions using simple and non-emotive language. The following anecdote from Dermon-Sparks et al. (1989, p. 41) shows how simple explanations can be. Misha is three-years-old and has had a tracheotomy. On her first day in the centre at group time the teacher allows children to raise any questions they want to ask about Misha, and explains the tracheotomy as follows:

> . . . Misha sings and talks. She gets air for singing and talking through a special tube in her throat.

Dermon-Sparks et al. (1989) suggest that staff check with the parents of children with disabilities to find out what they want staff to tell other children about their child. This can ensure that you use words with the children without disabilities that are meaningful to the child that has a disability.

REFLECTING ON TELLING AND INSTRUCTING TECHNIQUES

1   Briefly explain the differences between 'telling about' and 'telling what to do'.
2   How could telling be used as a technique to help toddlers learn how to wash their hands after toileting? What words would be best employed to achieve this aim?
3   Is telling an appropriate teaching technique to use with babies?
4   To what extent do you believe that telling is an appropriate technique to use in early childhood settings?
5   List five occasions on which you think it would be important for children to learn something by being told about it rather than discovering it for themselves.
6   What words might you use to tell a child why people have different skin tones?

7   What words might you use to tell a child why another child had one arm shorter than the other and had no fingers on the hand of this arm?

8   What words might you use to tell a child what a vagina is?

9   Research suggests that young children are more likely to do things when staff use storytelling or metaphors rather than through direct instruction. How might you tell a child what he needs to do on the following occasions through a short story or metaphor?
  ➔ Tying shoelaces?
  ➔ Rubbing hands with soap to get them clean?
  ➔ Putting away blocks on the shelf?

10   Observe an early childhood staff member during a routine time with toddlers. How and how often did she tell the children about the routine in order to help them learn about it? How did the children respond to this? Would it have been possible to tell the children what they needed to do through a short story or metaphor?

11   Observe an early childhood staff member as he works with a small group of preschool children. How and how often did he tell the children about the group experience and group rules in order to help them learn about both? How did the children respond to this? Would it have been possible to tell the children what they needed to do through a short story or metaphor?

IMPROVING TEACHING IN PRACTICE

1   Record (using a tape-recorder or written notes) the verbal teaching interactions you had with children during several half-hour teaching periods.

2   How often did you:
  ➔ tell the children how to do things?
  ➔ tell the children about things?

3   When telling children, did you:
  ➔ use your tone of voice and gesture to emphasise what you were saying?
  ➔ ensure that they understood what you were telling them by using clear, simple, descriptive language?

4   Tell a group of toddlers a simple story about an event that has recently happened in the centre. What did the toddlers learn from the story?

5   Tell a baby a simple story. Did the baby listen to and learn about how language is patterned and how meaning is associated with language?

6   What are your areas of strength and weakness in using telling and instructing as teaching techniques to promote children's learning?

7   How can you improve your teaching techniques in practice?

Further reading

Cole, P. and Chan, L. 1990, *Methods and Strategies for Special Education*, New Jersey, Prentice Hall Inc. [refer to pp. 170–91].

Kissinger, K. 1994, *All the Colours We Are*, St. Paul, Minnesota, Redleaf Press.

Seefeldt, C. 1980, *Teaching Young Children*, New Jersey, Prentice Hall Inc. [refer to pp. 146–59].

Smyth, J. 1996, 'Let's tell stories: sharing stories with young children', *Australian Early Childhood Association Resource Book Series*, 3(3), pp. 1–14.

Spodek, B. and Saracho, O. 1994, *Right from the Start: Teaching Children Ages Three to Eight*, Boston, Allyn and Bacon [refer to pp. 16–19].

References

Arthur, L., Beecher, B., Dockett, S., Farmer, S. and Death, E. 1996, *Programming and Planning in Early Childhood Settings*, second edn, Sydney, Harcourt Brace and Company.

Castle, K. 1990, 'The second year: 12–24 months', in E. Surbeck and M. Kelly, eds, *Personalizing Care with Infants, Toddlers and Families* (pp. 23–32), Wheaton MD, Association for Childhood Education International.

Dermon-Sparks, L. and the Anti-Bias Task Force 1989, *The Anti-Bias Curriculum*, Washington DC, National Association for the Education of Young Children.

Hass Dyson, A. and Genishi, C. 1993, 'Visions of children as language users: language and language education in early childhood', in B. Spodek, ed., *Handbook of Research on the Education of Young Children* (pp. 122–36), New York, Macmillan Publishing Company.

Hendrick, J. 1990, *Total Learning: Developmental Curriculum for the Young Child*, 3rd edn, Toronto, Merrill Publishing Company.

Hintz, B. F. and Stomfay-Stitz, A. 1999, Peace education and conflict resolution through expressive arts in early childhood education and teacher education, Paper presented at the *Annual Conference of the Eastern Educational Research Association*, Hilton Head, SC, February 26, ED433105.

Hughes, A. and Hughes, E. 1937, *Learning and Teaching: An Introduction to Psychology and Education*, London, Longmans.

Kissinger, K. 1994, *All the Colours We Are*, St. Paul, Minnesota, Redleaf Press.

Perlmutter, J., Bloom, L. and Burrell, L. 1993, 'Whole math through investigation', *Childhood Education*, 70(1), pp. 20–4.

Seefeldt, C. 1980, *Teaching Young Children*, New Jersey, Prentice Hall Inc.

Seifert, K. 1993, 'Cognitive development and early childhood education', in B. Spodek, ed., *Handbook of Research on the Education of Young Children* (pp. 9–23), New York, Macmillan Publishing Company.

Smyth, J. 1996, 'Let's tell stories: sharing stories with young children', *Australian Early Childhood Association Resource Book Series*, 3(3), pp. 1–14.

Spodek, B. and Saracho, O. 1994, *Right from the Start: Teaching Children Ages Three to Eight*, Boston, Allyn and Bacon.

Turney, C. 1985, *Anatomy of Teaching*, Sydney, Novak Publishing.

Wilkes, G. (ed.) 1979, *Collins Dictionary of the English Language*, Middlesex, Penguin Books.

Part Three
Specialist Teaching Techniques

Chapter 19

Co-constructing

Construct: to put together substances or parts, assemble.

> (*Collins Dictionary of the English Language*, p. 323)

Co: prefix together, joint or jointly, mutual or mutually.

> (*Collins Dictionary of the English Language*, p. 289)

The key to construction of knowledge is interaction

(Williams 1994, p. 158).

. . . it is the presence of an intended message that motivates children to negotiate shared meanings and to co-construct knowledge

(Forman 1996a, p. 90).

WHAT?

In everyday language to construct something is to form or build 'it'. To co-construct is to form with others. As a teaching strategy, co-construction refers to staff and children forming meaning and building knowledge about the world with each other. Staff and children co-construct their meanings and their knowledge.

THEORETICAL BACKGROUND

CONSTRUCTIVISM, SOCIAL CONSTRUCTIVISM AND CO-CONSTRUCTION

The strategy of co-constructing derives from the constructivist philosophical tradition in which it is believed that '. . . to understand this world of meaning one must interpret it . . .' (Schwandt 1994, p. 118). This philosophical tradition has led early childhood education to two approaches to understanding children's cognition: constructivism and social constructivism. Constructivism is evident in the work of Piaget and social constructivism in the work of Vygotsky. The difference between these approaches lies in the emphasis each one places on the role of the social and cultural world in children's construction of meaning.

Constructivists, building on Piaget's work, believe that children learn through active engagement with their physical environment. In particular, they believe that concrete activities which encourage children to explore and search for meaning help them to form their own knowledge about the world (Morrison 1995). As children interact with the concrete world around them and make sense of this interaction they form (construct) their own '. . . personal understandings and knowledge . . .' (Arthur et al. 1996, p. 88). Children create their knowledge about the world through direct physical experience of it (Spodek and Saracho 1994).

Social constructivists, building on Vygotsky's work, also believe that children are active in constructing (forming) their own knowledge about the world and that this occurs as children interact with their physical world. However, social constructionists see social interaction as the critical element in young children's meaningful construction. They believe that '. . . all knowledge emerges in the process of self- and social construction' (Rinaldi 1993, p. 105).

This theory holds that children become knowledgeable and are able to give meaning to their world by negotiating meaning with others.

The difference between the two theoretical traditions is summarised by Morrison (1995, p. 74) as follows:

Vygotsky believed that children's mental, language, and social development is supported and enhanced by others through social interaction. This view is the opposite from the Piagetian perspective in which children are much more solitary developers of their own intelligence and language.

Wertsch (2001, p. 1) also discussed a key difference between Piaget and Vygotsky:

. . . their views concerning the importance of culture, in particular, the role of mediation of action through artifacts, on the development of the mind.

Piaget emphasised the role of artifacts, Vygotsky emphasised the role of social interaction in the contruction meaning.

It is this belief in the collaborative nature of learning derived from social constructivism that underpins the belief in co-construction as an effective teaching strategy.

HOW?

Staff can co-construct knowledge with young children through emphasising the study of meaning rather than the acquisition of facts. Meaning is how we make sense of, understand, interpret or give significance to our world. To study meaning involves studying this process. To acquire facts involves gathering descriptions, information, data and figures about our world.

For example, an adult studying the meaning of sound with children would study how children understand sound, how children interpret different sounds and which sounds children see as significant. To do this, the adult needs to encourage the children to share what they think and know. The adult could encourage children to talk about which sounds they like, which sounds make them feel happy and which sounds make them feel sad. Talking with children would be one way for the adult to study the meanings children give to sound. However, the meaning children give to sound could also be studied by the adult asking children to express being happy through voice-sounds or for the children to make musical and non-musical sounds. Additionally, the meaning children give to sound could be studied by encouraging children to draw or mime a sound. Irrespective of how the adult chooses to study this, it would be necessary for her to access and reflect on the child's meanings.

On the other hand, a person wanting children to acquire facts about sound would encourage them to gather descriptions, data, information and figures. To do this, the adult would need to teach the child to listen to and recall the sounds the child experienced and made. This could involve encouraging a child to learn the names of sounds, to describe a particular sound or to react in particular ways to specific sounds. For an adult to teach a child the facts about sound requires the child to observe, listen and remember what they are told by the adult.

In summary, the study of meaning involves uncovering, expressing and sharing meaning, and the acquisition of facts involves observing, listening and remembering. Staff can help children study meaning by encouraging them to:

- uncover, express and share their meanings with others. Forman (1996a) suggested that children be encouraged to do this through symbolisation, communication, narrative and metaphor
- uncover, read and acknowledge the meanings of others (Forman 1996a).

The study of meaning becomes the co-construction of meaning when children's and adults' understandings, interpretations and sense of significance are developed in negotiation with each other. As Forman (1996a, p. 1) explained:

In this co-constructivist curriculum the teachers form a community of learners with the children and with the parents and other teachers . . . They discuss the social and symbolic processes by which meanings are negotiated toward some level of shared understanding.

Co-construction is supported through a negotiated curriculum based on design, documentation and discourse. Forman (1996a) defined these three elements of a negotiated curriculum as follows:

Design refers to any activity in which children make records of their plans or intended solutions (p. 2).

Discourse connotes a deep desire to understand each others' words . . . a struggle to understand, where speakers constructively confront each other, experience conflict, and seek footing in a constant shift of perspectives (p. 3).

Documentation refers to any activity that renders a performance record with sufficient detail to help others understand the behaviour recorded (p. 3).

Design and documentation enable children to uncover, express and share their ideas with others. They also enable children to see and acknowledge other people's ideas. Discourse is the process through which meaning is expressed, shared and negotiated with others as they struggle to understand each other's designs and documentation of a problem, issue or phenomenon. Discourse, in this sense of the word, is talk with children about meaning. Staff need to look for and discuss children's theories, assumptions, contradictions and misunderstandings about what is being studied to ensure that their talk supports the children's study of meaning rather than their acquisition of facts. For this reason, documenting (Chapter 22) is an important part of the process of co-constructing meaning with young children. It allows staff to examine in detail children's discourse and their own.

Co-constructing knowledge about sand properties.

Hughes (2002, p. 139) details the importance of documentation to the processes of co-constructing meaningful curriculum with children in the early years of school:

> Written transcripts and drawings of the children's experiences allow teachers to examine their teaching practices. In addition, teachers can review their questions and comments, and study the ways their responses influence the children's actions or thinking.

As staff review children's discourse and their own they can begin to map the exchange of ideas and triggers and barriers to the development of shared understandings between themselves and children. They can then reach deeper insights about how meanings were negotiated with children to build shared understandings, and draw on those insights in their future teaching with young children.

During the process of negotiating meaning with children, staff need to remember that children co-construct meaningful knowledge with each other when they share an interest in a particular phenomenon or issue (Hill 1994) and when they have the time to work together on it in some depth (Forman 1996b).

Harris (2000) studied a toddler and preschool children's art exhibition in which the images and constructions of children between 17 months and 6 years of age were exhibited. She described how this exhibition was used to facilitate a process of co-construction with the children and early childhood student-teachers. She described four phases in the study that highlight the process of co-construction in action:

- ➲ Phase 1—Children's responses to, and interactions with, the three-dimensional artworks at the exhibition.
- ➲ Phase 2—Student teachers' exploration of symbolic representation within the context of the exhibition.
- ➲ Phase 3—Student teachers' extension of the children's representations (i.e. art, stories and enactments) through a process of sharing their own symbolic representations with children.

Phase 4—Children/student teacher exchanges of creative works within their respective contexts (Harris 2000, p. 188).

While these phases describe a research process they also offer a process of co-construction that can be used by staff within early childhood services to proactively engage in co-construction with young children.

WHEN AND WHY?

Co-constructing meaning with adults helps children to learn how to problem-pose and problem-solve with others. Hence, co-constructing is a relevant teaching technique for extending children's current level of understanding and expression in any area of development. It is particularly pertinent when staff want to challenge children to predict and explain their world through a variety of symbolic media. Research suggests that co-construction may be a more powerful way for young children to learn than self-discovery and individual construction of meaning. Summarising this work Crowley and Siegler (1999, p. 314) noted:

> The current findings suggest that knowing the right explanation is what makes learning powerful, regardless of where the explanation came from. This conclusion is generally consistent with the broader literature on co-construction of knowledge during collaborative problem-solving and expert teaching.

Goal relevance

When staff and children co-construct meaning, children can learn that:

- there are multiple ways of explaining and representing the world (Forman 1996b)
- meanings are socially shared and negotiated (Forman 1996a)
- there are many ways to explore the one problem, issue or phenomenon (Forman 1996b)
- ideas can be transformed and extended (Harris 2000)
- it is possible to exchange ideas (Harris 2000)
- it is possible to enrich and deepen their understandings (Kolbe and Robertson 1996)
- mutual involvement between adults and children in meaning-making is exciting and enriching (Nimmo 1994).

Developmental considerations

The co-construction of meaning is possible whenever children are struggling to give meaning to their world. Research suggests that children do this from the moment they are born (DeRue-Durkin and Davey 1996). To co-construct meaning, children need to be given a wide range of media through which to express their understandings of the world and through which to share these understandings with others. They also need to have access to adults who listen for, watch and interact with them as they struggle to represent their meanings to others.

The forms of expression children can use to represent and discuss their meanings will vary from child to child and within each child as they grow and develop. A baby cannot dance, tell stories and make models in the ways that older children can. However, babies can express themselves through gesture, movement and sound. Staff need to offer children media for self-expression that are relevant to the current and emerging capacities of the child for self-expression. Pointers for staff on how to do this include:

➲ Babies are exploring the world via their senses and they can best share and express the meanings they give to their explorations via sensory play (DeRue-Durkin and Davey 1996). An environment which allows babies to touch, smell, move, listen, feel and taste will enable staff to listen for, watch and interact with them as they struggle to represent their meanings to others. The following extract describes how one centre approached the challenge of offering a rich and safe sensory environment for babies to explore:

> A shallow plastic wading pool was filled with scented water, pink camellias floating on the surface. Wind chimes hung from the ceiling above mountains of fat cushions covered by fluffy old bedspreads. Here the infants could venture across a landscape of satisfying textures and big soft bumps. There were fruit fingers and sorbet to satisfy the youngest palate (DeRue-Durkin and Davey 1996, p. 68).

➲ Toddlers are rapidly acquiring the ability to explore and express their meanings through language, images, models and constructions. They have a wide range of gestures they use to help them express their meanings and discoveries to others, and are beginning to be able to use the symbolic languages of music, drama, story, image-making and movement to discover other people's meanings and to share their own. The following extract shows how staff can draw on these abilities to study and negotiate meaning with toddlers:

> The farm in the storm and the zoo under the rainbow . . . it was rainbows which had captured their further interest. One of the books we had been using illustrated medieval ideas about the structure of rainbows, and Simon and Jesse chose to illustrate these. However, a dilemma faced them. They both wished to use brown and black, and Phoebe, pink, but wherever they looked in the books they could not find evidence of these colours in rainbows. Each would take a turn, flipping through the pages, as if not trusting the other to have looked hard enough . . . Their drawings were sophisticated, showing that they understood the schema of rainbows and the spectrum (Kolbe and Roberston 1996, p. 154).

➲ Preschool children's capacity for meaning-making and meaning-negotiation becomes increasingly complex and well-developed. They develop a growing competence in using the symbolic languages of music, drama, story, image-making and movement to discover other people's meanings and to share their own. The following extract shows how staff can draw on these abilities to study and negotiate meaning with preschool children:

Trees and forests

This investigation which ultimately involved five boys (and on one occasion one girl) for several weeks, was initially prompted by one child's spontaneously-made vertical structure which he identified as a tree. A second child seemed fascinated by the challenge of making a similar vertical structure . . . and was inspired to make two more trees. From then on, various further versions were made . . . As each new version was created the innovations were duly acknowledged by the group and often emulated and incorporated within the shared vocabulary of tree-making. Staff encouraged and extended this interest by discussing the discoveries with the children, displaying and photographing the clay trees, as well as encouraging the investigation and drawing of trees in the bush outside the centre . . . in terms of developing shared understandings about building vertical structures, and in developing each other's skills in communication, their knowledge about the appearance of trees through clay and graphic media . . . I was delighted with the progress made (Kolbe and Robertson 1996, p. 164).

Sharing meaning with others enables children to re-construct their own meanings. Through this co-construction and subsequent reconstruction, children can enrich their understandings of how to represent the world for themselves and to others. Gardner proposed that children have seven intelligences through which they can make and express meaning. They are logical–mathematical, linguistic, musical, spatial, bodily-kinaesthetic, interpersonal, and intrapersonal. Gardner defines them as follows:

- Logical–mathematical intelligence '. . . began as sheer pattern ability in infancy and developed through symbolic mastery of early childhood education and the notations of the school years'.
- Linguistic intelligence is about sensitivity to word order and meaning, sounds, rhythms and inflections, and to the different ways in which language can be used.
- Musical intelligence is about the ability to enjoy and replicate music.
- Spatial intelligence is about the ability to '. . . perceive the visual world accurately, to perform transformations and modifications . . . and to be able to re-create aspects of one's visual experience'.
- Bodily-kinaesthetic intelligence is the ability to use and control the body to express meaning.
- Interpersonal intelligence is the ability to '. . . understand and work with others'.
- Intrapersonal intelligence is the ability to '. . . understand and work with oneself'.

Source: Gardner, H., *Frames of Mind: The Theory of Multiple Intelligences*, 1993. © Basic Books. Reproduced by permission of Perseus Books Group.

Gardner's idea that children have multiple intelligences can be used to expose children to an enormous variety of opportunities for making, sharing and negotiating meaning. His work suggests that children of all ages have diverse forms of intelligence they can use to symbolise their world and thus make, share and negotiate meaning. They can do this on a specific topic using the categories listed above. Staff can encourage children to see and understand a specific issue or phenomenon through one or several of these intelligences.

When children explore meaning through several forms of intelligence they confront different ways of knowing, and therefore, different meanings (Forman 1996b). For example, exploring trees musically might involve trying to replicate the sounds made by them. Exploring trees spatially might involve looking at how to build a model of a tree. Each form of intelligence about trees brings forth different understandings of them. As children confront different ways of knowing about trees they revisit their original concepts and reform them. As children share this changing understanding with others they engage in the co-construction of meaning.

Children in the bayside Doandale Kindergarten have been co-constructing their knowledge of the sea. The project has progressed over several weeks and the children are now representing their knowledge in different ways. In dance they explore the movements of the tides, in modelling they make models of sea creatures with clay, and in painting they explore how to represent the colours they have observed in the water. At each stage of the project they have shared their representations of the sea with each other and their teacher.

Children's ability to uncover, represent, share and negotiate meaning will increase as they progress through childhood. In the early years of schooling, children are more able to understand the perspectives and feelings of others and use words to help them in their negotiation of meaning. However, children in the early years of school should still be provided with lots of opportunities to explore the diverse forms of intelligence they can use to symbolise their world and negotiate meaning. Experiences such as dance and music, which allow them to express and negotiate meaning spatially and kinaesthetically, can be powerful in contributing to their learning and in enriching their capacity to construct meaning.

EQUITY CONSIDERATIONS

The co-construction of meaning is often presented as a way to bring young children's voices and perspectives more powerfully into the curriculum (for example, Harris 2002). To that extent it relies strongly on children's active expression of their understandings, feelings and experiences. In considering the power of this for building more equitable curriculum with young children it is also important to note the equity alerts associated with adults seeking children's voice as a source of curriculum. Those alerts arise from diverse sources (for example, MacNaughton 2003; Viruru and Cannella 2001) but they raise similar points that staff may wish to reflect on as they attempt to co-construct meaning with young children. The privileging of voice as a curriculum goal assumes that silence is less valued and valid. Yet silence may not always mean a child is not being heard or is feeling ignored. Silence may be a strategy used by children to resist adults and a strategy for learning. Consider the comments by Viruru and Cannella (2001, pp. 167–168) as you reflect on the equity considerations in co-constructing meaning with young children:

> Are there ways to hear the voices of children, to regard them as human beings, without imposing our voices, expectations or our agenda on them? Do we have the right to question, observe, and interpret them? How do our methods create those who are younger as objects of colonizing power? What of silence? Do we place too much emphasis on oral and behaviour expression? Even when we have the best of intentions, how do our attempts to hear children serve as colonization? Are there ways that those of us who want to work with other human beings can learn to know each other without inadvertently working as colonizers?

'Race' and culture

Children's 'racial' identity can influence their desire to co-construct meaning with others. To contribute to group meaning-making, children need to have positive self-esteem and a belief that their contributions will be taken seriously by others (Hill 1994). Children who have experienced racism may have poor self-esteem and believe that their contributions will be dismissed or ignored by the group (Dermon-Sparks et al. 1989; Sleeter and Grant 1999). Children who have to negotiate their sense of self within two cultural groups are particularly vulnerable to low self-esteem because '. . . they assume that they cannot be successful in either society' (Ramsey 1987, p. 117). Two aspects of co-construction support the development of positive self-esteem for these children. Children are more likely to develop positive self-esteem when they can construct meanings rather than learn facts and when adults show interest in their ideas. However, staff should be alert to the fact that children may not feel comfortable to express their experiences of and feelings about racism towards them if they are working with staff who have not had similar experiences themselves.

Positive attitudes to racial diversity develop from a willingness to understand and respect other people's points of view. To do this children need an awareness of difference in others, the ability to notice other people's point of view, experience working with others and positive social interactions with others (Ramsey 1987). Co-construction supports these experiences in very active ways because it teaches children how to uncover, express, share and negotiate meaning. Children can be encouraged to engage in such meaning-making in relation to 'race'. They can be encouraged to uncover their understandings of 'race', express these through a variety of media, share them with others and to negotiate new meanings if and when they represent racist understandings.

Gender

Young Australian boys tend to solve the social problems they encounter with physical force and aggression. This tendency develops early and is well established by the time boys are eight years old. For example, by two years of age boys are often more unco-operative, non-compliant and aggressive than girls (Sanson et al. 1993). In contrast, young girls tend to solve the social problems they encounter through verbal reasoning and negotiation.

Young boys' tendencies towards violent social problem-solving strategies have implications for staff encouraging children to co-construct knowledge with each other and with staff. First, in mixed-gender groups girls may feel inhibited in expressing, sharing and negotiating meanings with boys. When girls fear that a difference of opinion may be resolved physically rather than verbally they become silent or move away from the conflict (MacNaughton 1997, 2000). Girls' meanings may be silenced or marginalised as a result. This turns co-construction of meaning into male-only meaning construction. Staff can guard against this by allowing girls to work in girls-only groups or by actively seeking and supporting girls' meaning-making in mixed-gender groups. Second, staff may be able to reduce boys' tendencies to use violent problem-solving strategies by improving their verbal reasoning skills (Sanson et al. 1993). Staff can work with young boys on ways to uncover, express, share and negotiate meaning verbally. This may be in boys-only groups until boys have gained the skills necessary to negotiate meaning with girls in less aggressive ways.

Disability and additional needs

Co-constructing meaning in a group of children with diverse abilities can be made exciting and enriching for all children if staff ensure children have a diverse range of media through which to discover, represent, share and negotiate meanings. Staff need to honour diverse ways of representing the world and encourage children to do the same. Talking with the children about how differently each person sees and understands the world helps build respect for diversity. It is through active involvement with each other's struggles to make meaning that children can learn to communicate with each other in innovative ways. Children can learn to listen to and read meaning in a wide variety of ways as they become familiar with the meanings in each other's images, sounds, gestures and computer messages. Consider the richness of meaning-making in the following scenario in which children of diverse abilities struggled to co-construct meaning:

> Children were trying to understand the night and its darkness. Several had been talking about what they could see at night and how it differed to what they could see during the day. In the group there was a child (Tanya) whose vision impairment resulted in reduced acuity (ability to see detail) and reduced colour vision. She could only see shades of grey. Staff encouraged children to paint the night

and the day and to then explore what was similar and different about their images. Tanya's images of the night and the day were full of lots of colour. For the remainder of children in the group their pictures of night were full of lots of grey and black. This led to lots of discussion about why Tanya's night looked different. The children struggled to understand each other. Tanya struggled to understand how what she saw as grey others saw as colour. The rest of the children struggled to understand how if Tanya's world was grey she painted it in colour. However, as the children started to talk about the content of their paintings they learned about what understandings of night they shared in common. Many, including Tanya, had painted bedtime. They started to see that night means more than colour.

Children with disabilities who have difficulty communicating via spoken language should be encouraged to find other ways of uncovering and representing their meanings to others. Children should have the opportunity to experiment with many media to find which ways of symbolising their meanings work best. For some children, clay, paint, chalk, blocks, movement, dance or music might be relevant. For other children, computer-enhanced communication might be best. The challenge for staff who want to co-construct meaning with children who cannot speak is to find another language through which the child can communicate.

REFLECTING ON CO-CONSTRUCTING TECHNIQUES

1 Define co-construction.
2 How does co-construction differ from construction?
3 What is the study of meaning?
4 How does the study of meaning differ from the acquisition of facts?
5 Identify five ways in which you could encourage children to uncover their understandings about shade and light. Would these be appropriate for children of all ages?
6 Identify five ways in which you could encourage children to share their understandings about shade and light. Would these be appropriate for children of all ages?
7 What do you see as the main gender equity issues in co-constructing knowledge with children?
8 What do you see as the main 'race' equality issues in co-constructing knowledge with children?
9 How might co-construction be used to support anti-discriminatory perspectives on disability?
10 To what extent do you believe that co-construction relies too heavily on forms of expression that devalue a child's silence?

IMPROVING TEACHING IN PRACTICE

1 Record (using a tape-recorder or written notes) several occasions on which you co-construct meaning with a small group of children.
2 What was your current style of co-construction? How and how well did you encourage children to:
     uncover, express and share their meanings with others?
     uncover, read and acknowledge the meanings of others?
     negotiate their meanings with others?

3 How and how well did you take account of developmental and equity considerations?
4 What are your areas of strength and weakness in using co-construction to promote children's learning?
5 How can you improve your co-construction techniques in practice?
6 What do you see as the hardest part of improving your co-construction techniques?

Further reading

Ebbeck, M. 1996, 'Children constructing their own knowledge', *International Journal of Early Years Education*, 4(2), pp. 5–27.

Forman, G. 1996a, Design, documentation and discourse: cornerstones of negotiated curriculum, Paper presented to the *Weaving Webs: Collaborative Teaching and Learning in the Early Years Curriculum Conference*, Melbourne, July.

——1996b, 'A child constructs an understanding of a water wheel in five media', *Childhood Education*, 72(5), pp. 269–73.

Harris, V. 2000, 'A unique pedagogical project contextualised within a children's art exhibition', *Contemporary Issues in Early Childhood*, 1(2), pp. 153–70.

Hughes, E. 2002, 'Planning meaningful curriculum: a mini story of children and teachers learning together', *Childhood Education*, 78(2), pp. 134–9.

Video

The Amusement Park for Birds, Forman, G. and Gandini, L. Amherst MA, Performanetics Press, 1994

Socially constructed learning in early childhood, Faculty of Education, University of Canberra, 1992.

Theories of Development. Studies of the child, Magna Systems, 1997, available from Marcom Projects at www.marcom.com.au [refer to section on Vygotsky's theories of development].

Websites—extending learning online

Department of Psychology, Massey University, has an introduction to Vygotsky's work by Trish Nicoll at http://www. massey.ac.nz/~Alock/virtual/trishvyg.htm

Cole, M. and Wertsch, J., Beyond the individual–social antimony in discussions of Piaget and Vygotsky, pp. 1–7 at http://www.massey.ac.nz/~Alock/virtual/colevyg.htm

There is an excellent source of resources on Vygotsky's work at http://www.kolar.org/vygotsky/

References

Arthur, L., Beecher, B., Dockett, S., Farmer, S. and Death, E. 1996, *Programming and Planning in Early Childhood Settings*, second edn, Sydney, Harcourt Brace and Company.

Crowley, K. and Seigler, R. S. 1999, 'Explanation and generalisation in young children's learning strategy', *Child Development*, 70(2), pp. 304–16.

Dermon-Sparks, L. and the Anti-Bias Task Force 1989, *The Anti-Bias Curriculum*, Washington DC, National Association for the Education of Young Children.

DeRue-Durkin, Y. and Davey, A. 1996, Empowering Infants, *Weaving Webs Conference*, Melbourne, July, pp. 65–76.

Forman, G. 1996a, Design, documentation and discourse: cornerstones of negotiated curriculum. Paper presented to the *Weaving Webs: Collaborative Teaching and Learning in the Early Years Curriculum Conference*, Melbourne, July.

——1996b, 'A child constructs an understanding of a water wheel in five media', *Childhood Education*, 72(5), pp. 269–73.

Gardner, H. 1993a, *Frames of Mind: The Theory of Multiple Intelligences*, New York, Basic Books.

——1993b, *Multiple Intelligences: The Theory in Practice*, New York, Basic Books.

Harris, V. 2000, 'A unique pedagogical project contextualised within a children's art exhibition', *Contemporary Issues in Early Childhood*, 1(2), pp. 153–70.

Hill, S. 1994, 'Co-operative communities in early childhood', *Australian Journal of Early Childhood*, 19(4), pp. 44–7.

Hughes, E. 2002, 'Planning meaningful curriculum: a mini story of children and teachers learning together', *Childhood Education*, 78(2), pp. 134–9.

Kolbe, U. and Robertson, J. 1996, The farm in the storm and other stories from Mia-Mia: children's collaborative learning, Paper presented to *Weaving Webs Conference*, Melbourne, July.

Morrison, G. 1995, *Early Childhood Education Today*, 6th edn, New Jersey, Merrill.

MacNaughton, G. 1997, 'Who's got the power? Rethinking gender equity strategies in early childhood', *International Journal of Early Years Education*, 5(1), pp. 57–67.

——2000, *Rethinking Gender in Early Childhood*, Sydney, Allen & Unwin; New York, Sage Publications; London, Paul Chapman Publishing.

——2003. 'Eclipsing voice in research with young children' *Australian Journal of Early Childhood*, 28(1) pp. 36–43.

Nimmo, J. 1994, 'Emergent curriculum', in the conference proceedings of *The Challenge of Reggio Emilia: Realising the Potential of Children* (pp. 199–214), University of Melbourne.

Ramsey, P. 1987, *Teaching and Learning in a Diverse World: Multicultural Education for Young Children*, Columbia, Teachers' College Press.

Rinaldi, C. 1993, 'The emergent curriculum and social constructivism: an interview with Lella Gandini', in C. Edwards., L. Gandini. and G. Forman, eds, *The Hundred Languages of Children: The Reggio Emilia Approach to Early Childhood Education* (pp. 101–11), New York, Ablex.

Sanson, A., Prior, M., Smart, D. and Oberklaid, F. 1993, 'Gender differences in aggression in childhood: implications for a peaceful world', *Australian Psychologist*, 28(2), pp. 86–92.

Schwandt, T. 1994, 'Constructivist, interpretivist approaches to human inquiry', in N. Denzin and Y. Lincoln, eds, *Handbook of Qualitative Research* (pp. 118–37), Thousand Oaks, CA, Sage Press.

Sleeter, C. and Grant, C. 1999, *Making Choices for Multicultural Education: Five Approaches to Race, Class and Gender,* third edn, New Jersey, Merrill Prentice Hall.

Spodek, B. and Saracho, O. 1994, *Right from the Start: Teaching Children Ages Three to Eight*, Boston, Allyn and Bacon.

Viruru, R. and Cannella, G. 2001, 'Postcolonial ethnography, young children and voice', in S. Grieshaber and G. Cannella, eds, *Embracing Identities in Early Childhood Education: Diversity and Possibilities*, pp. 158–72, New York, Teachers College Press.

Wilkes, G. (ed.) 1979, *Collins Dictionary of the English Language*, Middlesex, Penguin Books.

Wertsch, J. 2001. Beyond the individual-social ?? in discussions with Piaget and Vygotsky http://bion.psy.ed.ac.uk/lorenzo/Docs.

Williams, L. 1994, 'Developmentally appropriate practice and cultural values', in B. Mallory and R. New, eds, *Diversity and Developmentally Appropriate Practice: Challenges for Early Childhood Education* (pp. 155–65), New York, Teachers' College Press.

Chapter 20

Community building

Community: a feeling of belongingness within a group.

(Osterman 2000, p. 323)

[T]he community is the site of the mediating structures that intervene between the domain of the everyday life of individuals and the larger social, political and economic context . . . The word community conveys a sense of connectedness between people and their [our emphasis] organisations . . . The community is a social space, a sector made up of informal and relatively unmanaged associations.

(Casswell 2001, pp. 3–4)

WHAT?

A community can 'refer to a territorial or geographic unit' (Osterman 2000, p. 323) or 'the quality or character of human relationships' (Osterman 2000, p. 323). Building is the process of putting something together to create a new object. Community building is, however, a slippery term to define. The literature concerning community building and early childhood education is marked by the absence of a shared definition of 'community', and a shared understanding of how to build one.

There are two possible reasons for this. First, the multitude of socially, culturally and geographically based groups referred to as 'communities' is so broad and the social processes of building them are so complex that they may just defy definition. Second, 'community' is in such widespread use that it may preclude the need for definition—why consciously define a term that appears everywhere and is used by anyone to mean anything?

There is also a range of different ways in which community building is linked to learning. Terms such as learning communities and communities of learners populate the literature on building communities in educational settings.

Learning communities describes a collection of individuals, groups and organisations—a community—that is evolving or developing through learning, rather as a living organism does (Graves 1992). 'Communities of learners' describes collections of individuals who are learners. Jilk (1999, pp. 2–3) distinguished communities of learners from learning communities thus:

A community of learners . . . is a community that is a good place to live, work and play, and where everyone is engaged in lifelong learning . . . A learning community . . . is continually expanding its capacity to create its future; the community itself is a learner; and it is a community that responds to needs much faster than others.

For example, 'learning communities' could be used to refer to an early childhood centre where parent involvement is embedded in their children's learning and in the life of the centre, rather than being just an add-on. By contrast, communities of learners is often applied to programs around early childhood centres that seek to involve parents as learners. Fidler (1995, p. 4) described a learning community in terms of the relationships within it:

> A group of colleagues who come together in a spirit of mutual respect, authenticity, learning and shared responsibility to continually explore and articulate an expanding awareness and base of knowledge. The process of learning community includes inquiring about each other's assumptions and biases, experimenting, risking and openly assessing the results.

In this chapter we focus on what is meant by building learning communities in early childhood services and how this work might be approached to enhance young children's learning.

HOW?

> Shared work and common purpose are the basic elements that form the cornerstone of community (Balaban 2003, p. 87).

Building a learning community is a multifaceted teaching technique that draws on many of the other teaching techniques in this book including:

- ❥ encouragement (of co-operative learning)
- ❥ grouping (for co-operative and small group learning)
- ❥ co-operative problem-solving
- ❥ questioning to develop and excite curiosity and wonder
- ❥ collecting diverse resources to support flexible and open-ended learning
- ❥ facilitating learning rather than telling children the answers.

The first step in community building is to make a conscious commitment to it (Pascarella 1998). Campbell et al. (2002) provide an example of how one children's service has expressed this commitment:

Our philosophy

We are all people with unique historical, cultural and economic backgrounds living in a social world of shared and unshared meanings. We believe that access to knowledge and power is important in ensuring equity for everyone. Therefore, the service is committed to creating a critically reflective and collaborative learning environment by:

- ❥ providing an environment in which all participants have equal access to knowledge, space and time regardless of gender, culture, 'race', class and sexuality
- ❥ collaborating with parents, children and teachers in implementing a critical curriculum
- ❥ actively challenging bias and inequity in language, practices and relationships
- ❥ using different theories of learning as a curriculum frame that acknowledges the multiplicity of people within the service. These include: developmental psychology, critical theory, post-structuralism, feminist post-structuralism and post-colonialism.

Source: Campbell, Coady, Lawrence, MacNaughton, Rolfe, Smith & Totta, *Our Part in Peace*, 2002. Reproduced with the kind permission of the Australian Early Childhood Association Inc.

Once commitment is made then staff can develop a set of principles to guide their work with children and with each other. Identifying the critical features of learning communities offers the basis for developing a set of guidelines to guide staff's community building with young children. The following features of learning communities are taken from Harada et al. (2002/03, pp. 66–7):

➤ The focus is on the process of learning, rather than on mastering isolated skills.
➤ Learning is viewed as a social experience, with opportunities for co-operative problem-solving.
➤ Engagement involves wrestling with real-life problems.
➤ Learning is a demonstrated performance . . . through such acts as explaining, creating analogies, and generalising.
➤ Students have access to diverse resources. The environment is open and flexible . . . .
➤ Asessessment is continuous and in context. Time for reflection is an integral part of the process.
➤ Roles for instructors shift back and forth . . . Adults still ask questions, but they are doing so to arouse curiosity or to stretch children's thinking.

Within these broad principles for organising teaching and learning in a specific centre or classroom it is also important that staff build a strong sense of belongingness for each child within the group. Research suggests that specific classroom practices can be used to enhance children's sense of belongingness. These include:

➤ Emphasising co-operative learning rather than competition in learning. For instance, grouping older children (see Chapter 9) so that they are regularly interacting with each other and relying on each other to complete tasks, helping each other and caring about each other's learning is important (Anderman and Maehr 1994).
➤ Using dialogue as a tool for learning and as a way for children to learn about different ideas and feelings within the group (Osterman 2000).
➤ Building adult–child and child–child relationships that are caring and supportive (Osterman 2000).
➤ Taking care to include each child in positive social exchanges, as peer rejection leads to loneliness and a sense of not belonging (Osterman 2000).
➤ Building meaningful and reciprocal relationships with children's parents that involves them actively in learning (Konzal 2001). For instance, the recognition that parents have their own learning needs as well as being invaluable to their children's learning is regarded by Whalley et al. (2001) as central to the success of one of the Early Excellence Centres in the UK—Pen Green Centre in Corby:

Over 17 years we had been able to develop a comprehensive parent partnership programme. More than 6,000 local parents had been involved and staff had established a model of co-operative working that respected both the learning and support needs of parents, and children's right to high-quality early years education with care (p. 8).

➤ Using materials and experiences that 'promote opportunities for children to work and think together' (Balaban 2003, p. 85) and that encourage co-operation between children.
➤ Using group and classroom meetings to celebrate learning (Sterling 1998). The following extract from Sterling (1998, p. 68) provides insights into the active skill development teachers can focus on in order to ensure that classroom meetings support rather than undermine community building within a service.

> We teach directly the skill of being an audience: quiet listening, still bodies, patience when a presenter has an awkward moment, and applause at an appropriate time . . . Our students' abilities to keep still, to watch with an attentive attitude, and to refrain from chatting with neighbors are important to guarantee every current and future presenter a respectful and caring audience.

Ramsey (1987) offered useful guidelines about how to incorporate co-operative learning into everyday activities with young children:

- Select experiences that require the group to work together so that they build the skills of working as a group rather than learning to work as individuals.
- Include experiences that enable children to learn to focus on other people's actions, words and feelings so that they become interested in what others do, say and feel.
- Focus on finishing activities together so that children don't attempt to be the first to finish.
- Avoid games in which children eliminate each other till only one person is left as this leads to competition to be the last rather than co-operation.
- Organise the environment so that children can work in groups easily.

Whalley et al. (2001, p. 8) also highlighted the need within a learning community to build the capacity of 'children, parents and staff . . . to be good decision-makers, able to question, challenge and make choices'.

Some writers see the deepening of democratic practices as central to building communities in which reciprocal and meaningful learning can flourish. To deepen democracy in learning requires that the teacher 'practise "democratically wise" professional judgements' (Henderson 2001, p. 19). Henderson described the principles upon which these practices are based in the following ways:

> (1) they work in the inquiry spirit of 'not knowing', (2) they approach their work as a democratic 'calling', and (3) they embrace the artistry of their challenge (Henderson 2001, p. 19).

To work in the inquiry spirit of not knowing, a teacher must be open to new ways of thinking and understanding in the world and relinquish their role as the expert who knows all. To approach work with a democratic calling the teacher must work as a morally engaged teacher and act 'out of a deep sense of integrity or conscience' (Henderson 2001, p. 19). To embrace the artistry in this work the teacher must seek to work with imagination, creativity, sensitivity and intelligence.

For Goldstein (1997), commitment to teaching with love is central to building community within early childhood settings. She characterised building community as 'the development of intimacy, a critical component of teaching with love' (p. 80) and sees the development of deep connections with children as core to community building.

So, in summary, building learning communities involves:

- making a commitment to community building
- developing learning processes and materials that are democratic and that centre on co-operation, real-life problem-solving, and the use of flexible and open learning resources
- using dialogue to explore diverse ideas and feelings within the group
- building learning processes that are inclusive of all children
- building deep, caring, responsive and meaningful relationships with children
- working with the whole group for periods of time

➔ celebrating achievements within the group

➔ honoring a spirit of inquiry.

These processes take time and a community doesn't just build itself overnight. Cuffaro emphasised this point vividly in her exploration of building community within early childhood classrooms from within a Deweyian perspective:

> For a spirit of unity to exist within an ensemble we must add the factor of time—time to define purpose, to share activity, to experiment and to risk, to learn from success and failure, to open up each other's possibilities. The unity created by an ensemble grows out if its history (Cuffaro 1995, p. 28).

THEORETICAL BACKGROUND

LEARNING COMMUNITIES AND DEWEY'S DEMOCRATIC SCHOOLING

John Dewey (1859–1952) was a philosopher whose work became widely known in educational circles because he used philosophy to study education. His work was important to the Progressive movement in education.

In the United States in the 1920s and 1930s the Progressive education movement challenged the then dominant approach to education which was based on principles of scientific management theory and social efficiency with a call for democratic, child-centred, and social reform-oriented education. Dewey's ideas were core to this challenge (Henniger 1999). Two of Dewey's texts that were key to the Progressive movement were *School and Society* (1899), in which he linked schooling with social change and *Democracy and Education* (1916), in which he outlined in detail how he understood the relationship between schooling, democracy and social change. He linked social change with social improvement. Dewey strongly argued that education and democracy are intimately linked and that education should be used to change society (Pinar et al. 1995). More specifically, Dewey argued for a shift from the mental restrictions he saw within classical approaches to curriculum to a more meaningful and enriching curriculum drawn from the child's own experiences. Pinar et al. (1995, p. 105) described Dewey's arguments against classical curriculum as 'insightful and unrelenting' in the following summary of his position on curriculum:

> Routinization, memorization, and recitation characterized the classical curriculum for mental discipline. Dewey's criticism of the classical curriculum was insightful and unrelenting. He insisted that the child's experience must form the basis for the curriculum, and in so doing synthesize the apparent antagonism between the two.

In 1896 Dewey had established a laboratory school at the University of Chicago (USA) in which the development of a democratic social community in the school was core. Longstreet and Shane (1993, p. 71) characterised the curriculum of the school as follows:

> The curriculum was to be based on life itself, on such fundamental human characteristics as socializing, constructing, inquiring, and creating. The school tried to replicate a miniature society including occupational activities typically found in the real world . . . It was the teachers' responsibility to harmonize adult ends and values with the individuality of each child.

Dewey's work offers a rich basis for exploring the idea that community building is important to children's learning and for exploring how to build a learning community with young children. Dewey believed that learning grows through social interaction (Osterman 2000) and subsequently high quality education rests on the extent to which a community forms within the classroom and within the school. Community is 'realized in the degree in which individuals form a group' (Dewey 1958, p. 65). This group included the teacher and the children and it was at the heart of building democracy in and through education:

When the school introduces and trains each child of society into membership within such a little community, saturating him with the spirit of service, we shall have the deepest and best guarantee of a larger society which is worthy, lovely and harmonious (Dewey 1958, p. 49).

For Dewey, central to the capacity to build a democratic community of learners was communication (Cuffaro 1995). Communication was the mechanism through which meaning was created and shared. Without communication it was not possible to understand how others thought or understood the world and therefore it was not possible to build a shared understanding of what is valued and valuable for a group (community) of learners. He linked communication and community in the following way:

To be a recipient of a communication is to have an enlarged and changed experience. One shares in what another has thought and felt and in so far, meagerly or amply, has his own attitude modified (Dewey 1916, pp. 5–6).

WHEN AND WHY?

Goal relevance

Community building can be usefully employed by staff to assist children's learning in many ways. Osterman (2000) reviewed research on the links between children's sense of belonging in a school community and learning. She highlighted the following links between children's learning and children's sense of belonging in a school:

- ➲ Being part of a community in which children have a sense of belongingness can reduce stress and help produce a sense of well-being.
- ➲ Children's sense of community is linked to their motivation to learn. Intrinsic motivation to learn can be greater in children who have a sense of belonging.
- ➲ Pro-social behaviour is more likely when children have a sense of belongingness.
- ➲ Children's sense of identity is stronger when they are accepted as part of a community.
- ➲ Children are more able to regulate their own behaviours when they feel a sense of belongingness.
- ➲ Children are more likely to be actively engaged with the curriculum when they are accepted by peers and have a sense of being part of the community.

Osterman (2000, p. 343) concluded:

Children who experience a sense of relatedness have a stronger supply of inner resources. They perceive themselves to be more competent and more autonomous and have higher levels of intrinsic motivation. They have a stronger sense of identity but are also willing to conform to and adopt established norms and values. These inner resources in turn predict engagement and performance.

There is also considerable research evidence that the pro-social skills required for co-operative learning will benefit children's long-term learning and well-being. In particular, if children have positive social relationships with others in the early years it can enhance their long-term academic achievement and cognitive development (Bowman et al. 2001).

Developmental considerations

Children of all ages thrive when they have a sense of belonging, when they and their ideas are valued and when they have reciprocal relationships with others around them. The foundation for children's sense of belongingness in an early childhood setting and thus for building community is that babies and toddlers have time with responsive and sensitive adults and opportunities for play that comes from the children's interests and pleasures. Babies and toddlers are learning about the 'needs, rights and feelings of others' (Stonehouse 1999, p. 160) through their play and through their relationships with the adults in their lives. They can learn what it means to be part of a respectful and caring community if staff 'response to their interests and explorations, play with them, support them and enjoy them' (Stonehouse 1999, p. 160).

Research strongly suggests (Bråtan 1996) that children have pro-social capacities from their first year of life. It is therefore possible for staff to actively include the youngest of children in building a learning community. Adult behaviours that will help to support the development of caring and co-operative relationships in babies and toddlers are those that show babies and toddlers that adults care and respond to others, and they include:

- ❯ being encouraging of children's interests
- ❯ being nurturing by responding to the needs and interests of individual babies and toddlers
- ❯ showing immediate sensitivity to children's distress
- ❯ being immediately responsive to children in distress
- ❯ demonstrating concern for children's feelings (Bråtan 1996).

These adult behaviours can help in building an emotional memory in babies and toddlers that forms the basis for their own pro-social behaviours towards each other in the present and in the future.

Preschoolers also learn about social relationships through their play with each other. Children's capacity for complex socio-dramatic play in which relationships are formed and negotiated grows through their preschool years. It is through this play that they explore what it means to be part of a social group, and how it is possible to build groups in which sharing and learning is possible. Socio-dramatic play therefore offers staff an important vehicle through which to build communities of learners with preschool children. It is through play that preschool children can:

. . . problem-solve, put ideas together to form new meanings and develop symbolic capacities . . . practise being grown-up, exercise judgement, develop new and more complex physical skills and increase their strength, balance, speed, endurance and control (Glover 1999, p. 14).

They also learn about rights, rules and the negotiation of relationships that are fundamental to the development of a democratic learning community:

In staging these play episodes, the children explore their rights and duties and practise the skills necessary for good citizenship. They enact negotiations and various arguments and formulations. In doing so, they reconsider their place in the world, they work out the points of view which count in their 'real' discussions with adults. They give evidence of an attitude which Dewey deemed of great importance for citizenship and a democratic society: 'a personal interest in social relationships and control, and the habits of mind which secure social changes without introducing disorder' (Dewey 1916, p. 115 cited in Elbers 1996, p. 512–13).

Children from a very early age can also engage in co-operative learning. For instance, Ramsey (1987) highlighted the capacity of toddlers to physically co-operate with each other in games that require physical co-ordination:

> . . . 'Turtle' is played by having several children lie on the ground under a large blanket or mat. The 'turtle' has to move in a co-ordinated fashion so that the 'shell' (blanket) stays on everyone (Ramsey 1987, p. 135).

Hasan is alert to toddlers' capacity to physically co-operate with each other and draws on this knowledge in his work with them:

> Hasan works in the Bradley Park Family Centre with toddlers and preschool children. He is keen to build co-operative learning skills within his group but has noticed that the preschool children don't seem to invite the toddlers into their games in their outside play area. Hasan and his co-workers talk about this and decide to introduce the children to some new games which require the children to physically co-operate with each other. One of the games is called 'Snails'. It requires several children to hold onto a cardboard snail's shell that one of Hasan's co-workers has made as a line of children 'slither' like a snail around the silver snail's trail. Hasan has found some old silver cloth for the snail's trail and laid it out in a complex pattern in an underused part of the outside play area.

As children's language capacity grows they can also engage in more complex co-operative learning experiences such as putting on plays, writing group stories and making puppet shows. For children in the early years of schooling, video production can offer a powerful vehicle through which children can co-operate with each other in bringing diverse perspectives into the classroom. For instance, Grace and Tobin (1997) described in detail a three-year research project tracking how elementary school children make videos in their classroom and the issues and dilemmas for teachers involved in the project. It powerfully highlights the capacity of children in these early years of school to be video producers and to bring their meanings forward in the classroom through video making:

> Video production in the Waiau classrooms provided an opportunity for students to incorporate their own interests, experiences, and desires into the school world. A space was allocated in which they could explore the limits of speech, behaviour, and humor allowed in the classroom (Grace and Tobin 1997, p. 160).

EQUITY CONSIDERATIONS

Equitable learning communities rest on equitable processes and equitable participation. Staff can assess equity in their learning community processes and participation by using some simple questions that explore whose ideas drive the understandings and knowledge generated within a specific community. For instance:

- ➡ Whose voice is heard in this community?
- ➡ What is this voice inviting us to do, think and feel?
- ➡ Who benefits from this voice being heard?
- ➡ Who else may have a voice on this issue that we are not currently hearing?

'Race' and culture

Strategies such as co-operative learning open up larger questions about how groups relate to each other (Sleeter and Grant 1994, p. 105).

There is a close relationship between community-building strategies in an early childhood classroom and multicultural and anti-racist education (Kaltsounis 1997). They are linked by a commitment to democracy where there is equity of participation for all in their community and where all children have 'the right to dream' (Nieto 1995, p. 160).

It is important for children from diverse cultural, 'racial' and linguistic backgrounds to find 'safe places' where they can 'discover and develop commonalities across difference' (Lankshear et al. 1995, p. 176). This does not mean that staff should attempt to create learning spaces in which children all share the same views and visions of the task at hand. Instead, they need to create spaces for learning in which diversity is possible in what is thought, how a topic is approached, what skills are used and what knowledge is valued within the group. Exploring cultural and 'racial' differences and commonalities is an important part of building communities in early childhood settings. A community does not mean we are all the same but that we know how to be respectful of our differences. As Mattai (2002, p. 27) put it:

The teacher should become culturally synchronized with students so that they understand the cultural repertoire of their classroom and work to expand their own cultural horizons.

A community of learners will also be a safe space within which to express differences. Within this, staff need to be watchful of whose ideas come to the fore by asking the questions, 'Whose ideas are dominant within this community?', 'Whose ideas are silenced?', 'Whose ideas are marginalised?'. Such questions can help staff to reflect on the potential for one cultural group's ideas to dominate and they can alert them to moments when racist views emerge that may silence the voices of children from culturally, 'racially' and linguistically diverse backgrounds. Learning to 'listen to, rather than talk about or speak for, those who are at the margins of the culture of power' (Swadner Blue 2000, p. 127) is a critical task for staff wishing to build equitable learning communities.

Tijerina Revilla (1998) offered six basic concepts for building communities in areas where children are having to traverse more than one culture. They represent a 'whole school' approach to community building. These concepts are taken directly from her paper and they are:

1 Vision. There is a clear, compelling, shared image of what should, must and can be provided to promote learning at the highest levels for students.
2 Leadership and Governance. Highly creative and imaginative decisions are encouraged. Co-ordinated efforts from school board to parents, teachers and students exist with optimum level of involvement of all concerned.

3   Responsive Pedagogy. Creative and imaginative classroom teaching programs and practices effectively utilise relevant curriculum, state-of-the art instructional methods, and materials and assessments that clearly support a positive learning environment that meets the needs of individuals, builds upon the culture and past experiences, and addresses the development and 'readiness' stages of students.

4   Family and Community. Parents, businesses and community agencies are actively involved with school affairs, providing support and special services and networking to assure co-ordination.

5   Capacity Building. Ongoing utilisation of knowledge bases and unique cultural contexts guide staff development, aggressive program design and appropriate resource allocation.

6   Schooling Practice. There is concerted, orchestrated use of only the most effective programs and classroom practices supported by research, professional wisdom, and unified campus and district commitments.

The principles can be used as a checklist for those staff working at community building with children from culturally and linguistically diverse backgrounds. For instance, in my community-building efforts with this group of children have I:

- ➲ developed a clear vision of what needs to be provided to support all children to excel?
- ➲ co-ordinated my efforts with all adults involved with this group of children?
- ➲ developed a responsive teaching and learning environment that is building on all children's strengths and using the very best resources and knowledge available to me at this time?
- ➲ included families and communities in my vision-making and efforts?
- ➲ actively attempted to build the capacity of all staff to be involved in the process?
- ➲ attempted to act wisely at all times?

Staff working with young children who are learning English as a second language need to be alert to the ways in which they can proactively support their sense of belonging and inclusion in co-operative learning. Key dimensions to this work include:

- ➲ supporting the maintenance of children's first language to support children's sense of self-worth and connection with their family and wider cultural contexts
- ➲ introducing the second language using models of best practice that include the infusion of bilingual staff, resources and learning experiences throughout the curriculum (Siraj-Blatchford and Clarke 2000).

Gender

Communities of learners require reciprocal and respectful relations between children and between children and adults. To achieve reciprocity and respect between all children in a group staff will need to be alert to the prevailing gender dynamics and relations in their group and/or classroom. Research shows that disrespectful behaviours between girls and boys such as bullying and teasing are often missed or ignored by early childhood staff (Gropper and Froschl 2000). These behaviours can be strongly gendered, with one study of 231 children in early years classrooms showing that boys initiated bullying behaviours three times more often than girls in the study did (Gropper and Froschl 2000). Children in this study were keen for staff to intervene and to set rules that established that bullying and teasing were not acceptable within the classroom. The researchers highlighted the importance of adult vigilance of and intervention in children's gender relations to build a positive climate for learning within early childhood classrooms and concluded:

> . . . when teachers do not intervene, which is true of the majority of incidents we observed, it is conceivable that children perceive that this is condoning the behaviour. Since boys are the predominant initiators of these incidents, children may also see teachers' lack of response as giving boys a license to behave in these ways (Gropper and Froschl 2000, p. 55).

For staff who wish to build communities of learners in which gender equity flourishes, it is critical that they pay close attention to setting rules and limits that make bullying and teasing unacceptable. Given that children's gender identity construction is linked to the cultural ideas about gender that they encounter, it is important that staff offer boys and girls diverse ways to think about and respond to the idea that 'boys can bully' and 'girls can put up with it'.

Brani was a teacher working with 6–8 year old children in small country school. She was concerned that three of the girls in her classroom were resistant to working with the boys on any of the co-operative learning tasks she had planned. She had heard from one of the boys in the group that some older boys had been heard teasing the girls in the playground at break time. Brani decided to work with the children to set rules and limits that would make teasing unacceptable in the playground and in doing so strengthen the sense of a safe community in her classroom. To do this she walked the girls around the playground and asked them to talk about the places where it was nice to play and the places they didn't like playing. She then talked to the girls about why they didn't like playing in particular places. The girls talked about the 'rude names' they had been called by the boys. Brani held a classroom meeting where she shared what she had learnt and her concerns about it. She asked the children what they could do to make the playground a nicer place for everyone. This question became the focus of a project in which the children developed rules for a nicer playground. They made posters of their rules and the reasons for them that they shared with the rest of the school.

Research exploring the learning skills of boys and girls in mathematics and technology tasks also provides insights into how gender may influence children's co-operative learning in the classroom. Yelland (1998) found that girl pairs had more success in completing novel tasks on computers than did boy/girl pairs and boy pairs. Yelland linked these difference to the fact that girls:

➤ were planful in how they approached the task before and after it began
➤ took time to reflect on their progress
➤ predicted outcomes before acting
➤ engaged in dialogue as they worked co-operatively on the tasks (Yelland 1998).

Encouraging boys and girls to use these skills as they engage in co-operative learning tasks can help to support their success in these tasks and help to build a positive sense of community for children within the group.

Disability and additional needs

Community building rests on staff fostering a climate of co-operative learning. Co-operative learning strategies can be particularly powerful in improving the learning experiences and outcomes for many children with diverse disabilities (Sleeter and Grant 1994). However, some staff may inadvertently undermine the capacity of children with disabilities to learn from co-operative learning. Research has suggested that some early childhood teachers are more likely to interrupt the activities of children with disabilities than children who did not have identified disabilities, to offer them more information and directives and to be more generous with praise (Creaser 1999, p. 127). In this context, it is important to note that self-determination for children with disabilities may be supported if children are able to make choices and to do this within social contexts (Algozzine et al. 2001). Co-operative learning strategies could provide these opportunities.

REFLECTING ON COMMUNITY-BUILDING TECHNIQUES

1 What does research suggest are the keys to successful use of community building to optimise children's learning?
2 How would you define a learning community?
3 To what extent do you agree with the statement, 'In a truly dynamic learning environment, the process of inquiry is lived both by children and adults' (Harada et al. 2002/03, p. 71)?
4 Are there any times when you think community building is inappropriate with young children?
5 What do you think the 'practice of democractically wise professional judgements' (Henderson 2001, p. 19) means? How might such practice support the possibility of community building with children and families?
6 Develop a plan for a learning experience for four- to five-year-old children in which you wanted to support a sense of belongingness for each child.
7 Imagine you were working with a four-year-old child who was having difficulty completing a puzzle. How might community building help you help the child to learn skills for completing this and other puzzles?
8 Design a new game you could use to encourage toddlers to physically co-operate with each other.
9 What do you see as the hardest part of improving your community-building techniques?

IMPROVING TEACHING IN PRACTICE

1 Record (using a tape-recorder or written notes) small group learning with children during several half-hour teaching periods.
2 What was your approach to developing a sense of belongingness for individual children? Did you:
    ➋ emphasise co-operative learning rather than competition between children?
    ➋ use dialogue as a tool for learning?
    ➋ support children to share different ideas and feelings with each other in the group?
    ➋ show care for each child in a proactive way?
    ➋ take care to include each child in positive social exchanges with their peers and with you?

3 How and how well did you take account of developmental and anti-bias considerations?
4 What are your areas of strength and weakness in facilitating learning communities in your teaching and learning?
5 How can you improve your community-building techniques in practice?

Further reading

Fidler, M. 1995, Building a learning community. *Association Management*, 47(5), pp. 40–7.

Harada, V., Lum, D. and Souza, K. 2002/03, Building a learning community: students and adults as inquirers, *Childhood Education*, 79(2), pp. 66–71.

Lubeck, S. and Post, J. 2000, Creating a Head Start Community of Practice, in L. Diaz Soto, ed., *The Politics of Early Childhood Education* (pp. 33–58), New York, Peter Lang Publishing.

Osterman, K. 2000, 'Students' need for belonging in the school community', *Review of Educational Research*, 70(3), pp. 323–68.

References

Algozzine, B., Browder, D., Karvonen, M., Test, D. and Wood, W. 2001, 'Effects of interventions to promote self-determination for individuals with disabilities', *Review of Educational Research*, 71(2), pp. 219–78.

Anderman, E. and Maehr, M. 1994, 'Motivation and schooling in the middle grades', *Review of Educational Research*, 64(2), pp. 287–309.

Balaban, N. 2003, Creating a caring, democratic classroom community for and with young children, in J. Silin and C. Lippman, eds, *Putting the Children First: The Changing Face of Newark's Public Schools*, (pp. 82–90), New York, Teachers' College Press.

Bråtan, M. 1996, 'When toddlers provide care: infants' companion space', *Childhood*, 3(4), pp. 449–66.

Bowman, B., Donovan, M. and Burns, S. 2001, (eds), *Eager to Learn: Educating our Preschoolers*, Washington DC, National Academy Press.

Campbell, S., Coady, M., Lawrence, H., Smith, K., Totta, J., Siatta, S. and Rolfe, S. 2002, *Our Part in Peace*, Watson, ACT, Australian Early Childhood Association.

Casswell, S. 2001, 'Community capacity building and social policy—what can be achieved?' *Social Policy Journal of New Zealand*, December, pp. 22–36.

Creaser, B. 1999, 'The place of play for young children with disabilities in mainstream education', in E. Dau, ed., *Child's Play: Revisiting Play in Early Childhood Settings* (pp. 111–30), Sydney, Philadelphia and London, Maclennan and Petty.

Cuffaro, H. 1995, *Experimenting with the World: John Dewey and the Early Childhood Classroom*, New York, Teachers' College Press.

Dewey, J. 1916, *Democracy and Education*, New York, Macmillan Company [Reprinted 1966, the Free Press].

——1958, *Experience and Education,* New York, Macmillan.

Elbers, E. 1996, 'Citizenship in the making: themes of citizenship in children's pretend play', *Childhood*, 3(4), pp. 499–514.

Fidler, M. 1995, Building a learning community, *Association Management*, 47(5), 40–7.

Fowler, R. C. and Corley, K. K. 1996, 'Linking families, building communities', *Educational Leadership*, 53(7), pp. 24–7.

Glover, A. 1999, The role of play in development and learning, in E. Dau, ed., *Child's Play: Revisiting Play in Early Childhood Settings* (pp. 4–15), Sydney, Philadelphia and London, Maclennan and Petty.

Goldstein, L. 1997, *Teaching with Love: A Feminist Approach to Early Childhood Education*, New York, Peter Lang Publishing.

Grace, D. and Tobin, J. 1997, 'Carnival in the classroom: elementary students making videos', in J. Tobin, ed., *Making a Place for Pleasure in Early Childhood Education* (pp. 159–87), New Haven and London, Yale University Press.

Graves, L. 1992, 'Cooperative learning communities: context for a new vision of education and society', *Journal of Education*, 174(2), pp. 57–9.

Gropper, N. and Froschl, M. 2000, 'The role of gender in young children's teasing and bullying behaviour', *Equity and Excellence in Education*, 33(1), pp. 48–56.

Harada, V., Lum, D. and Souza, K. 2002/03, 'Building a learning community: students and adults as inquirers', *Childhood Education* 79(2), pp. 66–71.

Henderson, J. 2001, 'Deepening democratic curriculum work', *Educational Researcher*, 30(9), pp. 18–21.

Henniger, M. 1999, *Teaching young children: an introduction*, New Jersey, Merrill Prentice Hall.

Jilk, B. A. 1999, 'Schools in the new millennium', *American School & University,* 71(5), pp. 46–7.

Kaltsounis, T. 1997, 'Multicultural education and citizenship education at the crossroads: Searching for common ground', *The Social Studies*, 88(1), pp. 18–25.

Konzal, J. 2001, 'Collaborative inquiry: a means of creating a learning community', *Early Childhood Research Quarterly*, 16, pp. 95–115.

Lankshear, C., Peters, M. and Knobel, M. 1995, 'Critical pedagogy and cyberspace', in H. Giroux, C. Lankshear, P. McClaren and M. Peters, eds, *Counternarratives: cultural studies and critical pedagogies in postmodern spaces* (pp. 149–188), New York, Peter Lang Publishing.

Longstreet, W. and Shane, H. 1993, *Curriculum for a new millennium*, Needham Heights, MA, Allyn and Bacon.

Nieto, S. 1995, 'From brown heroes and holidays to assimilationist agendas: reconsidering the critiques of multicultural education', in C. Sleeter and P. McLaren, eds, *Multicultural Education, Critical Pedagogy and the Politics of Difference* (pp. 191–220), Albany, State University of New York Press.

Osterman, K. 2000, 'Students' need for belonging in the school community', *Review of Educational Research*, 70(3), pp. 323–68.

Pascarella, P. 1998, Cultivating the power of community, *Management Review*, 87(4), pp. 52–4.

Pinar, W., Reynolds, W., Slattery, P. and Taubman, P. 1995, *Understanding Curriculum*, New York, Peter Lang Publishing.

Ramsey, P. 1987, *Teaching and Learning in a Diverse World: Multicultural Education for Young Children,* New York, Teachers' College Press.

Mattai, R. P. 2002, 'A teacher educator responds', in N. Quisenberry and G. Duhon, eds, *Racism in the Classroom: Case Studies*, Olney, MD, Association of Teacher Educators and Association for Childhood Education International.

Siraj-Blatchford, I. and Clarke, P. 2000, *Supporting Identity, Diversity and Language in the Early Years*, Buckingham and Philadelphia, Open University Press.

Sterling, M. 1998, Building a community week by week, *Educational Leadership*, 56(1), pp. 65–9.

Stonehouse, A. 1999, 'Play, a way of being for babies and toddlers', in E. Dau, ed., *Child's Play: Revisiting Play in Early Childhood Settings* (pp. 152–63), Sydney, Philadelphia and London, Maclennan and Petty.

Swadner Blue, B. 2000, '"At risk" or "at promise"? From deficit constructions of the "other childhood" to possibilities for authentic alliances with children and families', in L. Diaz Soto, ed., *The Politics of Early Childhood Education* (pp. 117–34), New York, Peter Lang Publishing.

Tijerina Revilla, A. 1998, 'Schools As Communities of Learners: An Initiative Toward Creating Democratic Education', *IDRA Newsletter by the Intercultural Development Research Association*, February.

Whalley, M. and the Pen Green Team, 2001, *Involving parents in their children's learning*, London, Sage Publications.

Yelland, N. 1998, 'Gender issues in mathematics and technology', in N. Yelland, ed., *Gender in Early Childhood* (pp. 249–73), London, Routledge.

Chapter 21
Deconstructing

Construct: to put together substances or parts, assemble.

(Collins Dictionary of the English Language, p. 323)

De: prefix, removal of or from something specified. Reversal of something.

(Collins Dictionary of the English Language, p. 381)

To deconstruct the context of a text is to consider its purpose; that is, what it is trying to achieve.

(Zammit 1994, p. 28)

Deconstruction, or putting a concept or a word under erasure, is a political act. It reveals the generally invisible but repressive politics of any particular forms of representation.

(Davies 1993, p. 8)

WHAT?

Deconstruction is a specialist term that has not entered into everyday language to any large extent. However, we can understand the broad meaning of the term by looking at its two parts—'de' (implies reversal or removal) and 'construct' (meaning to put something together). To *de*-construct something is to take it apart, to 'unconstruct' it. In social theory deconstruction refers to the process of taking apart concepts and meanings.

More specifically, deconstruction is a form of critical thinking about social relations that involves questioning the meanings of words or concepts that normally go unquestioned. According to Alloway (1995, p. 106) it is '. . . a form of analysis which exposes the multiplicity of possible meanings, contradictions and assumptions underlying our understandings and ways of knowing'. Deconstructionism exposes the internal contradictions in particular systems of thought (Weiner 1994), and in doing so helps us question who benefits, and how, from particular taken-for-granted understandings of our social world. As such, it helps us examine the power relations that can be created and maintained through our ways of thinking and knowing. In other words, it can be used to help us understand the politics of the daily world. It also serves to remind us of those politics and our part in creating them and re-creating them through the decisions we choose to take or not to take:

Every decision involves potentially endless levels of choice which we can contrive to forget or conceal but which deconstruction is always ready to uncloak. We are responsible for those decisions in a most extreme way. We have a responsibility for our decisions that the world cannot excuse since the world is, itself, an outcome of our deciding so to take it (Parker 1997, p. 144).

As a teaching strategy, deconstruction can be used to help children take apart what is fair or not fair in the world and to understand the politics of their day-to-day relations with each other and in the world around them. It is, therefore, a teaching strategy that is suitable for those early childhood staff wishing to implement anti-discriminatory or anti-bias perspectives into their work with children.

THEORETICAL BACKGROUND

JACQUES DERRIDA AND THE THEORY OF DECONSTRUCTIONISM

The process of deconstruction derives from the work of a French poststructuralist language theorist called Jacques Derrida (1930–). For Derrida, meaning in language is ruled by the principle of 'differance'. This principle declares that meaning in language can never be finally fixed, that there is no final meaning we can give to any one word. Meaning depends on differences between words and images (signifiers), and so can only be relational, not essential or inherent. Meaning is constantly in a process of deferral (differance) to the moment when new meanings are constructed. These new meanings are constructed through changing relations of difference between signifiers that are de/reconstructed.

Within much modernist thought, notions of differences between signifiers rely on dichotomies (sharp divisions into two) and binary (paired) oppositions. To illustrate, the meaning of gender is constructed through dichotomies such as male and female, or boy and girl. There are seen to be sharp divisions between male and female. The difference in meaning between girl and boy relies on this sharp division. We know a girl is a girl because a girl cannot be a boy. In addition, meaning is constructed through pairing girl and boy and seeing them as opposite to each other. They form in Derrida's terms a binary opposition. We cannot understand what a girl is without the concept of a boy. Boy and girl are binary opposites. Each side of the opposition depends on the other for its meaning.

In other words, 'binary opposites' are 'binary intimates': without 'wrong', 'right' has no meaning, and the same is the case for 'male' and 'female', 'good' and 'bad', 'rich' and 'poor'. Modernism tends to seek final, fixed meanings for words (images etc.) through these oppositions. We can finally fix the meaning of male because it is paired with female, it is the opposite of female and there are clearly known sharp divisions between them. Everything male is obviously so because it is not female.

By fixing the meaning of words in this way Derrida argued that an equally fixed and equally final 'Other' is created. A pair always has two, one part of the pair therefore always has an 'Other'. You cannot have meaning without having the opposite or the 'Other'. The 'Other' for female is always male and the 'Other' for good is always bad. *For Derrida, binary oppositions always contain within themselves the impossibility of a definitive 'Other'.* The meaning of the 'Other' is always capable of deconstruction and therefore is never finally fixed

The importance of understanding binary oppositions and their 'Other' is that they are often organised hierarchically. The pairs are not equal. The 'Other' is not equal to the main part of the pair. The pairs are always ranked in some way that gives one part of the pair a higher order or place in the ranking. In other words, within the binary opposition some meanings are privileged (given advantages and status) and some meanings are given the lesser status of 'Otherness'. In other words, using binary oppositions places some meanings in a secondary and subordinate position. Think of the following pairs of words:

➔ man/woman
➔ white/black
➔ straight/gay
➔ slim/fat.

In each of these pairs we know what each part of the pair means because they are opposite to each other. Slim people are not fat. Slim is the opposite of fat. In each of these pairs the first word is often given more status or advantage in our society. For instance, being a man holds more status than being a woman. However, this status is not inherent in the word and thus not inevitable or accidental. It is socially determined and constructed. The part of a binary opposition that assigned the secondary and subordinate position of 'Other' is socially constructed. For example, in our society in the binary opposition of man and woman the secondary and subordinate position is given to 'woman'. Woman is not inherently secondary and subordinate to man. We socially determine and construct this subordination.

Deconstruction is about showing how pairs gain their meanings from each other, how one word (meaning) has more advantage and status than the other and how this advantage is not inevitable but socially decided. So, the aim in deconstructing meanings is to show the relations of power between the binary oppositions and to show '. . . that the privileged term derives its position from a suppression or curtailment of its opposite or other' (Grosz 1990, p. 95). Deconstructing (taking apart) binary oppositions is done by showing that each side depends on the other ('Other') for its meaning.

For example, the meaning of the word beauty comes from the way in which it is paired with ugly (in binary opposition to ugly). It is only possible to have a meaning for beauty if we have a meaning for not beautiful (ugly). Once we identify the word that is paired with beauty to give its meaning we know its 'Other'. Once we know a word's 'Other' we understand what is seen as secondary and subordinate in our social world. When we understand that the 'Other' to beautiful is ugly we can see that being ugly will be secondary and subordinate to being beautiful if this opposition is maintained. By doing away with binary oppositions new meanings and new desires become possible. Hence, if we see woman and man as linked rather than opposite then a third gender of woman/man becomes possible and thus desirable. Or, if we turn the binary opposition on its head we could make woman a more advantaged meaning than man.

Derrida believed that finding the 'Other' involves taking a particular word or concept and using reversal or displacement to create a new term which Derrida calls a 'hinge word' (Grosz 1990). Thus, reversing the binary opposition between beautiful and ugly involves giving ugly the privileged position, and creating a new term involves hinging them to show their links rather than their opposition. The hinge word becomes ugly/beauty. A new word, such as a hinge word, makes new meanings possible.

The aim in deconstruction is '. . . not so much to demonstrate the errors, flaws, and contradictions in texts, but . . . to reveal the necessity with which what a text says is bound up with what it cannot say' (Grosz 1990, p. 97). Identifying what is not said involves looking at what knowledge is privileged within the text/discourse using two Derridian concepts: of difference/'differance' and the notion of 'Otherness'. Through this process we come to create new meanings that can challenge the current relations of power within our ways of understanding the world. Deconstruction is tied to a politics of possibilities as it offers us ways to imagine new ways and to 'continuously wonder other forms of knowledge' (Hyun 2001, p. 24).

HOW?

Deconstruction is a complex and sophisticated process based on critical thinking about our language and the ways in which it constructs and constricts meaning for us. Language not only makes it possible to give meaning to our world, it also limits how we give meaning to it. The aim with deconstruction is to show how language limits meaning, explore in whose interests these limits are and open up the possibility of new meanings. For example, the aim is to show how the ways in which pairs of words are linked, in particular how their linking privileges one word, limits how we understand the world. By making new pairs and changing the ranking within pairs we can make new meanings.

It is possible at a very simple level to begin to help children grasp the idea that language both creates and constricts meaning. They can begin to think about how words are paired and how the ranking of words within pairs gives some meanings more power or status.

Staff can begin to deconstruct social meaning in language with young children through encouraging them to put their current meanings under question, to explore how these meanings limit their desires and understandings, to expand the meanings they have, to imagine new language and hence new meanings, and to think about the political implications of their meanings. The following points identify some of the specific developmental abilities of babies, toddlers and preschoolers that relate to their capacity for self-expression and indicate how staff can take account of these capabilities in their teaching:

❯ Question children's meanings of words or concepts that are key to their understandings of social relationships. Get children to identify pairs and ranking within pairs of words that are important to their understanding of social relationships. These words or concepts might be present in their everyday language, in the stories they read or in the popular media they watch. How do the children understand what it means to be poor, rich, male or Vietnamese? Zammit (1994) suggests asking children what words make them see and feel.

> Despina works with a group of four-year-old children at a centre in Footscray, a suburb in Melbourne with a high migrant population. She is having a discussion with the children about what it means to be rich and poor. Despina asks the children a series of questions such as: 'What does being rich mean?', 'What does being poor mean?'; 'Who is rich?'; 'If you're rich, how are you different?'; 'What other words could we use to describe poor?'. She listens carefully to the children's answers and uses these to extend children's thinking and to help the children begin to deconstruct their notions of poor and rich.

❯ Question if children's meanings are the only meanings possible. Are there other ways of understanding what it means to be, for example, poor, rich, male, Vietnamese? Turning the ranking in pairs upside down or linking a word in the pair in new ways can help this process. Staff can present children with images, ideas and stories that show them ways of understanding that are different to their own: 'What happens when poor is seen as having more status than rich?'; 'When and why might it be good to be poor?'; 'What things do poor people do better than rich people?'. Such questions help children to begin to understand the idea of what Jacques Derrida (refer above) called the 'Other', that is, the marginalised or silenced meanings that are possible within a word or concept.

- Expand the meanings that children are prepared to consider. Staff can use children's playful approach to language to encourage them to make up their own hinge words and think about what they might mean. For example, staff wanting to talk with children about being male and female could encourage them to think of a word for someone who is like a girl and like a boy. What could they call this person? What would they be like?

- Explore with the children how different meanings lead to taken-for-granted assumptions about each other, especially how they limit what children consider possible for themselves and for others. Talk with the children about the meaning of how we act and how we expect others to act if we talk about good people. How does being good limit what we do? What does it mean about how we expect stories to end, what games we expect to play with each other, who we expect to be friends with, what we think other people can do and enjoy doing. How different would it be if we talked about good/bad people? What would a good/bad person be like? What could we call them? Would they be limited in the same ways as a good person? What could they do differently?

> Three-year-old children at the Lupin Centre are concerned with fairness. Their teacher Hisham has noticed the frequent cry of 'it's not fair' when a group of children dominate the home corner and get to play with the new equipment. Hisham has a discussion with the children about fairness. She asks them to say what they think fairness is and leads them through a series of questions which challenge their notion that fair means everyone gets the same all the time.

- Look with the children at who benefits from specific taken-for-granted assumptions. This involves getting them to think about who might feel sad, hurt or angry by the understandings we have. Who might feel sad if we expect all good people to do certain things? Which children might be happy with this? What does it mean for children who are not good? Who will be their friends?

- Talk with the children about who has the power to decide who is good and what good means. Children can think about who creates word pairs, who can change them and what would happen if they tried to change the meanings within a pair. For example, what would happen if they tried to make a new dictionary or a new language? Who would listen to them? Where could they go? What would they be stopped from doing? Talk to the children about the extent to which it is fair, or not fair that some people control meaning-making. Work with the children to think about who gets their way because of the assumptions we have about others, and who does not? Is this fair? Is it unfair? Which meanings seem fair, which seem unfair? Would it be fairer if they used their new words to describe people rather than the usual words?

By way of illustration, if staff wanted to work with children to deconstruct (take apart) the class politics of their relations with each other they would need to develop ways of:

- uncovering children's meanings of being rich or being poor
- talking with the children about how the words are paired and how they rank things that happen within this pairing
- offering children alternative meanings of being rich or being poor

Dom and the children discuss fairness.

❯ encouraging children to think about new words that include rich and poor in describing people

❯ examining with the children the assumptions they have about what it means to be rich or poor

❯ exploring with the children who benefits from assumptions they have about being rich and being poor

❯ talking with the children about the extent to which their understandings mean that rich people have most power and the extent to which this is fair, or not fair. Would alternative meanings be fairer?

To accomplish these tasks with children staff will need to use a variety of general teaching techniques such as questioning and specialist teaching techniques such as co-constructing, problem-solving and task analysis.

WHEN AND WHY?

Goal relevance

Deconstruction can be used to help children understand the politics of their day-to-day relations with each other and in the world about them. This may include the gender, 'race', class and disability politics of their daily life and the world about them. Deconstruction can be used to:

❯ examine the politics (power relationships) present in children's relationships with each other to imagine other possibilities

❯ examine the politics in the stories they read to imagine other possibilities

❯ examine the politics in the images about them to imagine other possibilities

➔ examine the politics of the knowledge in the world about them and imagine other ways to understand and value different forms of knowledge

➔ examine the politics in current events in their local community to imagine other possibilities

➔ examine the politics in television programs and videos they watch to imagine other possibilities.

This helps children to think more critically about their relationships and the world about them, and helps them imagine a fairer world in which there is respect for diversity. Some specific strategies staff could use follow.

EXAMINE THE POLITICS (POWER RELATIONSHIPS) PRESENT IN CHILDREN'S RELATIONSHIPS WITH EACH OTHER TO IMAGINE OTHER POSSIBILITIES

Staff could use the following questions to decide if relationships between the children and between the children and the curriculum offered might be in need of deconstruction:

➔ Who has access to specific areas of the curriculum because of what they know or the language they have?

➔ Whose voices do you listen to most?

➔ Whose voices do you seem to not hear?

➔ Who is engaged in specific areas of the curriculum?

➔ How do the children show respect for each other?

➔ Who co-operates with each other? What are the effects of their co-operation for other children? (Adapted from McMillan 2001; MacNaughton 2000)

These questions can be re-formed and put to the children to begin discussions with them about what happens currently, what is fair or not fair in that and what else might be possible.

➔ What things do you like to do most?

➔ What things are hardest for you?

➔ What things are tricky to do?

➔ Who listens to you most?

➔ Who doesn't listen to you?

➔ Who has special places?

➔ Who do you play with?

➔ Who would you like to play with?

➔ Are there any places you can't play?

Using questions to begin talking with children about what's fair or not fair about what they share with you and how else you might do things can help staff to begin to deconstruct with children.

EXAMINE THE POLITICS IN THE STORIES THEY READ TO IMAGINE OTHER POSSIBILITIES

To engage children in a critical examination of the politics of the stories they read they will need to have access to books that present different perspectives and contradictory perspectives on a particular topic or issue (Swindler Boutte 2002). For instance, to explore gender expectations and possibilities with children around the topic of what boys do and don't like it would be helpful to have books that show boys who do and don't like to play with dolls, dress-ups, etc. These books should be read to the children more than once so that they can become familiar with the story and its messages and then staff can begin to analyse these critically with children. Swindler Boutte (2002) offers helpful guidance on how to approach critical discussions about books with children. She suggests:

- ➲ using probing questions to explore with children what they liked and didn't like about it, what sounded the same as what they thought and what was different
- ➲ reading different versions of the same story by changing endings, feelings, etc. of the characters. Children can be encouraged to do this and to take different roles in the story and imagine different ways for the story to develop.

These strategies open children up to multiple perspectives on the same topic, enable them to play with different approaches and ideas and to experiment with changing meanings and narratives. As they do this they can begin to imagine other possibilities and become critical meaning-makers in their own lives.

> Zeta, a teacher in a prep grade class in a middle-class suburb of Melbourne, searches the library for books that show men and women in stereotypical roles. She uses these books as a starting point for discussions about the politics of gender with the children. She challenges the assumptions portrayed in the books with the children and encourages them to think of different ways of presenting roles of men and women.

EXAMINE THE POLITICS IN THE IMAGES ABOUT THEM TO IMAGINE OTHER POSSIBILITIES
Staff can also use other tools such as cameras to begin a process of deconstruction with children. Children can be asked to take photographs of when they think children are enjoying playing/working and/or having a hard time or photos of things that happen that are not fair. These can then be used to talk with individual children and small groups of children about why these photos are not fair and how they would like to see things change. Photos can highlight diverse perspectives on classroom life and begin to engage children with the idea of multiple perspectives. This knowledge is central to a child's capacity to deconstruct and reconstruct the world and its meanings. As Whitin and Whitin (1998, p. 125) explained:

> One of the ways that learners can appreciate multiple perspectives is to understand that information can change in different contexts.

Using photos can also begin a discussion with children about what's fair or not fair about what they share with you and how else you might do things, and can help staff to begin to deconstruct with children.

EXAMINE THE POLITICS IN CURRENT EVENTS IN THEIR LOCAL COMMUNITY TO IMAGINE OTHER POSSIBILITIES
To act for fairness in the world we need to critically engage with the world. Young children have a capacity to act for fairness, and deconstruction can help them to engage critically with their world. Current events such as war, terrorism, violence, working for peace, standing up against racism, fighting for jobs and working for a sustainable environment offer staff events through which children can critically engage with their world. Campbell et al. (2002) described how an early

childhood service engaged young children in critically examining what peace means as a way of building a peaceful and respectful community. It was a centre in which bullying and aggression between the children had become an issue. They decided to start with asking children what they thought a peaceful community looked like. Here is what some of the children had to say:

A peaceful world

There would be peace, grass, sea, birds, whales, lots of people, big birds, seeds around. The world for all the trees and plants, the sun and yellow seeds all around sprinkled for peace. (Ashika, age 5, November 2000)

If other people take your things you have to say peace, and other people will give it back. The house has windows to look out the house at grass or flowers and others playing peacefully. (Lily, age 5, September 2000)

The Peace Town

The world would look nice if there were only goodies in it and there wouldn't be any Hurt or any killing or anything Broken. There would be lots of pretty colours and everyone will feel happy and safe. They will laugh. Well sometimes. They try to be friendly and the world looks pretty and peaceful. There will be cats and dogs and little parrots and grass and sky and flowers and people. That's my favourite things if it's peaceful because it feels nice. (Lauren, age 4, February 2001)

A peaceful world

Our world would have people. I like all people. I like animals and I like butterflies too and giraffes and elephants. There will be schools and kinders and creches. (Gabriel, age 3, March 2001)

Children, staff and parents discussed and represented their understandings of peace to each other and in doing so brought forth multiple and diverse perspectives on peace that enabled those involved to imagine what a peaceful world might look like in their own service and how aggression and bullying got in the way of peace.

EXAMINE THE POLITICS IN TELEVISION PROGRAMS AND VIDEOS THEY WATCH TO IMAGINE OTHER POSSIBILITIES

Popular culture is rich with examples of the politics of relationships in children's worlds. Children's understandings of and responses to popular culture can offer staff and children a pleasurable starting point for deconstructing cultural meanings with young children. Grace and Tobin (1997) highlight how the exploration of popular culture in primary school classrooms can disrupt the privileging of teacher knowledge in the classroom and in doing so expand the range of meanings and forms of pleasure that are articulated and circulate within a classroom. This is particularly so if the children control the conditions under which the meanings are produced and circulated. Grace and Tobin (1997, pp 165–6) described how student video production can achieve this:

When popular culture is brought into the curriculum, lines are crossed between high and low (*culture*), the official and unofficial (*curriculum*), the authoritative discourses of the school and the internally persuasive discourses of children . . . Our goal, therefore, should be to validate the popular culture interests of children without appropriating them. Student video production provides an arena for this to occur.

Student videos could provide a rich and extensive source of discussion about how they and other children and adults see what is fair and not fair in their lives and why.

Developmental considerations

Deconstruction is a teaching technique that relies on symbolic language, it is therefore suitable to use with children who have reached this stage in their language development and who have the ability to talk about what words mean. Deconstruction is therefore most likely to be suitable to use with older preschool children and children in the early years of school who are able to use the language(s) spoken by adults in the classroom. However, it is important to note that deconstruction is about critical meaning-making and that all children have the capacity and the desire to make meaning about their world and themselves.

EQUITY CONSIDERATIONS

'Race' and culture

Staff can teach children to deconstruct (take apart) their understanding of 'racial' and cultural stereotypes. To do this staff need to:

- ➲ uncover children's 'racial' meanings. For example, what meanings do the children give to being black or white?
- ➲ offer children alternative 'racial' meanings
- ➲ examine with children their 'racial' assumptions and who benefits from these. For example, what assumptions do they have about what it means to be black or white and who benefits?
- ➲ talk with children about the extent to which their understandings mean that some people have more power than other people. For example, do their understandings mean that black people or white people have most power? Encourage the children to think about the extent to which this is fair, not fair and whether alternative understandings are fairer.

Tiger Woods, a young black golf pro, has just won a prestigious golf tournament. This is a landmark for black people in the United States, who are still excluded from some golf courses. Several of the children have been talking about Tiger Woods and how 'cool' he is. David brings the newspaper to his Grade 2 class and uses the headline as a starting point for the children to discuss what it means for a young black person in America to win such a well-known tournament. David extends the discussion from the particular to a general talk about power and privilege in the United States. He talks with the children about how fair life is there for black people and if all black people live the same sorts of lives. He also talks about what is common in the lives of black people in the United States. He plans to use this to extend children's understandings about 'race', power and privilege in Australia.

To illustrate how staff can approach these tasks we will look at how they might encourage children to deconstruct their ideas about Native Americans. We have chosen this topic because stereotypes about Native Americans still abound in the Australian context. They can be still be seen in children's games of 'Cowboys and Indians', in children's literature often in alphabet books where 'I' is for 'Indian', and we have also seen several centres that have 'Indian' dress-up clothes available for the children. While Australian children have been playing this game for many decades, the release of the Disney film *Pocahontas* has revived this. In this revival many negative stereotypes about Native Americans have been re-created and reinforced. These stereotypes have been summarised by York (1991, p. 170) in the following way:

Native Americans: take scalps, have red skin, use tepees as houses, speak in grunts, wear feathers and costumes, ride horses, don't live now.

These stereotypes are often created and re-created through children's literature. Common stereotypes found include the idea that male Indians are 'savage, hostile warriors; drunken thieves; evil medicine men; loyal brave followers; lazy unemployed loafers' (Smardo Dowd 1992, p. 221) and female Indians are 'either heavyset, workhorse squaws or Indian princesses' (Smardo Dowd 1992, p. 221). Such stereotypes ignore the current and historical diversity and richness of the lives and lifestyles of Native Americans. As Reese (1996, p. 2) reminds us:

The term 'Native American' includes over 500 different groups and reflects great diversity of geographic location, language, socioeconomic conditions, school experience, and retention of traditional spiritual and cultural practices.

To begin to deconstruct stereotypes about Native Americans with young children, staff could:

● Question children's meanings of words or concepts that are key to their understandings of Native Americans. Ask the children what the following words make them see and feel: Indian, Red Indian, cowboys, savages. What words do they pair with them? One four-year-old child was asked by her mother who Indians are and the responses she got included the following:

'Indians eat animals like elephants and deer.'

'Indians don't wear any clothes and they don't wear underwear. They just wear cloths over their butts.'

'Indians wear feathers and they kill people.'

'Indians live in stick houses' (Brady and Bisson 1995, p. 19).

The four-year-old told her mother she had learned these things about Indians from the film *Pocahontas*. Realising how children make sense of the words they know helps staff to see what meanings they need to explore further to challenge them.

● Offer children alternative understandings of what it means to be Native American. To do this staff need to build their own knowledge base of the historical and contemporary ways of Native Americans. Reese (1996) offers some ways of doing this.

● Explore with children how their meanings about being Native Americans lead to taken-for-granted assumptions. For example, talk with them about how people react if they think that Native Americans 'wear feathers and kill people'. Do we want to be with people who wear feathers and kill people? Do we think that all people who wear feathers kill people? How would you feel if you met a Native American Indian wearing feathers? Would you want to be friends? What else might we expect a Native American to wear or to do?

● Explore with children how their ideas about Native Americans influence how we expect stories to end, what games we expect to play with each other, who we expect to be friends with, what we think other people can do and enjoy doing. The following extract from Brady and Bisson (1995, p. 19) shows how children's games can be influenced by the meanings they give to the word 'Indian' and how these meanings are influenced by films such as *Pocahontas*. Chris had seen the movie three times:

> One morning two-and-a-half-year-old (European American) Chris came in wearing a headband with a feather in the back. One of the teachers greeted Chris at the door with a 'Hi Chris!'. Chris' response was to furrow his brow, cross his arms, and in an angry, loud voice shout 'No! I'm an Indian', and run away 'growling' . . . Later, when a teacher asked Chris about who Indians are, he replied 'They shoot bows and arrows and they shoot people.' The teacher . . . asked, 'What else?' to which he replied, 'That's all.' Then the teacher asked, 'Well, do Indians go to the grocery store?' Chris answered, 'No' . . . 'Do they go to school?' Chris emphatically responded, 'No! It's too expensive' (Brady and Bisson 1995, p. 19).

To deconstruct Chris' understandings of being an Indian would involve taking the discussion further to explore the implications of his views. His teacher could ask him to think about what games he expects to play with other children about being Indian, who might want to be his friends and play these games, what he thinks Indian people can do and enjoy doing. These questions need to encourage Chris to think about the implications of his assertions about Indians. Questions such as: 'If Indians only shoot bows and arrows and shoot people, then is that the only game you can play if you are an Indian?'; 'Are there any other games you could play if you were an Indian?'; 'Who will be your friend if that is the only game you play as an Indian?'. Books that could help Chris' teacher extend his thinking about being Indian can be found in Slapin and Seale (1992) and Smardo Dowd (1992).

➲ Look with the children at who benefits from their specific taken-for-granted assumptions about Native Americans. This involves asking children: 'Who might feel sad, hurt or angry by the expectations we have?'; 'Who might feel sad if we expect all Native Americans to shoot bows and arrows and not wear clothes?'; 'Which Native Americans might be happy with this?'; 'What does it mean for the Native Americans who wear suits, jeans etc. and who go to the supermarket for their food?'; 'How would you feel about the idea that Indians shoot people if you were a Native American who went to school and shopped at the grocery store?'.

➲ Talk with the children about who has power and the extent to which this is fair, or not fair. Staff need first to do their own research. They need to learn about what is fair or not fair about how Native American Indians are portrayed in books and films such as *Pocahontas*. There were many inaccuracies in the film that staff would need to know about to show how unfair the representations of Native Americans were. For example, *Pocahontas* was eleven years old, never kissed John Smith and did not look like the person in the film (Brady and Bisson 1995). Armed with accurate information, staff can encourage children to think about if it is fair to have films made about people when they are not true and to think about who made the film. Did they make the film to tell the truth or to make money? Is it fair that people make money from films about Native Americans when they are not true?

Deconstructing children's ideas about Native Americans can take time. Children will need time to express and think about their own ideas. They will also need time to think about alternative ideas staff may present them with. The aim in deconstructing meanings with children is not to tell them what to think but to help them understand that the meanings they give to words such as Indian have implications for their own play and how they feel about others, and that these implications may be unfair to other people.

Gender

Staff can also work with children to deconstruct the gender politics of their relations with each other by:

- uncovering children's meanings of being a girl or boy
- offering children alternative meanings of being a girl or boy
- examining with children the assumptions they have about what it means to be a boy or girl
- exploring with children who benefits from assumptions they have about being boys and/or being girls
- talking with children about the extent to which their understandings mean that boys or girls have more power and the extent to which this is fair, or not fair.

Davies (1989) argues that deconstructing gender relations with young children frees them from the constraints that current dominant understandings of gender place on children. She believes that children need to:

> . . . have access to imagery in which new metaphors, new forms of social relations, and new patterns of power and desire are explored . . . and wonder how the social world could ever have been reduced to two types of people related to relatively minor pieces of anatomy (Davies 1989, p. 141).

Teaching children to deconstruct their gender understandings and to thus imagine new ways of being male and female involves the same processes as teaching them to deconstruct their 'racial' understandings. To show what this might mean in practice we will draw on questions from Dally and Lindstrom (1996, p. 83) about how to help children deconstruct the gender meanings in toys. To do this staff need to do the following:

- Question children's meanings of gender words or concepts associated with toys. Questions that might do this are: 'What are girls' toys and what are boys' toys?'; 'What toys do people buy for girls?'; 'What toys do people buy for boys?'.
- Encourage children to think of other ways of thinking about toys for boys and girls. Questions that might do this are: 'Would people always buy the same types of toys for all girls?'; 'Would people always buy the same types of toys for all boys?'; 'What other types of toys might they buy?'.
- Encourage children to find a name for toys that both boys and girls might enjoy. What would such toys be? What would they look like?
- Explore with children how the gender meanings around toys lead to taken-for-granted assumptions about boys and girls. For example, talk with the children about what it means for how we act and how we expect others to act if we think that all girls love dolls and all boys love train sets. What does it mean about what games we expect to play with each other, who we expect to be friends with, what we think other people can do and enjoy doing when people buy toys especially for girls or especially for boys?
- Look with the children at who benefits from their specific taken-for-granted assumptions about gender and toys. This involves getting children to think about who might feel sad, hurt or angry

by the toys they are given. Who might feel sad if all boys are given a football to play with? Which boys might be happy with this? What does it mean for the boys who hate playing football? What will the girls or boys learn from the toys they are given? What can they do with them? What can't they do with them? What might boys miss out on playing with and learning from their toys? What might girls miss out on playing with and learning from their toys?

❯ Talk with the children about who has power to choose toys and the extent to which this is fair, or not fair. Make the children think about who gets their way because of the assumptions we have about gender and toys, and who does not? Is this fair? Is it unfair? Who decides that boys should play with certain toys and girls with different toys? Is it fair that boys miss out on some toys? Is it fair that girls miss out on some toys?

There are a host of gender concepts that children can be encouraged to deconstruct in this way and through such deconstruction begin to imagine different ways of being a girl and being a boy. Dally and Lindstrom's (1996) suggestions about concepts and issues that children can deconstruct include rhymes and chants that give very 'gendered' messages about children (for example, Fire-cracker, firecracker and King Kong), dolls, advertisements for toys, stories about men and women in the news, and caring for babies.

Disability and additional needs

Discriminatory and offensive ideas about disability can also be deconstructed. Staff can teach children to deconstruct their understanding of disability by:

❯ uncovering children's meanings of being disabled and not being disabled
❯ offering children alternative meanings of being disabled and not being disabled
❯ examining with children the assumptions they have about disability and ability
❯ exploring with children who benefits from their assumptions about disability
❯ talking with children about the extent to which their understandings of disability means that people without disabilities have more power than those with disabilities, and the extent to which this is fair, or not fair.

We will focus on the issue of beauty to explore how this might happen in practice. Images of beauty powerfully influence what we see as the best way to look. Children learn about what is beautiful from a variety of sources. From an early age children are entered into baby shows and 'Little Miss . . .' shows. These shows judge children against prevailing norms about what is a desirable way to look and enforce these norms. Children learn that princesses are beautiful in traditional tales such as *Snow White* and *Sleeping Beauty* and that to be beautiful involves looking a particular way. Children also learn that models are beautiful and that real princesses are judged to be beautiful, as Princess Diana was.

In our society the dominant image of being beautiful that young children are introduced to totally excludes images of people with visible disabilities. Children with visible disabilities learn that they are not included in society's dominant concepts of beauty. This makes it hard for them to develop a positive sense of their own body. Children without visible disabilities construct their understanding of beauty in ways that excludes people with visible disabilities. Children who have parents who have a visible disability find their parents are not considered by the rest of society to be beautiful. This constructs for children an overall concept of people with disabilities as different, less valued and less valuable. As Hall (no date, p. 73) reminds us:

Prejudice and discrimination are based on appearance. People are judged not on their ability but on the way they look. Disabled people [often] look different from other people. The difference is caused by disability. Discrimination results when this difference triggers off the negative attitudes towards disability that are held by the other person.

One of the alternatives to being beautiful is to be considered ugly. This is a label that many people with visible disabilities have experienced.

He had called me ugly. There was more to beauty than wearing makeup and stockings, or the right clothes. I was ugly and not because my legs were too skinny, my bust undeveloped, or my face too plain. I was ugly because I was a disabled person. I was ugly and I would get uglier as my disability progressed (Hall, no date, p. 68).

Deconstructing children's understandings of beauty and ugliness can contribute to reducing the experience that Lesley Hall described above. To deconstruct children's understandings of beauty and ugliness staff would need to do the following:

- Question children's meanings of words or concepts associated with being beautiful and ugly. Questions that might do this are: 'Who do you see when you think about beautiful people?'; 'Who do you see when you think about ugly people?'.
- Encourage children to think of other ways of thinking about beauty and ugliness. Questions that might do this are: 'What makes you like a person?'; 'Does a person have to look a certain way for you to like them?'; 'What sort of person makes a good friend?'; 'Can people with no legs be beautiful?'; 'Would people with no legs think people with legs are beautiful?'; 'Does beauty come from inside a person and how they feel and act or does it come from outside and how they look?'.
- Explore with children how the meanings around being beautiful and being ugly lead to taken-for-granted assumptions about people. For example, talk with the children about what it means for how we act and how we expect others to act if we think that some people are ugly and some people are beautiful. What does it mean about those who we expect to be friends with? What do we think other people can do and enjoy doing? Can we be friends with people we call ugly?
- Look with children at who benefits from their specific taken-for-granted assumptions about beauty and ugliness. This involves getting children to think about who might feel sad, hurt or angry by being called ugly. What do we miss out on if we make friends only with people who are beautiful? Why would we want to call people ugly?
- Talk with children about who has the power to decide who is beautiful and who is ugly, and the extent to which this is fair, or not fair. Where do the children's ideas about being beautiful come from? Do you have to have a crown and lots of money to be beautiful?

There are a host of body image concepts that children can be encouraged to deconstruct in this way and through such deconstruction begin to imagine different ways of judging people. Concepts of body size, body shape, body weight and body style can all be explored in anti-discriminatory ways through deconstruction. Such explorations help children learn to respect physical diversity and to feel pride in their own body.

REFLECTING ON DECONSTRUCTING TECHNIQUES

1   Define deconstruction.

2   What does research suggest are the keys to using deconstruction to optimise children's learning?

3   When do you think deconstruction should be used in your teaching?

4   Are there any times when you think the use of deconstruction is inappropriate with young children?

5   Find one historical poster and one contemporary poster of Aboriginal and Torres Strait Islander people. How could you use these posters to deconstruct non-Aboriginal and Torres Strait Islander children's understandings of Aboriginal and Torres Strait Islander people? What questions might you ask? What research would you need to do to challenge any stereotypes that emerged?

6   What are some topics/ideas/concepts you could use to deconstruct negative stereotypes of people with disabilities?

7   'The fact is that while people, including young children, are thought of as fat by our society, the word fat is used only in disgust' (Whitney 1995, p. 8). How might you teach children to deconstruct the idea of fatness?

8   Find one television advertisement you could use with young children to deconstruct the idea that only mothers should care for babies.

9   Find one storybook about diverse family lifestyles you could use with young children to deconstruct the idea that all families have one mum and one dad.

IMPROVING TEACHING IN PRACTICE

1   Record (using a tape-recorder or written notes) an occasion on which you were deconstructing a social issue or idea with a small group of children.

2   What was your current style of deconstruction? Did you:
   ➲   question children's meanings of words or concepts that were the key to their understandings of social relationships?
   ➲   explore with the children how these meanings led to taken-for-granted assumptions about each other?
   ➲   look with the children at who benefited from specific taken-for-granted assumptions?
   ➲   talk with the children about who had power and the extent to which this was fair, or not fair?

3   How and how well did you take account of developmental and equity considerations?

4   What are your areas of strength and weakness in using deconstruction to promote children's learning?

5   How can you improve your deconstruction techniques in practice?

6   What do you see as the hardest part of improving your deconstruction techniques?

Further reading

Alloway, N. 1995, *Foundation Stones: The Construction of Gender in Early Childhood*, Melbourne, Curriculum Corporation.

Davies, B. 1993, *Shards of Glass: Children Reading and Writing beyond Gendered Identities*, Sydney, Allen & Unwin.

Slapin, B. and Seale, D. 1992, *Through Indian Eyes: The Native Experience in Books for Children*, Philadelphia, New Society Publishers.

Smardo Dowd, F. 1992, 'Evaluating children's books portraying Native American and Asian cultures', *Childhood Education*, 68(4), pp. 219–24.

Swindler Boutte, G. 2002, 'The critical literacy process: guidelines for examining books, *Childhood Education*, 78(3), pp. 147–52.

Zammit, K. 1994, 'Strictly stories: teaching narrative', *EQ Australia*, Autumn, (1), pp. 27–30.

References

Alloway, N. 1995, *Foundation Stones: The Construction of Gender in Early Childhood*, Melbourne, Curriculum Corporation.

Brady, P. and Bisson, J. 1995, 'Disney's *Pocahontas* will haunt us: impact on young children and anti-bias opportunities', *The Web Journal: The Culturally Relevant Anti-Bias Early Childhood Educators Network*, 2(3), pp. 16–24.

Campbell, S., Coady, M., Castilino, T., Lawrence, H., MacNaughton, G., Page, J. and Rolfe, S. 2002, *Our Part in Peace*, Australian Early Childhood Association.

Dally, S. and Lindstrom, H. 1996, *Girls and boys come out to play: teaching about gender construction and sexual harassment in English and Studies of Society and Environment*, Adelaide, South Australia, Department for Education and Children's Services.

Davies, B. 1989, *Frogs and Snails and Feminist Tales: Preschool Children and Gender*, Sydney, Allen & Unwin.

——1993, *Shards of Glass: Children Reading and Writing beyond Gendered Identities*, Sydney, Allen & Unwin.

Grace, D. and Tobin, J. 1997, 'Carnival in the Classroom: Elementary Students Making Videos', in J. Tobin, ed., *Making a Place for Pleasure in Early Childhood Education*, New Haven and London, Yale University Press.

Grosz, E. 1990, 'Contemporary theories of power and subjectivity', in S. Gunew, ed., *Feminist Knowledge: Critique and Construct* (pp. 59–120), London, Routledge.

Hall, L., no date, 'Beauty quests: a double disservice', in Women with Disabilities Feminist Collective, eds, *Women and Disability: An Issue* (pp. 68–74), Melbourne, Women with Disabilities Feminist Collective.

Hyun, E. 2001, Cultural complexity that affects young children's contemporary growth, change and learning, Paper presented at the *Annual Meeting of the Educational Research Association*, Seattle, WA, April 10–14, ED451941.

MacNaughton, G. 2000, *Rethinking Gender in Early Childhood*, Sydney, Allen & Unwin; New York, Sage Publications; London, Paul Chapman Publishing.

McMillan, A. 2001, *Deconstructing Social and Cultural Meanings: a model for Education Research Using Postmodern Construct*, Australia, Common Ground Publishing.

Parker, S. 1997, *Reflective Teaching in the Postmodern World: A Manifesto for Education in Postmodernity*, London, Routledge.

Reese, D. 1996, 'Teaching young children about Native Americans', *ERIC Digest, EDO-PS-96-3* (May), pp. 1–4.

Smardo Dowd, F. 1992, 'Evaluating children's books portraying Native American and Asian cultures', *Childhood Education*, 68(4), pp. 219–24.

Swindler Boutte, G. 2002, 'The critical literacy process: guidelines for examining books, *Childhood Education*, 78(3), pp. 147–52.

Weiner, G. 1994, *Feminism in Education: An Introduction*, Buckingham, Open University Press.

Whitin, D. and Whitin, P. 1998, 'Learning is born of doubting: cultivating a skeptical stance', *Language Arts*, 76(2), pp. 123–9.

Whitney, T. 1995, 'Respecting body size: differences in the classroom', *The Web Journal: The Culturally Relevant Anti-Bias Early Childhood Educators Network*, 2(2), pp. 8–9, 20.

Wilkes, G. (ed.) 1979, *Collins Dictionary of the English Language*, Middlesex, Penguin Books.

York, S. 1991, *Roots and Wings: Affirming Culture in Early Childhood Programs*, Minnesota, Toys'n Things Press.

Zammit, K. 1994, 'Strictly stories: teaching narrative', *EQ Australia*, Autumn, (1), pp. 27–30.

Chapter 22

Documenting

Document: a piece of paper, booklet, etc. . . . providing information.

(Collins Dictionary of the English Language, p. 433)

Documentation, in the forms of observation of children and extensive recordkeeping, has long been encouraged and practised in many early childhood programs.

(Katz and Chard 1996, p. 1)

. . . documentation—the written descriptions, transcriptions of children's words, photographs, and now the videotapes—becomes an indispensable source of materials that we use everyday to be able to 'read' and reflect critically . . . the project we are exploring.

(Vecchi 1993, p. 122)

WHAT?

In everyday language, to document a process or event is to gather and organise information about it. Documenting something provides a written or pictorial record of what has occurred. As a teaching technique, documentation refers to gathering and organising information to provide a written or pictorial record of children's learning.

As Katz and Chard (1996) indicated, documentation has been a practice used in many early childhood programs for some time. As part of the overall planning process, all early childhood staff are familiar with written record-taking and observation of children's development in order to help them to plan techniques and learning experiences for a particular child or group of children. This process is described in many early childhood texts that concern themselves with program planning, such as Read et al. (1993), Arthur et al. (1996) and Faragher and MacNaughton (1990). This kind of documentation is a support or adjunct to teaching; that is, it gives staff important information from which they devise goals, techniques and learning experiences for the children.

However, in recent years documentation as a teaching technique has become strongly associated with, and given particular meaning through, the pre-primary schools of the northern Italian city of Reggio Emilia. For this reason it is called the Reggio Emilia 'Approach' to documentation and the work that has developed from it will provide the focal point for the discussion in this chapter. This tradition of documentation '. . . refers to any activity that renders a performance record with sufficient detail to help others understand the behaviour recorded' (Forman 1996, p. 87).

Such documentation can enhance children's learning by exciting their interest in their own learning and by demonstrating to children that their work is being taken seriously (Malaguzzi 1993).

HOW?

Documentation builds from staff observing children's learning and making decisions about when and how to document this learning (New 1990). Staff need to think about what they want to document and why. In making this decision Katz and Chard (1996, p. 3) argued that staff should document children's learning when '. . . children are engaged in absorbing, complex interesting projects worthy of documentation'. The decision about what to document should arise from consultation between staff over what they deem to be worthwhile learning projects. Increasingly there is an interest in children being consulted as part of this decision-making process (Dixon 2001).

Once staff (and/or children) decide what specific project work will be documented, they need to set aside time for careful observation of children's learning throughout the project. Alongside this they need to develop techniques for recording, organising and displaying their observations. There are many techniques staff can use to record their observations of children's learning, including:

- ➲ photographing children's work, including the use of digital camera photographs of children's drawings, sculptures, paintings, buildings and other constructional work. Children can assist in this process (Dixon 2001)
- ➲ making written observations of children's work, including recording children's language

Marissa documents what Elenor says about her drawing.

- ➔ audio-recording children's comments and conversations
- ➔ making overhead transparencies of children's representations
- ➔ video-recording the processes and products of children's learning
- ➔ transcribing children's comments and observations
- ➔ collecting a portfolio of children's work (Trepanier-Street 2000; Dixon 2001).

At a kindergarten in Brisbane's outer western suburbs the children are involved in a project about snakes. It is summer and the children have all seen snakes in the grasslands adjacent to the suburb. They have become interested in these animals and have decided with the teacher to explore them through a project which is progressing and evolving.

Mardie, the teacher, sits with a group of children as they reflect on and recall their knowledge of snakes. She asks stimulus questions and provides children with time to speculate about aspects of snakes. She records the conversation on audiotape.

At the end of the day Mardie transcribes the tape onto paper. She interprets and analyses the transcript in order to increase her knowledge of what the children have said. Mardie then makes notes and uses them the next day when she is with the children to deepen and further their knowledge and interest in the subject.

Access to tools such as photocopiers, digital cameras or tape-recorders is important for this work. New technologies are making the process of documentation easier and speedier for many staff. Trepanier-Street et al. (2001, p. 182) highlighted a number of advantages of using a digital camera to document children's project work and the learning they gained from it. They point to the many ways in which a digital camera and the photographs it produces can be used in project work. They include the following:

Diana records aspects of social play during a session.

➔ Immediately printing photos taken of children's work in a specific area or on a specific day allows staff and children to discuss what has happened almost as it happens.

➔ Printing digital photos is cheaper than conventional photographs and so it is possible to build a store of photos of a project that children can revisit and use in their project work.

➔ Transparencies can be made of digital photographs and, using an overhead projector, projected to all children to revisit work and discuss progress.

➔ A classroom book is easily made via A4 prints of the photos that can be used to help children sequence the learning that has occurred during the project and support emergent literacy learning.

Videotaping children's learning offers a rich source of information about their language and interactions. However, revisiting videotape can be time-consuming and staff should bear this in mind if they choose to use it as part of their documentation process. Videotaping can also be used to revisit moments with parents and children:

> Videotapes serve a purpose not only for the teacher but also for the children and parents. Children can revisit with the teacher the section of the videotape that contains a significant advancement in their learning. Such revisiting can help children to connect their previous learning with current project exploration (Trepanier-Street et al. 2001, p. 183).

After the information on children's learning has been recorded, staff must interpret and organise it in ways that explain children's learning (Forman 1996). Interpreting children's learning is a collaborative process within the Reggio Centres. As Millikan et al. (1996, p. 211) explained:

> . . . collaboration is essential to interpretation because observation is never neutral, never objective, and is only partial. Therefore, the collaboration provides the opportunity for considering different points of view, and the possibility to move closer to reality.

Once staff have identified significant moments in a given project and explored ways of interpreting these, they can organise the documents for display to others. At this point captions often need to be added to pictures or transcripts of children's learning that:

➔ provide a commentary on what has occurred. This commentary often highlights the activities children have been involved in and how their learning has developed through the activities (Gandini 1993a)

➔ raise questions about children's learning and how they are being taught (Forman 1996)

➔ interpret what children have been learning (Forman 1996)

➔ provide a basis for 'further inquiry, discussion, and analysis' (Forman 1996, p. 95).

The intention in this phase of the documentation process is to produce documents (photographs, captions etc.) that enable staff, children and parents to reflect on the processes and issues associated with children's learning around a particular event and to '. . . pursue what is important to the child in constructing meaning' (Hertzberg 1995, p. 8). Such reflection is prompted by public display of the 'documents' in the centre. To excite the interest and reflection of children, staff and parents the display should be easily accessible, well-designed, aesthetically pleasing, and displayed with flair and care (Gandini 1993a).

Campbell et al. (2002) detailed a project in which children, staff and parents used documentation and children's artwork to explore what a peaceful community looks and feels like. Central to their processes of reflecting on the meanings of peace was a gallery space that enabled families, children, teachers and others to make sense of shared concerns and differences about how a peaceful and respectful community looks and feels to them and to:

- ➔ spontaneously discuss and reflect upon how hurtful behaviours have occurred, and how they imagined peace and respect would be practised in the centre
- ➔ share, admire and provoke different ways of understanding issues of peace and respect in conversations with each other
- ➔ encourage and support visitors to share and reflect on how their ideas and understandings of peaceful and respectful communities could be used in their own communities and their own lives
- ➔ revisit how their understandings, questions, concerns, and ideas about peaceful and respectful communities change, and why (Campbell et al. 2002).

Staff will need to set aside time to develop effective techniques for gathering information, to organise the information into meaningful documents and to display these with care. While such time can be hard to find, the effort involved will be rewarded as documenting produces information that enables staff to assess individual learning, plan curriculum and assess their own teaching (Forman et al. 1996, Ratcliffe 2001/02). The reasons for this are outlined by Ratcliffe (2001/02, p. 68) within the context of documenting children's emergent literacy skills:

> For an authentic assessment approach to be successful, a teacher must take time to think about what children already know and are able to do, and about what skills they will need to develop further . . . Regularly scheduling a time to review and reflect will allow teachers to achieve the insight they need to develop a clear understanding of the progress each child is making, and to plan appropriate experiences . . .

The process of review and reflection can occur with staff and between staff and children. The aim may not always be to find the most accurate assessment of children's learning, but to explore multiple perspectives on children's learning and project work as a provocation and invitation to further work and exploration of a topic. Review and reflection in this instance is not a final point in the documentation process but embedded in it as a driver for further learning. Some questions that can assist in this process include:

- ➔ Whose ideas and actions have we documented?
- ➔ Whose ideas and actions are missing from our documentation?
- ➔ What is similar and what is different in what we learn from different learners?
- ➔ What are the differences in how we each see what is significant? This question is especially important to ask if children and adults are sharing the review and reflection cycle and when there is social, cultural and linguistic diversity within the group of reviewers and reflectors.
- ➔ What of signficance to me is not captured in what has been documented?
- ➔ What learning seems worth exploring further?
- ➔ What actions do we want to take as a result of this review and reflection?

Some staff document children's learning to support their assessment of children's learning and organise the documentation into portfolios (for example, Shores and Grace 1998; Beeth et al. 2001).

THEORETICAL BACKGROUND

LORIS MALAGUZZI AND THE PRE-PRIMARY SCHOOLS OF REGGIO EMILIA

Loris Malaguzzi (1920–1994) was an Italian educator who founded and for many years directed the Reggio Emilia system of early childhood education in the northern region of Italy known as Emilia-Romagna. Malaguzzi worked with parents, children and colleagues to develop an approach to educating young children that has been acclaimed internationally and that has become known as the Reggio Emilia Approach. In this approach to early childhood education, children's learning is supported and enriched through in-depth, short- and long-term project work in which 'responding, recording, playing, exploring, hypothesis-building and testing, and provoking occurs' (New 1990, p. 3).

One of the features of the pre-primary schools in Reggio Emilia is the care that is taken to document and display the project work of the children in the schools. Malaguzzi sees this documentation and its display as central to the educational culture of the schools because it tells the school community what has happened and provokes further learning and exploration. For instance, walls and other spaces are used to exhibit the children's work to others.

The documentation is seen as integral to the children's learning and provides them with a reference source of what they have done and a source of information to provoke additional learning (Edwards et al. 1993).

More discussion of the philosophy and practices of Reggio Emilia pre-primary schools is presented in Chapter 29.

WHEN AND WHY?

Goal relevance

Documentation can be used as a teaching technique to support and enrich children's learning in a variety of ways. Specifically, documentation can be used by staff to:

 develop and deepen children's interest and curiosity in a project (Katz and Chard 1996)

 deepen children's understanding about their own learning (Malaguzzi 1993)

 support children's meta-cognitive learning by enabling them to revisit their ideas and view them from different perspectives (Doverborg and Pramling Samuelsson 1999)

 stimulate children's interest and curiosity in each other's interests, techniques, learning and achievements (Katz and Chard 1996)

 encourage children to plan and work together (Katz and Chard 1996)

 enable children to revisit their own learning (Forman 1996)

 encourage collaboration between parents, staff and children (Gandini 1994)

 help build communities of learners (Dixon 2001)

 make visible to the children their own learning journey (Wilson Gillespie 2000)

 enable children to 'examine their own thinking and the thinking of others on a project' (Trepanier-Street et al. 2001)

 encourage children to shape their own learning environment (Gandini 1994)

 help children gain a sense of history and evoke children's memories of past experiences (LeeKeenan and Nimmo 1994).

A documentation/display of photos has been put up in the foyer of the Panay children's centre. The photos trace the evolution of a project the children have completed about dinosaurs which has culminated with a large sculpture of a brontosaurus. The first photo shows a teacher–child discussion about the project. The following photographs show the remaining stages of the project and in particular children researching and making the sculpture. The children are looking at the photos with delight and talking animatedly. They recall the different aspects of the project and point out which parts of the project involved them. A teacher sits quietly and takes notes of what the children are saying. These notes will be used at a later time in a discussion with them.

Documentation can also help staff and parents reflect on teaching and learning in their centre, as it provides them with a detailed record of what has been accomplished by children over time. It also shows how children's learning has unfolded and provides adults with an awareness of what children are learning and how the centre supports their learning (Gandini 1993b, p. 146).

Angela uses photos to record the children at work.

Developmental considerations

Documentation of children's learning is relevant for children of all age groups and for learning across all developmental domains. However, children's ability to make sense of different forms of pictorial and written documentation will vary. The younger the child the more important it is to present information to them in a concrete way. For example, LeeKeenan and Nimmo (1994) argue that photographic documentation is particularly useful with two- and three-year-old children as photographs act as a more effective memory trigger with this age group than written representations of events:

> Staff at the Millgrove Children's Centre take photographs of all the children in their toddler group at the beginning of the year and put these up on the wall at the children's height. The staff then take care to play games with the children using the photos so that the children get to know each other and remember each other's names more easily. They also take photographs of the work of each child and add this to the display during the year. This acts as a point of conversation for the toddlers and helps them begin to reflect on their changing interests and accomplishments as the year progresses.

In their work with toddlers they also found that involving the children in taking the photographs was important to gain a sense of the children's perspective on the world. By contrast, many preschool children and children in the early years of school will be at a point where their own words, drawings and sketches may trigger memories and comments and further interest in a particular project. For example, in a research project in which the documentation of children's learning was traced (see Tinworth 1996), preschool children often requested that their words be written down as part of the documentation process. In a project on housing in the United States involving children in the early years of schooling, models and written reports made by children played a major role in the documentation process (Abramson et al. 1995).

Staff can judge which forms of pictorial and written documentation most effectively stimulate children's thinking and help them revisit their own learning by documenting children's reactions to documentation and by taking the symbolic and expressive language abilities of the children into account. In the project on families described below, the children relied strongly on the visual arts to express what they knew about families:

> In the foyer of the Waikia Children's Centre, the staff have documented the children's project on families. Several of the five-year-olds used photographs of their families and photographs from magazines to help them think about what it means to be a family. Six of the children have made a large collage of families that forms part of the foyer documentation. The collage has several family portraits within it that represent all the different types of families they know. There is a family with a dad, two dogs and one son; a family with one mum and two children; a family with an aunt, a dad, three children and a cat; a family with a mum and a dad and a step-dad and six children; a family with two mums and two children; and a family with a mum and a dad, a grandma, a new baby, a daughter and a parrot.
>
> Two children painted a frame for the collage and each family portrait they made. One of the children who is able to write has written the title they gave their collage on the top and the names of the families on each of the portraits. The other three children have selected the images that go inside each of the portrait frames to reflect all the families they know. The children are now getting ready to draw what they like most about their families.

It is important that staff develop criteria for assessing their documentation to assist their decision-making about which projects or learning experiences might be most valuable and meaningful within their specific context. These criteria could address the specific characteristics of the children they work with including the age of children, children's prior experience of the topic, its cultural relevance and the availability of appropriate resources to support and extend children's learning on the topic. Sloane (1999) provides detailed criteria for evaluating what kind of project might be suited to a specific group of children.

As children become older they become more able to collaborate with staff in documenting projects. Dixon (2001) described how children were actively involved in documenting their learning about water. The children produced drawings, diagrams, writing, photographs and models of their understandings of water as they researched in their classroom. Their research questions included:

➲ Where does water come from?
➲ Where does water go?
➲ What can water do?
➲ How does water support life?

EQUITY CONSIDERATIONS

Documentation develops from staff decisions about what they believe to be important to convey to others about children and their learning. It therefore conveys powerful messages about who and what is valued by the staff. In deciding what to document, how to document and how to interpret what is documented, staff need to be alert to the ways in which bias can enter their work and how this can be challenged.

'Race' and culture

'Racial' and cultural bias can enter into several phases of the documentation process. Staff can check against such bias in their own work on documentation by ensuring that:

➲ all children in the group have an opportunity to have their work valued through documentation
➲ the projects (themes or topics) chosen for documentation challenge rather than reinforce 'racial' and cultural stereotypes
➲ the techniques chosen to record observations are culturally inclusive and culturally sensitive
➲ the interpretations of children's learning display cultural awareness and sensitivity
➲ the displays of children's projects and learning are accessible to parents, staff and children from a variety of language backgrounds.

Staff should ensure that the black and ethnic minority children have the same opportunities for documentation as the ethnic majority children in the group. This means that the words and thoughts of all children in the group need to be represented and that all children's ideas and traditions should be valued. To achieve this goal, staff may need to find people who can translate the words and thoughts of children from language backgrounds other than their own.

Staff need to think carefully about which projects they choose to document. Some projects can overtly or covertly reinforce or challenge racism. For example, if several children in the group became interested in golliwogs it would be important to ensure that any project work arising from this interest involved the children in exploring how and why golliwogs are offensive to people of African descent. Offence arises because golliwogs 'reinforce a negative stereotype of black people—childlike, happy-go-lucky, with fuzzy hair, huge round eyes and thickened lips' (Brown 1995, p. 15). Images and text of children thinking about golliwogs should not merely represent any stereotypes the children have, but show how staff and children are working to challenge these stereotypes.

Documenting projects that build children's understanding of and respect for cultural and 'racial' diversity will be those that:

- ➲ develop and deepen children's interest and curiosity in cultural and racial differences and similarities. For example, projects that develop from children's questions such as, 'Where do people get their colour from?' or 'Why are her eyes different to mine?' offer lots of opportunity to build respect for 'racial' diversity
- ➲ encourage children from different 'racial' and cultural backgrounds to plan and work together
- ➲ encourage collaboration between parents, staff and children from different 'racial' and cultural backgrounds
- ➲ encourage children from a variety of 'racial' and cultural backgrounds to shape their own learning environment
- ➲ help children from different 'racial' and cultural backgrounds to gain a sense of history of working positively together.

Parents should be involved in discussions about the techniques staff wish to use to record children's learning, and staff should not proceed without parental approval. Staff discussion with parents will enable any cultural reservations parents may have about the proposed documenting to surface and for alternative techniques to be explored. It is also important that staff check that parents are happy for their children's images, words, thoughts and actions to be shared publicly. Cultural beliefs and traditions may influence parent's feelings about this.

Interpretation is a very subjective process which is strongly influenced by our cultural values and beliefs, and by those cultural values and beliefs that are dominant in our society. Our cultural values and beliefs can influence how we interpret children's body language, their accomplishments, their knowledge and their relationships. To counter the possibility of cultural misinterpretation or prejudice, staff can check their interpretations of children's learning with people from cultures other than their own and from other than the dominant culture. This collaborative interpretation can lead to better informed and more flexible ways of thinking about children and their learning as it can bring forth multiple and contrasting perspectives.

Accessibility to the project display if parents are not literate in English can be increased in several ways. Staff can ensure all written text is translated into the languages spoken by parents and use bilingual staff and parents for face-to-face interpretation of the text. In addition, staff can use pictures that reduce the need for textual translation and interpretation.

Children can benefit from seeing scripts of languages other than English. This can support or awaken their interest in such languages (Brown 1995) and add to the cultural richness of the centre.

In the foyer of the Topkapi Child Care Centre, the staff have documented the children's project on spaceships in English and in Turkish. The bilingual staff read this to the children in both languages. The Turkish parents are also able to read this documentation in their first language. Children who are not familiar with the Turkish language have begun to take an interest in the Turkish script and the sounds of the words when they are read out. Several of the five-year-old children are now beginning to incorporate different writing scripts in their spaceship representations. Staff have just found some photographs of spacecrafts from the former Soviet Union and the United States which clearly show the different scripts on each craft. They now plan to talk with the children about the photographs and the words that are often written on spacecraft.

In centres where children are learning English as a second language, bilingual documentation is especially beneficial. It shows children their first language is respected and it offers them ways of maintaining proficiency in it.

Gender

Gender bias can also enter into several phases of the documentation process. Staff can check against such bias in their own work by ensuring that:

- ➲ boys and girls in the group have an equal opportunity to have their work valued through documentation
- ➲ the projects (themes or topics) chosen for documentation challenge rather than reinforce gender stereotypes
- ➲ the interpretations of children's learning display gender awareness and sensitivity.

Staff will need to monitor the gender balance in their projects and take steps to counter any imbalances that develop over time. For example, gender can influence whether or not a particular child's interest becomes a group project (Tinworth 1996) and thus influence what staff might consider worthwhile to document over time. In the research reported by Tinworth (1996) boys' interests dominated over those of the girls' and led to a group project on reptiles and eagles. Other research suggests that the power relations between boys and girls often influences what children learn, how they approach their learning and how they express themselves (MacNaughton 1995, 2000) with boys often being more dominant than the girls. Given this, it is important that staff work particularly hard to develop and document the interests of girls as well as boys. This means staff need to value the traditional female domains of play, such as domestic play, as much as they value the traditional male domains of play, such as adventure play.

Developing and documenting projects with children that build their understanding of and respect for gender equity can:

- ➲ develop and deepen children's interest and curiosity in gender differences and similarities
- ➲ encourage boys and girls to plan and work together
- ➲ encourage collaboration between male and female parents, staff and children
- ➲ encourage girls and boys to shape their own learning environment
- ➲ help boys and girls to gain a sense of history of working positively together.

As staff construct the messages they want to convey to children, parents and other staff about children's learning, they need to be sensitive to the potential for gender bias in their interpretations. Staff should be alert to the fact that adults often interpret similar behaviours in boys and girls differently (France 1986). For example, research has shown that when baby girls respond with a startle to a new situation adults interpret this behaviour as anxiety and interpret the same behaviour in baby boys as excitement, and when babies are restless adults interpret this as a desire to play in baby boys and interpret the same behaviour in girls as distress (Alloway 1995). These research results suggest that staff should critically evaluate their interpretations of children's learning for gender bias and make any adjustments as appropriate.

Disability and additional needs

Staff can check against disability bias in their documentation work by ensuring that:

- children with and without disabilities in the group have an equal opportunity to have their work valued through documentation
- the projects (themes or topics) chosen for documentation challenge rather than reinforce disability stereotypes
- the techniques chosen to record observations are inclusive and sensitive to children with varying abilities
- the interpretations of children's learning display disability awareness and sensitivity
- the presentations of children's projects and learning are accessible to parents, staff and children of varying abilities and disabilities.

Children with and without disabilities should have an equal opportunity to have their work valued through documentation. If staff regularly monitor whose work is being documented they can identify any inequalities. If any inequalities do exist, staff can take steps to ensure that children with disabilities are represented in future documentation. Equal representation is much easier to manage when a child attends a centre regularly. However, regular centre attendance may not be possible for children whose health is impaired in some way. Conditions such as asthma, severe allergies, heart problems, cancer, epilepsy and juvenile diabetes may affect children's ability to attend regularly, and when children do attend they may need regular periods of rest. Depending on the severity of the condition, a child may need to be hospitalised for periods of time. Staff need to ensure that irregular attendance at the centre, periods of absence and the need for rest does not lead to children's absence in any documentation. To guard against such exclusion, staff will need to record children's learning at times and on occasions when any children with health impairments are present. Staff may also be able to involve parents and other carers, such as hospital staff, in the process of recording a child's learning away from the centre to supplement the documentation that occurs there.

Developing and documenting projects with children that build their understanding of and respect for people with different abilities can:

- stimulate and deepen children's interest and curiosity in ability differences and similarities
- encourage children of different abilities to plan and work together
- encourage collaboration between parents, staff and children of different abilities
- encourage children of different abilities to shape their own learning environment
- help children of different abilities gain a sense of history of working positively together.

The techniques chosen to record observations need to be inclusive and sensitive to children with varying abilities. For example, if children have a disability that makes sharing their ideas, thoughts and feelings through speech difficult, they may communicate via sign language, body language or communication aids that enhance their speech. In such instances, recording children's learning through tape-recording is likely to be less valuable than a video-camera. The tape-recorder may miss most of what a child communicates and thus makes revisiting it difficult. On the other hand, video-recording can capture the complex and varied non-verbal ways in which a child may express themselves through dance, movement, facial expression, sign language and the visual arts such as painting and collage.

As mentioned above, interpreting children's learning is a value-based process. Judging what is a significant moment in children's learning or what is intended by children's actions or words is highly subjective. When staff are working with children with disabilities they need to be aware of and sensitive to the complexities of making judgements about what is significant learning. What staff believe to be significant will depend on their own values about what is important to learn, what they believe learning is and how they believe learning can be recognised. It will also depend on their understanding of a specific child and how a child's learning may be enhanced or limited by their particular level and form of disability. Getting to know each child will assist staff in making their judgements about what to document. However, the process of getting to know children can be difficult when children's ability to communicate is limited by their disability. In such instances, staff need to allow children many different ways of expressing themselves; for example, through painting, drawing, collage, dance, music, movement, drama, story or construction. Such opportunities will enhance the possibility of each child finding a 'language' to learn with and communicate through. If children can find such a 'language' it will enhance their staff's ability to sensitively interpret what and how they are learning.

When a child or a parent has a disability that may influence their ability to access the display, staff need to communicate with them about what they can do to ensure accessibility. For example, if a child or parent has a sight impairment, then adding sound, texture and Braille to the display could make the display more accessible to them.

REFLECTING ON DOCUMENTING TECHNIQUES

1   What is documenting?
2   What do you see as the main differences between observation and documenting?
3   What does Katz suggest are the keys to successfully using documenting to optimise children's learning?
4   What do you think are the pros and cons of using documenting in your teaching?
5   What do you see as the key equity issues in using documenting in your teaching?
6   View one of the videos listed below and answer the following questions. To what extent did documentation:
    ❯ stimulate children's learning?
    ❯ deepen and enrich their understanding of what they were learning?
    ❯ encourage co-operative learning between children?
    ❯ extend children's understandings of how they learn?

IMPROVING TEACHING IN PRACTICE

1   Use three different techniques to record children's learning during several half-hour teaching periods and examine the information you have collected and answer the following questions:
    ❯ What themes or issues about children's learning would you like to document?
    ❯ Which technique provided the most useful material on children's learning during this time?
    ❯ How could you display the material you have collected to provide a commentary on what has occurred, to raise questions and interpret children's learning and how they are being taught?

2   To what extent did equity issues emerge in the process of documenting children's learning?
3   What are your areas of strength and weakness in using documenting to promote children's learning?
4   How can you improve your documenting techniques in practice?

Further reading

Abramson, A., Robinson, R. and Ankenman, K. 1995, 'Project work with diverse students: adapting curriculum based on the Reggio Emilia Approach', *Childhood Education*, 71(4), pp. 197–202.

Dixon, B. 2001, 'Purposeful learning: a study of water', *Early Childhood Research and Practice*, 3(2), pp. 1–18.

Gandini, L. 1993, 'Educational caring spaces', in C. Edwards, L. Gandini and G. Forman, eds, *The Hundred Languages of Children: The Reggio Emilia Approach to Early Childhood Education*, pp. 135–49, New Jersey, Ablex Publishing Company [refer to p. 146].

Helm, J., Beneke, S. and Steinheimer, K. 1998, *Windows on learning: documenting young children's work*, New York, Teachers' College Press.

Katz, L. and Chard, S. 1996, 'The contribution of documentation to the quality of early childhood education', *ERIC Digest*, April, EDO-PS-96-2.

Ratcliffe, N. 2001/02, 'Using authentic assessment to document the emerging literacy skills of young children', *Childhood Education*, 78(2), pp. 66–9.

Video

Children Creating Curriculum, University of Melbourne, Faculty of Education, Department of Early Childhood Studies, Victorian College of the Arts Multi-media Production Unit, Melbourne 1996.

Mia Mia: A New Vision for Day Care. Part 1. The Program for 2- to 5-year-olds, Summerhill Films for the Institute of Early Childhood, Macquarie University Nth Ryde, Australia 1995.

My Kind of Place: Quality Care for Infants and Toddlers, Roger Neugebauer Publications, Child Care Exchange 1989.

Websites—extending learning online

Explore examples of projects with young children and their documentation at
http://www.ualberta.ca/~schard/projects.htm

Read a detailed account of a project about water and its documentation by young children at
http://www.ecrp.uiuc.edu./v3n2/dixon.html

References

Abramson, A., Robinson, R. and Ankenman, K. 1995, 'Project work with diverse students: adapting curriculum based on the Reggio Emilia Approach', *Childhood Education*, 71(4), pp. 197–202.

Alloway, N. 1995, *Foundation Stones: The Construction of Gender in Early Childhood*, Melbourne, Curriculum Corporation.

Arthur, L., Beecher, B., Dockett, S., Farmer, S. and Death, E. 1996, *Programming and Planning in Early Childhood Settings*, second edn, Sydney, Harcourt Brace and Company.

Beeth, M., Cross, L., Pearl, C., Pirro, J., Yagnesak, K. and Kennedy, J. 2001, 'A continuum for assessing science process knowledge in grades K–6', *Electronic Journal of Science Education*, 5(3), pp. 1–17.

Brown, B. 1995, *All Our Children: A Guide for Those who Care*, third edn, London, British Broadcasting Commission Education.

Campbell, S., Coady, M., Castilino, T., Lawrence, H., MacNaughton, G., Page, J. and Rolfe, S. 2002, *Our Part in Peace*, Australian Early Childhood Association.

Doverborg, E. and Pramling Samuelsson, I. 1999. Apple cutting and creativity as a mathematical beginning. Kindergarten Education, 4(2), 87–103

Dixon, B. 2001, 'Purposeful learning: a study of water', *Early Childhood Research and Practice*, 3(2), pp. 1–18.

Edwards, C., Gandini, L. and Forman, G. (eds) 1993, *The Hundred Languages of Children: The Reggio Emilia Approach to Early Childhood Education*, New Jersey, Ablex Publishing Corporation.

Faragher, J. and MacNaughton, G. 1990, *Working with Young Children: Guidelines for Good Practice*, Melbourne, TAFE Publications.

Forman, G. 1996, Design, documentation and discourse: cornerstones of negotiated curriculum, Keynote address presented to the *Weaving Webs Conference*, Melbourne, July.

Forman, G., Lee, M., Wrisley, L. and Langley, J. 1996, 'The city in the snow: applying the multisymbolic approach in Massachusetts', in C. Edwards, L. Gandini and G. Forman, eds, *The Hundred Languages of Children: The Reggio Emilia Approach to Early Childhood Education* (pp. 233–50), New Jersey, Ablex.

France, P. 1986, 'The beginnings of sex stereotyping', in N. Browne and P. France, eds, *Untying the Apron Strings: Anti-Sexist Provision for the Under Fives* (pp. 49–67), Milton Keynes, Open University Press.

Gandini, L. 1993a, 'Fundamentals of the Reggio Emilia Approach to early childhood education', *Young Children*, 49(1), pp. 4–8.

——1993b, 'Educational caring spaces', in C. Edwards, L. Gandini and G. Forman, eds, *The Hundred Languages of Children: The Reggio Emilia Approach to Early Childhood Education* (pp. 135–49), New Jersey, Ablex Publishing Company.

——1994, 'What can we learn from Reggio Emilia: an Italian–American collaboration', *Child Care Information Exchange*, (3), pp. 62–6.

Hertzberg, C. 1995, 'The image of the child', *The Challenge*, June, pp. 7–9.

Katz, L. and Chard, S. 1996, 'The contribution of documentation to the quality of early childhood education', *ERIC Digest*, April, EDO-PS-96-2.

LeeKeenan, D. and Nimmo, J. 1994, 'Connections: using the project approach with 2- and 3-year-olds in a university laboratory school', in C. Edwards, L. Gandini and G. Forman, eds, *The Hundred Languages of Children: The Reggio Emilia Approach to Early Childhood Education* (pp. 251–67), New Jersey, Ablex Publishing Corporation.

MacNaughton, G. 1995, 'A poststructuralist approach to learning in early childhood settings', in M. Fleer, ed., *DAPcentrism: Challenging Developmentally Appropriate Practice* (pp. 35–54), Watson, ACT, Australian Early Childhood Association.

——2000, *Rethinking Gender in Early Childhood*, Sydney, Allen & Unwin; New York, Sage; London, Paul Chapman Publishing.

Malaguzzi, L. 1993, 'History, ideas and basic philosophy', in C. Edwards, L. Gandini and G. Forman, eds, *The Hundred Languages of Children: The Reggio Emilia Approach to Early Childhood* (pp. 41–90), Norwood, NJ, Ablex.

Millikan, J., Mauger, M., Thompson, J. and Hobba, M. 1996, A collaboration in reconceptualising the roles of children and adults in children's learning and development, Paper presented to the *Weaving Webs Conference*, Melbourne, July.

New, R. 1990, 'Projects and provocations: preschool curriculum ideas from Reggio Emilia, Italy', *ED318565*.

Ratcliffe, N. 2001/02, 'Using authentic assessment to document emerging literacy skills of young children', *Childhood Education*, 78(2), pp. 66–9.

Read, K., Gardner, P. and Mahler, B. 1993, *Early Childhood Programs: Human Relationships and Learning*, ninth edn, Forth Worth, TX, Holt, Rinehart and Winston Inc.

Shores, E. and Grace, C. 1998, *The Portfolio Book: A Step-by-Step Guide for Teachers*, Beltsville, MD, Gryphon House.

Sloane, M. 1999, 'All kinds of projects for your classroom', *Young Children*, 54(4), pp. 17–20.

Tinworth, S. 1996, Octopus tales: perspectives on learning and teaching at the DECS Children's Centre. Paper presented to *Weaving Webs Conference*, Melbourne, July.

Trepanier-Street, M. 2000, 'Multiple forms of representation in long-term projects: the garden project', *Childhood Education*, 77(1), pp. 18–25.

Trepanier-Street, M., Hong, S. and Bauer, J. 2001, 'Using technology in Reggio-inspired long-term projects', *Early Childhood Education Journal*, 28(2), pp. 181–8.

Vecchi, V. 1993, 'The role of the *atelierista*: an interview with Lella Gandini', in C. Edwards, L. Gandini and G. Forman, eds, *The Hundred Languages of Children: The Reggio Emilia Approach to Early Childhood* (pp. 119–31), Norwood, NJ, Ablex.

Wilkes, G. (ed.) 1979, *Collins Dictionary of the English Language*, Middlesex, Penguin Books.

Wilson Gillespie, C. 2000, 'Six Head Start classrooms begin to explore the Reggio Emilia Approach', *Young Children*, 55(1), pp. 21–7.

Chapter 23

Empowering

Empower: to give ability to, to enable or permit.
To give or delegate power or authority.

(Collins Dictionary of the English Language, p. 408)

The objectives of empowerment should contribute to social justice and [ensure] positive discrimination in favour of the underprivileged to ensure equity.

(Rees 1991, p. 65)

Empowerment rests on the belief that we should all be able to . . . participate in the practice of freedom . . . and discover how to participate in the transformation of . . . [our] world.

(Freire 1972, p. 15)

WHAT?

To empower means to give others the power (or ability) to do something. In everyday usage empowering is often used to describe the process of giving someone the power to do something on our behalf. For example, we might empower someone to sign cheques in our place or empower someone to take decisions about what to do if our dog becomes ill when we are away on holidays.

Empowerment always involves people who have the power to do something by giving up or over their power to someone who does not have it. In the case of signing cheques, you give up or give over the power you had to sign your cheques to someone who would not normally have this potential. Empowerment always involves such a transfer between the powerful and powerless in a particular situation. As such, empowerment can only occur when one person or a group of people has more power than others. It is only necessary when there is an unequal distribution of power between people.

While empowerment can be used to describe any transfer of power it most often refers to the transfer of cultural, political, economic and social power between people. In this usage, empowerment is the process of giving greater cultural, economic, social and political power to those who have little access to such opportunities because of injustices and inequalities in a particular society. By giving people who have been treated unequally and unjustly more power (ability) they can take greater control over their lives and participate more equally in the cultural, social, political and economic life of their society. They have more freedom to choose in their daily lives (Wasserman 1991; Darder 2002). The aim of empowerment is to create greater social justice. As Bystydzienski (1992) explained, empowerment is:

Mimi and Fergus take turns at washing their own hands.

. . . a process by which oppressed persons gain some control over their lives by taking part with others in development of activities and structures that allow people increased involvement in matters which affect them directly (Bystydzienski 1992, cited in Yuval-Davis 1994, p. 179).

Put simply, people are empowered when they have the resources and the independence to direct their own lives in ways that they are free from discrimination and oppression.

As a teaching technique, empowerment has both a general and a specialist usage. In general usage, empowerment as a teaching technique involves giving children the power (or ability) to do things. For example, giving children the ability to (power to) decide which experiences they want to participate in or when they have milk and fruit.

> Riverbrook Kindergarten uses the High Scope Curriculum. One aspect of this allows the children to decide what they will do. The teacher holds a meeting with the children each morning and asks them what they'll play with first, second, third . . . The teacher has a magnet board where she writes the children's names and then the children stick symbols under their names for the activities that they have chosen each day.

The staff transfer the power they have of deciding what and when the children will do daily tasks. An example of this general usage of empowerment is also detailed by the New Zealand Ministry of Education in their curriculum guidelines for early childhood services. They believe that empowering children means staff will provide them with the following power (abilities):

The knowledge, skills, and attitudes fostered by the curriculum . . . to:

- ➲ take increasing responsibility for their own learning and care;
- ➲ continue learning with an enhanced sense of self-worth, identity, confidence, and enjoyment;
- ➲ contribute their own special strengths and interests;
- ➲ learn useful and appropriate ways to find out what they want to know;
- ➲ understand their own individual ways of learning and being creative (Ministry of Education (NZ) 1996, p. 26).

FREIRE: CRITICAL CURRICULUM AND EMPOWERMENT

Paulo Freire (1921–1997) was a Brazilian educator who strongly believed that all education has social and political consequences. He also believed that educators have a moral, social and political responsibility to be involved in education for social transformation which creates a more just and equal social world. These beliefs underpin current anti-discriminatory (or 'anti-bias') approaches in early childhood education and care.

It was Freire's work to eradicate adult illiteracy in Brazil that led him to these beliefs and led him to develop what has become known as a critical approach to literacy. In Brazil he was Secretary of Education and Co-ordinator of the National Plan of Adult Literacy. After this he spent time as a Visiting Professor at Harvard's Center for Studies in Education and Development, and served as a consultant to UNESCO (Freire 1972).

Friere's first book, *Cultural Action for Freedom*, was published in Brazil in 1967 and first appeared in English translation in 1970. Since the 1970s his view of literacy education has provided a powerful framework for understanding the relationship between teaching and learning, and his work has deeply influenced the development of what is known as critical or transformatory education (Sarup 1978).

Critical approaches to education start from the assumption that the world as it is now involves inequalities and injustices. They rest on the assumption that education must explore these inequalities and injustices in order to challenge and then change them. It is a view of education that sees:

> ... educational issues in a social-political context and attempts to identify the political-economic structures which shape educational provision and practices (Carr and Kemmis 1986, p. 24).

In particular, the factors that create inequalities and injustices need to be identified and worked against to create a more just and wise social future. In critical education teachers work against these injustices and towards empowerment of the oppressed by critically reflecting on the social consequences of what they teach. This requires recognition that all education, including early childhood education, is a social and political act and that knowledge is socially constructed. To do this, staff need to understand how particular knowledge is unjust and oppressive and use this understanding to guide teaching decisions. They need to think and act in ways that help solve injustices confronted in the daily life of students.

Freire believed that teachers can do this through praxis. Praxis is a process through which people take informed action to create human liberation (Sarup 1978) and it is based on developing a critical, self-reflective form of knowledge. Smith and Lovat referred to this knowledge as 'knowing from the inside':

> Self-reflective, or critical knowledge, would then cause us to ask whether the information we have received is reliable, whether we are in a position to learn or not to learn through it, or whether we might not be controlled somehow by the forces of propaganda which surround us: this is helping to satisfy our interest to be free.
>
> For Habermas, it is only when we have reached [critical knowledge] . . . that we are guaranteed true knowledge because true knowledge demands that we be free . . . the information which comes

from any subject can become a means of bondage, rather than emancipation, a way of oppressing people or keeping them in straitjackets (Smith and Lovat 1990, pp. 69–70).

Praxis involves linking teaching actions with critical knowledge of and reflection on these actions, producing a critical evaluation of teaching that informs what is done next. As Grundy (1987, p. 115) put it '. . . curriculum is not simply a set of plans to be implemented, but rather is constituted through an active process in which planning, acting and evaluation are all reciprocally related and integrated into the process'.

Praxis describes how staff process information about the daily actions of teaching, try to solve problems encountered in teaching and then decide the best way forward (Smith and Lovat 1990). Praxis involves staff:

- ➔ exploring the gap between intention and actuality in their teaching
- ➔ making explicit and deliberate choices after examining their options
- ➔ recognising the conflicts and contradictions in their teaching and resolving them in ways that empower children.

Ideally, in critical approaches to education, curriculum content is developed in collaboration with students. According to Freire, such collaboration should arise in and through students and teachers confronting real problems in their daily lives. He called this a 'problem-posing' approach to education and contrasted it with traditional education which he believed used a 'banking' approach to education. As Sarup (1978, pp. 58–9) explained:

In the 'banking' concept of education the scope of action allowed to students extends only so far as receiving, filing and storing the deposits. The teacher makes the deposits which the students patiently receive, memorise and repeat . . . [In] problem-posing education . . . students become critical co-investigators in dialogue with the teacher.

While children and teachers interact to choose the curriculum content, their content selection should contribute to the overall goals of greater social justice and equity. When this occurs a critical, collaborative and problem-posing approach to teaching and learning is seen to be empowering for both children and staff.

It should be noted that there is considerable debate about the extent to which one person or group can empower another.

The more specialised usage of empowerment as a teaching technique is associated with what are known as 'critical', 'transformative' or 'emancipatory' approaches to education. In early childhood education these are also known as anti-discriminatory or anti-bias approaches.

Critical education theorists drawing on the work of Freire see educators as 'cultural workers' (Darder 2002, p. 171) who can be actively involved in the transformation of their society to a more just society by challenging discrimination and its effects on learners and by opening up multiple possibilities for learners (MacNaughton, 2003). As Darder (2002, p. 171) explained:

As teachers we are cultural workers, whether we are aware of it or not. If teachers don't question the culture and values being promoted in the classroom, we socialize our students to accept the inequalities of our society along lines of race, class, gender, and ability.

HOW?

Empowerment involves transferring power from one group to another in order to create greater social justice and equity between groups in a particular society. This transference of power should give the less powerful a greater ability to control and participate in decisions about their lives. To achieve this transference of power with young children, staff need to:

 decide what skills children need to experience greater control and participation in their learning

> At the Potts Child Care Centre, when each child arrives at the centre a staff member carefully observes the self-help skill level of each child. They then develop a program which will help the child to learn how to feed, dress, toilet themselves and play independently of an adult. This is so that they do not have to rely on others. Once children are able to do this, staff plan lots of opportunities for the children to make choices about what they will do and how they will do it.

 choose teaching and learning techniques that enable children to experience greater control and participation in their learning

 choose content that is compatible with the goals of greater equity and justice underpinning empowerment.

Skills for empowerment

The aim when transferring power to children within a critical approach to education is to enable them to gain '. . . the intellectual and emotional ability to confront oppression and work together to create a more just society . . .' (Dermon-Sparks et al. 1989, p. 5). Young children can gain these abilities when staff:

 help children to feel good about themselves
 build children's capacity to participate in the program to their fullest potential
 build children's ability to have positive relationships with others
 teach children to problem-solve what is fair or not fair in their day-to-day relationships with each other   ·
 help children learn to stand up for themselves and others who are treated unfairly
 build children's capacity to think critically.

Strategies for empowerment

While there is no specific group of teaching techniques that will automatically develop children's skills for their own empowerment, staff can draw on the following critical educational teaching principles to guide their choice of teaching strategies.

Content compatible with equity, justice and empowerment

Much of the traditional curriculum content for young children has developed over time to serve the interests of particular groups of people. There are, therefore, biases built into this content and staff need to learn to recognise them. These biases will be evident in the children's literature, music, dance, maths and science resources (Siraj-Blatchford and Siraj-Blatchford 1995).

Skill development for children's empowerment	Criticial education principles	Teaching techniques discussed in other chapters
Help children to feel good about themselves.	Value children's answers and knowledge. Enable children and adults to interact to decide how and when something is to be learned.	Open questioning. Active listening. Scaffolding.
Build ability to have positive relationships with others.	Emphasise the adult's role as facilitator. Encourage self-reflective knowledge.	Careful positioning of adults. Modelling. Open questions about feelings. Co-constructing.
Build capacity to participate to their fullest potential. Teach to problem-solve what is fair or not fair.	Use open-ended materials ensuring bias is not inherent in them. Emphasise open, problem-posing questioning. Encourage self-reflective knowledge.	Organising the environment. Co-constructing. Problem-solving. Task-analysing. Open questions about feelings. Philosophising.
Help to stand up for themselves and others when unfairly treated.	Emphasise open, problem-posing questioning. Encourage self-reflective knowledge.	Problem-solving—social issues. Open questions about feelings. Recalling and revising.
Build capacity to think critically.	Emphasise open, problem-posing questioning. Emphasise the process of learning rather than its product. Emphasise doing rather than knowing facts.	Deconstructing. Open questions. Co-constructing. Experimenting. Documenting.

In working to empower children, staff should choose curriculum content that ensures that what is learned and taught is as fair and just as possible. This involves integrating equity issues into the content of what is taught through the topics, themes, stories and songs that staff introduce children to. Staff also need to evaluate the information about their social world contained in the formal and informal discussions between children and themselves. These discussions can contain information about various forms of inequalities and injustices in the daily lives of the children and they could be ignored.

Questions to help staff critically reflect on the content of their teaching are:

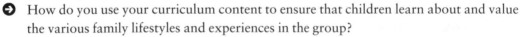 Have you checked the stories, poems and songs used with the children to ensure that they promote positive attitudes to human diversity?

➲ How do you use your curriculum content to ensure that children learn about and value the various family lifestyles and experiences in the group?

➲ How do you develop curriculum content to ensure that children learn that gender, 'race', ability, age and class stereotypes exist and that these are inaccurate and hurtful?

> How do you use your curriculum content to ensure that children learn how to be 'fair' to others?

> How do you ensure that your curriculum content assists children to learn how to stand up for themselves when injustices occur?

Evaluating for empowerment

Critical education theory emphasises staff collaboration with the children in judging progress towards empowerment. Staff can become involved in collaborative evaluation with children by checking if:

> the learning was comprehensible for all children
> everyone shared the same understandings
> everyone shared equally in developing understandings of the situation
> the staff's actions were appropriate given the differing needs and interests of children in the group
> power was shared in appropriate ways.

These reflections will highlight the:

> gap between intention and actuality in your work with children. Did you actually empower them?
> conflicts and contradictions in your work with the children. For example, what conflicts did you encounter between the need to empower boys and girls? Were their empowerment needs in conflict?

WHEN AND WHY?

To empower children, staff must be committed to creating a more just social world through transferring power from more powerful groups to less powerful groups. This commitment should build from an understanding of how power is currently distributed in a given society at specific points in time and an understanding of the connections between the wider social and political contexts of their work and their daily lives with the children in specific centres.

Commitment to progressive social change

To use empowerment as a teaching technique, staff must want to change the current distribution of power between different groups in society. They must have a belief that unequal and unjust power relationships currently exist between specific groups of people in their society and want to change this. Some questions to prompt staffs' thinking about their commitment to social change are:

> What groups do you currently belong to?
> What groups currently make up society?
> Do you believe that there should be a fair distribution of resources and experiences between all these groups in society? Do you think that there are? What examples do you have to support your views?
> Do you believe that there should be fair, respectful and non-exploitative relationships between all these groups in society? Do you think that there are? What examples do you have to support your views?

➡ Do you believe that there should be full participation by all these groups in society in social, economic, cultural and educational life? Do you think that there are? What examples do you have to support your views?

➡ Do you believe that all these groups in society should have the ability for self-expression and experience self-esteem? Do you think that they do currently? What examples do you have to support your views?

Answering these questions should give staff a sense of their level of commitment to progressive social change and of their understanding about the distribution of power in their society.

Understanding the social and political contexts

Commitment to social change builds from an understanding of the current distribution of power between different groups in their society. Staff, therefore, must be able to identify what is unfair and unjust about the distribution of power. For example, they need to understand who has the ability to actively contribute to, access and transform the cultural, economic, social and political life of their society and who does and who doesn't benefit from this.

Staff can find out more about the current distribution of power between different groups in society by exploring the specialist readings listed in the Appendix.

Understanding how inequities and injustices impact on children

Once staff understand how power is distributed within their society they have a basis from which to think about which groups of children are most likely to have less power than others. From these understandings staff can work with children to enable them to challenge the unfair and unequal as it touches their daily lives and the lives of those about them. Staff need to develop strategies to ensure that the groups of children with less power gain more. They also need to ensure that the children in the group with greater power learn to share their power with others. In early childhood settings this means:

➡ ensuring a fair distribution of resources and experiences

> Jane noticed that Sarah, a timid, shy child, was looking longingly at the blocks. She attempted to help Sarah join in the block play that was dominated by the boys in the group, but Sarah was reluctant to stay. After several sessions, when Jane encouraged Sarah to play with the blocks with or alongside the others, she decided to use a different approach. She told the children that the blocks would be off-limits to the girls and boys respectively on alternate days. In this way she was able to help Sarah play alongside the other girls in the block area.

➡ ensuring fair, respectful and non-exploitative relationships
➡ ensuring full participation by all
➡ ensuring children have the ability for self-expression and experience self-esteem.

Goal relevance

Historically, it is possible to identify five different approaches to issues of equity and social justice in teaching young children (see Corder and Quisenberry 1987; Dermon-Sparks et al.

Girls only in block play today.

1989; Beane 1990; Dermon-Sparks 1998; MacNaughton et al. 2002). To appreciate when and why to use empowerment teaching techniques, staff should understand the differences between these approaches. These differences are discussed below. Empowerment is used as a teaching technique when staff are committed to the goals of the fifth approach below.

1   Laissez-faire approaches. Staff ignore the social, cultural, racial, ability and gender differences between children and assume that treating children the same will lead to similarities. While this approach has been historically prevalent, it is not now.

2   Special provisions education approach. Specialist education is provided for the groups identified as different. The aim is to help equalise educational opportunity for children/groups who are seen as different to the 'norm'. Examples of education for the groups identified as different would include special educational provision for children with disabilities and for non-English-speaking background children. Such approaches tend to segregate the children identified as different to the norm. This segregation can reinforce notions of rejection and create a continued sense that the children being segregated are less valued than others by reinforcing the idea that only 'normal' children can participate in particular activities.

3   Cultural understanding approaches (Tourist approaches). The aim of these approaches to equity and diversity is to create understanding between diverse groups of children. Children are made aware of the fact that people dress, eat and live differently. Equality is assumed to come about through increased understandings of our similarities and differences as people by 'visiting' a disability or a cultural group for a day. This approach often leads to special experiences—such as pretending to be blind for the day, having Chinese food for lunch or adding chopsticks to the home corner for a day.

While it is important to educate children about difference, it is important to avoid some of the difficulties that have been identified when teachers rely solely on cultural understanding approaches. First, cultural understanding approaches can lead to simplistic and stereotyped understanding of other cultures and teaching children about disabilities often focuses on the negative aspects of disabilities, not on the positive aspects of the child as a whole. Second, there can often be a lack of understanding about the fact that there are differences within the abilities of people with specific disabilities or from specific cultural groupings. For example, people who cannot see do not all think, feel and act in the same way, just as all people who can see do not share the same values. Finally, often there is only seen to be a need to deal with diversity if there is social, cultural, racial or ability diversity in the children attending the centre.

4   Human rights approaches. The focus here is to teach children 'living together skills' such as sharing and caring. It is assumed that this will lead to an environment in which each individual is valued and treated with respect. This is a critical first step in building respectful relationships between children but is not sufficient in and of itself.

5   Anti-discriminatory approaches. Anti-discriminatory approaches to diversity and equity address more than individual people's differences and similarities. They also address the negative impact of discrimination on the lives of people and challenge this discrimination via the experiences and materials they offer. They aim to:

   ● make the different abilities, cultures and genders of the children visible via the curriculum
   ● enable all children to experience the richness and diversity of different parts of the curriculum
   ● develop non-discriminatory attitudes and understandings within the children towards disability, culture, social differences, 'race' and gender
   ● encourage children to value each other equally
   ● provide opportunities for children to express their own individuality and life experiences via a variety of curriculum experiences.

Empowerment is also used as a teaching technique when staff are committed to education for progressive social change in other areas of our social, economic, cultural and political life. This would include, for example, peace education, environmental education and education against homophobia, ageism and classism.

Developmental considerations

Empowerment will involve different aims and processes, depending on the age group of the children. The table below illustrates how children's age and developmental abilities may influence staff's work towards empowering children.

It should be remembered that attitudes to others and the formation of social values begin from the moment a child is born. Children learn about the world about them and the values placed on who they are from their first interactions with the world. Children can learn both fair and unfair perceptions about themselves and others. In an empowering approach to working with young children the emphasis is firmly on helping children to build fair perceptions about themselves and others. It is important to remember in this work that just as children can learn bias and unfairness they can unlearn it:

Skills underpinning empowerment	Age group			Concepts children can learn* [Will depend on developmental abilities.]
	Babies	Toddlers	3–8 years	
Help children feel good about themselves.	3	3	3	I'm me. I'm special. Each of us is special. My family is special.
Build children's capacity to participate in the program.	3	3	3	I'm capable; I can do things. I can use sounds, looks and words to express feelings and thoughts. If I try very hard I can do lots of things.
Build children's ability to have positive relationships with others.	3	3	3	I have lots of different feelings. There are lots of ways I can show and tell how I feel. I can take care of others. Friends like to be called by their names. Friends are people we especially like to be with. I can have friends. Friends share things and play together. Friends do special things for each other.
Teach children to problem-solve whether fair or not fair.		3	3	It's not fair . . . when someone takes my toy without asking, when someone calls people names, when you laugh and make people cry, when you use words to hurt people, when you say things about people that are not true. It's fair . . . when we all share, when we learn what's special about others, when we can all have a turn, when we can all have special times. People need to have food to eat, somewhere to live, clothes to wear, ways to travel from one place to another, and they need to love and be loved. Not everybody has the same amount of these things. Is that fair?
Help children learn to stand up for themselves and others who are treated unfairly.	Model to lay founda-tions	3	3	I can use my words to say how I feel. It's not fair to hurt others. It's not fair for others to hurt me. When my friend is sad I can try to help. When I'm sad my friends can help. We can join together to help each other. There is always something we can do to help.
Build children's capacity to think critically.			3	Is this true? Is this untrue? Is this fair?

Skills underpinning empowerment	Age group			Concepts children can learn* [Will depend on developmental abilities.]
	Babies	Toddlers	3–8 years	
			3	Is this unfair?
				How could we find out?
				Stereotypes are unfair because they are untrue.
				Stereotypes hurt real people because they stop them doing things.
				Can we always believe what we read in books?
				Can we always believe what we see on television?
				How might this picture/story/song hurt someone?
				What is this picture/story/song saying about people who look like this or dress like this or have skin this colour etc.?
				How might we find out more?
				Who could we talk to?
				What could we look at?
				What might we need to ask?

Source: Derman-Sparks, L., *Anti-bias Curriculum: Tools for Empowering Young Children*, 1989, 69–71, NAEYC, Washington

Even when children seem to hold unfair social perceptions of others . . . they have an intellectual capacity for un-doing their pre-existing unfair perceptions through personally meaningful experiences with others. (Hyun 2001, p. 11).

EQUITY CONSIDERATIONS

To empower children who face discrimination in their daily lives it is important that staff consciously work with children to support them to:

- ➡ take increasing responsibility for their own learning and care
- ➡ continue learning with an enhanced sense of self-worth, identity, confidence and enjoyment
- ➡ contribute their own special strengths and interests to the group
- ➡ learn useful and appropriate ways to find out what they want to know
- ➡ understand their own individual ways of learning and being creative.

The challenges and opportunities for doing this will differ according to the inequity and injustice staff are working on with children. The issues in relation to 'racial' inequalities, gender inequalities and inequalities for children with disabilities are different from each other and thus require different approaches to empowering children. For the children who experience discrimination because of their 'race', gender or disability, empowerment involves addressing the negative impact of discrimination on their lives and providing them with the skills to challenge unfair treatment of themselves and others in the future. However, staff cannot work towards empowering these children unless they understand how inequity and injustice is shaping children's lives.

'Race' and culture

Racial discrimination influences the lives of all children: those who are the victims of racial discrimination and those who perpetrate it. Children who have been the victims of racial discrimination need special support and encouragement to overcome the racially negative images they may develop about their own 'race'. Some black children may learn to value their skin colour and hair texture negatively. Children who have experienced racism will gain more power over their lives if staff:

➡ ensure that black children feel proud and confident about who they are. This involves building a strong group and personal identity (Dermon-Sparks et al. 1991; Dermon-Sparks 1998). Simple measures can be used to help children feel that their skin colour and physical characteristics are valued. For example, staff can ensure that children have access to paints which allow them to represent their own skin or hair colour. It is also important to think carefully about how colours are used and discussed within the curriculum. Is black always associated with negative or fearful images, for example, Halloween, witches, thunderstorms and monsters? Think of creative ways of helping children to rethink these associations, keeping in mind the following:

Help them to see that there is beauty in people of all physical types; develop language which expresses appreciation for people seemingly very different from themselves. Explore with even the youngest children similarities and differences. Use children's natural curiosity about their own peers and others they see around them, to challenge ideas of what's normal (Brown et al. 1991, p. 5).

➡ ensure that the children's group and personal identities are strengthened by a program in which their cultural heritage is celebrated on a regular basis
➡ regularly discuss and challenge 'racial' stereotypes
➡ provide children who have experienced racial discrimination with the skills and confidence needed to challenge any act of racism against themselves and others. They need to recognise what is fair and what is not, and to work with others for fairness. Games that help children practise telling others that what they are doing or saying is hurtful and stories that provide models of how to stop people hurting others can be useful. Dermon-Sparks et al. (1991, pp. 75–6) provide ideas for how these might be structured.

Gender

Traditional gender stereotypes can limit how boys and girls understand what they are capable of; how they should think, feel and behave; and limit how they view other people's capabilities. These gender stereotypes can lead to power imbalances in how boys and girls experience the early childhood program. How these power imbalances impact on the lives of particular boys and girls will differ from child to child. Not all boys will be powerful and not all girls powerless. For instance, a boy who practises being male in very non-traditional, non-sexist ways may not be very powerful within a group of traditionally gendered boys and girls. He may face teasing and rejection when he wants to play with dolls or dress in pink. For girls who are non-traditionally gendered there may be similar difficulties in gaining acceptance within the group. Children who are different to the gender norms of a particular group of children will gain more power over their lives if staff:

➡ make the different ways of being male and female visible via the curriculum. Stories, songs and images of boys and girls and men and women doing, dressing, feeling and trying out lots of different tasks can make children feel that the ways of being male and female are just one of many ways, and that their ways are equally valued in the centre

➔ enable boys and girls to experience the richness and diversity of different parts of the curriculum. Encourage all children to explore all aspects of the curriculum and ensure that the non-traditionally gendered children are supported when they try out new experiences. Being present to prevent and/or step in when teasing or exclusion is happening offers a simple way of ensuring that other children do not use their power to exclude non-traditionally gendered children from their play

➔ provide opportunities for girls and boys to express their own individuality and life experiences via a variety of curriculum experiences. Talking with children about gender stereotypes and encouraging them to act in non-stereotypical ways can help children feel more able to be 'different' to the norm and also to feel powerful in their differences. There are some excellent examples of how to do this in Dally and Lindstrom (1996).

Disability and additional needs

Empowering children with additional needs involves addressing the negative impact of discrimination and providing them with the skills to challenge this via the experiences and materials staff have. Children with disabilities will gain more power over their lives if staff:

➔ make the different abilities of the children visible via the curriculum. Music and movement can be used to make people with disabilities audible and visible. For example, the words: 'walking' and 'running' can be changed to 'moving' in songs such as 'Run, Sister, Run'

➔ enable all children to experience the richness and diversity of different parts of the curriculum. Movement can be used to ensure that constructive, open and sensitive attitudes develop about the children's own bodies and those of others. All children move in their own way, so don't feel that dance is an elitist art (see the reading list in the Appendix for further material on this issue)

➔ provide opportunities for children to express their own individuality and life experiences via a variety of curriculum experiences. For example, painting and drawing offer an opportunity to draw and paint images of one's self. It is important that children with disabilities, or children who have parents with disabilities, are encouraged and feel able to depict their bodies as they are and not feel that they need to reproduce images of able-bodied people.

> Con's father has had a serious car accident, and has lost the use of his lower limbs. Con's teacher, Lisa, has helped Con to learn how to draw wheelchairs so that Con is able to represent his family just as the other children do. She has done this by suggesting, describing and presenting Con with images of people in wheelchairs.

For children with disabilities to be empowered to participate to their maximum potential in the program it is also important that the children and adults around them actively display non-discriminatory attitudes and understandings towards disability. Stories, images and puppets offer very powerful opportunities for developing positive images and ideas about children with disabilities. Literature also conveys very powerful messages about people and the ways in which they are valued. It would be essential for children to have access to literature in which the heroine has a disability, for example, uses a wheelchair and in which a disability is not presented as an overwhelming handicap. For example, children's books can often contain powerful negative images of people with disabilities. Think of 'Captain Hook' and the one-legged pirates. Often people with disabilities are portrayed as being naughty or frightening. The checklist in Chapter 14, is designed to help early childhood practitioners critically evaluate the disability content of books from an anti-discriminatory perspective.

An image can say a thousand words. Visual images in posters, photographs and books can relay very powerful messages to young children. Within a disability equity curriculum those images should be positive—avoid images that encourage others to feel sorry for people with disabilities. Focus on the positive aspects of their lives.

Alongside this it is important that staff encourage children to value each other equally. Dramatic play is often the venue that children choose to gain an understanding of others—often by projecting and identifying with them. This must be handled sensitively so that tolerance and empathy develops. It can be developed in ways that show how different places can be geared to the needs of people with disabilities. Equipment such as walking sticks, wheelchairs and dolls with disabilities can be included as a matter of course so that children can use them in their play. This should be accompanied by open and clear discussion. By restricting and banning play of this type the early childhood educator can widen the gap between people with different abilities.

REFLECTING ON EMPOWERING TECHNIQUES

1   How would you define empowerment?
2   What is the relationship between general teaching techniques, such as questioning, and empowering?
3   Identify five general teaching techniques you will need to be familiar with in order to empower children.
4   Read the following extracts from Dermon-Sparks et al. (1989, pp. 69–70).

> A four-year-old White child asks a visitor to her day care center, 'What is your name?' The visitor answers, 'Rayko.' 'Yuck, yuck, yucky', responds the child. Her teacher admonishes, 'Be nice to our visitor'.
>
> As their teacher begins reading a story in Spanish to an English-speaking group, a few children begin to giggle. The teacher stops reading and tells the children, 'I am stopping because some children are giggling while I am reading. That is not OK—it is rude. I know Spanish is a new language to some of you. Sometimes we are not comfortable with something we do not know and we laugh to make ourselves feel better, but laughing at how people talk is hurtful and unfair. Laughing is not OK, but it is OK to raise your hand and ask me questions about what I am reading'.

What differences were there between how the teacher acted in each situation? Do you think the teacher's actions were empowering for the children? How else might the teacher have acted to empower the children in each situation?

5   Read the following extracts from Dermon-Sparks (1989, pp. 70–1).

> Billy, a White child, refuses to sit next to George, a Cherokee child. Billy cries to his teacher, 'I'm afraid that George is going to kill me.' To learn about the source of this fear, the teacher asks, 'Why do you feel that way?'. Billy says, 'Because Indians kill White people. I saw it on TV last night.' Teacher: 'Billy,

most TV programs are just make-believe, so there is no reason to be afraid of Indian people. The cowboy and Indian movies you see on TV do not tell the truth about Indian people. Many White people did mean things to Indian people, like taking away their land and their homes. That is why the Indian people fought back, to protect their homes and families. George is a member of our class. He and his family live in our neighbourhood, just like you and your family do. We will not insult him and his family by saying things about Indian people that are not true. Whenever I hear anyone saying untrue things about Indian people, I tell them to stop. I'd like you to help me do that.'

After building a house in the block area, Barbara and Lisa, two Black girls, have a disagreement about where to put the furniture. Unable to reach a compromise, Lisa screams at Barbara, 'Well, I don't like you anyway because you've got short nappy hair. My hair is good'. Teacher: 'Lisa, you are upset because Barbara wants to put the furniture one place and you want to put it some other place. However, you must not hurt Barbara's feelings by saying something that is mean and disrespectful. All hair grows differently. Many Black people's hair grows slowly. It is usually short and springy. How your hair grows depends on the kind of hair your family has. Lisa, in this classroom you may not call your hair better than anyone else's. Barbara, if some people say mean things about your hair, you just tell them that your hair is pretty just as it is. Now let's figure out a way to solve the problem of where to place the doll furniture. By learning to co-operate, you won't say mean things that hurt feelings.'

Which goals do you believe informed the teacher's action in each instance?

IMPROVING TEACHING IN PRACTICE

1   Identify a child in your group who you believe is facing unjust or unequal treatment. Observe the child and identify a problem that you can work with the child to solve. Plan at least three periods of time in which you work closely with the child on this problem. Implement and record these sessions.

2   After each session evaluate your own empowering skills by reviewing the extent to which you were able to promote the child's self-esteem and their ability to challenge unfairness.

3   What additional skills and knowledge do you need to consolidate and improve your empowering skills?

4   How and how well did you take account of the following considerations when empowering the child: the child's gender, ability levels, cultural and 'racial' background, and developmental age and stage?

5   Smith and Lovat (1990, p. 8) argued that practising critical reflection with 'critical friends' who can 'listen, clarify, challenge and confront within a trusting, acceptant but risking relationship' can improve our teaching for empowerment. Try the above tasks with a 'critical friend'.

Further reading

Critical curriculum and empowerment

Darder, A. (ed.) 2002, *Reinventing Paulo Friere: a pedagogy of love*, Boulder, Colorado, Westview Press.

Freire, P. 1972, *Pedagogy of the Oppressed* (Myra Bergman Ramos, Trans.), Middlesex, Penguin Books.

——1985, *The Politics of Education: Culture, Power and Liberation* (Donaldo Macedo, Trans.), Massachusetts, Bergin Garvey Publishers Inc.

Sleeter, C. and Grant, C. 1999, *Making Choices for Multicultural Education: Five Approaches to Race, Class and Gender* (third edn), New Jersey, Prentice Hall [Chapter 6 is of particular relevance].

Empowering young children

Brynes, D. and Kiger, G. 1992, *Common Bonds: Anti-Bias Teaching in a Diverse Society*, Wheaton, MD, Association for Childhood Education International.

Dally, S. and Lindstrom, H. 1996, *Girls and boys come out to play: teaching about gender construction and sexual harassment in English and Studies of Society and Environment*, Adelaide, South Australia, Department for Education and Children's Services.

Dau, E. (ed.) 2001, *The Anti-Bias Approach in Early Childhood*, Frenchs Forest, New South Wales, Australia, Pearson Education Australia.

Dermon-Sparks, L. 1992, '"It isn't fair!" Anti-bias curriculum for young children', *Alike and Different*, Washington DC, NAEYC [refer to pp. 2–10].

Dermon-Sparks, L. and the Anti-Bias Task Force 1989, *Anti-Bias Curriculum: Tools for Empowering Young Children*, Washington DC, NAEYC [refer to pp. 69–81].

Hopkins, S. and Winters, J. 1990, *Discover the World: Empowering Children to Value Themselves, Others and the Earth*, Gabriola Island, BC, New Society Publishers.

Jones, K. and Mules, R. 2001, 'Developing critical thinking and activism' in E. Dau, ed., *The Anti-Bias Approach in Early Childhood*, pp. 192–209, Frenchs Forest, New South Wales, Australia, Pearson Education Australia.

MacNaughton, G. 2003. *Shaping early childhood: learners, contexts and curriculum*. Open University Press [Chapter 9].

Ramsey, P. 1987, *Teaching and Learning in a Diverse World: Multicultural Education for Young Children*, Colombia, Teachers' College Press.

Wasserman, S. 1991, 'Louis E. Raths: theories of empowerment', *Childhood Education*, 67(4), pp. 225–39.

York, S. 1991, *Roots and Wings: Affirming Culture in Early Childhood Programs*, Minnesota, Toys'n Things Press.

Learning more about inequalities and injustices
Refer to the Appendix

Video

Anti-Bias Curriculum, Pacific Oaks College, Extension Services, 714 West California Bvd, Pasadena, CA91105.

Children Without Prejudice, BBC, London.

Empowered to learn: Te Whariki for infants and toddlers, published for the Ministry of Education by Learning Media, New Zealand, 2001.

Empowered to learn: Te Whariki for young children, published for the Ministry of Education by Learning Media, New Zealand, 2001.

What's the Difference, Free Kindergarten Association, Melbourne, Australia.

CD-ROM

MacNaughton, G., Campbell, S., Smith, K. and Lawrence, H. 2002, *Equity Adventures in Early Childhood*, Centre for Equity and Innovation in Early Childhood, University of Melbourne, available at http://www.mup.unimelb.edu.au/e-showcase/0-734-02679-X.html

Websites—extending learning online

Institute of Anti-bias Education Study Guide, which describes the aims of anti-bias education. Full text reading at http://www.adl.org/tools_teachers/tip_antibias_ed.html

Access to practical resources for implementing social justice and anti-bias curriculum with young children at http://californiatomorrow.org/

References

Beane, J. 1990, *Affect in the Curriculum: Toward Democracy, Dignity, and Diversity*, New York, Teachers' College Press.

Brown, C., Barnfield, J. and Stone, M. 1991, *Spanner in the Works: Education for Racial Equality and Social Justice in White Schools*, Staffordshire, England, Trentham Books.

Carr, W. and Kemmis, S. 1986, *Becoming Critical: Knowing through Action Research*, Geelong, Deakin University.

Corder, L. and Quisenberry, N. 1987, 'Early education and Afro-Americans', *Childhood Education*, February, pp. 154–8.

Dally, S. and Lindstrom, H. 1996, *Girls and boys come out to play: teaching about gender construction and sexual harassment in English and Studies of Society and Environment*, Adelaide, South Australia, Department for Education and Children's Services.

Darder, A (ed.) 2002, *Reinventing Paulo Friere: a pedagogy of love*, Boulder, Colorado, Westview Press.

Dermon-Sparks, L. 1998, (published 2001), Education without prejudice: goals, principles and practices, Paper presented to *Respect: education without prejudice, a challenge for early years educators in Ireland*, 16 October 1998, Dublin, Ireland, Pavee Point Travellors Centre, pp. 22–31.

Dermon-Sparks, L. and the Anti-Bias Task Force 1989, *Anti-Bias Curriculum: Tools for Empowering Young Children*, Washington DC, NAEYC [refer to pp. 69–81].

Dermon-Sparks, L., Gutierrez, M. and Phillips, C. 1991, *Teaching Young Children to Resist Bias: What Parents Can Do*, Washington, NAEYC.

Freire, P. 1972, *Pedagogy of the Oppressed* (Myra Bergman Ramos, Trans.), Middlesex, Penguin Books.

Grundy, S. 1987, *Curriculum: Product or Praxis*, London, The Falmer Press.

Hopkins, S. and Winters, J. 1990, *Discover the World: Empowering Children to Value Themselves, Others and the Earth*, Gabriola Island, BC, New Society Publishers.

Hyun, E. 2001, Cultural complexity that affects young children's contemporary growth, change and learning, Paper presented at the *Annual Meeting of the Educational Research Association*, Seattle, WA, April 10–14, ED451941.

MacNaughton, G., Campbell, S., Smith, K. and Lawrence, H. 2002, *Equity Adventures in Early Childhood*, Centre for Equity and Innovation in Early Childhood, University of Melbourne, Australia.

MacNaughton, G. 2003. *Shaping early childhood: learners, contexts and curriculum*. Open University Press [Chapter 9].

Ministry of Education (NZ), 1996, *Te Whariki: Early Childhood Curriculum*. Ministry of Education, New Zealand at http://www.minedu.govt.nz/

Rees, S. 1991, *Achieving Power: Practice and Policy in Social Welfare*, Sydney, Allen & Unwin.

Sarup, M. 1978, *Marxism and Education*, London, Routledge Kegan Paul.

Siraj-Blatchford, I. and Siraj-Blatchford, J. (eds) 1995, *Educating the whole Child: Cross Curriculum Skills: Themes and Dimensions*, Milton Keynes, Open University Press.

Smith, D. and Lovat, T. 1990, *Curriculum: Action on Reflection*, Sydney, Social Science Press.

Wasserman, S. 1991, 'Louis E. Raths: theories of empowerment', *Childhood Education*, 67(4), pp. 225–39.

Wilkes, G. (ed.) 1979, *Collins Dictionary of the English Language*, Middlesex, Penguin Books.

Yuval-Davies, N. 1994, 'Women, ethnicity and empowerment', *Feminism and Psychology*, 4(1), pp. 179–97.

Chapter 24

Philosophising

Philosophy: the rational investigation of being, knowledge and right conduct.

(*Collins Dictionary of the English Language*, p. 1101)

Philosophising: to make philosophising speculations.

(*Collins Dictionary of the English Language*, p. 1101)

Children are natural philosophers, and their curiosity sparks off philosophical discussion.

(DeHaan et al. 1995a, p. 4)

What distinguishes humans from other animals is their ability to think, to reason and to wonder ... The role of the educator is one of moving young children towards solving their own problems through active exploration, discovery and reflection.

(Latham 1996, p. 12)

WHAT?

Broadly speaking, philosophy is the study of truth. In studying truth, philosophers seek answers to questions such as, 'What do we know to be true?'; 'What is truth?'; 'How do we know this is true?'; 'How can we prove this is true?'. To answer these questions philosophers have to carefully look at, try to understand and to evaluate what we claim to be true about our world. They critically examine and take apart our truth claims to see if they are indeed true. For example, when scientists claim that the earth is round the philosopher of science examines this truth claim critically and asks, 'How do we know that the earth is round?'; 'How can we prove that this is true?'; 'Are the methods we use to prove that the earth is round the right methods to get to the truth?'. Philosophers ask such questions of all areas of knowledge about our social world. For example, philosophers can and do study the truths of medicine, geography, religion, psychology, mathematics, education, law, history and ethics.

In searching for what we know about our world (what we can claim to be true) philosophy uncovers problems in what we claim to be true. These problems often have an ethical and moral dimension to them. This is because what we claim as truth comes to be seen as the right and proper way to conduct ourselves; that is, when we ask philosophical questions about education, we question what we know to be the truth about how we should educate young children. We might find that there is no one truth about how to educate them, but many different versions of what is the best or truest way to do it arise. Parents may have one truth, politicians another and educators yet another. When philosophers probe our claims to truth they may find that we have no way to prove what we claim to be true.

As such, philosophy is a very particular form of critical reflection about the world. It can improve our ability to think carefully about what we do and what we say is right and true, and to think about the ethical and moral implications of this.

As a teaching technique, 'doing philosophy' or philosophising with children involves studying children's everyday truths and the truths of others in the world about them. In doing this children learn '. . . to articulate questions, comprehend carefully, evaluate reasons, uncover assumptions, clarify ideas and concepts, make judgements and draw inferences' (DeHaan et al. 1995b, p. 4).

Philosophising with young children improves their ability to think carefully about what they and others claim to be right and true.

How we see the world depends on how we look at it. Lets try cellophane.

Maria works as child care worker in an upper-class suburb in Melbourne. She cares for a group of four- and five-year-old children who will soon be going to school. Maria decides to use a current issue for discussion with them: the refugee camps in Africa. One of the children has described what he has seen on the TV news. Maria shows the children a photo of a crowded refugee camp.

Maria: 'Has anyone seen pictures like this on TV or in a newspaper? What questions do you have about these people?'

She takes notes of the ensuing questions:

Who are these people?

What are they doing there?

Why are there so many of them?

How did they get there?

What do they eat?

Where do they sleep?

Are they families?

Maria then encourages the children to reflect on their questions and to make connections between them. She then begins to explore some answers with the children.

Maria: 'What do you think they're doing there? Where might the food come from?'

Maria listens carefully to the children's suggestions, taking care to show them that she values all answers.

At the end of the session Maria feeds back to the children their initial questions and they all discuss how much they have found out about the refugees. Maria praises the children for being so curious and for sticking to the topic at hand.

HOW?

DeHaan et al. (1995a, b) detailed a fifteen-point plan for initiating and guiding philosophical discussion in groups with young children. Their guidance builds from the work of Matthew Lipman and the following points draw heavily on this guidance.

1   Select materials to stimulate discussion. These could include a storybook, song, poem or image.

2   Form small groups and organise them so that everyone can hear each other. Listening is an important part of learning about how others think.

3   Present the materials to the children.

4   Ask them what questions they have about what they have heard or seen.

5   Makes notes about the questions raised.

6   Make connections between the questions by asking if any of the questions are linked.

7   Encourage discussion by asking one of the children to explain why they asked a particular question and encourage others to join in. The children should decide which question to explore first.

8   Make distinctions between different answers so that children learn about the different ways in which questions can be answered.

9   Encourage different points of view on a question.

10 Ask children why they have the point of view they have.

11   Point out inconsistencies in their answers.

12   Talk about any disagreements and try to work out why they occurred.

13   Model careful listening.

14   Keep the children focused on the questions and the topic.

15   Evaluate with the children how they feel at the end. Were they happy with the answers to their questions? What else do they want to know about the topic?

THEORETICAL BACKGROUND

PHILOSOPHY WITH CHILDREN AND THE WORK OF MATTHEW LIPMAN

Matthew Lipman is an American educator who has developed an approach called 'Philosophy for Children'. Through this work Lipman has generated international interest (see, for example, Robinson 1995). The hallmarks of Lipman's approach are:

➤ Philosophical issues and discussion are generated with young children through narrative forms such as picture books, poems and stories.

➤ Workbooks with practical resources and exercises help guide teachers and children through their philosophical inquiries.

➤ The key aim of doing philosophy with children is to help them to become critical thinkers.

➤ Children learn critical thinking by inquiring, reasoning, forming concepts and communicating meanings to others in what Lipman calls a 'community of inquiry' (Lipman 1995, p. 69).

➤ A community of inquiry operates on democratic principles (based on Lipman 1995; Fields 1995).

Lipman (1989) pointed out that there are several misconceptions about what constitutes critical thinking and argued that critical thinking is not:

➤ about drilling children in how to think

➤ the same as logical thinking.

Critical thinking is a form of thinking that evolves over time through building a community of thinkers.

Successful group philosophy sessions rely on staff creating a climate in which children can enjoy sharing their theories of the world with others. This involves making a careful selection of stimulus materials and learning to ask appropriate questions.

Stimulus materials that generate philosophical discussion are those in which children have an active interest and in which there are puzzles, issues, dilemmas and problems to be solved (Sprod 1995). Suggestions for children's books, poems, songs and posters that could be used for this are at the end of this chapter.

When choosing stimulus material consider the following questions:

➤ Will the materials encourage the children to wonder about the issue or dilemma? For example, are there surprises in the storyline or image, or is more than one solution to the problem shown?

➤ Will the materials extend or challenge children's current understandings of the issue?

When deciding which questions to use to help children learn to think philosophically DeHaan et al. (1995a) recommended using a wide variety of open-ended questions that challenge children to problem-solve and seek innovative ways of viewing the world.

More informal opportunities for discussing children's theories of how the world works should also be sought. Children will share their theories with adults if their ideas are valued, if they have lots in their daily world to wonder about and they have the time and opportunity to share their wondering with others (Latham 1996). It is also important to be watchful for moments where children can be encouraged to explore different viewpoints on the same issue. Everyday problems between children offer many opportunities for this. When staff encounter differences of opinion between children they can help them learn about different viewpoints by saying, 'We have a problem. It seems that both Jane and Clara want to use the red spade. Does anyone have ideas about what we could do?'.

Involving children in public reasoning of the problem will help them see that there is more than one way to understand a situation (Carlsson-Paige and Levin 1985). This ability to understand the perspective of others is the foundation for making moral judgements about what is right, true and fair in our relationships with each other (Tan-Niam 1994). As such, it is an important component of philosophical reasoning with young children.

> Dia, a teacher of three-year-olds, helps two children to sort out who will use the wheelbarrow first. She asks questions about how they might resolve their dispute: 'What can we do when two people want the same thing at the same time? What are the different ways that we can share?'
>
> Jon is having a discussion with his second grade class about taking other people's lunches. He begins by telling the children that he has a problem. He explains it and invites them to help him solve it.

WHEN AND WHY?

Goal relevance

Philosophising with children enriches and extends their cognitive skills, and helps to build a strong disposition for curiosity and collaborative inquiry (Robinson 1995). Such dispositions are important across all areas of learning and across all disciplines. Specifically, philosophising with young children is appropriate when staff want them to learn to be curious about:

- ⊙ who they are and their place in the world
- ⊙ how the world works
- ⊙ how we relate to each other
- ⊙ what is fair, good and right in the world (DeHaan et al. 1995a, 1995b).

By applying philosophical thinking to their world children will learn to:

- ⊙ think creatively
- ⊙ use words to express their thoughts
- ⊙ understand different viewpoints in the world
- ⊙ ask questions
- ⊙ search for answers

'What do you think?'

>● use their memory to help them think
>● use other people's ideas (DeHaan et al. 1995a, 1995b).

Philosophising with children also enriches us as adults as we engage with children in what Matthews (1996, p. 13) described as the 'genuinely baffling questions of childhood'.

Developmental considerations

To share philosophical thinking with others requires language and abstract thought. For young children to share their philosophical thinking with others they need to have the cognitive and communicative capacity to use language to represent thought, the ability to engage in conversation with others and the ability to concentrate. This means that philosophising, as discussed in this chapter, is a teaching technique that will be most appropriately used with older preschool children and children in the early years of school.

However, it is important to remember that babies are struggling to make sense of their world from the moment they enter it. While babies cannot 'talk' of this struggle, staff can encourage and preserve this 'sense of wonder' by allowing them to play with their voices and their environment, and by showing delight in such play (Latham 1996). Such encouragement can help build in younger children the 'disposition' to wonder and to be curious, and can act as a spur for them to think philosophically in their preschool years.

Between 18 months of age and two years of age there is an increase in children's ability to use language to talk about feelings (Hinchcliffe 1996). This offers opportunities for staff to begin the process of talking with toddlers about how we feel and familiarising them with the meanings of words that are important in learning to think about such terms as: know, think, guess and remember. When adults use these terms with two-year-old children there is evidence that children will better understand the distinctions between them in their preschool years (Hinchcliffe 1996).

Eighteen-month-old Turc is finding life a little difficult as he wants things 'now' and he often has to wait his turn at the child care centre. He responds to this frustration by flinging himself on the floor and screaming. Shona, his designated child care worker, understands his frustration and helps by verbalising his feelings for him.

'I guess that you're a bit cross just now.'

'It's hard when you can't have what you want.'

'You're pretty angry at the moment.'

'Remember yesterday when you were cross and you waited and got the car after Jon had a turn?'

'Let's think about a way to wait.'

Suitable philosophical projects for preschool children will be those that interest them. Children's conversations, artwork and imaginative play will offer many clues as to what they have questions about and what they enjoy thinking about. For example, preschool children's self-portraits show an interest in themselves and how we represent what we look like to others, their paintings of their families show an interest in who their family is and what families do, and their paintings of their local community show an awareness of the world about them (Piscitelli 1993). Children's self-portraits can be used to provoke the question, 'Who am I?'. Children can be encouraged to think about the questios: 'How do I know this is me?'; 'What other things (apart from how I look) make me?'; 'What is the same about me and other children?'; 'What is different about me that makes me who I am?'. Some children's books that deal with these issues include: *The Trouble with Gran* by B. Cole, 1987, Heinneman, London; *Abby's Wish*, by L. St John, 1995, Stock Vaughan, Texas; and *Princess Smartypants* by B. Cole, 1986, Hamish Hamilton, London. Questions of identity and how we know who our 'true' selves are form the heart of much philosophical inquiry. Children can be encouraged to think about these questions in a concrete way that builds on the things they are already working with and thinking about each day. Davey Zeece (1996) provides a good overview of concept books for young children that can be used for philosophical inquiry.

Examples of questions preschool children ask and comments they make that staff can use to help them learn basic philosophical thinking processes are shown on the next page.

Children in the early years of schooling can be supported in their critical reasoning skills through language arts programs which have the following features:

- ➡ A strong relationship between what children are talking about and what they are reading.
- ➡ A stress on the meaning in children's reading and writing rather than its form.
- ➡ A link between children's language experiences and the folklore of their culture. This helps them learn what has been said with language and how language can be used to convey ideas.
- ➡ They stimulate the children to think about what they are reading.
- ➡ They make children very familiar with everyday words (Lipman 1988).

In addition, children's critical thinking skills will be improved by learning that everyday words have more than one meaning (Lipman 1988). Word games, puns and nonsense books help with this.

Comments by preschool children	Source	Issues echoed in 'adult' philosophy	Possible questions to further children's thinking (based on DeHaan et al. 1995a, b)
'I wonder who the first people were?'	Latham 1996, p. 13.	How did life on earth begin?	Why did you say that? How could we find out? What do other people know about that?
'You shouldn't smoke, you might die, it's naughty.'	Collins 1992, p. 12.	What is the relationship between life and death?	How do you know that? Can you think of a time when that wouldn't happen?
'We knocked down the leaves . . . we're trying to find out how many. How many down. How many on the tree.'	Mousley 1993, p. 4.	How is mathematical knowledge of the world verified?	What is it that puzzles you? How could we work that out?
'Being black is hard work.'	Brown 1995, p. 13.	What is the nature of racism?	What do you mean by that? What do others think? How do you know that?

Wing Han Lamb (2002, p. 9) identified ten philosophical questions that could be explored with young children. They were as follows:

1   Why do we exist?
2   How can we be sure that everything is not a dream?
3   Can we make time stand still?
4   What makes us human?
5   What does it mean to be alive?
6   Am I the same person as when I was a baby?
7   Why should I be kind to animals?
8   Should I be good when no-one is watching?
9   What is a friend?
10 What is art?

Fisher (1999) offers the following philosophical questions that have been used with children in primary schools in the UK to help children engage in philosophical thinking:

- How do you know you are not dreaming at this moment?
- How do you know when something is true or not?
- Is an apple dead or alive?
- Is it right to eat animals?
- What is the difference between pretending and lying?
- What is the difference between a real person and a robot?

➔ Is there a difference between your mind and your brain?

➔ Can animals think?

➔ Is it ever right to tell lies?

➔ What are the most valuable things in your life? (Fisher 1999, p. 60)

EQUITY CONSIDERATIONS

Preschool children and children in the early years of school can understand what is fair and what is not fair in their daily world. This ability to understand fairness can be used to explore what rules need to be developed in the centre to ensure fairness around issues of culture, 'race', gender and disability. Suggestions for specific ways in which the idea of fairness and people's rights can be explored using the techniques and processes above target some of the specific ways in which unfairness can manifest itself in relationships between children. The *Philosophy with Kids* (DeHaan et al. 1995a, 1995b) books listed at the end of the chapter offer many practical examples of how this might be approached in small group exercises and activities with young children.

In designing activities that require children to understand the perspectives of others, staff should be aware that children's fantasy play helps them develop their perspective-taking ability (Tan-Niam 1994). Fantasy play can be an important bridge between children's wonder about the world and their ability to think critically: it offers a place in which different ways of thinking about the world flourish.

'Race' and culture

Children's friendships can be very flexible and can quickly change from one day to the next. Also, there are many different factors that impact on whom children form friendships with. However, we do know that children can form friendships based on 'race' from their toddler years and can be racist in their friendship choices (Dermon-Sparks et al. 1989). Philosophical questions concerning how we think about what and who a friend is can help children reflect critically on and rethink these decisions. Questions that can prompt this rethinking include: 'How do you know someone is a friend?'; 'Can someone be a friend when they are different from you?'; 'How do we choose our friends?'; 'How do we feel when people are not friends with us?'; 'How would it feel to not have your friend talk to you because your skin was black?'.

Preschool children's thinking about racial difference is often inconsistent, based on how things look rather than logical reasoning and they often make incorrect generalisations. This means that young children can be very susceptible to believing the racial stereotypes they see in the world about them (York 1991). If children see images of Aboriginal Australians with boomerangs hunting kangaroos and wearing loin cloths they can quickly generalise that all Aboriginal Australians do this. Some of the racial stereotypes they see and read, and thus become susceptible to, include the following:

➔ Native Americans all ride on horseback and shoot bows and arrows.

➔ All people from China eat with chopsticks.

➔ All Italo-Australians love pasta.

➔ All Vietnamese people came to Australia in boats.

➔ All Anglo-Australians live in big houses and love barbecues.

Philosophising with children can be used to help them rethink their stereotyped racial beliefs. Questions such as the following can help children become critical thinkers about 'racial truths':

'How do you know Italo-Australians love pasta?'; 'Is someone who loves pasta an Italo-Australian?'; 'Can you be an Italo-Australian if you hate pasta?'.

Some children's books that question 'racial' stereotypes include:

- *All the Colors We Are* by K. Kissinger, 1994, Redleaf Press, Minnesota, prompts children's thinking about how people get their skin colour.
- *Look at Your Eyes* by P. Showers, 1969, Crowell, New York, prompts children's thinking about why eyes differ.
- *Living in Two Worlds* by M. Rosenberg, 1988, Lothrop, Lee & Shepard, New York, prompts children's thinking about what it means to be bi-racial.
- *You Be Me, I'll Be You* by P. Mandlebaum, 1992, Kane Miller, New York, prompts children's thinking about racism towards Chinese-American children.

When children are learning a language in addition to their mother tongue, developing philosophical thinking in the second language will take time. Children will need to have the concepts and ideas discussed in depth over time and have them supported with appropriate visual and verbal guidance (Sharma 1995). It is important to remember that fairness does not mean that everyone should have the same treatment all of the time. Sometimes, fairness will involve giving children special attention to ensure that they can contribute effectively to the group.

Gender

There is research that shows that boys and girls often contribute differently to packing away time in early childhood programs. Boys tend to do less of it and girls tend to do more of it. Often the girls tend to do it with fewer reminders from adults than do the boys. One way to encourage children to think about this and work out solutions to it is to engage children in a discussion about if they think this is fair and how they might make it fairer. For example, children could be asked to think about the following questions: 'Who packed away everyday?'; 'Can you tell me who packed up with you yesterday?'; 'How could we find out if everyone shared in packing away?'; 'How would you decide who should help with packing away?'; 'Do you think it is fair that some people pack away more than others?'.

Children have often developed strong and persistent gender stereotypes by the time they are three years of age (Alloway 1995). These stereotypes include:

- Only boys play with trains, blocks and bicycles.
- Only girls play with dolls and in the home corner.
- Boys are stronger than girls.
- Girls can't have short hair.
- Boys don't wear skirts. (Kilts could be a point of discussion here.)

Philosophising with children can be used to help them rethink their stereotyped gender beliefs. Questions such as the following can help children become critical thinkers about their 'gender truths': 'How do you know boys are stronger than girls?'; 'Is someone who is strong always a boy?'; 'Can you be a boy if you are not very strong?'.

Some children's books that challenge gender stereotypes include:

- *Feelings Alphabet* by J. Lalli, 1984, Winch & Associates, California, helps children from two years of age to think about realising their potential.

- *Women at their Work* by E. Betty, 1988, Dial, New York, helps children from three years of age to think about boys doing ballet.
- *Mommies at work* by E. Merriam, 1989, Simon & Schuster, New York, helps children from three years of age to think about the possibilities of women working in the paid workforce.
- *What is a girl? What is a boy?* by S. Waxman, 1989, Harper & Row, New York, helps children from four years of age to think about physical differences between boys and girls.

Disability and additional needs

All children approach and complete tasks such as painting or building in different ways. However, when a child with a disability is in a group with children without disabilities they can often be disadvantaged by how the task is presented. When staff are rethinking how activities offered in the centre can be made more appropriate for children with disabilities, they can involve all the children in the group. Children can explore the idea that there is no right way for completing most tasks and be encouraged to think about finding other ways of doing things that a child with a disability might find difficult. Staff can encourage children to think about what other ways things could be done, how activities could be adapted to suit a particular child's needs and what assistance might be offered. They can also be encouraged to think about how to find out if their suggestions are workable and if they would be welcomed by a particular child. For example, imagine there is a child in the group (let's call her Beth) with insufficient strength in her hands to hold a paint brush. All the children, including Beth, could be asked to think about how she could participate in painting. They could also be encouraged to think about how they could find out if Beth liked the agreed change.

More general discussion about the nature of hearing, seeing, moving, feeling and tasting things can also help children appreciate the different abilities and disabilities of people. The following questions about hearing and listening taken from DeHaan et al. (1995a, pp. 72–3) provide some starting points for such discussions. They can readily be adapted to talk about other sensory-motor abilities with preschool children.

- Is it hard to listen?
- Is listening the same as hearing?
- Can we hear without seeing?
- Can we see without hearing?
- Do we all hear the same things?
- How do we know what other people hear?

Some children's books that challenge 'disability' stereotypes include:

- *Doing Things Together* by C. James and E. James, 1975, Raintree Publisher, Milwaukee, helps children from four years of age realise that a girl with a hearing aid can be a gardener, adventurer, student and friend.
- *Someone Special, Just Like You* by T. Brown, 1991, Henry Holt, New York, helps children from three years of age think about physical differences between people.
- *Our Brother Has Down's Syndrome* by C. Shelley, 1985, Annick Press, Canada, helps children from three years of age think about the similarities between children with Down's syndrome and those without it.

REFLECTING ON PHILOSOPHISING TECHNIQUES

1　Briefly define philosophy.

2　Develop five philosophical questions you could ask if you were a philosopher of early childhood education.

3　To what extent do you agree with the statement that '. . . all children can remain active and curious philosophers and scientists throughout their lives'? (Latham 1996, p. 12).

4　What are the main things that early childhood staff need to do to ensure that children do 'remain active and curious philosophers' in the early childhood program?

5　To what extent have you been encouraged to be an 'active and curious philosopher' during your education?

6　Why do you think the following statement was made: 'Philosophers, like reporters, tend to disagree with everyone' (Romano 1995, p. 10)

7　Select a poem you could use with young children to engage them in philosophical thinking. What are some of the questions you think children might ask about the poem?

8　Read one of the following picture books. What questions might the book prompt from children?

- ❯ Gay, M.L. 2002, *Stella: Fairy of the Forest*, Groundwood Books, Toronto, Canada.
- ❯ Valentine, J. 1992, *The Duke Who Outlawed Jellybeans*. Boston, Alyson Publications.
- ❯ Ziefart, H. and Doherty, R. 2002, *Toes have wiggles, kids have giggles*. G.P. Putnam's Sons, New York.
- ❯ Baylor, B. 1998, *The Table Where Posh People Sit*, Aladdin Publishing Company, New York.
- ❯ *Princess Smartypants* by B. Cole, 1986, Hamish Hamilton, London.

9　If a child remarked to you, 'I wonder how the sky stays up?' how would you respond?

10　How might you use a photograph of a child's family to prompt philosophical discussion between yourself and the child? How might this be used to stimulate a group discussion session?

IMPROVING TEACHING IN PRACTICE

1　Plan, implement and record (using a tape-recorder or written notes) a group discussion session with children.

2　What was your style of philosophising with young children? Did you:

- ❯ stimulate discussion through your choice and presentation of materials?
- ❯ question the children in ways that promoted philosophical thinking?
- ❯ help children learn about different ways in which questions can be answered?
- ❯ encourage children to share their ideas and respect other children's viewpoints?
- ❯ encourage children to listen to a variety of viewpoints and reflect on differences between these viewpoints?

3　Plan, implement and evaluate a group philosophy session in which you talked with children about what a stereotype is. Focus on either 'race', gender or disability stereotypes.

4　What are your areas of strength and weakness in using philosophising to promote children's learning?

5　How can you improve your philosophising techniques in practice?

Further reading and resources

The Australasian Journal of Philosophy for Children and the Federation of Australian Philosophy for Children Associations, Sally Biskupic, 1/36 Mckeon St, Marouba 2035, NSW, Australia.

Centre of Philosophy for Children, Australian Council for Educational Research, Private Bag 55, Camberwell, Victoria, Australia, 3124. Tel. 03 9277 5555. Fax 03 9277 5500.

Davey Zeece, P. 1996, 'Just think of that: concept books in early childhood', *Early Childhood Education Journal*, 23(4), pp. 221–5.

DeHaan, C., MacColl, S. and McCutcheon, L. 1995a, *Philosophy with Kids. Book 1*, Melbourne, Longman.

——1995b, *Philosophy with Kids. More Ideas and Activities*, Melbourne, Longman.

Fisher, R. 1998, *Teaching thinking: philosophical inquiry in the classroom*, London, Cassell.

Institute for the Advancement of Philosophy for Children, Montclair State College, New Jersey, USA.

Latham, G. 1996, 'Fostering and preserving wonderment', *Australian Journal of Early Childhood*, 21(1), pp. 12–15.

Murris, K. 1992, *Teaching Philosophy with Picture Books*, London, Infonet Publications.

Pritchard, M. 1985, *Philosophical Adventures with Children*, USA, University of America Press.

Robinson, W. 1991, 'Rich seems of mind', *Support for Learning*, 6(3), pp. 119–23.

——1995, 'Why "philosophy for children"?', *Early Child Development and Care*, 107, pp. 5–15.

Websites—extending learning online

There is a WebForum titled Philosophy for Children that interested staff and students can access and contribute to at Northwest Center for Philosophy for Children http://depts.washington.edu/nwcenter

Thinking skills website: http://www.standarss.dfee.gov.uk/guidance/thinking

References

Alloway, N. 1995, *Foundation Stones: The Construction of Gender in Early Childhood*, Melbourne, Curriculum Corporation.

Brown, B. 1995, *All Our Children: A Guide for Those who Care*, third edn, London, British Broadcasting Commission Education.

Carlsson-Paige, N. and Levin, D. 1985, 'Helping young children understand peace, war and the nuclear threat', *Australian Journal of Early Childhood*, 10(4), pp. 3–15.

Collins, M. 1992, 'What do children think about smoking?', *Nursery World*, 92(3318), pp. 12–13.

Davey Zeece, P. 1996, 'Just think of that: concept books in early childhood', *Early Childhood Education Journal*, 23(4), pp. 221–5.

DeHaan, C., MacColl, S. and McCutcheon, L. 1995a, *Philosophy with Kids, Book 1*, Melbourne, Longman.

——1995b, *Philosophy with Kids. More Ideas and Activities*, Melbourne, Longman.

Dermon-Sparks, L. and the Anti-Bias Task Force 1989, *The Anti-Bias Curriculum*, Washington DC, National Association for the Education of Young Children.

Fields, J. 1995, 'Sleepers awake: the current debate about using philosophy with young children (Citizenship, philosophy and reasoning: Citizens of the twenty-first century)', *Early Child Development and Care*, 107, pp. 17–21.

Fisher, R. 1999, 'Thinking skills to thinking schools: ways to develop children's thinking and learning', *Early Childhood Development and Care*, 153, pp. 51–63.

Hinchcliffe, V. 1996, 'Fairy stories and children's developing theories of the mind', *International Journal of Early Years Education*, 4(1), pp. 35–46.

Latham, G. 1996, 'Fostering and preserving wonderment', *Australia Journal of Early Childhood*, 21(1), pp. 12–15.

Lipman, M. 1988, *Philosophy Goes to School*, Philadelphia, Temple University Press.

——1989, *Misconceptions on teaching for critical thinking*, New Jersey, Institute for Critical Thinking.

——1995, 'Moral education, higher-order thinking and philosophy for children', *Early Child Development and Care* (107), pp. 61–70.

Matthews, G. 1996, *The Philosophy of Childhood*, Cambridge, MN, Harvard University Press.

Mousley, J. 1993, 'Constructing number concepts in a problem-posing classroom', *Australian Journal of Early Childhood*, 18(3), pp. 3–11.

Piscitelli, B. 1993, *Our World: Young Children's Views of Life*, Brisbane, Queensland University of Technology.

Robinson, W. 1995, 'Why "philosophy for children"?', *Early Child Development and Care*, pp. 107, pp. 5–15.

Romano, C. 1995, 'Birds of a feather . . .?', *UNESCO Sources: First UNESCO Philosophy Forum*, April (68), pp. 10.

Sharma, C. 1995, 'Linguistic factors in critical thinking', *Early Child Development and Care*, pp. 107, 35–43.

Sprod, T. 1995, 'Cognitive development, philosophy and children's literature', *Early Child Development and Care*, 107, pp. 22–33.

Tan-Niam, C. 1994, 'Thematic fantasy play: effects on the perspective-taking ability of preschool children', *International Journal of Early Years Education*, 2(1), pp. 5–16.

Wilkes, G. (ed.) 1979, *Collins Dictionary of the English Language*, Middlesex, Penguin Books.

Wing Han Lamb, W. 2002, 'Philosophy for children and the philosophy of childhood', *Every Child*, 8(4), pp. 8–9.

York, S. 1991, *Roots and Wings: Affirming Culture in Early Childhood Programs*, Minnesota, Toys'n Things Press.

Chapter 25

Problem-solving

Problem: any thing, matter, person that is difficult to deal with, solve or overcome.

(Collins Dictionary of the English Language, p. 1165)

Solve: to find the explanation for or solution to (mystery, problem etc. . . .).

(Collins Dictionary of the English Language, p. 1386)

Problem-solving is the foundation of a young child's learning. It must be valued, promoted, provided for, and sustained in the early childhood classroom.

(Britz 1993, p. 2)

Whether it's a toddler, trying to find out what made the wet spot on the rug, or a scientist attempting to find a cure for cancer, the processes involved in thinking and problem-solving are the same.

(Seefeldt and Barbour 1986, p. 363)

WHAT?

As a teaching technique problem-solving involves helping children learn how to find answers to puzzles, questions, dilemmas, issues, predicaments and quandaries they face in their daily world. Britz (1993) sees this as the basis for young children's learning.

THEORETICAL BACKGROUND

DEWEY AND PROBLEM-SOLVING

John Dewey (1859–1952) was an American professor of philosophy whose theories of how we think and learn have had a strong influence on early childhood education. Dewey believed democratic life in the United States could be improved by schooling that could '. . . nurture individual differences among learners in a common learning community . . .' (Levin 1991, p. 73). He believed that the individual's learning should be nurtured through individualised learners tasks and small group project-based learning rather than standardised whole group tasks. He saw classrooms as 'scientific labs for knowledge making' (Greenberg 1992, p. 62). Small group projects were seen as an important technique for building children's problem-solving skills across discipline boundaries and improving their ability to collaboratively solve problems.

Dewey argued that thinking and problem-solving were integrated. To problem-solve was to think and vice-versa. For Dewey thinking was 'thus synonymous with inquiry' (Cahan 1992, p. 208). Dewey believed that thinking involved the following steps:

- recognition that the problem exists
- gathering data on the problem
- formulating solutions to the problem
- testing the solutions in practice
- collecting data on the tests
- summarising what happened
- formulating a new plan of action on the basis of what was learned (Seefeldt and Barbour 1986).

Dewey also believed that collaborative problem-solving could improve the capacity of each child to participate actively in the social and intellectual rights and responsibilities of living in a democracy and critically reflect on what this meant in practice. So, for Dewey, developing the ability to critically reflect on one's world was a key aim for education (Park Han 1995). Such reflection requires that children become skilled in the process of inquiry into their world through individual and collaborative problem-solving. Dewey strongly argued that, for young children, the process of inquiry should derive from first-hand experiences (Cahan 1992). This belief has strongly influenced the development of discovery-based learning which underpins many contemporary early childhood programs (Read et al. 1993).

Dewey's views on how learning should be fostered differed from many of his contemporaries at the turn of the century who believed in whole class activities and routine approaches to learning (Levin 1991). His legacy includes the University of Chicago's Laboratory Schools, the University of Michigan School of Education's Dewey Web and his collected works, which total over 37 volumes (Center for Dewey Studies 1996).

How?

Children need to learn how to problem-solve. To learn this Britz (1993) suggests children need staff who:

- facilitate a problem-solving climate
- create time to problem-solve
- create space to problem-solve
- use materials to encourage problem-solving
- show familiarity with how to problem-solve
- choose appropriate problems to solve.

We shall now look at each of these in more detail.

Facilitating a problem-solving climate

Staff can facilitate a climate in which children want to solve problems by valuing children's problems and valuing their solutions to them. Within this, staff should ensure that children feel psychologically safe (Tegano et al. 1989). To feel psychologically safe children need to know its 'OK' that being 'wrong' is not going to be punished and that their judgements are as valued as those of the adults. Children's judgements and solutions should never be ridiculed.

Their interest in problem-solving will be increased if staff pay attention to children's answers and encourage them to try out their ideas in practice. These processes act as positive reinforcers (see Chapter 26) for children's problem-solving (Hendrick 1990). Helping children to 'learn to listen, understand other perspectives, recognise problems, and look for alternative solutions' (Browning et al. 2000, p. 233) is the key to facilitating a problem-solving climate.

Creating time to problem-solve

Problem-solving takes time. Children need to think about how to solve a problem and to test their solutions in practice. Trial and error is an essential part of learning to solve problems (Moyles 1989). It is, therefore, important to plan large blocks of time for children to fully investigate problems and to give children opportunities to practise their problem-solving skills (Browning et al. 2000). Time for problem-solving also enables children to deepen their understandings and construct more complex knowledge about the problem they are attempting to solve (Lambert 2000).

Creating space to problem-solve

Testing out solutions to problems can take space. It is important that children have a suitable and safe space within which to experiment with solutions to problems. If several children are trying to solve a problem co-operatively it is especially important to set aside space that allows for social interaction between them as they try to solve their joint problem.

Using materials to encourage problem-solving

The development of problem-solving skills is associated with the opportunity to play in a wide variety of ways with a wide variety of materials (Moyles 1989). The flexibility of open-ended materials such as sand, water, blocks and art materials creates more opportunities for children to problem-solve than closed-ended materials. Children can test out solutions readily and shape the open-ended materials in lots of different ways as they explore their solutions (Goffin and Tull 1985). Staff can stimulate children's interest in problem-solving with open-ended materials by collecting materials together in areas such as special interest tables (Hendrick 1990) and by allowing children lots of opportunity to be involved in child-directed play.

Familiarity with how to problem-solve

Children can be introduced to a logical sequence for problem-solving. The steps in the process recommended by Britz (1993) echo those of Dewey but are simpler:

- identify the problem
- brainstorm possible solutions
- test out one solution
- evaluate what happened.

Pondering on a problem together.

Tan, a member of staff in an early learning centre, is very enthusiastic about using art as a medium for children to represent the world around them. The children have been discussing totem poles and have decided to make one that represents their group.

They are using papier maché and have built the base of the pole, but are having difficulty with making the base stand up—it keeps collapsing into itself.

Tan: 'I wonder what you could do to help it stand?'

Susie: 'We could make it solid with paper in the middle.'

Tan: 'That's one idea.'

Sam: 'We could use chicken wire and put the papier maché on the outside like we did when we built Lulu (Lulu was a full-sized 'person' that the children had constructed last term).

Tan: 'That could be a good way.'

Sulu: 'What about putting wood into the middle to make it strong.'

Tan: 'You're all getting some ideas together here.'

Simon: 'I wonder if we could use strips of paper to hold it all together.'

Tan: 'You've all come up with useful suggestions'—he reminds them of the ones they have just made—'Which one will you try first?'

The children elect to use the chicken wire; they know how to do this and they remember the previous experience of success. After a while Tan approaches the children and encourages them to evaluate what they have done.

Understanding the processes of thinking involved in problem-solving helps improve children's problem-solving skills (Moyles 1989; Browning et al. 2000). Staff can help children learn this process of thinking by talking aloud as they themselves solve problems. This should include telling children about the things they thought about when trying to solve problems and why a solution did or did not work (Arthur et al. 1996; Lambert 2001). Questions which will help stimulate creative problem-solving are those that are open-ended (see Chapter 13). Hendrick (1990) suggests questions similar to the following:

- ➲ How could this be made to work again?
- ➲ What else could you do?
- ➲ What might happen if . . . ?
- ➲ How could we find out?
- ➲ How could we do this?

Appropriate problems to solve

Finding appropriate problems to solve should not be difficult as children's daily lives are full of puzzles, dilemmas, issues and questions. If the children are interested in the problem, if there are many ways to solve it and if it is possible to evaluate the actions taken, then the problem is an appropriate one (Britz 1993). Problems may be related to how the physical world works or how the social world works. The physical and social world generate problems of movement, discussion, skill and strategy (Goffin and Tull 1985). Problems from the physical world could be:

- ➲ How to keep a balance scale level while adding weights to it?
- ➲ How to fill a bottle with water when there is a hole in the bottom?
- ➲ How to tie a shoelace?
- ➲ How to reach the top of the painting easel?
- ➲ How to make a tunnel in the sandpit without the castle falling down?

Problems from the social world could be:

- ➲ How to join in a chasing game that looks fun?
- ➲ How to help a friend stop crying?
- ➲ How to talk to a friend whose hearing is impaired?
- ➲ How to stop the boys knocking over your blocks?
- ➲ How to decide who comes to your party?
- ➲ How to stop a fight between children?

The problems will be appropriate if they come from the puzzles, dilemmas and issues that children are confronting and trying to find answers to. Using the everyday life experiences of children is important to their motivation to problem-solve. Children are more likely to problem-solve when they can define their own problems and their own goals for solving the problem (Lambert 2000). These turn into good opportunities for problem-solving when staff encourage the children to '. . . plan, predict possible outcomes, make decisions, and observe the results of their actions' (Goffin and Tull 1985, p. 30).

Several children at the Protea Downs Early Learning Centre were puzzled by a comment made by one of their peers, Sabrina, when she was telling them about her birthday party:

> Sabrina: 'The best present I got was a puppy. My mums helped me name her. She's called Daxina.'
>
> Toby: 'How many mums do you have?'
>
> Nida: 'One mum, you only ever have one mum, silly.'
>
> Sabrina: 'No, Nida, you can have two mums. I have two mums.'

Petra: 'I have two mums because daddy divorced one. I never see her now 'cos she lives in Coffy. I talk on the phone with her though. When you have two mums one lives a long way away.'

Toby: (to Sabrina) 'Are your mums divorced too? Which one do you speak to on the phone?'

Sabrina: 'My mums live together with me. We don't need the phone, I talk to them all the time.'

Petra: 'Where's your dad live then? Do you speak on the phone with him?'

Sabrina: 'I don't have any dad. My mums had me without a dad.'

Toby: 'No they didn't.'

Sabrina: 'Yes they did.'

Toby: 'You're silly, you can't have a mum without a dad.'

The argument continued until the children asked the teacher to arbitrate. The teacher, Cheryl, decided to help the children find the answer to their puzzle over how many mums you can have by acknowledging their problem and getting them to think about how to solve their puzzle. She asked the children how they might find out how many mums you can have and if you can have a mum without a dad. They had lots of ideas so they agreed that she would help test out their ideas. They decided to ask their own parents and come and tell everybody the next day, and to bring in photos of their parents and count how many mums and dads were in them, and how many had mums and no dads. Cheryl then provided them with:

- ❯ time to problem-solve. Each day they were able to spend time on sharing information about their research into families and thinking about new ways to solve their puzzle.
- ❯ space to problem-solve. Cheryl set up special interest areas on families. The first thing they put on the wall near the interest table were pictures of their parents.
- ❯ materials to encourage problem-solving. Cheryl found several books and images of different types of families to share with the children.

Source: Goffin, S. and Tull, C., 1985, 'Problem-solving: Encouraging Active Listening' in *Young Children* 40(3) 28–32.

WHEN AND WHY?

Goal relevance

Problem-solving skills are the foundation of all areas of knowledge including mathematics, the sciences and the arts. It is through learning to problem-solve that children build their intellectual skills in these areas. Hence, using problem-solving to help children learn is relevant to teaching and learning goals across all curriculum content areas. While problem-solving is an intellectual skill, staff may want to teach children to problem-solve to enhance children's emotional, social, physical, aesthetic and moral development. More specifically, learning to problem-solve has been shown to help children to:

- ❯ develop initiative (Marxen 1995)
- ❯ enhance their manipulative skills (Marxen 1995)
- ❯ develop their creativity (Moyles 1989)
- ❯ gain confidence in their ability to work things out for themselves (Marxen 1995)
- ❯ become resilient and cope successfully with their world (Mayr and Ulich 1999)
- ❯ take responsibility for conflict resolution (Browning et al. 2000)
- ❯ enhance their mathematical thinking (Groves and Stacey 1990)
- ❯ increase their social leadership skills (Hensel 1991).

Developmental considerations

As soon as young children begin to ask, 'Why?' and 'How?' they show an interest in learning through problem-solving. However, staff need to match the use of problem-solving to enhance children's learning with their developmental abilities and interests in two ways.

First, staff need to match their expectations of how long children can focus on a problem with their developmental abilities. The older the children the more they are likely to have sustained, focused attention on the problems they encounter. This is particularly the case in 'free' play. Ruff and Lawson (1990) found that three-year-old children were more able to sustain focused attention on problem-solving with toys during free play than one- and two-year-old children.

Second, staff also need to match the types of problems they encourage children to solve with children's developmental interests. Babies will be puzzled by many things in the world about them. However, the problems (puzzles) they can learn to solve for themselves are going to be simple puzzles about how the world works and how to make their body work in the world. By about four months of age, babies reach a stage in their cognitive development where they can intentionally begin to make things happen (Seefeldt and Barbour 1986). For example, they will use their hands to hit a mobile, or cry for a caregiver. It is the point at which intentionality begins that babies can learn to solve very simple, immediate, short-term problems about how to make things work and how to make things happen. Once babies reach this stage of cognitive development, staff can present babies with simple puzzles that they can solve. For example, moving a mobile that a baby can reach to a slightly different location so that baby has to work out anew how to use their hands to reach it. Or, offering a new toy to a baby requires that they work out what it does or what can be done with it. Remember, babies' concentration span is likely to be short and their frustration and distress levels can rocket quickly. Staff need to choose puzzles that are within the baby's grasp and do not cause distress or frustration. Learning to enjoy problem-solving at this age relies on having problems that are fun and of interest to the baby.

Suitable problems will depend on the particular interests and temperament of each baby. Some examples of the problems they can be encouraged to solve are presented in the following anecdotes:

Andrew, four months old, has rolled over several times but now seems to forget how to do it. His carer, Andrea, gently encourages him by assisting him to get his arm out of the way, and physically prompting him. All the while she is talking to him about how he can manage to roll over.

Hannah, five months old, is lying on her tummy and trying to reach a toy that is on the floor in front of her. Stephanie, the child care worker, comes over and says: 'Hannah, are you trying to get that rattle? You need to move forward, let me help you.' She gently prompts Hannah to move forward by putting her hands on Hannah's feet and pushing.

Mario, nine months old, is trying to transfer a small doll from one hand to the other (by crossing the mid-line). He seems to be having trouble, so his carer, Clare, gently guides his hand across the middle of his body to meet his other hand. She also talks to him and gives praise when he succeeds.

Anthony, ten months old, wants to reach a biscuit that he can see on the floor under a chair. He can't reach it by himself and screams for attention. His caregiver, Elly, comes over and talks him through a solution. She shows him how to go around the other side of the chair where he is able to reach the biscuit.

Toddlers encounter many puzzles and dilemmas in their constant exploration of the world about them. It is puzzling how shoelaces can be tied into bows; why someone cries when you borrow their toy; and there are constant dilemmas about what to play with, how to play with it and what happens when you stop playing with it. Toddlers' 'hunting, gathering, building up and knocking down activities' (Kowalski 1996, p. 8) will provide staff with repeated opportunities to encourage a disposition towards problem-solving. Toddlers can learn to enjoy solving problems as they 'hunt, gather, build and knock down' if adults show interest in what they find puzzling and show enjoyment in their attempts to find answers to the puzzles they confront. They are likely to enjoy looking for things that are hidden, will look in more than one place for such objects and invent ways of getting to them despite their being beyond reach (Seefeldt and Barbour 1986). It is, therefore, important to ensure that the environment is toddler-safe (see Chapter 1). Staff interest in and enjoyment of toddlers' own attempts to solve problems will encourage persistent exploration and enjoyment in the business of looking for solutions.

The problems toddlers encounter in social relationships with each other are likely to be disputes over objects such as who should have the new doll to play with or who should be able to push the trolley. Teaching children physical techniques for solving these problems, such as finding another doll or another trolley to push, are more likely to be successful than teaching verbal techniques at this stage (Wheeler 1994).

Preschool children are likely to encounter many problems in their increasingly complex social relationships with each other. Problems are likely to occur over possession of objects, name-calling, play decisions and facts about what has occurred or should occur. As preschool children quickly reach a point in their cognitive development where they can generalise from one situation to another (Seefeldt and Barbour 1986), they quickly learn to use the solutions they reached to solve a problem in one situation to solve a similar problem elsewhere. In social situations this means that preschoolers can learn to generalise about what to do if there is a disagreement over a storyline or if they have a fight over a piece of equipment. For example, a preschooler can learn that whenever another child takes their toy the best way to get the toy back is to name-call until the toy is returned, or to negotiate so each child has a turn with it. Children can generalise positive or negative problem-solving techniques.

To help preschool children learn constructive ways to solve social problems, staff need to encourage them to explain their actions to each other and to encourage children to come up with their own 'fair' solutions. Children who learn to 'use their words' to explain what they want and what they are doing to others are more likely to find solutions to their social problems. Children who reach their own solutions are more likely to abide by what has been agreed to than with solutions adults create for them (Wheeler 1994). However, it can be helpful if staff offer solutions when the children seem stuck. Solutions to disagreements in play and over materials such as changing the activity, creating new rules, forgetting the problem or changing the storyline can all lead to positive and workable outcomes for preschool children (Wheeler 1994).

Navaz is an early childhood teacher who believes it is important to encourage children to reach their own solutions to play disagreements through their own problem-solving:

A group of four-year-old girls playing in the home corner have developed a rule called 'no boys allowed'. Their teacher, Navaz, suggested that this might not be fair and helped the girls to think of other rules. After a lengthy discussion they came up with some new rules: 'No pushing, no taking other people's things.'; 'Let the boss decide who will play what role.'; 'No being silly.'.

Preschool children can also learn to generalise about solutions to problems in the physical world around them. They encounter many problems about the physical world that fascinate them and that need solutions for their play to continue. For example, preschoolers encounter problems about how to construct block buildings that stay standing as they build higher and more complex buildings, problems about how to get water from one place to another, problems about how to move objects from one place to another and problems about how to join objects together. Many of these problems can be readily solved by preschoolers, but to do so the children must have plenty of time and opportunity to explore the materials they are working with (Napper 1991). Unless children thoroughly explore the materials they will experience frustration in their attempts to independently solve problems about how to make the physical world work for them in their play with each other. Preschoolers use five strategies to solve problems successfully: recognising the problem, restructuring the problem, monitoring their own efforts at solving the problem, persistence and being planned in their approach to it (Lambert 2001). Staff can support preschoolers in their problem-solving by encouraging children to 'think aloud and verbalise their actions as they explore materials' (Lambert 2001, p. 27) and by modelling thinking aloud to children (Lambert 2001).

As children become older they become less egocentric and more able to solve problems that involve people having different points of view. By about six to seven years of age children are able to learn, remember and impose rules about how to play with each other. They are, therefore, likely to become involved in conflicts over who is obeying or not obeying the rules they have developed. Staff can use these conflicts as opportunities to encourage the children to problem-solve solutions (Castle 1990). Many six- and seven-year-old children will be able to develop workable solutions to their disagreements over rules with some help from teachers. Questions that act as suggestions or encourage them to think of ways to modify the rules of their games are most likely to be successful in prompting them to problem-solve for themselves. Browning et al. (2000) reported on action research they conducted in a primary school classroom in which they successfully introduced a 'Wheel of Choice' that enabled the children to make choices about how best to solve conflicts between them in the classroom. This research highlighted how the children were able to choose between several possible solutions to conflict resolution in the classroom and to learn to follow a simple step-by-step approach to problem-solving.

EQUITY CONSIDERATIONS

'Race' and culture

Inter-cultural and inter-racial relationships between children offer many opportunities for problem-solving. As children encounter each other's diversity they often flounder. We know that children can reject, ostracise, silence and hurt each other because of 'racial' difference. York (1991) offers a range of problem-solving activities to help children learn to respect and accept each other's diversity. These activities help children explore how they might respond to situations in which they or other children are treated unfairly.

One such activity is called, 'What would you do if . . . ?'. In this activity, children are shown a range of pictures of children from different racial backgrounds involved in everyday tasks in the early childhood centre. Children are told a story about the picture and asked what they would do if they were the person in the story. Stories are simple situations in which a child is rejected and hurt. For example, 'This is a picture of a little girl called Khan Tho who is from Vietnam. She was very upset when Sally didn't want to sit with her yesterday at milk and fruit time. Sally said she had funny eyes. What would you do if you were Khan Tho?'.

Gender

Research revealed that preschool girls tend to perform less well at problem-solving tasks when they are in mixed-gender groupings (Parkin 1991). The reasons for this were centred on boys' assertiveness. This intimidated the girls, causing their concentration to waver and their preparedness to become involved in group discussion to reduce. On the other hand, in girls'-only problem-solving sessions the girls concentrated better and contributed more to discussion. Research (Browne and Ross 1991) has also shown that girls' persistence and confidence in solving problems can be quickly undermined by boys, as the following extract highlights:

> . . . a four-year-old girl was in the process of grappling with a problem with a construction toy when a boy approached. He watched for a moment and then said, 'That's not how you make a car. I know how.' He then began to tell her what to do. The girl responded by adopting a helpless demeanour and made no comment. Following the boy's intervention the adult tried to encourage her to continue but she refused, saying 'I can't do it' (Browne and Ross 1991, p. 44).

Staff need to be alert to the potential difficulties in mixed-group problem-solving and plan for it by positioning themselves close to such groups to monitor relationships within the group. This will enable staff to intervene quickly if and when the gender dynamics prove problematic.

Boys' and girls' confidence in problem-solving may begin to be shaped in infancy. Leipzig (1992) noted that when boys were distressed staff would often direct them into doing activities, while staff would often cuddle and talk to girls who were distressed. This provided boys with strong messages that they are doers and solvers of problems and girls that they should be passive rather than active. Staff should actively plan to avoid such gender differences in how they deal with children's distress. They should also ensure that both girl and boy infants and toddlers have lots of simple problem-solving opportunities.

Observing who has had the opportunity to successfully solve problems each day and noting any gender imbalances in this can provide important information about the extent to which there is gender equity in problem-solving opportunities in the group. Once any inequalities have been identified, staff can plan to overcome them. In this process it is important to focus problem-solving on everyday problems. It has been found that girls tend to improve their problem-solving skills in mathematics and science when they understand that they are being given tools to help them solve everyday problems (Chira 1992).

Disability and additional needs

There are two dimensions to anti-discriminatory approaches to disability to consider when using problem-solving as a teaching technique. First, problem-solving can be used to build, enrich and extend the cognitive development of children with disabilities in the group. To do this it is important to focus on problems of interest and relevance to individual children and to provide the time, opportunity and support for individuals to solve problems in their own ways. For some children, such as those who have sensory impairments, the ways in which they solve a problem might be quite different to someone without a sensory impairment. Taking care to respect different ways of solving problems helps build children's confidence in their own ability to be active problem-solvers. Part of learning such confidence is gained through support for developing autonomy and independence as learners (Dermon-Sparks 1992). A balance needs to be struck between allowing children with disabilities the time to explore different solutions and take risks, and allowing them to experience enough frustration in this process that they are reluctant to try again.

Second, problem-solving can be used to build positive, respectful relationships between children with and children without disabilities in the group. Activities which York (1991) suggested for building such ties between children in relation to culture and 'race' can be adapted for similar work with regard to disability. For example, the 'What would you do if . . .?' activity outlined above could be adapted to disability issues by showing children a range of pictures of children of differing abilities involved in everyday tasks in the early childhood centre. Children can be told a story about the picture and asked what they would do if they were the person in the story. Stories are simple situations in which a child is rejected and hurt.

The following anecdotes show how everyday situations offer opportunities for children to practise anti-discriminatory problem-solving:

> This picture is of a little girl called Jane who has Down's syndrome. She was very upset when Sam didn't want to play with her this morning. Sam said she looked funny. What would you do and how would you feel if you were Jane?
>
> At a child care centre in Brighton, a bayside suburb in Melbourne, the children are getting excited about a forthcoming excursion to the zoo. Their teacher, Penny, has had several discussions with the children about what they might see.
>
> Osker: 'Steve can't come.' (Osker is referring to Steve who is blind.)
>
> Penny: 'Of course Steve can come. Why do you think he can't?'
>
> Osker: 'He can't see!'
>
> Penny: 'That's right, he can't see but he can do other things—what does he use instead of his eyes?'
>
> The group of children come up with a variety of answers such as: 'He uses his ears to hear different sounds'. 'He uses his nose to smell.' 'He can touch things.'

It can be particularly useful to initiate discussions about what children believe that those with particular disabilities can and cannot do. Young children can develop very stereotyped and mistaken ideas about what it means to have a disability. Dermon-Sparks et al. (1989) described some of these misconceptions which include the belief that people in wheelchairs can't be parents and that people who are sight-impaired can't move because they can't see where to go. Problem-solving can be used to work through with children about how people in wheelchairs can be parents, and how you might find out where to go and how you might get there if you have a sight-impairment.

REFLECTING ON PROBLEM-SOLVING TECHNIQUES

1 What is a problem?
2 How would you define problem-solving?
3 What is the relationship between problem-solving and discovery learning?
4 What are the key factors that contribute to good problem-solving with children?
5 What is the relationship between general teaching techniques, such as questioning, and problem-solving?

6 Identify five general teaching techniques you will need to be familiar with in order to practise problem-solving with children.

7 What problems have you solved over the past week? To what extent did you follow the process of problem-solving outlined above? Are there any suggestions from this chapter that might have improved your problem-solving skills?

8 'Children take responsibility for their interactions and generate their own solutions more often when an adult is absent' (Wheeler 1994, p. 3). What implications does this research finding reported by Wheeler have for your role in teaching children appropriate social problem-solving skills?

9 Design a problem-solving activity you could use with four-year-old children to help them learn how to stand up for themselves when they are bullied by another child.

10 Observe one baby, one toddler and one preschool child for ten minutes each. What problems (puzzles, dilemmas etc.) did they encounter in this time? To what extent did the children successfully solve the problems they encountered? To what extent did the children need adult assistance to solve the problems? What form of adult assistance were they offered? Is there anything you could have done to improve the children's ability to solve the problems they encountered?

11 Observe staff in an early childhood centre working with a small group of three-year-old children for a period of thirty minutes. To what extent did staff members:
   ➲ encourage children to problem-solve issues of interest to them?
   ➲ organise time, space and materials to help children problem-solve?
   ➲ use clear steps to help children problem-solve?

IMPROVING TEACHING IN PRACTICE

1 Identify a child you could involve in your problem-solving techniques. Observe the child closely and identify a problem of interest to them that you can work together to solve. Plan at least three periods of time in which you work closely with the child on this problem. Implement and record these sessions.

2 After each session evaluate your own problem-solving skills by reviewing the extent to which you were able to:
   ➲ recognise problems
   ➲ think of different solutions to these problems
   ➲ choose your preferred solution to a problem and try it out
   ➲ reflect on what happened
   ➲ work with the children at each step in the problem-solving process.

3 What additional skills and knowledge do you need to consolidate and/or improve your problem-solving skills?

4 How and how well did you take account of the following considerations when problem-solving?
   ➲ developmental
   ➲ culture and 'race'
   ➲ gender
   ➲ disability.

Further reading

Cahan, E. 1992, 'John Dewey and human development', *Developmental Psychology*, 28(2), pp. 205–14.

Cohen, S. and Trostle, S. 1990, 'This land is our land: promoting ecological awareness in young children', *Childhood Education*, 66(5), pp. 304–10.

Cuffaro, H. 1995, *Experimenting with the World: John Dewey and the Early Childhood Classroom*, New York, Teachers' College Press.

Goffin, S. and Tull, C. 1985, 'Problem-solving: encouraging active learning', *Young Children*, 40(3), pp. 28–32.

Groves, S. and Stacey, K. 1990, 'Problem-solving: a way of linking mathematics to young children's reality', *Australian Journal of Early Childhood*, 15(1), pp. 5–11.

Lambert, B. 2000, 'Problem-solving in the first years of school', *Australian Journal of Early Childhood*, 25(2), pp. 32–8.

Tegano, D., Sawyers, J. and Moran, J. 1989, 'Problem-finding and solving in play: the teacher's role', *Childhood Education*, 66(2), pp. 92–7.

Tudge, J. and Caruso, D. 1988, 'Cooperative problem-solving in the classroom: enhancing young children's cognitive development', *Young Children* (November), pp. 46–52.

Websites—extending learning online

Center for Dewey Studies. Contact Dr Larry Hickman, Director of Center for Dewey Studies: lhickman@siu.edu

John Dewey Discussion Group on the Internet. To subscribe send a message to: listserv@vm.sc.edu. Leave the subject line blank. In the body of the text type: subscribe jdewey-1 YOUR NAME

References

Arthur, L., Beecher, B., Dockett, S., Farmer, S. and Death, E. 1996, *Programming and Planning in Early Childhood Settings*, second edn, Sydney, Harcourt Brace and Company.

Britz, J. 1993, *Problem-solving in early childhood classrooms*, ERIC, ED355040.

Browne, N. and Ross, C. 1991, '"Girls' stuff, boys' stuff": young children talking and playing', in N. Browne, ed., *Science and Technology in the Early Years* (pp. 37–51), Milton Keynes, Open University Press.

Browning, L., Davis, B. and Resta, V. 2000, 'What do you mean "think before I act?": conflict resolution with choices', *Journal of Research in Childhood Education*, 14(2), pp. 232–8.

Cahan, E. 1992, 'John Dewey and human development', *Developmental Psychology*, 28(2), pp. 205–14.

Castle, K. 1990, 'Children's invented games', *Childhood Education*, 67(2), pp. 82–5.

Center for Dewey Studies, 1996, John Dewey, http://www.siu.edu/~deweyctr/

Chira, S. 1992, 'How boys and girls learn differently', *Redbook*, September, pp. 191–2, 194–5.

Dermon-Sparks, L. 1992, '"It isn't fair!". Antibias curriculum for young children', in B. Neugebauer, ed., *Alike and Different: Exploring our Humanity with Young Children* (pp. 2–10), Washington DC, National Association for the Education of Young Children.

Dermon-Sparks, L. and the Anti-Bias Task Force 1989, *The Anti-Bias Curriculum: Tools for Empowering Young Children*, Washington DC, National Association for the Education of Young Children.

Goffin, S. and Tull, C. 1985, 'Problem-solving: encouraging active learning', *Young Children*, 40(3), pp. 28–32.

Greenberg, P. 1992, 'Why not academic preschool (part 2), Autocracy or democracy in the classroom', *Young Children* (March), pp. 54–64.

Groves, S. and Stacey, K. 1990, 'Problem-solving: a way of linking mathematics to young children's reality', *Australian Journal of Early Childhood*, 15(1), pp. 5–11.

Hendrick, J. 1990, *Total Learning: Developmental Curriculum for the Young Child*, 3rd edn, Toronto, Merrill Publishing Company.

Hensel, N. 1991, 'Social leadership skills in young children', *Roper Review*, 14(1), pp. 4–6.

Kowalski, H. 1996, 'What should we do with toddlers?', *Every Child*, 2(1), pp. 8–9.

Lambert, B. 2000, 'Problem-solving in the first years of school', *Australian Journal of Early Childhood*, 25(2), pp. 32–8.

——2001, 'Metacognitive problem solving in preschoolers', *Australian Journal of Early Childhood*, 26(3), pp. 24–9.

Leipzig, J. 1992, 'Helping whole children grow: non-sexist childrearing for infants and toddlers', in B. Neugebauer, ed., *Alike and Different: Exploring our Humanity with Young Children* (pp. 32–41), Washington DC, National Association for the Education of Young Children.

Levin, R. 1991, 'The debate over schooling: influences of Dewey and Thorndike', *Childhood Education*, 68(2), pp. 71–5.

Marxen, C. 1995, 'Push, pull, toll, tilt, swing: physics for young children', *Childhood Education*, 71(4), pp. 212–16.

Mayr, T. and Ulich, M. 1999, 'Children's well-being in day care centres: an exploratory empirical study', *International Journal of Early Years Education*, 7(3), pp. 229–40.

Moyles, J. 1989, *Just Playing: The Role and Status of Play in Early Childhood Education*, Milton Keynes, Open University Press.

Napper, I. 1991, 'The development of technological capability in young children', *Australian Journal of Early Childhood*, 16(3), pp. 23–7.

Park Han, E. 1995, 'Reflection is essential in teacher education', *Childhood Education*, 71(4), pp. 228–30.

Parkin, R. 1991, 'Fair play: children's mathematical experiences in the infant classroom', in N. Browne, ed., *Science and Technology in the Early Years* (pp. 52–64), Milton Keynes, Open University Press.

Read, K., Gardner, P. and Mahler, B. 1993, *Early Childhood Programs: Human Relationships and Learning*, 9th edn, Forth Worth, TX, Holt, Rinehart and Winston Inc.

Ruff, H. and Lawson, K. 1990, 'Development of sustained, focused attention in young children during free play', *Developmental Psychology*, 26(1), pp. 85–93.

Seefeldt, C. and Barbour, N. 1986, *Early Childhood Education: An Introduction*, Toronto, Merrill.

Tegano, D., Sawyers, J. and Moran, J. 1989, 'Problem-finding and solving in play: the teacher's role', *Childhood Education*, 66(2), pp. 92–7.

Wheeler, J. 1994, 'Peer conflicts in the classroom', *ERIC Digest, EDO-PS-94-13*.

Wilkes, G. (ed.) 1979, *Collins Dictionary of the English Language*, Middlesex, Penguin Books.

York, S. 1991, *Roots and Wings: Affirming Culture in Early Childhood Programs*, Minnesota, Toys'n Things Press.

Chapter 26

Reinforcing

Reinforce: to give added strength or support.
(*Collins Dictionary of the English Language*, p. 1231)

Rewarding the target behaviour in children will reinforce it and increase the probability of their maintaining it.
(Spodek and Saracho 1994, p. 193)

Whilst most teachers do not think of themselves as behaviourists, they use reinforcers to ensure that desired behaviours will recur or to make the child feel good about himself or herself.
(Robison and Schwartz 1982, p. 47)

WHAT?

In everyday language, to reinforce something means to make it stronger. For example, when concrete is reinforced it is made stronger through the addition of steel mesh or steel rods. This positively reinforces the concrete. In educational language, to positively reinforce a child means to make particular behaviours stronger or more likely to occur. When a child's behaviour is reinforced it is made stronger or more likely to occur through the use of rewards (or reinforcers). Rewards can be social, such as praise, or material, such as food (Spodek and Saracho 1994). It is also possible to negatively reinforce a child's behaviour to make it less strong or less likely to occur. As a teaching technique, reinforcement is, therefore, used to increase or decrease the likelihood of a child displaying a particular behaviour.

HOW?

Reinforcement as a teaching technique is based on the theories of behaviourist psychologists. Behaviourists believe that people's behaviour can be changed by rewarding and hence reinforcing it.

To change children's behaviour using reinforcement techniques, the following steps are recommended by Seefeldt and Barbour (1986), Moyles, (1989) and Spodek and Saracho (1994):

 Observe children to identify the specific behaviour (or behaviours) that you want to increase or decrease. In this way staff can target their reinforcement more specifically.

THEORETICAL BACKGROUND

SKINNER AND BEHAVIOURISM

Burrhus F. Skinner (1904–1990) was a North American academic who, along with Pavlov and Watson, significantly contributed to the psychological theory of behaviourism. Reinforcement as a teaching technique is derived from behaviourism.

Behaviourists believe that:

➜ development occurs as a result of different types of learning experiences children have

➜ differences in children's development occur as a result of the different learning opportunities children have, not as a result of biological differences between them

➜ children can be taught by the same principles of learning, irrespective of age

➜ learning occurs as a result of reinforcement of particular behaviours by the child's social and physical environment

➜ the child's motivation to learn will be controlled by the type of reinforcement the child receives in a range of situations (Faragher and MacNaughton 1990; MacNaughton 2003).

Skinner's work provides the theoretical basis for using reinforcement as a teaching technique. He claimed in the 1930s that he had developed techniques that enabled him to accurately shape and, therefore, predict human behaviour. He called these techniques operant conditioning.

The fundamental principle of operant conditioning is that if a person gives a response or demonstrates a behaviour (the response or the behaviour is known as the operant) which is immediately rewarded then the strength of the response or behaviour will be increased in the future. The future strength and predictability of a given response or behaviour will be dependent on the schedule of rewards that is used.

Skinner's work on operant conditioning has had significant impact on theories of teaching and learning, particularly in the 1950s and 1960s. At this time machines (human teaching machines) were designed to provide feedback to learners when they made a response to a specific instruction As Chaplin (1968, p. 460) explains:

Skinner's basic teaching techniques of operant conditions have been extended into the use of human teaching machines which operate on the principle of self-reinforced learning.

Skinner's work has influenced the development of programmed instruction and highly structured early childhood curriculum because he strongly believed that to control the learning that takes place in any given situation the environment also needs to be controlled. The materials used to direct learning need to be highly structured and in practice programs based on behaviourist principles have tended to concentrate on cognitive development to the exclusion of other areas of development (MacNaughton 2003).

In the 1990s the influence of Skinner's work on operant conditioning was most noticeable in the early childhood curriculum in the 'application of technology to curriculum and instruction' (Morrison 1995, p. 573). Many software programs for young children are based on operant conditioning with clear reinforcers for correct answers and the opportunity to redo if incorrect. For example, when children select particular responses to a question or a problem posed in the software they are rewarded with a computer voice saying, 'Well done' or 'Good job'.

Morrison (1995) notes that controversy exists concerning the extent to which software programs based on operant conditioning are appropriate in the early years. Some people argue that open-ended software which promotes discovery learning is preferable (Yelland 1998).

> Habous, a child care worker, was keen to find out why one of the babies in her care was 'fussing' such a lot. After a discussion with a co-worker she decided to look more carefully at what the baby was doing when he was fussing. After several observations at different times of the day she distinguished three types of fussing behaviours; namely, crying loudly, head-banging and moaning to himself. She decided to target the head-banging behaviour first—when this was extinguished she looked at the other two behaviours.

- Note down the context within which the desired or undesired behaviours occur so that you have a clear picture of when, why and how often it is occurring.
- Develop clear goals for what you want to have happen. This should specify the behaviours desired (or not), the context in which you expect them to happen (or not) and when you expect them to happen (or not). This should be specific and limited to very few behaviours in the first instance.
- Decide on rewards that can be used to reinforce desired behaviours. They should be something valued by the child. These might be simple, such as a smile or a pat on the back, or more complex, such as reading a favourite book with a child (refer below for more detail).
- Develop a plan of action that rewards desired behaviours and ignores undesired behaviours. Reinforcing a behaviour intermittently is a very effective way to ensure it continues.
- Observe again and evaluate the success or otherwise of your program. Modifications to the reward may be necessary if the program has not worked.

Rewards or reinforcers need to vary according to the age, abilities and interests of the child. Research (see Turney 1985) has shown that the following reinforcers can be used to successfully change behaviour:

- Verbal—telling a child that you are pleased with what they have done. These reinforcers can be very simple:

> Gracie always shows the children in her care that she is pleased with their achievements. She often says 'Well done!' and combines this with a smile, and some sort of physical reinforcement such as a pat, a rub or a hug.

- Gesture—showing a child you are pleased with what they have done through non-verbal signs such as smiles or nods.
- Proximity—showing a child you are pleased with what they have done by moving closer to them.
- Contact—showing a child you are pleased with what they have done through contact such as a gentle touch on the arm.
- Activity—showing a child you are pleased with what they have done through allowing them to be involved in an activity they enjoy, such as bike-riding or helping with story time.
- Tokens—showing a child you are pleased with what they have done by giving them a special token such as a star or a stamp.

Research shows that rewards work best when they are given as soon as the behaviour is seen, when the child likes the reward, when the child is clear why they are being rewarded and when there are a variety of rewards used (Turney 1985).

> Erica comes into the kindergarten and shows her teacher her star chart. Her mother has set up a token reward program for Erica. She has a new star on her chart every time she has a dry bed. When she has seven stars she will be going for a special tea to her grandfather's. Erica loves having tea with her grandfather but as he lives out of town she can't visit him very often. Erica has not wet the bed for a week and is proud of her achievements. She excitedly tells her teacher that tomorrow she is going to her grandfather's for tea because she has seven stars on her chart.

There are several reasons why reinforcement may be unsuccessful in modifying children's behaviour. Robison and Schwartz (1982, p. 51) cite the following reasons:

- The reinforcement was not appropriate or adequate.
- The reinforcement occurred too often or too infrequently.

Reinforcement has been shown to be a consistently powerful teaching technique which modifies children's behaviour in the short term, rather than the long term. There is now considerable evidence to suggest that behaviour modification programs based on rewards and praise rarely produce any lasting changes in children's attitudes or behaviours (Kohn 1994). However, because reinforcement can be so effective in changing children's behaviour in the short term it can be tempting to use. We believe that it should be used very cautiously and only in very unusual circumstances. Caution is advised for the following reasons.

- Children can quickly learn which behaviours are being reinforced by staff and they can come to resent being manipulated. Seefeldt and Barbour (1986) cite an instance where a child who learned that desirable behaviour was rewarded with a sweet crushed hers underfoot when she was given one for finishing a painting.

> Adam, a kindergarten teacher in a private boys-only school in Melbourne was shocked to hear Jasper say 'What will you give me if I help you pack up the blocks?'. He decided to rethink his approach to encouraging children to pack away as he had relied on rewards to date.

- Children can become motivated via reinforcement to learn to get rewards rather than motivated to learn (Kohn 1994; Deci et al. 2001).
- When children are not rewarded they can learn to feel they are failures. Children can wonder about what is wrong with them that they never get the rewards that others do.
- Children can learn to resent those children who are receiving rewards (Seefeldt and Barbour 1986).
- Children's feelings and the reasons for their behaviours are ignored. Hence only surface change in behaviours, not feelings occur (Robison and Schwartz 1982).
- Children can learn to become dependent on adult rewards for learning rather than independent learners (O'Brien 1990).

➲ Children who are encouraged to work for rewards become 'less inclined to explore ideas, think creatively, and take chances' (Kohn 1994, p. 2).

➲ When praise is used as a reinforcer of children's behaviour it can lower children's confidence in themselves (Hitz and Driscoll 1988).

➲ Young children do not always understand negative reinforcement, such as time out, in the ways that adults intend. Children can feel hurt and anxious when they experience time out and these feelings can lead to an increase in negative behaviours (Readdick and Chapman 2000).

➲ Rewards can undermine children's motivation to learn rather than increase it (Deci et al. 2001).

WHEN AND WHY?

Goal relevance

Reinforcement can be used to enhance children's learning in several ways:

➲ Reinforcement can be used to increase children's attention on a particular activity or experience (Turney 1985), especially when they have an initial interest in the task (Cameron 2001).

➲ Reinforcement can be used to enhance social learning (Spodek 1987; Slee 1998; Guss and Jackson 1999). Generally, this would be done to increase a desirable behaviour such as sharing and to decrease an undesirable behaviour such as hitting.

➲ Reinforcement can be used as part of programmed learning instruction. As Morrison (1995, p. 573) explains:

> . . . what students are to learn is programmed or arranged in a progressive series of small steps from simple or basic to complex. Students are rewarded or reinforced for the right answer after each small step . . .

➲ Reinforcement can be used to increase children's interest and motivation in a particular experience (Turney 1985; Cameron 2001).

Reinforcement is a useful technique to use for short-term changes in children's behaviour. Staff should remember that long-term changes in children's learning are unlikely to occur if reinforcement is the sole teaching technique employed.

Developmental considerations

Behaviourists studied learning and how it occurs, and then applied the general principles of learning they developed to explain the process of development. They did not propose a stage theory of development and argued that all the basic principles of learning are equally applicable to children irrespective of their developmental abilities. However, they did recognise that children's ability to learn will vary, depending on their level of maturity and their existing skill base.

Hence, reinforcement can be used effectively to develop many of the skills babies and toddlers are striving towards in the early years, such as self-help skills, problem-solving, autonomy and independence, and to help teach preschool children more complex pro-social and cognitive skills.

From a developmental perspective it is important to consider two things when using reinforcement as a teaching technique. First, it is important to only try to reinforce those skills and dispositions relevant to the child's developmental age and stage. The following discussion between a teacher and a parent shows how important this can be:

A teacher–parent discussion is taking place in a child care centre. Trish is talking with Sara, the mother, an intelligent high achiever who works in business. Trish is a very experienced child care worker. They are discussing Sara's daughter, Isobel, who is three years old.

Sara: 'Isobel has started wetting the bed again. I've tried telling her that she's a big girl now and that she'll get a present when she stops completely, but this has been going on for months and it doesn't seem to make any difference. She doesn't seem to care.'

Trish: 'When she wets the bed what do you do?'

Sarah: 'I'm usually very cross with her and I remind her that big girls don't wet beds. I also tell her that if she's good until Easter she can have a Barbie Doll.'

Trish: 'Easter is a long way away for a three-year-old [four weeks]. Perhaps you could reward Isobel for being dry more frequently and not make such a fuss when she wets the bed. I know it's hard sometimes when it's the middle of the night not to react crossly. What rewards does Isobel respond to?'

Sara: 'She loves praise, and she likes having breakfast in bed with me on the weekends.'

Trish: 'I wonder if you could reward her for dry nights by praising her and on Saturday morning by making a big fuss of her and allowing her to have breakfast with you in bed?

'When she does wet, the best thing to do is to simply acknowledge that she has wet the bed, then change the bed and put her back to sleep in a matter-of-fact way. She'll look forward to praise and to the treat on the weekend.'

Second, it is important to choose rewards appropriate to children's differing developmental abilities and interests. For example, while proximity rewards might be suitable across all age groups, tokens are only likely to be of interest to older children who have reached an appropriate level of symbolic thought. Similarly, the activity rewards that might be enjoyed by babies are likely to be different to those enjoyed by preschoolers and children in the early years of school. Research suggests that intrinsic motivation in school-aged children can be undermined by tangible rewards so it is especially important to reflect carefully on when and how to use reinforcement as a teaching technique in the early years of schooling (Deci et al. 2001).

It is also important to bear in mind the concerns raised above about using reinforcement as a teaching technique. It should be used selectively and with great care with all age groups. This will ensure that children's learning does not become dependent on external rewards at the expense of intrinsic pleasure from success and striving to achieve.

EQUITY CONSIDERATIONS

'Race' and culture

As mentioned above, reinforcement can be an effective teaching technique for increasing and decreasing specific targeted behaviours. It can be used to decrease children's negative comments and reactions to each other based on 'racial' bias and to increase children's respectful behaviours. For example, staff may have a white child in the group who has refused to play with one of the black children in the group. Staff may have told the white child they find this unacceptable and find as a result that very occasionally he is beginning to play with the black child. Staff may be looking for ways to increase this play and decide that reinforcement might assist. Positive reinforcement can also be used by staff if a child is being rejected by others because of her 'racial' or ethnic background. Staff can increase inter-group contact by reinforcing the positive behaviours of the rejected child in front of other children (Ramsey 1987). However, once again caution should be exercised in relying on this teaching technique. There is some evidence that children whose social behaviour is regularly shaped by adults through rewards tend to be less generous to others than children whose behaviour has not been shaped in this way (Kohn 1994).

When deciding on rewards for children for specific behaviours it is important to consider the cultural relevance of the rewards being chosen. Special care should be given to using proximity and gesture as rewards when the children are from a cultural group different to that of the staff because non-verbal signals such as eye-contact and touching can be understood differently. For example, for some Indigenous Australian children eye contact could be read as threatening rather than as supportive (Colbung and Glover 1996). The level of comfort people feel standing or sitting next to each other can also differ between cultural groups. In some cultures it can be considered extremely impolite to be very near someone and, therefore, children from these cultures may see this as a negative reward. In other cultures, the opposite can be true (Millam 1996). It is important for staff to take time to learn from the children and their families how body language might be read by the children. This can prevent rewards and praise being misread and can help staff to choose rewards that are culturally sensitive and appropriate.

Information on general patterns of non-verbal interaction in specific cultures can be found in *Caring For Every Child*, published by the Sydney Lady Gowrie Children's Centre in 1996, and in *Childrearing and Background Information Sheet*, prepared by the FKA Multicultural Resource Centre in Melbourne. The Appendix has contact details for each of these agencies.

It is important that staff do not rely strongly on reinforcement as a teaching technique for increasing pro-social behaviour between children from different 'racial' groups. Research (Krebs 1983) suggests that there are only a very few pro-social behaviours that are learned effectively via reinforcement.

It may also be the case that what is considered anti-social behaviour by adults is in effect a child resisting what they believe to be unfair expectations placed on them. Sleeter and Grant (1999, p. 195) make this point well:

> Most people, often as part of a group, oppose on a daily basis what they see as unfair authority or restrictions imposed by someone else. In school, this may take countless forms, such as girls resisting being viewed as sex objects, students in wheelchairs ganging up against those who tease them, or students living below the poverty line who refuse to obey middle-class teachers with low expectations of them.

Gender

There is considerable research to suggest that girls and boys partly learn their gender through adult reinforcement of their gender behaviours. Boys are more likely to be reinforced for the following behaviours than are girls: playing outside, moving away from the adult, being involved in rough-and-tumble play, helping with DIY chores, not crying when upset and taking up lots of physical space (France 1986). When staff interact with young children it is important to reflect on the extent to which they may be reinforcing gender stereotyping and the extent to which girls and boys are being reinforced for similar behaviours.

There is some evidence (see Browne and Ross 1991) that adults can increase non-traditional gender behaviours through using proximity rewards. For instance, if boys are playing in a caring and enjoyable way with dolls, having an adult nearby makes it more likely that the behaviour will be strengthened and occur again.

One of the outcomes of the gender differences in adult reinforcement is that boys are likely to be more involved in aggressive behaviour than girls (Moyles 1989). It is also likely that much of boys' aggressive behaviour will be directed towards the harassment of girls (Alloway 1995). Harassment may take the form of hitting girls, knocking over their blocks, pinching their bottoms and pulling their hair. When such harassment occurs girls will often shy away from the harassment and relinquish any play areas in which the harassment occurs (MacNaughton 1994, 2000; Alloway 1995). Staff can use negative reinforcement to reduce the boys' aggression towards the girls and to increase the girls' determination to challenge the harassment and maintain involvement in their chosen play areas. In planning to use reinforcement for these goals, staff need to remember that there may be differences in what boys and girls will find rewarding. For example, boys are likely to have been rewarded for playing without adults nearby (France 1986). This may mean that proximity rewards may be less effective than with girls who are likely to have been rewarded for playing near adults.

Research (Browne and Ross 1991) also indicates that rewarding preschool girls with praise for their involvement in non-traditional areas such as play with construction materials can be counterproductive. Girls quickly learn that producing a construction with minimal effort and complexity can produce considerable praise from staff. This can teach them that not much is expected of them in the area of construction. The girls also learn that once they have received praise for the efforts nothing much else is expected and they move quickly on to other learning areas.

It is important to remember that reinforcement may change behaviours but not change how children feel. Moreover, reinforcement does not enable children to understand why staff see some behaviours as more acceptable than others. It is, therefore, not prudent for staff to rely heavily on it as a teaching technique in implementing gender equity programs.

Disability and additional needs

When children with and without disabilities first meet there will be a lot to learn about each other and about how to build relationships. Careful use of simple reinforcement techniques can help them build positive relationships. Simple rewards for children without disabilities appropriately helping those children with disabilities can strengthen such behaviours. It is important that such helping does not reduce the possibilities for independence for children with disabilities (Palmer 1995).

There is considerable debate about the best way to help give children with disabilities appropriate social interaction skills (see Bordner and Berkley 1992). Many teaching techniques rely heavily on behaviourist learning principles in which children are taught specific social skills in a highly programmed way. One effective method of building social interaction between children with and without disabilities is to provide opportunities for social play that is fun—this 'becomes a natural reinforcer as it is more likely to be repeated' (Bordner and Berkley 1992, p. 39).

REFLECTING ON REINFORCEMENT TECHNIQUES

1 Consider the following concerns about the use of reinforcement as a teaching technique raised by Spodek and Saracho (1994, pp. 192–3):

Some feel that the focus on behaviour leads to a concern for symptoms rather than causes. Others object to the use of rewards, equating it with bribery. Still others feel that this technique places the control of behaviour outside the individual and does not help the children learn to judge what is proper behaviour, thus limiting autonomy.

To what extent do you agree with the comments? Why? To what extent do you disagree with the comments? Why?

2   Kohn (1994, p. 1) writes:

A child promised a treat for learning or acting responsibly has been given every reason to stop doing so when there is no longer a reward to be gained.

To what extent do you agree with the comments? Why? To what extent do you disagree with the comments? Why?

3   Imagine you are working with a four-year-old boy who always tries to be the leader when he is playing with other children. If he isn't allowed to be the leader he often hurts the other children verbally or physically. His favourite places to play are in the outside play area and he loves all types of water play. What else would you need to know about this child before deciding to use reinforcement to change his behaviour in group settings?

4   Review an 'educational' software program for children under five years of age. To what extent is the program based on learning through reinforcement? Would you use the program with young children? Why? Why not?

5   Choosing appropriate reinforcers is an important part of using reinforcement as a teaching technique. Consider what might be some appropriate reinforcers to use for children of different ages by completing the following table.

Reinforcer	Babies	Toddlers	Preschoolers
Verbal			
Gesture			
Proximity			
Activity			
Token			

IMPROVING TEACHING IN PRACTICE

1   Identify a child for whom reinforcement techniques may be appropriate in the short term. Observe the child closely and identify a behaviour that you would like to positively reinforce. Plan at least five periods of time in which you work closely to reinforce this behaviour. Implement and record these sessions.

2   At the end of the fifth session evaluate your own reinforcing skills by reviewing the extent to which you were able to increase the desired behaviour.

3   What additional skills and knowledge do you need to consolidate and improve your reinforcing skills?

4   How and how well did you take account of the following considerations when reinforcing the desired behaviour with the child you selected?

- ➔ developmental
- ➔ cultural and 'race'
- ➔ gender; and
- ➔ disability.

Further reading

Cole, P. and Chan, L. 1990, *Methods and Strategies for Special Education*, New Jersey, Prentice Hall Inc. [refer to pp. 94–106].

Duncan, T., Kemple, K. M. and Smith, T. 2002, 'Developmentally appropriate practice and the use of reinforcement in inclusive early childhood classrooms', *Childhood Education*, 76, pp. 194–203.

Hitz, R. and Driscoll, A. 1988, 'Praise or encouragement? New insights into praise: implications for early childhood teachers', *Young Children*, July, pp. 6–13.

Kohn, A. 1994, 'The risks of rewards', *ERIC Digest, EDO-PS-94-14*.

O'Brien, S. 1990, 'Praising children: five myths', *Childhood Education*, 66(4), pp. 248–9.

Readdick, C. and Chapman, P. 2000, 'Young children's perception of time out', *Journal of Research in Childhood Education*, 15(1), pp. 81–7.

Robison, H. and Schwartz, S. 1982, *Designing Curriculum for Early Childhood*, Boston, Allyn and Bacon Inc. [refer to pp. 47–51].

Salkind, J. 1985, *Theories of Human Development*, 2nd trans., New York, John Wiley & Sons [refer to pp. 138–48].

Turney, C. 1985, *Anatomy of Teaching*, Sydney, Novak Publishing [refer to pp. 181–3].

Websites—extending learning online

Home page of the B. F. Skinner Foundation. This has extensive links to publications and summaries of his work and is at http://www.bfskinner.org/

References

Alloway, N. 1995, *Foundation Stones: The Construction of Gender in Early Childhood*, Melbourne, Curriculum Corporation.

Bordner, G. and Berkley, M. 1992, 'Educational play: meeting everyone's needs in mainstreamed classrooms', *Childhood Education*, 69(1), pp. 38–42.

Browne, N. and Ross, C. 1991, '"Girls' stuff, boys' stuff": young children talking and playing', in N. Browne, ed., *Science and Technology in the Early Years* (pp. 37–51), Milton Keynes, Open University Press.

Cameron, J. 2001, 'Negative effects of reward on instrinsic motivation—a limited phenomenon: comment on Deci, Koestner, and Ryan (2001)', *Review of Educational Research*, 71(1), pp. 29–42.

Chaplin, J. 1968, *Dictionary of Psychology*, New York, Dell Publishing.

Colbung, M. and Glover, A. 1996, 'In partnership with Aboriginal children', in M. Fleer, ed., *Conversations about Teaching and Learning in Early Childhood Settings* (pp. 33–40), Canberra, Australian Early Childhood Association.

Deci, E., Koestner, R. and Ryan, M. 2001, 'Extrinsic rewards and intrinsic motivation in education: reconsidered once again', *Review of Educational Research*, 71(1), pp. 1–29.

Faragher, J. and MacNaughton, G. 1990, *Working with Young Children: Guidelines for Good Practice*, Melbourne, TAFE Publications.

France, P. 1986, 'The beginnings of sex stereotyping', in N. Browne and P. France, eds, *Untying the Apron Strings: Anti-Sexist Provision for the Under Fives* (pp. 49–67), Milton Keynes, Open University Press.

Guss, C. and Jackson, I. 1999, 'Behaviour management strategies in the preschool: teacher strategies in current use', *Australian Journal of Early Childhood*, 24(3), pp. 38–41.

Hitz, R. and Driscoll, A. 1988, 'Praise or encouragement? New insights into praise: implications for early childhood teachers', *Young Children*, July, pp. 6–13.

Kohn, A. 1994, 'The risks of rewards', *ERIC Digest, EDO-PS-94-14*.

Krebs, D. 1983, 'Commentary and critique: psychological and philosophical approaches to prosocial development', in D. Bridgeman, ed., *The Nature of Prosocial Development: Interdisciplinary Theories and Strategies* (pp. 205–17), New York, Academic Press.

MacNaughton, G. 1994, 'It's more than counting heads in block play: rethinking approaches to gender equity in the early childhood curriculum', in *20th Triennial conference Australian Early Childhood Association*, Perth, WA.

MacNaughton, G. 2000, *Rethinking Gender in Early Childhood Education*, Sydney, Allen & Unwin; New York, Sage Publications; London, Paul Chapman Publishing.

——2003. Eclypsing voice in research with young children, Australian Journal of Early Childhood, 28(1), 36–43.

Millam, R. 1996, *Anti-Discriminatory Practice: A Guide for Workers in Childcare and Education*, London, Cassell Books.

Morrison, G. 1995, *Early Childhood Education Today*, 6th edn, New Jersey, Merrill.

Moyles, J. 1989, *Just Playing: The Role and Status of Play in Early Childhood Education*, Milton Keynes, Open University Press.

O'Brien, S. 1990, 'Praising children: five myths', *Childhood Education*, 66(4), pp. 248–9.

Palmer, A. 1995, 'Responding to special needs', in B. Creaser and E. Dau, eds, *The Anti-Bias Approach in Early Childhood* (pp. 71–83), Sydney, Harper Educational.

Ramsey, P. 1987, *Teaching and Learning in a Diverse World: Multicultural Education for Young Children*, Columbia, Teachers' College Press.

Readdick, C. and Chapman, P. 2000, 'Young children's perception of time out', *Journal of Research in Childhood Education*, 15(1), pp. 81–7.

Robison, H. and Schwartz, S. 1982, *Designing Curriculum for Early Childhood*, Boston, Allyn and Bacon Inc.

Seefeldt, C. and Barbour, N. 1986, *Early Childhood Education: An Introduction*, Toronto, Merrill.

Slee, J. 1998, 'Understanding and responding to children's antisocial behaviour', *Every Child*, 4(2), pp. 8–9.

Sleeter, C. and Grant, C. 1999, *Making Choices for Multicultural Education: Five Approaches to Race, Class and Gender*, Columbus, Ohio, Merrill.

Spodek, B. 1987, The knowledge base of kindergarten education, Paper presented to *Five-Year-Olds in School Conference*, East Lansing, MI, 9 January.

Spodek, B. and Saracho, O. 1994, *Right from the Start: Teaching Children Ages Three to Eight*, Boston, Allyn and Bacon Inc.

Turney, C. 1985, *Anatomy of Teaching*, Sydney, Novak Publishing.

Wilkes, G. (ed.) 1979, *Collins Dictionary of the English Language*, Middlesex, Penguin Books.

Yelland, N. 1998, Gender issues in mathematics and technology. In N. Yelland (Ed.) *Gender in Early Childhood*. (pp. 249–73) Routledge, London.

Chapter 27

Scaffolding

Scaffold: a temporary structure or framework that is used to support (people) during erection, a repair of a building or other construction.

(Collins Dictionary of the English Language, p. 1300)

Teachers should . . . be sensitively attuned to children's abilities, interests and strengths, and remain accessible enough to provide appropriate scaffolding.

(Smith 1996, p. 332)

The support of adults and more competent peers provides the necessary assistance or 'scaffold' that enables the child to move to the next level of independent functioning.

(NAEYC 1991, p. 26)

WHAT?

In everyday usage scaffolding describes a temporary structure of support that is used by construction workers to assist with constructing or with repairing buildings. Jerome Bruner developed the metaphor of 'scaffolding' children's learning to describe the process through which a more competent peer or adult helps a less competent child to become more competent and eventually function independently of the original person's help (Meadows and Cashdan 1988).

As a teaching technique, scaffolding describes the process of providing temporary guidance and support to children moving from one level of competence to another. The guidance may be verbal or non-verbal (Burns-Hoffman 1993). 'Scaffolds' (or the support of more competent people) can help increase children's level of competence in all areas of development. Edwards and Knight (1994) view scaffolding as an 'apprenticeship' view of teaching and learning because the expert adult supports the less competent child's learning. The 'scaffold' in teaching is the social environment (Arthur et al. 1996). This environment supports the child's exploration of new meanings, relationships and knowledges, and it consolidates what is nearly known by the child. Scaffolding is a teaching technique that has been developed from the work of Leo S. Vygotsky and Jerome Bruner.

THEORETICAL BACKGROUND

VYGOTSKY AND SCAFFOLDING

Leo Semenovich Vygotsky (1886–1934) was a Russian academic whose theory of cognitive development in the 1920s and 1930s provided a powerful framework for understanding the relationship between teaching and learning. It also provided a '. . . fresh perspective on children's development . . .' (Berk and Winsler 1995, p. 3).

Vygotsky's work reached Western, English-speaking scholars only recently. His work was banned in the Soviet Union until 1953, and the Cold War between the United States, its allies (including Australia) and the Soviet Union limited the possibility of the academic exchange of his ideas (Berk 1994a).

The following beliefs about learning and development held by Vygotsky's work provide the theoretical rationale for scaffolding as a teaching technique. He believed:

- ➔ child development occurs as a result of natural and cultural activity. Natural activity refers to the biological growth and maturation of the person. Cultural activity refers to the social processes through which we learn to use cultural tools and to think
- ➔ thought processes occur on a lower and a higher plane. The lower plane we share with other mammals. The higher plane involves the use of language and cultural knowledge, and its existence distinguishes us from other animals
- ➔ each plane of learning requires the assistance of a more experienced learner to maximise learning
- ➔ higher plane thought processes (cognition) are highly dependent on language
- ➔ 'Education leads development' (Berk and Winsler 1995, p. 17) and thus learning on the higher plane of thinking.

More specifically, Vygotsky believed that learning occurred most effectively on the higher plane of thinking through competent adults interacting with a child in a theoretical zone of development called the Zone of Proximal Development (ZPD). The ZPD referred to a region in which a child could work at higher levels of competence in relation to a particular skill, understanding or disposition when working with more competent peers or adults than working by herself (Meadows and Cashdan 1988, p. 53). In the ZPD there is a transfer of ability from a more competent person to the child.

Vygotsky defined the ZPD as the '. . . distance between the actual developmental level as determined by independent problem-solving and the level of potential development as determined through problem-solving under adult guidance or in collaboration with more capable peers . . .' (Vygotsky 1978, cited in Berk and Winsler 1995, p. 38). Once children develop cognitive competencies in a social context they are internalised by the child. At this point a child no longer needs adult guidance and support for their newly acquired competency. However, there will be new competencies that now can be practised in the ZPD and will through adult support and guidance be internalised.

Vygotsky's work supports a play-based early childhood curriculum because he strongly believed that imaginative play was important in building young children's intellectual and social competencies. He saw play as a '. . . leading activity which determines the child's development . . .' (Vygotsky 1932, p. 552). Vygotsky believed that imaginative play expresses children's zone of proximal development as it allows the child to perform tasks, experience feelings and test competencies not possible in non-imaginative play (Jones and Reynolds 1992).

In imaginative play children can imagine themselves beyond what they can accomplish in ordinary interactions with themselves and others (Moyles 1989; Fimreite et al. 1999). This idea gains support through research showing that children involved in child-directed fantasy play produce more varied and alternative uses for objects than children who have not had this experience (Moyles 1989). In addition, while involved in imaginative play, children regulate their behaviour according to the rules of the play and thus learn to regulate their impulsive actions (Berk 1994b). Vygotsky believed each of these attributes of imaginative play supports the emergence of a wide range of competencies and thus it should be fostered.

Vygotsky's beliefs on imaginative play are increasingly supported by research which shows that it enhances children's imagination and creativity, improves their ability to reason about the impossible or absurd, extends all aspects of children's conversational competence, and promotes children's story-telling and story-memory abilities (Berk 1994b; Fimreite et al. 1999).

How?

The role of staff in scaffolding children's learning is threefold:

 First, staff need to judge when children are ready to move from one level of competence to another (Read et al. 1993). Staff need to carefully observe and note the social, cognitive and communicative competencies of the child. This may mean joining in children's imaginative play and intervening in children's other learning experiences to find out what they can or cannot currently do without assistance (Meadows and Cashdan 1988). Staff need to ask themselves: 'Have I seen . . . do this before?'; 'How easily can . . . do this?'; 'What would present the child with a challenge in this situation?'; 'What is the next level for the child in this situation?'.

 Second, staff need time to support, guide and assist children's moving from one level of competence to another (Smith 1996). Successful scaffolding rests on staff spending time with children on a one-to-one basis or in small groups (Fleer 1996).

 Third, staff need to judge how best to assist children's movement to increased competence. This involves using a variety of verbal and non-verbal general teaching techniques to extend children's understandings and skills. Staff may use a single technique or a combination of techniques. Teaching techniques that support scaffolding include several of the general teaching techniques discussed in previous parts of this book. For example, questioning, prompting, praising, confirming, pointing out things to children and modelling (Madsen and Gudmundsdottir 2000).

Maria has drawn on general techniques such as questioning, encouraging, praising and non-verbal suggesting as part of her scaffolding process with Adrian:

Adrian: 'How do you draw a person?'
    Maria: 'Can you make a shape for the head?' She makes a round motion around her head. Adrian makes a roundish shape.
    Maria: 'That's good—now what shape is the body?' She indicates length in front of her body. Adrian makes a long oval shape below the head.

> Maria: 'Well done—now what else does a person have?' She holds out her arms. Adrian draws lines off the body.
>
> Maria: 'And . . .' She holds up her legs.
>
> Adrian draws the legs off the body. They have a further discussion about body parts and Adrian adds hands and hair. Maria enthusiastically praises him.

According to Berk and Winsler (1995) good quality scaffolding involves the following features:

- joint problem-solving
- inter-subjectivity
- warmth and responsiveness
- keeping the child in the ZPD
- promoting self-regulation.

We shall now look at each of these in turn.

Joint problem-solving

The first feature in quality scaffolding is that two or more people (child–child or child–adult) try to solve a problem together. They must each be interested in the problem and the problem must be culturally meaningful to them (Berk and Winsler 1995).

Inter-subjectivity

The meaning of inter-subjectivity can be easily understood by splitting the word into two: 'inter' and 'subjectivity'. Inter means mutual or reciprocal. Subjectivity means a person's consciousness (thoughts) or perception (feelings/senses). Hence, inter-subjectivity involves trying to reach shared (mutual) understandings between adult and child or child and child of how each thinks and feels. Inter-subjectivity 'creates a common ground for communication as each partner adjusts to the perspective of the other' (Berk 1994a, p. 256). This means interacting to find out what the other thinks and feels, and negotiating a common understanding—sometimes through compromise. This common understanding must be within the child's ZPD (Berk and Winsler 1995).

> Zone of Actual Development (ZAD) is the term that can be used to describe the level of competence a child has reached in relation to a particular skill, understanding or disposition when working by her or himself.
>
> Zone of Proximal Development (ZPD) is the term used by Vygotsky to describe the level of competence a child can potentially reach in relation to a particular skill, understanding or disposition. This potential is reached when working with more competent peers or adults. It is easy to think of the ZPD as the zone of 'next development' (Meadows and Cashdan 1988, p. 53).

Warmth and responsiveness

Scaffolding involves social collaboration between child and adult to enhance children's learning. Its effectiveness as a teaching technique is, therefore, strongly dependent on the 'emotional tone' (Berk and Winsler 1995, p. 41) of the relationship between learner and teacher. A positive 'emotional tone' is more likely when staff acknowledge children's efforts and understandings. Staff need to take notice of what children are doing and saying, positively comment on children's work and stay closely attuned to children's need for additional support.

> Pia works with Leo, a four-year-old, in the block area. She sits close to him and makes several suggestions as to how he can make the structure he is building stronger. She has observed Leo in the blocks over time and has noticed that he gives up easily when his structures fall over. She continues to support his learning in this way until he has completed the structure. As she sits next to him she takes care to encourage his efforts.

Keeping the child in the ZPD

Learning for the child will be at its most intense and most effective when she is regularly working within her ZPD. In other words, children's learning is maximised when they are regularly working at the upper level of their competence. To enable this to happen, staff need to ensure that children's learning experiences and their learning environment challenge them to do and think beyond what they can currently do unaided by others. This involves staff encouraging children to try new tasks and skills, use equipment in novel ways, and it requires that staff be close by to adjust their level of support accordingly. As Berk and Winsler (1995, p. 41) stated, this means staff need to assist children less as their level of competence increases.

Once a child is able to verbalise his thoughts, staff can judge if a task is within a child's ZPD by listening to the child's private speech. Private speech is the chatting children do with themselves when working on a task. Private speech generally happens when a task is challenging enough for a child to need to talk his way through it. If a child is using clear, task-related private speech then it is likely that the task being attempted is within the child's ZPD (Berk and Winsler 1995).

Promoting self-regulation

When children self-regulate they are in control of their own learning. In successful scaffolding, staff are actively involved in promoting this via the distancing techniques they use. In low-level distancing, staff pose questions and comment on the immediate problem at hand. In medium-level distancing, staff compare and contrast what is happening currently. In high-level distancing, staff encourage children to think hypothetically about what might happen in a particular task or situation (Berk and Winsler 1995).

To decide how much assistance to offer children during play with each other Berk and Winsler (1995) suggested that staff ask themselves what they have seen children do before, how much help children need to successfully achieve their goals and what staff–child interactions will keep the children focused on each other.

> The children in Grade 1 are cooking Easter buns. They have written out the recipe, shopped for the ingredients and are now in the process of mixing the dough. Jo, their teacher, leaves them alone to do this because she knows from previous cooking sessions that they are capable. Once mixed, the dough must be kneaded for ten minutes. Jo knows that the children have little experience of kneading or of timing their work. She stays near where they are working and occasionally comments on what they are doing to keep them focused on their task with each other. She is also watching for the time when they will need assistance with kneading the dough and when they may need suggestions about how best to time this process.

One child scaffolds another as she learns a new skill.

In summary, scaffolding involves staff using a variety of verbal and non-verbal general teaching techniques to identify children's current levels of competence in specific developmental domains and to challenge the children to move beyond their original level of competence.

When and why?

The staff's aim when scaffolding is to move children to a point where they can do something without help from a more competent adult or peer (Meadows and Cashdan 1988). Hence, scaffolding is a relevant teaching technique to use whenever staff want to extend children's current level of understanding and skill in any area of development. It is particularly pertinent when staff want to lead development rather than allow children to discover something for or by themselves.

Klaus has chosen to lead the children's physical co-ordination skills as he feels that the older preschool children in his group are ready for some new physical skill challenges:

> Klaus is keen to teach the children to do somersaults. He guides them by verbal instruction and physical prompting. He also demonstrates the different steps involved in doing somersaults as each child attempts them.

Scaffolding is, therefore, a teaching technique that is highly interventionist in children's learning.

Goal relevance

According to Burns-Hoffman (1993), verbal scaffolding can be used to enhance children's factual knowledge about the world. Such factual knowledge includes children's claims and questions about what things are, their key attributes, how things work and how they are related. Verbal scaffolding in these instances can have the following aims and involve the following processes:

Teaching aim	Scaffolding process
Shaping a child's understandings.	Giving verbal feedback which affirms, negates, recasts, models or hints at what has been said or should be said to be accurate.
Reinforcing a child's proposition.	Restating or expanding what the child has said.
Maintaining joint attention and involvement between child and adult.	Requesting clarification of what the child has said, reflecting on what has been said or done, or by asking the child questions.
Linking thoughts and actions through using language.	Commenting on the present, on what the child or the adult remembers about the situation, or on what the adult thinks about what is happening, and comparing and contrasting thoughts and actions.
Extending understandings beyond the current situation.	Questioning through closed and open questions, modelling new understandings, expanding what is said by the child, talking about the implications of what is said, comparing and contrasting thoughts and actions.

Fleer (1996) described three case studies in which teachers used scaffolding with preschool and school-age children to develop their ability to think technologically about the space in which they were learning and living. For example, one teacher set up the play area as an architect's studio and the children used this space to investigate what architects do and how to build. The relationship between scaffolding and the development of technological thinking involved:

➲ the provision by the adult of a meaningful context in which children could solve technological problems and develop an extensive technological vocabulary through conversation with adults and each other
➲ the encouragement by the adult of children to orally report, evaluate and, hence, learn to reflect on what had happened as they solved their technological problems.

The emphasis within Vygotsky's work on the relationship between thought and language means that scaffolding is a particularly pertinent technique to use when extending children's cognitive and linguistic competencies. Recent research (for example, Berk and Spuhl 1995) suggested that scaffolding can stimulate children to chat to themselves as they work on problems or play. Vygotsky called this their 'private speech' (Berk and Winsler 1995). Private speech contributes to children's ability to solve problems. When children talk to themselves during a task, they are more able to solve problems related to it than when they don't (Berk and Winsler 1995). Scaffolding can also be used to build children's literacy skills. Boyd Ingram (2000) described a literacy program in a home-based child care setting in which the carer scaffolded children's literacy learning by reading to the children and allowing them to complete words that were missing.

Developmental considerations

The existence of inter-subjectivity between adults and young babies is evident in their ability to finely tune themselves to each other through such activities as jointly gazing at the same objects (Seifert 1993). By the second year of life, inter-subjectivity is possible in relation to play, language and problem-solving skills (Berk 1994a). As Pelligrini and Boyd (1993, p. 110) reported:

> Infants, it seems, can attend to those parental suggestions relevant to tasks that they are in the process of mastering and ignore comments relevant to skills already mastered or beyond their capabilities.

This suggests that staff can scaffold with young babies and toddlers by presenting them with objects and experiences that challenge them. Good scaffolding with babies involves the same five factors as mentioned earlier. However, as the following discussion illustrates, the process will be of a shorter duration, maybe only a few minutes, and will be focused on less complex 'problems' than with other children:

- ⟫ Joint problem-solving—find a problem that interests you and the baby. For example, 'How can a particular toy be taken apart?'; 'Where do the pictures go when the book is closed?'; 'Where does the sound come from when you drop the keys on the floor?'.
- ⟫ Inter-subjectivity—establish joint interest by taking note of a child's reactions. Are you both looking and listening for the same thing or is the baby interested in something else?
- ⟫ Warmth and responsiveness—establishing a positive relationship is as important to babies' learning as it is to that of older children. Pelligrini and Boyd (1993) argued that secure attachment to the adult involved in scaffolding a baby's learning is an important precursor to successful scaffolding. This is because secure attachment is an important factor in infants' disposition to explore and gather information about their environment.
- ⟫ Keeping the child in the ZPD—do you know the child's current level of development in various developmental domains? Staff need to know this in order to challenge baby beyond what is known or understood. Simple scaffolding can occur when staff have this knowledge.

> April is twelve months old, she is attempting to climb up the steps to the slide. Dominic, her carer, comes over and holds her hand so that she won't over balance.

- ⟫ Promoting self-regulation—staff can do this once a baby can successfully drop the keys on the floor and anticipate the sound they will make. Babies will show that they can do this by being attentive to the floor and showing delight when the sound happens. Staff can then watch for the child's desire to continue with this or test out new understandings. Take the cue from the child. Do they want you to make the sound? Do they want to try something else out with the keys? Are they checking your reaction to the noise the keys make when they fall?

Infants and toddlers can also benefit from the support and guidance of more competent peers. Staff can scaffold infants' and toddlers' growing language and cognitive abilities through providing opportunities for imaginative play in mixed-age groupings. Older children add new scripts to toddlers' imaginative play and through directing the play they extend the range of materials used (Arthur et al. 1996). Grouping children to enable older children to scaffold younger children's learning can be a powerful technique because children close to each others' developmental stage are '. . . able to use more appropriate concepts, language and communications . . .' (Arthur et al. 1996, p. 169) than those used by adults.

Adding novel and surprising items to the imaginative play of toddlers is another important way in which adults can challenge children to move to their ZPD during socio-symbolic play. Studies have also shown that the acquisition of syntax and vocabulary in the first two years of life is facilitated through the use of scaffolding (Bowman et al. 2001).

Scaffolding is also a useful technique for developing older children's skills as written language users. Staff–child discussions about the processes and outcomes of children's efforts at writing can be used to scaffold these skills. It seems that when staff ask children questions about how they write, and comment to children about their own writing processes, children begin to internalise these questions and comments (Hass Dyson and Genishi 1993; Bowman et al. 2001). As children internalise staff questions and comments about writing processes, they begin to use these questions and comments to reflect on these processes. This reflection helps the children become more competent in using written language.

Scaffolding can also be used with older children to support friendship building in classrooms where there are children with disabilities. Specifically, teachers can create a structured environment in which they scaffold children's friendship building skills such as joining in group activities, negotiating roles in play, exchanging ideas, offering to help each other and sharing (McCay and Keyes 2001/02).

As more competent peers can act as effective scaffolders of learning for children of any age, it is important to group children to allow opportunities for peer scaffolding to occur (Fimreite et al. 1999; Bowman et al. 2001) (see Chapter 9 for further discussion of this point).

EQUITY CONSIDERATIONS

'Race' and culture

Research on scaffolding is primarily limited to children in Western industrialised countries and it often ignores the influence of culture on scaffolding techniques:

> This approach implies a 'deficit model' assumption in which Western middle class mother–child interactions are the ideal norm and any variations are aberrations that produce deficits. (Kermani and Brenner 2000, p. 31).

There is now some research emerging that is beginning to explore how culture and teaching techniques interact. For instance, research exploring the similarities and differences in how mothers of preschool children from an Anglo-American background and from an Iranian immigrant background scaffolded children's learning suggested minimal cross-cultural differences in their scaffolding strategies in relation to their sensitivity to children's competence. The researchers found that each group of mothers scaffolded children's learning by adapting their interactions with children to the demands of the task and the competence of the child. However, Iranian mothers were often more directive in their teaching than the Anglo-American mothers when specific goals had to be achieved (Kermani and Brenner 2000).

Given the lack of culturally specific work on scaffolding it is important to think carefully about cross-cultural use of scaffolding and to remember that different cultural groups may scaffold children's learning in different ways.

There is some evidence that scaffolding can be useful in promoting co-operative play between children in multicultural settings (Doolittle 1995).

Scaffolding can also be used to promote anti-discriminatory 'racial' attitudes through adapting the general process of scaffolding to this work:

Teaching aim	Scaffolding process
To increase children's vocabulary for talking about different hair texture.	Activity in which children are pretending to be hairdressers. They are brushing the hair of dolls that represent children from a variety of 'racial' backgrounds.
Shaping a child's understandings of hair texture. Give children words for different hair texture: silky, springy, smooth, flat, crinkly, bristly, spiky.	Giving verbal feedback as children comment on the hair texture which affirms, negates, recasts, models or hints at what has been said or should be said to be accurate.
Reinforcing a child's proposition that the hair they are brushing is hard to brush because it is very springy.	Restating or expanding what the child has said. For example, 'Yes, I can see that it's hard to brush the doll's lovely curly hair because it's so springy'.
Maintaining joint attention and involvement between child and adult about the different hair textures the child is experiencing and the implements he or she is using to care for the doll's hair.	Requesting clarification of what the child has said, reflecting on what has been said or done or asking the child questions. For example, 'Do you think that it might be easier to care for the doll's springy hair using an "Afro"-comb?'.
Linking thoughts and actions by using language to describe them. As the child puzzles over how to tie long, straight, slippery hair into a pony-tail, staff can comment on how the child is attempting the task and describe the sequence of actions.	Commenting on the present, on what the child or the adult remembers about the situation, or on what the adult thinks about what is happening and comparing and contrasting thoughts and actions. For example, 'It's hard to make a pony-tail when the doll's hair is so shiny and slippery. Asking Patrick to open the scrunchy for you while you hold the hair together seems to have worked.'
Extending understandings beyond the current situation. Staff can talk with the children about scientific explanations for differences in hair texture, such as the role of hair shape in determining hair texture and the role of melanin in determining hair colour. Children can learn that hairs grow up from the skin and melanocytes (the cells that produce melanin) in the root of the hair produce more or less melanin, making the hair darker or lighter. Carotene helps give red hair its redness.	Questioning using closed and open questions, modelling new understandings, expanding what is said by the child, talking about the implications of what is said, and comparing and contrasting thoughts and actions. For example, staff can encourage children to make a chart of the differences in hair colour they have in their group. They can talk about whose hair has lots of melanin and whose hair has less melanin.

Gender

We have been unable to find any published research that specifically examines the gender implications of scaffolding as a teaching technique. However, general research about gender relations in early childhood settings offers some pointers as to how gender might influence some parts of the process of scaffolding in mixed-gender groups of children:

- Joint problem-solving—finding a problem that interests adults and the children is the beginning part of scaffolding. It is important that staff monitor which children are taking the lead in defining problems to be investigated and ensuring that there is an opportunity for both boys and girls to lead such decisions.
- Inter-subjectivity—establishing joint interest in and understandings of the problem offers the potential for the more vocal or assertive children in the group to establish their meanings and interest as paramount. If there are more boisterous boys in the group this could lead to many of the girls losing interest in the task at hand. It is important that staff monitor the gender implications of any children who leave such group work.
- Promoting self-regulation—in learning to take the cue about what has been learned from the children it is important to check once again who is taking the lead. What room has there been for boys and girls to self-regulate?

Good scaffolding begins with a shared problem that needs solving. There are many areas of gender relationships between children that offer fruitful ground for problem-solving between children and teachers. Think of the often-discussed problem of boys and girls not playing together or defining particular learning areas as 'no-go' areas for the 'other' gender. This could include:

- the boys always rushing for the bicycles and the girls missing out
- the boys being bored with playing dad whenever they go into the home corner with the girls
- the boys and the girls laughing at one of the boys who loves dressing in pink
- one of the girls being upset because none of the girls will play superhero games with her
- the boys and girls always wanting to sit apart at snack time.

The emphasis in scaffolding is not for the adult to tell the children how to solve the problem (for example, by establishing girls-only days in the block area), but to build on children's interests to help them solve the problem for themselves. What do the girls want to do about the fact that the boys won't let them in the block area? What do the boys want to do about the fact that the girls won't let them play in the sandpit? The following conversation provides some flavour about how this might happen. It is an adaptation of a teacher–child discourse reported in Berk and Winsler (1995).

> Problem: A group of four-year-old girls has just talked to an early childhood staff member about the fact that the boys have barricaded the block corner and said that they don't want the girls playing in it. The girls are cross and want the adult to do something about it. The adult is also concerned.
>
> Adult: 'I can see that you want to play with the blocks and that you are cross about what the boys have done. I am upset too. What would you like to do about it?'
>
> Sally: 'You tell them that they can't do it.'
>
> Adult: 'I'd like you to think about what we could do together.'

> Sally: 'Too hard.'
>
> Adult: 'Well, how about we talk about some different things we could do. I could tell the boys to leave but I'm not sure they would be happy. Is there anything else we could do with all of us helping?'
>
> Mei Thu: 'We [pointing to the girls] could tell them?'
>
> Adult: 'How could you tell them?'
>
> Sally: 'We could all tell them together, you [to the adult] could help?'
>
> Adult: 'I could be with you when you tell the boys but you could do the talking. Would you all like to talk at the same time? Would that mean you were telling them together?'
>
> Clara: 'We could sing all at once, that would be together.'
>
> Adult: 'What do you think? Do you want to try?'
>
> Girls in unison: 'Yeah, let's try.'
>
> Adult: 'What would you want to tell them in your song?'

The conversation continues until the children and the adult have a song worked out. They then try out their technique and reflect on what happens. The cycle of learning starts again at this point with the girls having learned to tell the boys how they feel without total reliance on the adult. The aim would be to move them to a point in their relationships with the boys that they felt able to try out different ways of telling them how they felt. This process could be used to build fairer gender relations between the children in many areas of daily life.

Disability and additional needs

The development of competence and self-regulation of learning is just as important for children with disabilities as it is for children without them. However, McCollom and Blair (1994) caution that scaffolding is likely to be a more complex and difficult process with many children with disabilities. One of the main reasons given for this is that establishing mutuality with some children with disabilities (inter-subjectivity) and assuming that children can be the major initiators in their own learning may be less appropriate in some instances. As they explained:

> For children who may initiate interactions less frequently, such as those with Down's Syndrome or visual impairment, the adult's role may require more aggressive recruitment . . . Thus, for the child with a disability, the appropriate balance of support and challenge may look quite different from that which is appropriate to a child who frequently initiates and independently pursues encounters with object or events in his environment (McCollom and Blair 1994, pp. 98–9).

However, this does not mean that scaffolding is inappropriate to use with children with disabilities. For instance, research on use by teachers of different forms of scaffolding strategies with seven-year-old children with Down's syndrome shows that the children were more responsive to strategies that involved the use of gestures than they were to those using words (Wang et al. 2001).

In promoting positive attitudes to children with disabilities, scaffolding offers an interesting way forward. The adult can act as a strong lead in teaching children without disabilities how best to interact with children with disabilities. The Burns-Hoffman (1993) framework for using verbal scaffolding (see above) to enhance children's factual knowledge of the world could provide a guide to this. In particular, it is important that staff take a lead in scaffolding friendship building skills with all children in a group to help build an inclusive climate within the group (McCay and Keyes 2001/02).

REFLECTING ON SCAFFOLDING TECHNIQUES

1 How would you define scaffolding?

2 What is the relationship between scaffolding and Vygotsky's idea of the ZPD?

3 What are the key factors that contribute to good scaffolding by adults concerned with children's learning?

4 What is the relationship between general teaching techniques such as questioning and scaffolding?

5 Identify five general teaching techniques you will need to be familiar with in order to practise scaffolding with children.

6 Clements and Nastasi (1993) argued that computers provide an important scaffolding tool for early childhood staff. They can allow children to perform a variety tasks that they are unable to perform by themselves. What do you see as the pros and cons of using computers as a scaffolding tool in early childhood settings? In what ways could computers achieve the requirement for good scaffolding outlined by Berk and Winsler (1995)? What, if any of these factors, are not met by computers?

7 Read the following conversation between a two-year-old child and her mother. How is the mother scaffolding Melinda's learning? What else might she have said or done to scaffold Melinda's learning on this occasion?

> McDonald's is the family's favourite restaurant.
>
> Mother: 'You're going to McDonald's.'
>
> Melinda: 'Yeah!'
>
> Mother: 'Is Andrew the cook?' (Andrew is a four-year-old friend who is playing with Melinda's sister.)
>
> Melinda: 'Yep . . . My cook.'
>
> Mother: 'You're the cook? You can cook with your dishes, right? Do you have some pots and pans?'
>
> (Extract based on Berk and Winsler 1995, p. 74.)

IMPROVING TEACHING IN PRACTICE

1 Identify a child you could practise your scaffolding techniques with. Observe the child and identify a problem that you could work together to solve. Plan at least three occasions in which you work closely on this problem. Implement and record these sessions.

2 After each session evaluate your own scaffolding skills by reviewing the extent to which you were able to:

- ➲ jointly problem-solve with the child
- ➲ achieve inter-subjectivity between yourself and the child
- ➲ establish warmth and responsiveness in your relationship with the child
- ➲ keep the child in her ZPD
- ➲ promote the child's self-regulation of the problem-solving.

3 What additional skills and knowledge do you need to consolidate and improve your scaffolding skills?

4 How and how well did you take account of the following considerations when scaffolding?
- ➡ developmental
- ➡ cultural
- ➡ gender
- ➡ disability and additional needs.

Further reading and resources

Berk, L. 1994, *Child Development*, 3rd edn, Boston, Allyn and Bacon [refer to pp. 254–61].

Berk, L. and Winsler, A. 1995, *Scaffolding Children's Learning: Vygotsky and Early Childhood Education*, Washington DC, National Association for the Education of Young Children.

Bodrova, E. and Leong, D. 1996, *Tools of the Mind: The Vygotskian Approach to Early Childhood Education*, Englewood Cliffs, New Jersey, Merrill.

Fleer, M. 1992, 'Identifying teacher–child interaction which scaffolds scientific thinking in young children', *Science Education*, 76(4), pp. 373–97.

——1996, 'Talking technologically in preschool and school: three case examples', *Australian Journal of Early Childhood*, 21(2), pp. 1–6.

Video

Centre-Based Infant Care: Session 1, Open Training and Education Network, TAFE, NSW, Australia 1992.

Communicating with Young Children: Guidelines for Good Practice, Lady Gowrie Children's Centre, Melbourne, Australia, 1993.

Play: A Vygotskian Approach, Davidson Films Inc., 231 E. Street, Davis, California, 1996.

Scaffolding: self regulated learning in the primary grades, Davidson Films, 1996. Distributed by Educational Media Australia.

References

Arthur, L., Beecher, B., Dockett, S., Farmer, S. and Death, E. 1996, *Programming and Planning in Early Childhood Settings*, second edn, Sydney, Harcourt Brace and Company.

Berk, L. 1994a, *Child Development*, third edn, Boston, Allyn and Bacon.

——1994b, Vygotsky's theory: the importance of make-believe play', *Young Children*, 50(5), pp. 30–9.

Berk, L. and Spuhl, S. 1995, 'Maternal interaction, private speech and task performance in preschool children', *Early Childhood Research Quarterly*, 10, pp. 145–69.

Berk, L. and Winsler, A. 1995, *Scaffolding Children's Learning: Vygotsky and Early Childhood Education*, Washington DC, National Association for the Education of Young Children.

Bowman, B., Donovan, M. and Burns, S. 2001, *Eager to Learn: Educating Our Preschoolers*, Washington DC, National Academy Press.

Boyd Ingram, H. 2000, 'Literacy contexts in family day care', *Australian Journal of Early Childhood*, 25(3), pp. 19–24.

Burns-Hoffman, R. 1993, 'Scaffolding children's informal expository discourse skills', in *Biennial Meeting of the Society for Research in Child Development*, ED362292, New Orleans, LA, ERIC.

Clements, D. and Nastasi, B. 1993, 'Electronic media and early childhood education', in B. Spodek, ed., *Handbook of Research on Early Childhood Education* (pp. 251–75), New York, Macmillan Publishing Company.

Doolittle, P. 1995, Understanding cooperative learning through Vygotsky's Zone of Proximal Development, Paper presented to the *Lilly National Conference on Excellence in College Teaching*, Columbia, SC. ED36055.

Edwards, A. and Knight, P. 1994, *Effective Early Years Education: Teaching Young Children*, Milton Keynes, Open University Press.

Fleer, M. 1996, 'Talking technologically in preschool and school: three case examples', *Australian Journal of Early Childhood*, 21(2), pp. 1–6.

Fimreite, H., Flem, A. and Gudmundsdottir, S. 1999, 'Peer interactions among preschool children in play', Paper presented at the *8th European Conference for Research on Learning and Instruction*, August 24–28, Goteborg, Sweden.

Hass Dyson, A. and Genishi, C. 1993, 'Visions of children as language users: language and language education in early childhood', in B. Spodek, ed., *Handbook of Research on the Education of Young Children* (pp. 122–36), New York, Macmillan Publishing Company.

Jones, E. and Reynolds, G. 1992, *The Play's the Thing: Teachers' Roles in Children's Play*, New York, Teachers' College Press.

Kermani, H. and Brenner, M. 2000, 'Maternal scaffolding in the child's Zone of Proximal Development across tasks: cross-cultural perspectives', *Journal of Research in Childhood Education*, 15(1), pp. 30–52.

Madsen, J. and Gudmundsdottir, S. 2000, 'Scaffolding children's learning in the Zone of Proximal Development: a classroom study', Paper presented at the *Annual Meeting of the European Conference on Educational Research*, September 19–21, Norway.

McCay, L. and Keyes, D. 2001/02, 'Developing social competence in the inclusive primary classroom', *Childhood Education*, 78(2), pp. 70–8.

McCollum, J. and Blair, H. 1994, 'Research in parent–child interaction: guidance to developmentally appropriate practice for young children with disabilities', in B. Mallory and R. New, eds, *Diversity and Developmentally Appropriate Practices: Challenges for Early Childhood Education* (pp. 84–106), New York, Teachers' College Press.

Meadows, S. and Cashdan, A. 1988, *Helping Children Learn: Contributions to a Cognitive Curriculum*, London, David Fulton Publishers.

Moyles, J. 1989, *Just Playing: The Role and Status of Play in Early Childhood Education*, Milton Keynes, Open University Press.

NAEYC 1991, 'Guidelines for appropriate curriculum content and assessment in programs serving children ages 3 through 8. Position statement of the NAEYC and the National Association of Early Childhood Specialists in State Departments of Education', *Young Children*, 46(3), pp. 21–8.

Pelligrini, A. and Boyd, B. 1993, 'The role of play in early childhood development and education: issues in definition and function', in B. Spodek, ed., *Handbook of Research on the Education of Young Children* (pp. 105–121), New York, Macmillan Publishing Company.

Read, K., Gardner, P. and Mahler, B. 1993, *Early Childhood Programs: Human Relationships and Learning*, ninth edn, Forth Worth, TX, Holt, Rinehart and Winston Inc.

Seifert, K. 1993, 'Cognitive development and early childhood education', in B. Spodek, ed, *Handbook of Research on the Education of Young Children* (pp. 9–23), New York, Macmillan Publishing Company.

Smith, A. 1996, 'Quality programs that care and educate', *Childhood Education*, 72(6), pp. 330–5.

Vygotsky, L. 1932, *Thought and Language*, Massachusetts, MIT Press.

Wang, X., Bernas, R. and Eberhard, P. 2001, 'Effects of teachers' verbal and non-verbal scaffolding on everyday classroom performances of students with Down's Syndrome', *International Journal of Early Years Education*, Vol 9(1) pp. 71–80.

Wilkes, G. (ed.) 1979, *Collins Dictionary of the English Language*, Middlesex, Penguin Books.

Chapter 28
Task analysis

Task analysis: to analyse: to break down into component features.

(Collins Dictionary of the English Language, p. 50)

If teachers are to plan for each child on the basis of his or her needs they must . . . understand task analysis, how to break a task down into its component parts and present the steps in an orderly sequence.

(Allen 1982, p. 3)

The chief purpose of task analysis is to help the teacher determine the optimum learning conditions for the various tasks the student must learn to perform.

(De Cecco 1968, p. 45)

WHAT?

A task is a piece of work that needs to be carried out to achieve something. A task may refer to a small job such as picking up a piece of paper or a large job such as building a house. Analysis is the detailed study of the key elements or processes in something or someone. Task analysis is the detailed study of the key elements or processes involved in a particular piece of work that needs to be done. As a teaching technique, task analysis is used to help children understand the key steps involved in a particular task they are about to tackle. For example, to help them understand the key steps involved in tying shoelaces. Task analysis may be used to help children learn skills and knowledge. It allows children to have early success in learning certain things.

HOW?

There are two main dimensions to task analysis. The first dimension involves analysing the child's abilities in relation to a given task. Staff need to ask: 'What can the child do currently?'; 'What does the child need to learn to successfully complete the task?'. The second dimension involves analysing the task itself. Staff need to ask: 'What are the steps involved in this task and how are they sequenced?'. The following points summarise the key steps involved in task analysis and suggest a sequence in looking at these steps:

- ➲ Identify the task that you wish a child to learn.
- ➲ Identify the sub-steps involved in the task.
- ➲ Sequence the key steps in a logical way.

An example:

> Snack time. Key steps:
> Child to get plate and mug from trolley.
> Take plate and mug to table.
> Sit at table.
> Pour drink.
> Select fruit or other snack and put on plate.
> Eat and drink.
> Take empty plate and mug to trolley.

- ➲ Sequence the key steps developmentally to minimise the difficulty of successfully learning and completing the task.
- ➲ Check what the child can currently do and not do in relation to the task.
- ➲ Present the steps to the child through direct instruction.
- ➲ Teach the child one step at a time until it is successfully mastered.
- ➲ Offer extra guidance if the child has difficulty with the task. This guidance could involve child or adult modelling and verbal guidance.
- ➲ Restructure the task, if necessary, to assist with successful completion. (Based on Lerner et al. 1987; Cole and Chan 1990; Petriwskyj 1992)

Some of the more lengthy and complex tasks that a child may need to or may wish to learn can be taught through backward chaining (Lerner et al. 1987). In backward chaining, staff complete each of the steps involved for the child until the last step in the task is reached. The child completes the last step. When the child has learned the last step the child can then be taught the second-last step. The teaching of the steps continues 'backwards' until the skill or knowledge has been learned. To work successfully, backward chaining should be accompanied by direct positive reinforcement as each step in the chain is learned.

An example:

> Tying a shoelace. Steps:
> Hold one lace in each hand.
> Cross one lace over the other.
> Tie a granny knot.
> Form a bow with each lace.
> Knot bows.
> Pull tight.

In backward chaining, the child would be taught each of the steps separately and then taught to put the steps together backwards. The teacher would perform all of the steps for the child except the last one (pull tight). The child would then be encouraged to carry out the last, the second-last step and so forth until all of the steps have been achieved.

THEORETICAL BACKGROUND

TASK ANALYSIS AND GAGNE'S CLASSES OF BEHAVIOUR

Robert Mills Gagne (1916–) graduated with a major in psychology from Yale University in 1937. From that time he held various research and academic posts as a psychologist, including eight years with the US Air Force, a professorship in psychology at Princeton University and a professorship in education psychology at the University of California. He retired in 1992 (Morgan 1992).

Gagne's best known book *The Conditions of Learning* has been translated into most major languages. In this book, Gagne outlined a detailed range of behaviours that can be observed as people learn. These behaviours can be used to help analyse the different levels of learning that children may engage in. The behaviours described by Gagne are as follows.

1. Signal learning—refers to the learning that occurs when a person produces a particular behaviour when a particular signal is produced.
2. Stimulus response learning—refers to the learning that occurs when a person learns to reproduce a clear and specific physical response to a specific stimulus.
3. Chaining—refers to the learning that occurs when a person links two or more steps that have been learned via stimulus response learning to perform a more complex task.
4. Verbal association—refers to the learning that occurs when a person can associate several words with the one object and can link them in a phrase or a sentence.
5. Multiple discrimination—refers to the learning that occurs when a person is able to accurately distinguish what makes a specific object different from others that are similar to it. For example, what makes one car a station wagon and another a 4-wheel drive? The person can discriminate between the multiple characteristics of a car (it has tyres, four wheels etc.) and isolate those that discriminate one type of car from another.
6. Concept learning—refers to the learning that occurs when a person uses abstract properties of objects (for example, shape, size or position) to distinguish between things, people and events.
7. Principle learning—refers to when a person learns how to use several concepts to develop principles about how things work.
8. Problem-solving—refers to the learning that occurs when a person uses principles to achieve a particular goal. It always involves internal thinking processes (based on De Cecco 1968).

Gagne's work in *The Conditions of Learning* emphasised the hierarchical nature of learning. He stressed that more complex learning behaviours such as problem-solving built from simple learning behaviours such as chaining. Gagne's particular understanding of how learning behaviours were organised hierarchically underpins the sequencing of learning in task analysis. His theory details nine instructional events and corresponding cognitive processes that can be used to teach a task or concept:

1. gain the learner's attention (reception)
2. inform learners of the objective of the experience (expectancy)
3. stimulate recall of prior learning (retrieval)
4. present the stimulus for the learning (selective perception)
5. provide learning guidance by showing how to complete the task or experience (semantic encoding)

6   elicit performance by asking the learner to undertake specific tasks (responding)

7   provide feedback on the extent to which the learner has performed the task or understood it correctly (reinforcement)

8   assess the learner's performance and give them feedback on their level of performance (retrieval)

9   enhance retention and transfer by introducing material and experiences that support and reinforce the learning (generalisation) (Gagne et al. 1992).

WHEN AND WHY?

Goal relevance

Task analysis can be usefully employed by staff to assist children's learning across all developmental domains. Research has shown it to be useful in the following areas:

- building children's social interaction skills such as group entry skills and responding appropriately to peers (Murdock 1993)
- improving children's self-care ability in relation to tasks such as dressing, putting on shoes etc. (Petriwskyj 1992)
- developing children's skills such as pasting and stapling during construction activities (Petriwskyj 1992)
- improving children's physical skills such as climbing and balancing (Allen 1982)
- teaching children basic first aid skills (Marchan et al. 1991).

Developmental considerations

Children's ability to successfully learn complex tasks is related to their developmental skills and abilities. It is, therefore, important to ensure that the skills children are being encouraged to learn are appropriate to their developmental abilities and skills. Observing the children closely will provide information about the developmental abilities they have currently and what new skills they may be interested in acquiring. Remember the key questions are: 'What can the child do now?'; 'What do I want them to do?'; 'What are the steps involved in getting her to the desired point?'.

Paula is 14 months old. She is keen to do everything by herself. Tiziana, her caregiver, wants to help Paula achieve maximum independence at this stage of life. Tiziana task analyses 'eating with a spoon' and teaches this to Paula with backwards chaining — in that way Paula has success every time she feeds herself. Very soon she is able to eat with a spoon by herself. Both Paula and Tiziana are pleased with the results.

Patrick is learning to crawl, he has just begun to push himself on to his knees and he rocks back and forth, then collapses again. His caregiver watches his struggle and through task analysis of creeping, she is able to assist him to propel himself forwards, moving each leg in turn.

Sophie is sewing around a shape that she has cut out of material. She wants to add sequins to her creation. She finds it difficult to hold the sequin in one hand and to fasten it with the thread to the material. Her teacher analyses what Sophie is doing and helps her to hold the sequin in one hand as she manoeuvres the thread in the other.

Task analysis can also be useful with children in the early years of schooling as they learn new games and new skills. Staff may find it helpful to teach them the basic steps involved in a new game or in an activity in which they will be developing new skills. Bohning and Williams (1996/97) discuss how such instruction in the steps involved in quilting and using tangrams helped the children feel confident in using the materials. They were, with task analysis, able to quickly move to a point where they could use and create very complex mathematical shapes.

EQUITY CONSIDERATIONS

'Race' and culture

Learning about similarities and differences between people's cultures and learning to recognise stereotypes is a complex task. Task analysis can be used by staff to help sequence this learning into small, logical steps for the children. For example, teaching children about stereotypical images of different cultural and racial groups involves them learning that:

- pictures can make people feel happy or sad
- pictures can be fair or unfair
- pictures can give us true or false images of people
- pictures that show unfair and false images of people can make them feel sad. These pictures are called stereotyped pictures.

York (1991) provides many ideas for how to introduce these ideas to children using pictures from magazines. The process can begin with children being asked to find pictures that make them feel happy or sad and pictures that might make other people feel happy or sad. From this base, children begin to learn that images carry important messages and can influence how we feel. Once this concept has been understood, staff can move to the next step of talking about pictures that are fair or unfair. In this process it will be important for staff to talk about why they think particular pictures are unfair and encourage children to do the same. For example, staff may say that a picture of an Asian person that shows him looking silly is unfair and talk about why before moving on from this point to other groups. By breaking down the process of learning about racial and cultural stereotypes into discrete steps, teachers with practical activities can help children learn abstract and complex concepts.

Gender

There are gender differences in the ease with which girls and boys learn particular physical, social and linguistic skills. For example, preschool girls sometimes take longer than preschool boys to learn to throw and catch balls, and the reverse is the case with sewing skills. There is strong evidence to suggest that these skill differences are due to different expectations of boys and girls rather than a genetic difference between the two sexes. Task analysis can be used to help children gain competence and confidence in skill areas that they might otherwise miss out on. For example, if staff want girls who lack ball-handling skills to gain these skills and boys who lack sewing skills to gain these skills, then breaking skills into smaller components and working on these in a logical, sequential way can assist.

Task analysis can also be used to challenge preschool children's gender stereotypes about what men and women, boys and girls can do. If children in the group believe only men can change tyres, be doctors etc. staff can analyse with the children the tasks involved in these jobs. Changing tyres might involve getting the spare tyre and the jack from the car boot, undoing the tyre bolts, jacking up the car etc. Children can think about what skills are needed and if a woman can do it. The children may think a woman is not strong enough to lift the tyre from the car boot. This can be countered with the idea that women lift groceries out of the car boot and whether a tyre would be any heavier . . . Such detailed analysis of tasks that children believe can only be done by one gender is a good way to help them rethink their ideas.

Disability and additional needs

Task analysis has been widely used to help teach children with a variety of additional needs new skills. It is, therefore, an important teaching technique to help build the self-esteem of children with additional needs in the group through increasing their sense of competence and confidence. However, as much of this work is highly specific we will not focus on how to do this in this section. Books in the further reading list provide specialist information on skill building with children with a variety of additional needs.

Task analysis can be a positive support for teaching children in the group without specific disabilities how to assist and support those with them. Staff can observe what the children currently know about the specific needs of the child(ren) with a disability, think about what else they need to know and then sequence this into manageable steps. For example, if a child in the group (we will call Saul) has a communication disorder because his speech is impaired by a very husky voice, then Saul will need particular support and assistance from the other children to ensure that his needs and thoughts are understood. Children will need to learn to listen carefully when Saul speaks, to be particularly quiet when Saul is speaking, to have games with Saul that don't always involve talking and to let Saul have rests from speaking. Breaking each of these skills into smaller sub-skills and carefully planning experiences through which the children can learn them will help provide a strong supportive environment for Saul.

REFLECTING ON TASK ANALYSIS TECHNIQUES

1 What does research suggest are the keys to successfully using task analysis to optimise children's learning?
2 How would you define backward chaining?
3 When do you think task analysis should be used in your teaching?
4 Are there any times when you think that task analysis is inappropriate with young children?
5 Imagine you wanted to teach a toddler to pour her own drink at snack time. What are the sub-skills involved in this task? Would it be appropriate to teach a toddler these sub-skills? Why? Why not? Would backward chaining assist in teaching the toddler this task? How would this work?
6 Develop a plan for a learning experience for four- to five-year-old children in which you wanted to increase their balancing skills. How could you use task analysis as a teaching technique to do this?
7 Imagine you were working with a four-year-old child who was having difficulty completing a puzzle. How might task analysis help you help the child to learn skills for completing this and other puzzles? What sub-skills for completing puzzles could help you answer this question?
8 What do you see as the hardest part of improving your task analysis techniques?

IMPROVING TEACHING IN PRACTICE

1 Record (using a tape-recorder or written notes) a task analysis session with children during several half-hour teaching periods.

2 What is your current style of task analysis? Did you:

- ➔ decide on a specific task you wanted the children to learn?
- ➔ make a written or mental list of the sub-tasks involved?
- ➔ plan a logical sequence to introduce the sub-tasks to the children?
- ➔ take account of the children's current ability and developmental levels in planning the sub-task sequence?
- ➔ demonstrate the sub-tasks to the children one step at a time until each was successfully mastered?
- ➔ support the children's attempts at task mastery through using appropriate reinforcement and restructuring of the task when necessary?

3 How and how well did you take account of developmental and anti-bias considerations?
4 What are your areas of strength and weakness in using task analysis to promote children's learning?
5 How can you improve your task analysis techniques in practice?

Further reading

Allen, K. 1982, *The preschool program: adaptation to the individual child*, ERIC Document 015407.

Casey, K. 1994, *Teaching Children with Special Needs: An Australian Perspective*, Sydney, Social Science Press [refer to pp. 72–3].

Gagne, R., Briggs, L. and Wager, W. 1992, *Principles of Instructional Design* (fourth ed), Fort Worth, TX, HBJ College Publishers.

Lerner, J., Mardell-Czudnowski, C. and Goldenberg, D. 1987, *Special Education for the Early Childhood Years*, second edn, New Jersey, Prentice Hall [refer to pp. 140–2 and pp. 223–4].

Martella, R. and Marchand, A. 1991, 'Teaching elementary first-aid skills via interactive storytelling', *Exceptional Children*, Fall, pp. 30–3.

Websites—extending learning online

The following websites provide further information about Gagne and his work:
http://www.psy.pdx.edu/PsiCafe/KeyTheorists/Gagne.htm
http://www.ittheory.com/gagne1.htm

References

Allen, K. 1982, *The preschool program: adaptation to the individual child*, ERIC Document 015407.

Bohning, G. and Williams, R. 1996/97, 'Quilts and tangrams: linking literature and geometry', *Childhood Education*, 73(2), pp. 83–7.

Cole, P. and Chan, L. 1990, *Methods and Strategies for Special Education*, New Jersey, Prentice Hall Inc.

De Cecco, J. 1968, *The Psychology of Learning and Instruction: Educational Psychology*, New Jersey, Prentice Hall.

Gagne, R., Briggs, L. and Wager, W. 1992, *Principles of Instructional Design*, fourth edn, Fort Worth, TX, HBJ College Publishers.

Lerner, J., Mardell-Czudnowski, C. and Goldenberg, D. 1987, *Special Education for the Early Childhood Years*, second edn, New Jersey, Prentice Hall, pp. 140–2.

Marchand-Martella, N., Martella, R. and Marchand, A. 1991, 'Teaching elementary first-aid skills via interactive storytelling', *Exceptional Children*, Fall, pp. 30–3.

Morgan, R. 1992, 'Robert Mills Gagne', in D. Ely and B. Minor, eds, *Educational Media and Technology Yearbook 1992* (pp. 148–51), Englewood, Colorado, Libraries Unlimited Inc.

Murdock, A. 1993, 'Social interaction: developing skills of a child with disabilities in an integrated kindergarten setting', *Australian Journal of Early Childhood*, 18(3), pp. 17–25.

Petriwskyj, A. 1992, 'Integrating children with special needs into early childhood centres', *Australian Early Childhood Resource Booklets*, 3, pp. 1–16.

Wilkes, G. (ed.) 1979, *Collins Dictionary of the English Language*, Middlesex, Penguin Books.

York, S. 1991, *Roots and Wings: Affirming Culture in Early Childhood Programs*, Minnesota, Toys'n Things Press.

Part Four
Educational Philosophies, Goals and Teaching Techniques

Chapter 29

Building a strategic approach to teaching techniques

Strategic: of, relating to, or characteristic of strategy.

(*Collins Dictionary of the English Language*, p. 1437)

Strategy is the determination of basic long-term goals and objectives together with the adoption of courses of action and the allocation of resources for carrying out those goals.

(Pugh et al. 1983, p. 50)

. . . strategy is concerned with those decisions which determine the direction which an enterprise is taking. The formulation of strategy is thus a primary determinant of the character of an organization.

(Minkes 1987, p. 132)

STRATEGIES AND STRATEGIC DECISIONS

A strategy is a broad plan of action for achieving a goal. Strategic decisions are those in which people decide the general approach they will need to take to gain something they want. In other words, strategic decisions determine how a person will achieve their organisational goals.

Strategic decisions provide organisations with purpose and direction because they require the people within them to be clear about what they want to achieve (their goals) and how they might successfully achieve what they want (their general approach). To take a strategic approach to decision-making, people in organisations need to have several things in place. They need:

- ➔ a clear vision of what they want to do. Organisations often have different names for their vision. Some organisations talk of their mission statement, others their philosophy and others their organisational goals, objectives or purposes
- ➔ a general approach (or strategy) for putting their vision into practice. This involves deciding what is permissible or not (policies), and how people and resources will be organised to achieve the goals (resource management)
- ➔ a match between their vision and their general approach to making it a reality.

Therefore, when people in an organisation are being strategic they are being deliberate about what they want to do and how they will get there. They are being purposeful in making plans to ensure that their vision becomes a reality.

Not all organisations are strategic. Some organisations do not have a clear sense of what they want to do and how they will do it. Some organisations have a clear vision of their work but do not have a set of tactics they can use to make their vision a reality. These organisations tend to take decisions in an ad hoc rather than a strategic way. Ad hoc decision-making makes it harder to turn an organisational vision into a reality.

Strategies and strategic teaching

Applied to teaching and learning, strategic decisions are those in which staff decide the general approach they will use to help children learn. They then draw on this general approach to choose the specific teaching techniques that best reflect their educational vision.

Strategic teaching decisions in an early childhood setting give staff purpose and direction because they require staff to be clear about what they want to achieve with children (their educational vision) and how they might successfully achieve what they want (their educational approach or strategy). To take a strategic approach to teaching, staff need to have several things in place. They need:

- ➤ a clear educational vision
- ➤ a general approach (or strategy) for making their vision a reality
- ➤ a match between their vision, their general approach (or strategy) and their specific teaching techniques.

We shall now consider the first two points (the following section considers the third point in some detail).

A clear educational vision

EDUCATIONAL VISION

A statement about your broad, long-term educational goals for the children. Goals are based on your vision of the child as a learner and your vision of what it is valuable for children to learn.

A coherent educational vision embraces a vision of who the child is, how the child learns, what the child should learn and what the adult's role in children's learning should be. This vision is described in various ways, including a mission statement, an educational philosophy or educational goals, objectives or purposes. Staff generally name their vision according to their personal preference and/or their centre's preference.

Staff's vision of the child as learner, their role in the child's learning and their beliefs about what the child should be learning will be influenced by their personal and professional knowledge base and their value systems. Staff's knowledge and values will influence how they view:

- ➤ the role of the child's developmental achievements and challenges in learning
- ➤ the role of the individual child's cultural, personal and political characteristics in learning
- ➤ what is educationally, culturally, socially, morally, politically and ethically appropriate for young children to learn.

Developing an educational vision involves grappling with these issues in order to decide:

- what is to be learned by the child
- when it is to be learned
- how it is be learned (Katz 1995).

In addition, staff need to have some sense of how they will know when a child has learned what they believe she can and should learn. They therefore need to also ask: 'How will I know when the child has learned what is to be learned?'

Answering this question will result in clear goals about how staff can and should support the child as a learner.

A general approach (or strategy)

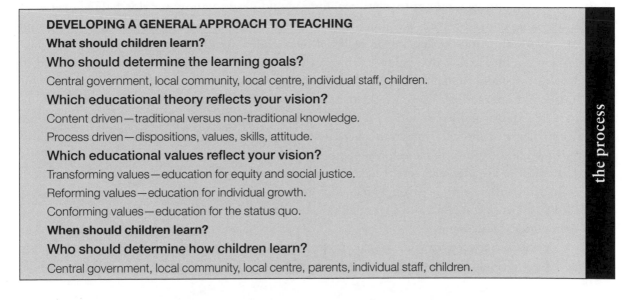

A GENERAL APPROACH TO TEACHING

A general or strategic approach to teaching is a broad description of how your vision will be made to happen which can guide your choices about:

- how you organise the learning environment
- which specific range of teaching techniques you use to support children's learning
- how you will evaluate children's learning.

definition

Making an educational vision a reality involves developing a general approach to teaching to ensure that:

- children learn what staff believe needs to learned
- children learn what is to be learned when it is appropriate to be learned
- children learn what is to be learned in the ways staff believe are appropriate
- staff can assess what has been learned and how they have assisted or not in that learning.

Staff can use the following questions to determine an overall approach to teaching that reflects their educational vision.

DEVELOPING A GENERAL APPROACH TO TEACHING

What should children learn?

Who should determine the learning goals?

Central government, local community, local centre, individual staff, children.

Which educational theory reflects your vision?

Content driven—traditional versus non-traditional knowledge.

Process driven—dispositions, values, skills, attitude.

Which educational values reflect your vision?

Transforming values—education for equity and social justice.

Reforming values—education for individual growth.

Conforming values—education for the status quo.

When should children learn?

Who should determine how children learn?

Central government, local community, local centre, parents, individual staff, children.

the process

Which educational theory reflects your vision?

Age driven—all children learn the same at a given age.

Developmentally driven—individual differences: what is learned when.

How do children learn?

Which learning theory reflects your vision?

Maturationist, behaviourist, interactionist, psychodynamic, constructivist.

Which general teaching strategy bests suits your vision?

Child-directed via free play and self-discovery.

Adult-directed via formal learning experiences and adult instruction.

Which general teaching environment best suits your vision?

Open-ended or closed-ended materials.

Highly structured or flexible use of time, people, materials and space.

How can children's learning be evaluated?

Who should evaluate children's learning?

Central government, local community, parents, local centre, individual staff, children.

Which general evaluation strategy bests suits your vision?

Highly structured observation or flexible individualised observation.

Highly structured standardised testing or flexible individualised assessment.

Answering these questions will enable staff to develop an overall approach to teaching young children that reflects their educational vision. This overall approach to teaching young children can then be used by staff to choose the specific teaching techniques that are in theoretical and practical harmony with their vision.

To illustrate: an early childhood practitioner who has a vision of the child as an active learner may decide that constructivist learning theory best suits their educational vision. Drawing on constructivist theory the practitioner would want to develop an overall approach to teaching young children in which there was a balance between adult-directed and child-directed learning. The teaching techniques that would be most in harmony with their theory of learning and general approach to teaching would need to allow for this balance between adult- and child-directed learning. The specialist teaching techniques of scaffolding and co-constructing and the general strategies of open-ended questioning, demonstration and suggestion could provide this balance. To use these techniques the practitioner would need to develop a schedule and an approach to positioning people that allowed lots of opportunities for staff–child interaction. There would also need to be an environment that allowed the child to actively explore and hence construct their own knowledge. This would require the practitioner to emphasise open-ended materials and to develop scheduling which allowed for long periods of time for child exploration and for in-depth staff–child interactions. As the practitioner believes that children are active in constructing their own meanings, the general approach he takes to evaluation will need to be strongly individualised and flexible. Teaching techniques that would allow him to evaluate a child's learning in a flexible way include documenting, listening and open-ended questioning.

A match between an educational vision and a general approach to teaching and learning increases the possibility that a vision may become a reality. The next part of the chapter shows how this match can work in theory and in practice. We will look at the theoretical match between the educational visions and teaching techniques underpinning five well-known approaches in early childhood education and care:

- The High/Scope Preschool Curriculum
- Montessori Education
- The Reggio Emilia Approach
- Rudolf Steiner and Waldorf Schooling
- Anti-Bias Curriculum.

MATCHING EDUCATIONAL VISIONS AND TEACHING TECHNIQUES

The High/Scope Preschool Curriculum

> . . . High/Scope curriculum . . . is an approach to education and not a specific curriculum. Thus, it is a method that helps organise the day, frames teacher–child relationships and interaction, encourages use of child development principles . . . (Morrison 1995, p. 149).

The High/Scope Preschool Curriculum (formerly known as the High/Scope Cognitively Orientated Curriculum) was first developed in 1962 by the staff at the High/Scope Educational Research Foundation based in Michigan, USA. The curriculum model is widely used within the United States and it has been the most widely used curriculum model to emerge from the Head Start program in the USA (Bowman et al. 2001). There is also growing international interest in the High/Scope Curriculum model with High/Scope programs being formally developed in fifteen other countries. These include the United Kingdom, the Netherlands, Singapore, Finland and Mexico (Weikart 1995/96).

OVERVIEW OF EDUCATIONAL VISION

High/Scope curriculum is strongly based on Piagetian theories of development and learning. The Piagetian base to the curriculum is evident in three major ways. First, the curriculum goals focus on the development of children's cognitive skills. Second, the cognitive skills that are prioritised (language, experiencing and representing, classification, seriation, number, spatial relations and time) directly reflect Piaget's understandings of cognition. Specifically the curriculum is designed to:

> . . . allow children to develop meaningful representational abilities and to see relationships between objects and events (Spodek and Saracho 1994, p. 106).

These cognitive skills are nurtured through key learning experiences in which children learn to be active learners; to use language; to represent experiences and ideas; to classify objects; and to use number, space and time concepts. These skills help children become problem-solvers and independent thinkers (Schweinhart and Hohmann 1992; Henniger 1999).

Third, the teaching techniques encouraged in High/Scope are based on Piaget's assumption that children are active learners who need direct personal interaction with the world to learn from it and that children need to reflect on this experience and to use their reflections to increase their understanding of the world about them. Hence, the philosophy of learning that underpins High/Scope is that children learn best when they have time to experience and explore their world for themselves and time to reflect on what they have learned from this. As such, children's learning can best be supported by allowing them to plan and implement and reflect on their concrete experiences of the world about them (Weikart and Schweinhart 1987).

TEACHING TECHNIQUES

In High/Scope curriculum, staff support children's active learning in several ways:

- Positioning equipment and materials: Staff select and arrange materials and experiences to encourage children's active exploration and reflection.
- Scheduling: Staff develop a daily schedule based on what is known as the 'Plan–Do–Review' cycle of learning. The schedule generally includes a planning time for children to decide who and what they will work with; a work time in which these plans can be implemented and represented in some way (for example, via a model, photograph, collage or story); a time to pack away; and a time to recall and reflect on the plans, experiences and representations of the day. This recall and reflection may occur in small and/or large group times. The aim is to create a schedule that allows children to initiate, plan, carry out, reflect on and discuss their experiences and ideas.
- Verbal interaction: Staff develop content around key learning experiences (refer above) that help children develop rational thought. To develop rational thought via the key learning experiences, staff need to be actively involved in open-ended questioning of the children, listening to the children's responses to these questions and problem-solving with them. Using these teaching strategies throughout each part of the 'Plan–Do–Review' learning cycle in each of the key learning experience areas, the teacher builds rational thought by helping the '. . . children learn to place things in categories, to rank things in order, [and] to predict consequences . . .' (Weikart and Schweinhart 1987, p. 253).

Sample plans of small group and large group experiences within a High/Scope preschool from Hohmann and Weikart (2002) show the following sequencing of learning for the children:

- Staff identify an idea or concept to explore with the children that originates from their interests—known as the originating idea—and this is what begins a 'Plan-Do-Review' sequence.
- Staff gather suitable learning materials that will allow children to physically explore the idea or concept.
- Staff identify potential key learning experiences for the children.
- Staff plan a way to begin the experience—samples offered by Hohmann and Weikart (2002) illustrate a strong use of staff questioning to begin the experience. For instance, in a sample small group plan in which staff wish to help clarify children's understandings of coconuts staff offer children a coconut and various materials with which to explore it, such as a hammer, and then begin with the question, 'What can you find out about your coconut?'
- Staff then allow children to explore the materials with staff listening and observing children's explorations.
- The experience ends with staff asking children to review what they have learnt and plan what they might do to extend their experiences. For instance, in the small group

experience in which coconuts were explored, it was suggested that staff end with the question, 'What could we do with these pieces tomorrow at work time?'. The aim is to motivate children 'to reach higher levels of understanding' (Henniger 1999, p. 64).

➋ The staff then plan how to extend the experience with the children on the following day.

Evaluation of children's learning focuses on staff observation in which they track children's learning by using the key learning experiences areas. Observational checklists which detail the developmental steps involved in progressing through each of the key learning experiences are used to record children's progress. These checklists are specific and detailed. For example, the number concepts observation checklist includes the following:

> The child compares continuous quantities in terms of more versus less (or fewer).
> The child judges that continuous quantities are the same . . .
> The child can recite the number series by rote from '1' to '3' (Weikart and Schweinhart 1987, p. 261).

A CD-ROM is available from the High/Scope Foundation (see end of chapter) which supports staff as they build their skills in tracking children's learning.

In summary, teachers in the High/Scope curriculum support children's active learning by identifying children's developmental level, by providing a physical environment relevant to their developmental level, by scheduling the day in ways that respect children as active learners and by interacting with children in ways that enable them to become decision-makers and problem-solvers. Interactions centre on staff:

➋ collecting together appropriate materials
➋ asking questions of children that prompt them to problem-solve
➋ observing children's problem-solving and concept development
➋ listening to and evaluating children's explorations so that they can be further extended.

Montessori Education

> With my methods . . . the teacher teaches little and observes much; it is her function to direct the psychic activity of the children and their physiological development. For this reason I have changed the name of the teacher into that of directress (Montessori 1936, pp. 96–7).

OVERVIEW OF EDUCATIONAL VISION

Maria Montessori (1870–1952) was an Italian doctor who initially developed her educational goals and methods when working with children with intellectual disabilities (Catron and Allen 1993) who at the time were considered mentally 'deficient' and were living in the Rome asylum. Her main educational goals in this and her later work were to improve the individual child's practical daily living skills and to develop each child's intellectual potential to the full.

Current Montessori programs have a wide range of goals aimed at developing the individual child's practical daily living skills and intellectual potential. Such goals include encouraging the child's independence and problem-solving skills, developing children's concentration skills, encouraging children to respect themselves and others, and helping children to become responsible group members (Morrison 1995) through work experiences in the classroom (Henniger 1999).

Montessori's ways of achieving her educational goals derived from three interrelated beliefs she held about children's growth and development. First, she believed that from birth children are active, self-motivated learners who have moments in their development when they are best able to learn some concepts more easily than others. Montessori called these moments sensitive periods. In this belief, Montessori differed from several of her contemporaries who believed that children do not learn during infancy (Brewer 1992).

Second, Montessori believed that children learn best through active involvement in their physical and sensory environment because in her view sensory learning was the foundation of all other learning. This idea is captured powerfully in the following statement:

> Set the children free, let them have fair play, let them run out when it is raining, take off their shoes when they find pools of water, and when the grass of the meadows is damp with dew let them run about with bare feet and trample on it; let them rest quietly when the tree invites them to sleep in its shade . . . (Montessori 1948/1962, p. 100).

In forming this belief she drew on the ideas of two Parisian doctors, Jean-Marc-Gaspard Itard and Edouard Seguin, whose work with children considered to be 'mentally defective' emphasised the success of sensory training in developing the children's intellectual skills (Kramer 1988).

Third, Montessori believed that children best learn when they are free to self-educate. Such beliefs earned her the title in the United States of '. . . the Italian apostle of a new libertarian education . . .' (Kramer 1988, p. 227).

Using her understandings about children's growth and development and her own experiences of working with children with intellectual disabilities, Montessori developed her program of education for young children. It strongly emphasised the educational potential of allowing children's sensory and physical exploration of self-correcting materials and using carefully sequenced exercises appropriate to each of their sensitive periods. To support her program Montessori used a range of self-correcting materials which provided children with physical and sensory feedback about whether or not they had used the materials correctly, and she developed a number of exercises targeted at maximising children's learning during their sensitive periods. The materials Montessori used were first developed by Seguin and Itard, but she modified them in the light of her experiences in Rome. These initial materials borrowed from the work of Seguin and Itard, included '. . . three-dimensional shapes and letters to be felt, matched, set into holes of corresponding shapes . . . [and] a whole series of objects of differing sizes, shapes, colours, [and] textures . . .' (Kramer 1988, p. 86) that children sorted, matched and joined together. Many of the materials Montessori used, such as the three-dimensional shapes and letters, were the forerunners of current educational materials for young children such as inset puzzle boards.

TEACHING TECHNIQUES

The Montessori approach to curriculum design relies strongly on structured skill-acquisition activities in which staff model the skills to be acquired (Robison and Schwartz 1982) using the prescribed exercises and materials developed by Montessori in the early 1900s. However, children can choose which of these materials they use and when they use them. To optimise children's capacity to self-educate, staff draw strongly on the following teaching techniques:

 Positioning equipment and materials: as Montessori believed strongly in the child's ability to self-educate, staff need to position equipment and materials to maximise the child's choice and independence. This involves arranging equipment and materials in a highly ordered way so that children can readily access and choose the equipment and materials they wish to work with, and easily identify where the materials should be returned. Equipment and materials should be positioned neatly, in an orderly manner and respectfully (Jackson 1997). The materials should be chosen with 'careful attention to concept development . . . graduated difficulty/complexity . . . [be] self-correcting . . . [and] sensory-oriented (Henniger 1999, p. 55).

- ❯ Scheduling: the child's self-paced, self-directed learning is also supported within a Montessori program by staff scheduling large blocks of uninterrupted time for the children to explore the learning materials and exercises at their own pace (Morrison 1995; Kahn 1997).

- ❯ Non-verbal interaction: staff involvement in children's activities is minimal because Montessori believed that children self-educate if the environment is appropriately prepared. When staff do interact with children there is often a strong emphasis on indirect, non-verbal teaching techniques such as modelling and redirecting. Montessori emphasised that modelling should only be provided when children need assistance with a skill or new piece of equipment, and that redirection is only needed when children are behaving inappropriately (Brewer 1992).

- ❯ Verbal interaction: once staff have selected developmentally appropriate self-educating materials, Montessori suggested that they should 'leave [their] . . . little scholars in liberty' (Montessori, cited in DeCecco 1968, p. 139). Hence, in a Montessori program, verbal interaction between staff and children is kept to a minimum. However, recent research suggests that Montessori teachers are likely to intervene when children make errors in their understandings of mathematical concepts and when they use incorrect language (Chattin-McNichols 1991).

Montessori's belief that there are key periods when children's readiness to learn a particular skill is at its height means that staff need to observe for the emergence of these periods and provide materials appropriate to them. It is through this observation that children's learning is evaluated. As Kahn (1997, p. 1) puts it:

> . . . the child can only be free when the adult becomes an acute observer. Any action of the adult that is not a response to the children's observed behaviour limits the child's freedom.

The Reggio Emilia Approach

> One of the most challenging aspects of the Reggio Emilia approach is the solicitation of multiple points of view regarding children's needs, interests, and abilities, and the concurrent faith in parents, teachers, and children to contribute in meaningful ways to the determination of school experiences (New 1993, p. 2).

As mentioned in Chapter 22, Loris Malaguzzi (1920–1994) founded and for many years directed the Reggio Emilia system of early childhood education in the northern Italian region of Emilia-Romagna. The approach he developed to educating young children has been acclaimed internationally and is known as the Reggio Emilia Approach. In recent years there has been considerable international interest in the Reggio Emilia approach to early childhood education and its influence can be seen in early childhood programs in the United States, United Kingdom and Australia.

OVERVIEW OF EDUCATIONAL VISION

The educational vision underpinning the schools of Reggio Emilia is not fixed. It constantly evolves as staff, parents and children reflect on how best to promote children's learning. However, Malaguzzi (1993) identified wide and disparate sources of inspiration for the vision that has evolved to date. They included names familiar to early childhood educators in Australia such as Vygotsky, Erikson, Piaget, Brofenbrenner, Montessori and Dewey. There were also many European theorists less well known in Australia such as Decroly, Freinet and Chaperade. Of the multiple and diverse sources of inspiration for the educational vision underpinning the schools of Reggio Emilia, Malaguzzi said that staff have learnt how versatile research and theory can be (Malaguzzi 1993).

This versatility has led to a complex and changing vision of the child as a competent learner and of the way in which the child can best be supported in her learning. There is a strong vision of the child as an active constructor of knowledge:

> What children learn does not follow as an automatic result from what is taught. Rather, it is in large part due to the children's own doing as a consequence of their activities and our resources (Malaguzzi 1993, p. 59).

The child is seen to learn through being actively engaged in a rich and complex set of relationships and interactions with the adults around them, the peer group and an 'amiable' learning environment.

The vision of the child as a competent learner strongly influences how curriculum is decided. The child's ability to construct knowledge positions the child as a person who has the right and capability to direct his own learning. A strong child-directed curriculum model which places the child in the centre of curricula negotiations has evolved. However, negotiation is a critical word within the Reggio Emilia approach to curriculum as there is a strong belief that children learn through relationships with others, including parents and staff. This belief in part derives from the work of Vygotsky (see Chapter 27) and his belief that children learn through interaction, modelling and support from competent others at critical periods in the acquisition of new skills and knowledge.

While Vygotsky's ideas on children's learning and the role of social relationships in this learning have influenced the vision of the child as competent learner, they have also been modified through the experiences and theory building of staff in the schools of Reggio Emilia. The relationship between adult and child in the child's learning is seen as highly complex and Vygotsky's ideas as somewhat problematic. The idea that an adult can help a child gain competence when the child is not yet competent is seen as problematic and the idea that there is just the right moment to offer help is also seen as problematic. However, the need for adults to carefully time their interventions in children's learning is seen as a critical issue to grapple with.

The shape, style, tone, focus and content of the curriculum evolves from the day-to-day happenings in the lives, experience and interests of children and adults in the centre. The emphasis is on communication and interaction to deepen children's inquiry and theory building about the world around them and building a community of inquiry between adults and children through which this can happen (Knowles Kennedy 1996). Children's learning is supported and enriched through in-depth, short- and long-term project work in which 'responding, recording, playing, exploring, hypothesis-building and testing, and provoking occurs' (New 1993, p. 3). Within the project work the arts play a powerful role. The children are encouraged to use many forms of symbolic language to express their ideas and further their understandings in their project work, and the aesthetics of the schools have led to the claim by Malaguzzi (1993, p. 57) that the 'walls speak and document'.

TEACHING TECHNIQUES

One of the key techniques used in the pre-primary schools in Reggio Emilia is the documentation and display of children's project work. The specialist technique of documentation is seen as essential to the process of children being able to express, revisit, construct and reconstruct their feelings, ideas and understandings. Community building is also critical to the teaching and learning experiences within Reggio Emilia pre-primary schools.

Documentation is discussed further in Chapter 22 and community building is discussed further in Chapter 20. However, alongside the technique of documentation several other general and specialist techniques support staff in implementing their educational vision of the child as a competent learner. These techniques include:

➲ Positioning equipment and materials: staff select and organise equipment and materials in ways that invite children's discovery, that enable children to express their ideas in multiple ways and that enable children to revisit their work. Equipment and materials are also positioned to enable children's long-term project work to take place. It is also important that the physical space 'foster communication and relationships' (Henniger 1999, p. 70) and be alive with children's representations of the world around them. A workshop area in which children can engage in project work is often present:

One special space found in Reggio classrooms is called the atelier. The teacher sets aside this special workshop as an area for recording in visual form what students learn as they engage in projects of their own choosing . . . The atelier contains a wealth of tools and resource materials that children can use for their documentations (Henniger 1999, p. 71).

➲ Scheduling: children's learning is supported and enriched through scheduling time for in-depth project work. There is also a minimum of six hours per week provided for staff to engage in planning, inservice training and reflection on their work with children and their families (Henniger 1999).

➲ Verbal and non-verbal interaction: staff actively interact with children to encourage expression of their ideas and theory construction. The role of the adult is in part a participant observer in children's learning and in part it is to be an agent provocateur. To a large extent Vygotsky's view of the child learning through scaffolding with competent others informs this sense of the role of the teacher (Malaguzzi 1993). Open-ended questioning, problem-solving, recalling, feedback, demonstrating and describing help staff participate in and provoke children's learning. Dialogue is central to the teaching and learning experience within Reggio Emilia:

Reggio Emilia educators commonly study conversations among children and between children and adults . . . They believe such conversations allow children to reflect on their ideas and extend their thinking . . . (Hughes 2002, p. 137)

Robertson (1995) describes a project she observed at the Diana school in Reggio Emilia and how staff's organisation of the environment and their interaction with the children respected the vision of the child as a competent learner:

> . . . a group of three five-year-old children had been give a bucket, a Plexiglas mirror and asked if they could make a rainbow. Eventually, after sorting out they needed water and light, and a great deal of trial and error they achieved the result . . . In the Reggio Emilia tradition the whole event is documented closely with photographs (Robertson 1995, p. 14).

Rudolf Steiner and Waldorf Schooling

> When the Waldorf curriculum is carried through successfully, the whole human being—head, heart, and hand — has been truly educated (Barnes 1991, p. 54).

Rudolf Steiner (1861–1925) was an Austrian intellectual who widely researched and wrote on the scientific and philosophical thinking of his time. As part of his writing and research he developed a spiritual science called Anthroposophy. Steiner became involved in education in 1919 when he was asked by a German factory owner, Emil Molt, to create an educational program for Molt's Waldorf-Astoria cigarette factory workers and their families based on Steiner's anthroposophical views. By the 1990s approximately 550 schools in over 30 countries had been established using Waldorf educational principles established by Steiner in 1919 (Barnes 1991). Several of these schools have a preschool component.

OVERVIEW OF EDUCATIONAL VISION

Steiner's educational philosophy was derived from humanistic philosophy and emphasised the importance of education for life and education for the whole being. For Steiner, the spiritual, physical and intellectual being were equally the concern and responsibility of education. This meant that Steiner was a strong advocate of an integrated and a holistic approach to education.

Steiner also believed that each person attains their spiritual, intellectual and physical potential as an adult by passing through three developmental stages: early childhood, middle childhood and adolescence (Barnes 1991). Writing about his approach to curriculum in 1919, this developmental approach is clear:

> Knowledge of the special needs of each life period provides a basis for drawing up a suitable curriculum. This knowledge also can be a basis for dealing with instructional subjects in successive periods. By the end of the 9th year, one must have brought the child to a certain level in all that has come into human life through the growth of civilization. (Steiner 1919, p. 3)

In each developmental stage the concerns, interests, capacities and ways of knowing of a person differ. Accordingly, Steiner argued that the nature of the educational content and methods should differ in each developmental stage. For example, in the phase of early childhood it is the physical being that is pre-eminent. Children are absorbing the world through their senses and their major way of learning and knowing is through imitation. The responsibility of adults educating children in their early childhood years is to nurture the positive development of the physical being by ensuring that the child has a sensory world of sounds, sights, gestures, actions, aesthetics and feelings that are worthy of imitation (Barnes 1991).

Each developmental stage lays the foundations for the concerns and ways of knowing in the next phase. Hence, inappropriate educational content or methods in the early childhood stage can harm the later development of the child. As Barnes (1991, p. 52) explains:

Drawing the child's energies away from this fundamental task [their physical development] to meet premature intellectual demands robs the child of the health and vitality he or she will need for later life.

Conversely, the experience of Waldorf teachers is that matching curriculum content with the developmental stage enhances children's enjoyment in and capacity for learning across a range of content areas including mathematics (Mollet 1991).

While many of Steiner's beliefs paralleled those of several other educationalists influenced by humanistic philosophy, his anthrosophical views provided his pedagogy with a distinctive philosophical, educational and spiritual coherence lacking in the writings of other educationalists:

Steiner's emphasis on the development of the normal child's inner capacities at the proper times has much in common with Montessori, Neill, Ashton-Warner, even Dewey, but Steiner is unique in that this emphasis is underpinned by an entire cosmology so that students sense their interconnection with everything: earth and planets, body and spirit, past and present, life and death (Reinsmith 1989, p. 82).

His approach to education was linked powerfully to spirituality:

Steiner Education is an explicitly spiritual approach. The teacher nourishes the soul of the child through story, art, music, and movement. The kindergarten class remains together through to the eighth grade with the same teacher from 1–8. A strong set of relationships and sense of community is formed (Lawrence and Coady 2002, p. 18).

TEACHING TECHNIQUES

Steiner formed his views on the nature of development and learning into the five principles which guided the curriculum content and teaching methods of the Waldorf schools. The curriculum was integrated, developmental, spiritual, drew strongly on artistic method and processes, and taught students the art of eurhythmy. Eurhythmy was described by Steiner (1970) as a form of language based on gesture and movement. While individual Waldorf schools may now differ in the detailed content of their curricula, these five principles still exemplify the essential components of the Waldorf approach to education (Reinsmith 1989; Pinar et al. 1996).

Waldorf teaching involves learning specialist teaching methods (for example, for teaching eurhythmy). However, it also draws on several generalist teaching techniques to support its distinctive approach to education in the early childhood years. These techniques include:

- Positioning equipment and materials: staff select and arrange materials and experiences to encourage children's sensory exploration of their environment and to stimulate their artistic sense of being. Natural materials are used as these are seen to '. . . breathe and enhance the life forces' (Linden Steiner Kindergarten, no date, p. 8).
- Scheduling: activities requiring mental concentration are scheduled early in the day. There is also a strong rhythm to the scheduling of activities for the week and of the year. At the Linden Steiner Kindergarten they describe their schedule as follows:

> All the children participate in a mixed-age, play-centred curriculum with a strong emphasis on rhythm . . . Each day the children participate in a rhythmic circle time, often seasonally based, which includes songs, verses and movement. At the end of each morning session the children are told a story, most often a fairy story. Eurhythmy and various artistic activities and crafts are offered during the week (Linden Steiner Kindergarten, no date, p. 8).

In addition, there is strong emphasis on providing long blocks of time for children's free play to allow children to fully explore their environment and express themselves.

- ❯ Non-verbal interaction: as imitation is seen to be the young child's main form of learning, teachers must think carefully about the physical, spiritual and intellectual model they provide for the children. As Steiner strongly believed that children are affected by their teacher's inner being, it is important that teachers are positively committed to learning and personal growth (Reinsmith 1989). Staff need to model social skills such as sharing and co-operation and work hard to model '. . . positive, quiet and calm behaviour' (Linden Steiner Kindergarten, no date, p. 6). Facilitation of opportunities for the child's self-expression is also emphasised, with particular stress placed on encouraging and nourishing children's imaginative play (Linden Steiner Kindergarten, no date).
- ❯ Verbal interaction: as children's learning is seen to occur through imitation, direct instruction is kept to a minimum. When staff need to tell children to do something for reasons of their own or for other people's safety the direction is given in short, simple sentences. Staff are involved in daily story-telling and singing with the children as a way of enhancing children's sense of wonder and connection with the spiritual world.

Evaluation of children's learning happens via observation. Daily observation of the child based on the teacher's knowledge of anthroposophy builds a deep spiritual knowledge of each child which the teacher uses to individualise her teaching and alter her teaching methods and content as appropriate. Steiner refers to this process as 'learning to observe in the most intimate way . . .' (Steiner 1970, p. 28) the young child's '. . . gift of imitation' (Steiner 1970, p. 31).

Anti-Bias Curriculum

> Anti-bias curriculum embraces an educational philosophy as well as specific techniques and content. It is value-based: Differences are good: oppressive ideas are not. It sets up a creative tension between respecting differences and not accepting unfair beliefs and acts (Dermon-Sparks et al. 1989, p. x).

The Anti-Bias Curriculum was first developed in the late 1980s by a task force of early childhood educators from Pasadena and Los Angeles in California, USA. The task force wanted to develop a curriculum for working on issues of diversity with young children. They met for two years, shared their ideas and experiences, and eventually developed an approach to diversity which they named the Anti-Bias Curriculum. The philosophy, goals and techniques of their approach to diversity were first published by the National Association for the Education of Young Children (NAEYC) in 1989 as the *Anti-Bias Curriculum: Tools for Empowering Young Children*. This publication has since sold over 100 000 copies.

OVERVIEW OF EDUCATIONAL VISION

The educational philosophy underpinning the Anti-Bias Curriculum shares much in common with other approaches to early childhood education. It is premised on the beliefs that early childhood education should be developmentally appropriate and that its goal should be 'the development of each child to her or his fullest potential' (Dermon-Sparks et al. 1989, p. x).

However, the ABC task force also argues that early childhood education should be culturally and socially appropriate and that much early childhood education is not. This is because much mainstream early childhood education fails to acknowledge the real and continuing ways in which children's development is constrained by the inequalities and oppression they notice and experience in their daily lives.

Specifically, children's development is constrained by racism, sexism, handicappism, classism and heterosexism from an early age. In support of this claim the Anti-Bias Task Force cite their own experiences and research about young children's awareness that specific forms of difference, such as racial difference and physical abilities, are connected with status, privilege and power in their society (see Dau 2001). They believe that children come to understand the way different groups are privileged in their society through observing the spoken and unspoken messages that adults and other children provide about differences between people. Drawing on their work, they argue that children need:

- ➋ a future free from the constraints of racism, sexism, classism and handicappism
- ➋ early childhood education which directly addresses equity issues in, and through, the early childhood curriculum.

To build a curriculum that met these goals the task force drew on their own educational experiences as early childhood educators and on the philosophy, goals and techniques of critical or transformative education (see Chapter 23: Friere and empowerment—also refer to MacNaughton forthcoming). Dermon-Sparks (1998, p. 22) describes how the anti-bias curriculum began:

> The term 'anti-bias' has a similar meaning to 'education without prejudice'. We chose it because we wanted to say that this work requires a very active stance in relationship to challenging racism, sexism and all other forms of systematic oppression . . . We also need to look at the power relationships that interfere with the possibility of true diversity—the institutional structures and beliefs that systematically result in less resources, power and status for large numbers of people because of their racial and ethnic group membership, their gender, their class, their sexual orientation.

The aim of critical curriculum is to develop educational processes which create a more just and wise social world. Within this there are two broad goals: challenging discrimination and empowering children. Translating and developing these goals for within early childhood education led the task force to argue that early childhood education needs to help children to:

- ➋ take increasing responsibility for their own learning and care
- ➋ continue learning with an enhanced sense of self-worth, identity, confidence and enjoyment
- ➋ contribute their own special strengths and interests to the group
- ➋ learn useful and appropriate ways to find out what they want to know
- ➋ understand their own individual ways of learning and being creative
- ➋ be active in confronting and challenging inequality and injustice.

The challenges and opportunities for doing this differ according to the inequity and injustice staff are working on with children. The issues in relation to racial inequalities, gender inequalities and inequalities for children with disabilities are different from each other and thus require different approaches to empowering children. For children who experience discrimination because of their 'race', gender or disability, empowerment involves addressing the negative impact of this discrimination on their lives and in providing them with the skills to challenge unfair treatment of themselves and others in future. More detailed discussion of these issues and practical strategies related to them can be found in Dau (2001).

The Anti-Bias Task Force named their approach to tackle social inequality and discrimination with young children an anti-bias approach for the following reasons:

> In a society in which institutional structures create and maintain sexism, racism, and handicappism, it is not sufficient to be non-biased (and also highly unlikely), nor is it sufficient to be an observer. It is necessary for each individual to actively intervene, to challenge and counter the personal and institutional behaviours that perpetuate oppression (Dermon-Sparks et al. 1989, p. 3).

Anti-Bias Curriculum is, therefore, a political, activist approach to the education of young children.

Teaching techniques

While empowerment is the prime technique used in the Anti-Bias Curriculum, staff also draw on several generalist and specialist teaching techniques to support this distinctive approach to education in the early childhood years. These techniques include:

- ❯ Positioning equipment and materials: while there is no specific direction given to staff about how to position equipment and materials in an Anti-Bias Curriculum, there are clear guidelines for the creation of an anti-bias learning environment in which selection of equipment and materials are the key (see Jones and Dermon-Sparks 1992). Equipment and materials should be anti-discriminatory, culturally inclusive and relevant, and they should enable children to explore issues of human diversity and anti-discriminatory (anti-bias) ways of being. Collecting equipment that supports this work is an important part of anti-bias teaching.
- ❯ Non-verbal interaction: staff are actively involved in children's activities because children's biased ideas and behaviours need to be challenged and confronted. However, there is also a strong emphasis on staff modelling anti-biased ways—children are seen to learn many of their biased and anti-biased attitudes from the adults around them.
- ❯ Verbal interaction: staff develop anti-bias content around the children's daily experiences. As Dermon-Sparks (1993/94, p. 71) explains:

Critical thinking and activism activities should rise out of real-life situations that are of interest to the children.

Staff use a variety of verbal teaching techniques to build this content and to enable the children to engage with it and with each other in anti-biased ways. Staff need to be actively involved in open-ended questioning of the children around issues of diversity and equity, listening to the children's responses to these questions, problem-solving with the children what is fair and unfair, and empowering the children to think critically about their social world and to take action against inequalities and injustices. Story-telling and story-reading are seen as powerful ways to raise issues of equity and diversity with young children. A specialist story-telling technique using dolls has also been developed to support the development of children's critical thinking and problem-solving abilities around issues of diversity and equity. This was developed by Kay Taus, a member of the Anti-Bias Task Force, and is known as the 'Persona Doll' technique. A key element of the Persona Doll technique involves introducing children to 'personalised' storylines about equity and diversity that extend, enrich and challenge their current knowledge and attitudes. Examples of this technique can be found in Dau (2001), Brown (2001) and MacNaughton et al. (2001).

Evaluation of children's learning is through observation of their interactions with each other and with educational materials, and through staff discussion with the children about their values and attitudes towards diversity.

CONCLUSION

When early childhood staff take a strategic approach to their teaching and children's learning they are being educationally purposeful and make plans to ensure that their educational vision becomes a reality.

Not all early childhood staff are strategic about teaching and learning. Some staff do not have a clear sense of what they want to do and how they will do it. Some staff have a clear vision of their work but do not have a coherent approach to their teaching that harmonises with their vision. When staff are not being strategic they tend to take ad hoc educational decisions that may not achieve what is best for children. Program-planning on a daily, weekly or fortnightly basis can be an ad hoc approach to teaching when it is not based on an overall approach that reflects an educational vision.

There are clearly many different educational visions that influence curriculum for young children. Staff must choose between a staggering array of competing philosophies, educational goals and processes when deciding what and how they will teach. Sometimes staff have to make their choices in isolation, sometimes in consultation with parents and other staff. Irrespective of who is involved in these decisions, the decision about what and how to teach is strongly value-based. As Elliot and Hatton (1994, p. 55) stated:

> Teaching is not a value-neutral activity. It is premised on certain values and promotes certain, although not always the same, values.

Understanding the values that underpin teaching decisions is an important component of excellence in teaching (Elliot and Hatton 1994). However, it is equally important for staff to know how to build their own educational and professional values into a strategic approach to teaching and learning. We borrow from the writing of Lillian Katz to summarise our argument:

> The main argument in this chapter is that consideration of what young children should learn, and when and how they should do so, have to be addressed together in order to formulate an appropriate pedagogical approach for any of them (Katz 1995, p. 115).

By staff being strategic in this way, it is more likely that the educational vision of excellence in teaching for all young children, as outlined in this book, can become a reality.

REFLECTING ON BEING STRATEGIC

1 What is the difference between strategic decision-making and ad hoc decision-making?

2 How can strategic decision-making help you achieve your teaching and learning goals with young children?

3 Do you have a clear educational vision? What are your current beliefs and values about:
   - how children's development influences their learning?
   - how children's learning is influenced by their cultural, social and political background?
   - what cultural, social, moral, political and ethical goals should underpin an educational program for young children?

4 What are your current ideas about:
   - what children should learn?
   - when children should learn?
   - how children should learn?

5 Which of the following general teaching techniques do you feel are best suited to your own educational vision for young children?
   - demonstrating
   - describing
   - encouraging, praising and helping
   - facilitating
   - feedback
   - grouping
   - listening
   - modelling
   - positioning people
   - questioning
   - reading
   - recalling
   - singing
   - suggesting
   - telling.

6 Which of the following specialist teaching techniques do you feel are best suited to making your own educational vision for young children a reality?
   - co-constructing
   - community building
   - deconstructing
   - documenting
   - empowering
   - philosophising
   - problem-solving
   - reinforcing
   - scaffolding
   - task-analysing.

7 Visit one of the following websites and answer the following questions:

> To what extent is there a clear philosophy underpinning teaching and learning practices in the service?

> In which ways do the teaching techniques discussed link with the service's philosophy?

> How strategic is this service being in its approach to teaching and learning?

> Sheridan College Early Childhood centres
http://www.sheridan.on.ca/academic/edserv/miss.htm

> Education Review Office http://www.ero.govt.nz/Publications/pubs2002/Montessori.htm

> I Live and Learn Private Preschool and Day Care Centres http://www.preschoolnz.co.nz/
This site leads to several specific centres whose philosophy you can analyse.

Further reading and resources

The High/Scope Preschool Curriculum (USA and Singapore)

Bredekamp, S. 1996, '25 years of educating young children: the High/Scope Approach to preschool', *Young Children*, 51(4), pp. 57–61.

Hohmann, M. and Weikart, D. 1995, *Educating Young Children: Active Learning Practices for Preschool and Child Care Programs*, Ypsilanti, Mich., High/Scope Education Research Foundation.

Morrison, G. 1995, *Early Childhood Education Today*, sixth edn, New Jersey, Merrill. [refer pp. 136–53].

Post, J. and Hohmann, M. 1995, 'Planning the day in infant and toddler programs', *Extensions*, 10(3), pp. 1–3.

Weikart, D. 1995/96, 'High/Scope in action: the milestones', *High/Scope Resource, Special Edition* [refer to pp. 4–6].

Weikart, D. and Schweinart, L. 1987, 'The High/Scope cognitively orientated curriculum in early childhood', in J. Roopnaarine, ed., *Approaches to Early Childhood Curriculum* (pp. 253–67), Ohio, Merrill Publishing Company.

The following information and resources are available from the High/Scope Educational Research Foundation, 600 North River St, Ypsilanti, MI 48198-2898, USA. Telephone 1 (313) 4850704:

Extensions Newsletter of the High/Scope Curriculum.

High/Scope Resource: A Magazine for Educators.

Other resources

Extensive information and resources are available from the High/Scope Educational Research Foundation, 600 North River St, Ypsilanti, MI 48198-2898, USA. The website for the Foundation contains detailed links to reading lists, videos (listed below), research, sample plans and newsletter updates: www.highscope.org

High/Scope COR Self-Study Guide on CD-ROM, High/Scope Foundation, 0-57379-084-9

Video (available from www.highscope.org)

High/Scope Curriculum. Its Implementation in Family Child Care Homes.

The High/Scope Curriculum. The Daily Routine.

The High/Scope Curriculum. The Plan-Do-Review Process.

Setting up the Learning Environment.

Supporting Children's Active Learning. Teaching Strategies for Diverse Settings.

Montessori Education

Albanseia, F. 1990, *Montessori Classroom Management*, New York, Crown Books.

Brewer, J. 1992, *Introduction to Early Childhood Education: Preschool through Primary Grades*, Boston, Allyn and Bacon [refer pp. 38–45].

Hainstock, E. 1986, *The Essential Montessori*, New York, New American Library.

Kramer, R. 1988, *Maria Montessori*, London, Hamish Hamilton Paperback.

Montessori Life is a journal which publishes current international research on Montessori education.

Morrison, G. 1995, *Early Childhood Education Today*, sixth edn, New Jersey, Merrill [refer pp. 91–119].

Other resources

Association Montessori International (AMI). This association was founded by Maria Montessori in 1929. AMI, 170 West Scholfield Road, Rochestor, New York, 14617, USA.

Montessori Connections. A website developed by the IntelleQuest Education Company that has links to other websites concerned with Montessori education, journals, teacher resources and details of Montessori schools: http://www.montessoriconnections.com/

Montessori Foundation. Email: timseldon@montessori.org or http://www.montessori.org

Montessori International Index with details about teacher training, environments and materials, lectures and conferences and online resources: http://www.montessori.edu/

Video

Maria Montessori: Follow the Child, Douglas Clark Associates, California 1994.

Montessori: Freedom in a Structured Environment, Reggio Emilia, University of Melbourne, 1991.

Practical Teaching Excerpts: Montessori Method, Sister Christine's Class, University of Melbourne, 1991.

Reggio Emilia

Edwards, C. 1993, 'Partner, Nurturer and Guide: The Roles of the Reggio Teacher in Action', in C. Edwards, L. Gandini and G. Forman, eds, *The Hundred Languages of Children: The Reggio Emilia Approach to Early Childhood Education* (pp. 151–69), New Jersey, Ablex Publishing Company.

Firlik, R. 1996, 'Can we adapt the philosophies and practices of Reggio Emilia, Italy, for use in American schools?', *Early Childhood Education Journal*, 23(4), pp. 217–20.

Gandini, L. 1993a, 'Educational caring spaces', in C. Edwards, L. Gandini and G. Forman, eds, *The Hundred Languages of Children: The Reggio Emilia Approach to Early Childhood Education* (pp. 135–49), New Jersey, Ablex Publishing Company.

——1993b, 'Fundamentals of the Reggio Emilia approach to early childhood education', *Young Children*, 49(1), pp. 4–8.

Hendricks, J. (ed.) 1997, *First steps towards teaching the Reggio way*, Columbus, Ohio, Merrill/Prentice Hall.

Hughes, E. 2002, Planning meaningful curriculum: a mini story of children and teachers learning together, *Childhood Education*, 78(3), pp. 134–9.

Katz, L. 1995, 'Lessons from Reggio Emilia: an American perspective', ED388425.

New, R. 2000, 'Reggio Emilia: catalyst for change and conversation', ERIC Digest, ED447971.

Other resources

Innovations in Early Education: The International Reggio Exchange is a journal through which subscribers can keep up to date with developments in the Italian programs and hear about how these programs are being adapted in other countries. Available from: The Merrill-Palmer Institute, Wayne State University, 71-A E. Ferry Ave, Detroit MI 48202, USA.

Selected resources about Reggio Emilia and its influences in early childhood education can be found at: http://www.members.aol.com/ouidameier/reggio/cavallo_bib.htm

Reggio Emilia LIST SERV – email REGGIO-L listserv@postoffice.cso.uiuc.edu

Reggio Emilia Information Exchange: http://reggio-oz.dd.com.au

Video

An Amusement Park for Birds, Perfomanetics, USA, 1994.

The Hundred Languages of Children, Lyon, M. S. A visit to the Reggio Emilia Exhibit, USA, 1995. Fax USA (415) 3978211.

The Long Jump, Perfomanetics, USA, 1992.

Rudolf Steiner and Waldorf Schooling

Barnes, H. 1985, *An Introduction to Waldorf Education*, Spring Valley, NY, Mercury Press.

——1991, 'Learning that grows with the learner: an introduction to Waldorf Education', *Educational Leadership*, October, pp. 52–4.

Blackwood, R. 1992, 'Alternative early childhood education: the Steiner way', *Journal of the Australian Early Childhood Association*, Victorian Branch, 10(3), pp. 25–6.

Masters, B. (ed.) 1989, *Rudolf Steiner: Waldorf Education*, Stourbridge, UK, The Robinswood Press.

Mollet, D. 1991, 'How the Waldorf Approach changed a difficult class', *Educational Leadership*, October, pp. 55–6.

Reinsmith, W. 1989, 'The whole in every part: Steiner and Waldorf schooling', *The Educational Forum*, 54(1), pp. 81–91.

Steiner, R. 1919, 'An introduction to Waldorf Education', an essay by Rudolf Steiner, downloadable from http://wn.elib.com/Steiner/Articles/IntWal_index.html

——1970, 'Education and the Science of Spirit (Lecture, 1921)', in P. Allen, ed., *Education as an Art* (pp. 19–49), New York, Rudolf Steiner Publications.

——1982, *The Roots of Education*, London, Rudolf Steiner Press.

Other resources

Useful links to a variety of sites associated with Steiner's educational philosophy: http://www.awsna.org

Steiner Waldorf Schools for Curriculum Choice in Scotland: http://www.steinerweb.org.uk

Video

Candle on the Hill, BBC TV, 1990.

Anti-Bias Curriculum

Byrnes, D. and Kiger, G. 1992, *Common Bonds: Anti-Bias Teaching in a Diverse Society*, Wheaton, MD, Association for Childhood Education International.

Dau, E. (ed.) 2001, *The Anti-Bias Approach in Early Childhood*, second edn., Sydney, Harper Educational.

Dermon-Sparks, L. 1992, '"It isn't fair!". Anti-bias curriculum for young children', in B. Neugebauer, ed., *Alike and Different: Exploring our Humanity with Young Children* (pp. 2–10), Washington DC, National Association for the Education of Young Children.

——1993/94, 'Empowering children to create a caring culture in a world of differences', *Childhood Education*, 70(2), pp. 66–71.

Dermon-Sparks, L. and the Anti-Bias Task Force 1989, *The Anti-Bias Curriculum*, Washington DC, National Association for the Education of Young Children.

Jones, E. and Dermon-Sparks, L. 1992, 'Meeting the challenge of diversity', *Young Children*, January, pp. 12–16.

Jones, K. and Mules, R. 2001, Developing critical thinking and activism, in E. Dau ed., *The Anti-Bias Approach in Early Childhood*, (pp. 192–209), Frenchs Forest, New South Wales, Australia, Pearson Education Australia.

LGCC, 1996, *Caring for Every Child: Ideas to Meet Diverse Needs in Child Care*, Sydney, Lady Gowrie Child Centre, Sydney.

Neugebauer, B. (ed.) 1992, *Alike and Different: Exploring our Humanity with Young Children*, Washington DC, National Association for the Education of Young Children.

Other resources

A child care centre in USA with an anti-bias philosophy: email address cshrc@stuaf.umass.edu

Equity Alliance – http://www.RootsforChange.net

CD-ROM: MacNaughton, G., Campbell, S., Smith, K. and Lawrence, H. 2002, *Equity Adventures in Early Childhood*, Centre for Equity and Innovation in Early Childhood, University of Melbourne, Melbourne, Australia. http://www.edfac.unimelb.edu.au/LED/CEIEC/

Web pages with extensive resources on anti-bias perspectives:

Access to practical resources for implementing social justice and anti-bias curriculum with young children available at http://californiatomorrow.org/

A journal on projects that foster equity, respect and understanding available at http://www.splcenter.org/teachingtolerance/tt-index.html

A great list of resources on equity and diversity available at http://www.ali.apple.com/naeyc/06.shtml

Institute of Anti-bias Education Study Guide which describes the aims of anti-bias education—full text available at http://www.adl.org/tools_teachers/tip_antibias_ed.html

A list of the articles produced by the National Network for Child Care on Diversity available at http://www.nncc.org/Diversity/divers.page.html

Video

Anti-Bias Curriculum, Pacific Oaks College, Extension Services, 714 West California Bvd, Pasadena, CA91105.

Fair Play: Anti-Bias in Action. A Training Kit, Lady Gowrie Children's Centre, Sydney, NSW, Australia, 1997.

References

Barnes, H. 1991, 'Learning that grows with the learner: an introduction to Waldorf Education', *Educational Leadership*, October, pp. 52–4.

Bowman, B., Donovan, S. and Burns, S. 2001, *Eager to Learn: Educating Our Preschoolers*, Washington DC, National Academy Press.

Brewer, J. 1992, *Introduction to Early Childhood Education: Preschool through Primary Grades*, Boston, Allyn and Bacon [refer pp. 38–45].

Catron, C. and Allen, J. 1993, 'Early Childhood Curriculum', New York, Macmillan Publishing Company.

Chattin-McNichols, J. 1991, 'Montessori teachers' intervention: preliminary findings from an international study', ED341499.

DeCecco, J. 1968, The Psychology of Learning and Instruction: Educational Psychology, New Jersey, Prentice Hall Inc.

Dermon-Sparks, L. 2001, Education without prejudice: goals, principles and practices, Paper presented to the Respect: education without prejudice, a challenge for early years educators in Ireland, 16th October, 1998, Dublin, Ireland, Pavee Point Travellors Centre Ireland pp. 22–31.

Elliot, R. and Hatton, E. 1994, 'Neutrality and the value-ladenness of teaching', in E. Hatton, ed., Understanding Teaching: Curriculum and the Social Context of Schooling, Sydney, Harcourt Brace.

Henniger, M. 1999, Teaching Young Children: An Introduction, Colombus, Ohio, Merrill.

Jackson, P. 1997, Orient express: intercontinental destinations for Montessori Education?, Paper presented to the 1997 Montessori Congress, downloaded from http://www.ilu.uu.se/ilu/montessori/MOrient.htm

Jones, E. and Dermon-Sparks, L. 1992, 'Meeting the challenge of diversity', Young Children, January, pp. 12–16.

Katz, L. 1995, Talks with Young Children: A Collection, New Jersey, Ablex Publishing Corporation.

Knowles Kennedy, D. 1996, 'After Reggio Emilia: may the conversation begin!', Young Children, July, pp. 24–7.

Kramer, R. 1988, Maria Montessori, London, Hamish Hamilton Paperback.

Lawrence, H. and Coady, M. 2002, 'Development of spirituality acknowledgement in education and early childhood thinking', Every Child, 8(4), pp. 18–19.

Linden Steiner Kindergarten, no date, Welcome to Linden, Melbourne, Linden Steiner Kindergarten.

MacNaughton (in press) Shaping Early Childhood; a learners Curiculum and Context, Open University Press.

MacNaughton, G. and Hughes, P. (2001). Creating interpretive communities through staff parent communication. Research paper presentation to the Association for Childhood International Conference, April 4–7, Toronto, Ontario, Canada.

Malaguzzi, L. 1993, 'History, ideas and basic philosophy', in C. Edwards, L. Gandini and G. Forman, eds, The Hundred Languages of Children: The Reggio Emilia Approach to Early Childhood (pp. 41–90), Norwood, NJ, Ablex.

Minkes, A. 1987, The Entrepreneurial Manager: Decisions, Goals and Business Ideas, NY, USA Penguin.

Mollet, D. 1991, 'How the Waldorf Approach changed a difficult class', Educational Leadership, October, pp. 55–6.

Montessori, M. 1936, The Secret of Childhood, London, Ballantine Books.

Montessori, M. 1948/1962, The Discovery of the Child, London, Ballantine Books.

Morrison, G. 1995, Early Childhood Education Today, sixth edn, New Jersey, Merrill.

New, R. 1993, Reggio Emilia: some lessons for US educators. ERIC Digest, EDO-PS-93-3.

Pugh, D., Hickson, D. and Hinings, C. 1983, Writers on Organisations, third edn, NY, USA, Penguin Books.

Reinsmith, W. 1989, 'The whole in every part: Steiner and Waldorf schooling', The Educational Forum, 54(1), pp. 81–91.

Robertson, J. 1995, 'Projects', The Challenge, June, pp. 12–15.

Robison, H. and Schwartz, S. 1982, Designing Curriculum for Early Childhood, Boston, Allyn and Bacon Inc.

Schweinhart, L. and Hohmann, C. 1992, 'The High/Scope K–3 curriculum: a new approach', Principal, 71(5), pp. 16, 18–19.

Spodek, B. and Saracho, O. 1994, Right from the Start: Teaching Children Ages Three to Eight, Boston, Allyn and Bacon Inc.

Steiner, R. 1919, 'An introduction to Waldorf Education', an essay by Rudolf Steiner, downloadable from http://wn.elib.com/Steiner/Articles/IntWal_index.html

Steiner, R. 1970, 'Education and the Science of Spirit', lecture 1921, in P. Allen, ed., *Education as an Art* (pp. 19–49), New York, Rudolf Steiner Publications.

Weikart, D. 1995/96, 'High/Scope in action: the milestones', *High/Scope Resource*, *Special Edition*, pp. 4–6

Weikart, D. and Schweinhart, L. 1987, 'The High/Scope cognitively orientated curriculum in early childhood', in J. Roopnaarine, ed., *Approaches to Early Childhood Curriculum* (pp. 253–67), Ohio, Merrill Publishing Company.

Wilkes, G. (ed.) 1979, *Collins Dictionary of the English Language*, Middlesex, Penguin Books.

Index